The
SOCIAL WORLD
of the
NEW TESTAMENT

The
SOCIAL WORLD
of the
NEW TESTAMENT

Insights and Models

Jerome H. Neyrey *and*

Eric C. Stewart, *editors*

The Social World of the New Testament: Insights and Models
© 2008 by Hendrickson Publishers, Inc.
P. O. Box 3473
Peabody, Massachusetts 01961-3473

ISBN 978-1-59856-128-9

Printed in the United States of America

First Printing — November 2008

The translations of the Bible are the authors' unless otherwise marked.

Cover art credit: A greengrocer. Relief on a funerary stele. (1st half 3rd CE). Museo Ostiense, Ostia, Italy.
Photo credit: Eric Lessing / Art Resource, N.Y.

Library of Congress Cataloging-in-Publication Data

The social world of the New Testament : insights and models / edited by Jerome H. Neyrey and Eric C. Stewart.
p. cm.
Includes bibliographical references (p.   ) and indexes.
ISBN 978-1-59856-128-9 (alk. paper)
1. Bible. N.T.—Social scientific criticism. I. Neyrey, Jerome H., 1940–
II. Stewart, Eric Clark.
BS2545.S55S64 2008
225.6′7—dc22

2008026193

To all the family and friends of the Context Group

Contents

PART THREE: CULTURE

PART FOUR: MODAL PERSONALITY

List of Figures

Acknowledgments

Chapter 1: Social-Scientific Criticism—Bruce J. Malina

Chapter 1 was originally published as "Rhetorical Criticism and Social-Scientific Criticism: Why Won't Romanticism Leave Us Alone?" Pages 72–101 in *Rhetoric, Scripture and Theology: Essays from the 1994 Pretoria Conference.* Edited by S. E. Porter and T. F. Olbricht. Journal for the Study of the New Testament: Supplement Series 131. Sheffield: Sheffield Academic Press, 1996. Used by permission.

Chapter 2: Kinship—K. C. Hanson

"All in the Family: Kinship in Agrarian Roman Palestine," by K. C. Hanson, from *Palestine in the Time of Jesus,* ed. by K. C. Hanson and Douglas E. Oakman. Copyright © 1998 Fortress Press. All rights reserved. Reproduced by permission of Augsburg Fortress.

Chapter 3: The Patron-Client Institution—Alicia Batten

Chapter 3 was originally published as "God in the Letter of James: Patron or Benefactor." *New Testament Studies* 50 (2004): 257–72. Reprinted by the permission of Cambridge University Press.

Chapter 4: Economics—Douglas E. Oakman

Chapter 4 was originally published as "Jesus and Agrarian Palestine: The Factor of Debt." Pages 57–73 in *Society of Biblical Literature 1985 Seminar Papers.* Edited by K. H. Richards. Society of Biblical Literature Seminar Papers 24. Atlanta: Scholars Press, 1985. Used by permission.

Chapter 5: Honor and Shame—Jerome H. Neyrey, SJ

Chapter 5 was originally published as "Loss of Wealth, Loss of Family and Loss of Honour: The Cultural Context of the Original Makarisms in Q." Pages 139–58 in *Modelling Early Christianity: Social-Scientific Studies of the New Testament in Its Context.* Edited by P. E. Esler. London: Routledge, 1995. Used by permission.

Chapter 6: Purity—John H. Elliott

Chapter 6 was originally published as "The Epistle of James in Rhetorical and Social Scientific Perspective: Holiness-Wholeness and Patterns of Replication." *Biblical Theology Bulletin* 23 (1993): 71–81. Used by permission.

Chapter 7: Social Location: Jesus—Douglas E. Oakman

Chapter 7 was originally published as "Was Jesus a Peasant? Implications for Reading the Samaritan Story (Luke 10:30–35)." *Biblical Theology Bulletin* 22 (1992): 117–25. Used by permission.

Chapter 8: Social Location: Jesus' World—Richard L. Rohrbaugh

Chapter 8 was originally published as "The Social Location of the Marcan Audience." *Biblical Theology Bulletin* 23 (1993): 114–27. Used by permission.

Chapter 9: Gender—S. Scott Bartchy

Chapter 9 was originally published as "Who Should Be Called Father? Paul of Tarsus between the Jesus Tradition and *Patria Potestas.*" *Biblical Theology Bulletin* 33 (2003): 135–47. Used by permission.

Chapter 10: Space—Jerome H. Neyrey, SJ

Chapter 10 was originally published as "'Teaching You in Public and from House to House' (Acts 20.20): Unpacking a Cultural Stereotype." *Journal for the Study of the New Testament* 26 (2003): 69–102. Used by permission of SAGE Publications.

Chapter 11: Healing—John J. Pilch

Chapter 11 was originally published as "Healing in Luke-Acts." Pages 89–117 in John J. Pilch, *Healing in the New Testament: Insights from Medical and Mediterranean Anthropology.* Minneapolis: Fortress, 2000. Used by permission.

Chapter 12: Evil Eye—John H. Elliott

Chapter 12 was originally published as "Paul, Galatians, and the Evil Eye." *Currents in Theology and Mission* 17 (1990): 262–73. Used by permission.

Chapter 13: Limited Good—Jerome H. Neyrey, SJ, and Richard L. Rohrbaugh

Chapter 13 was originally published as "'He Must Increase, I Must Decrease' (John 3:30): A Cultural and Social Interpretation." *Catholic Biblical Quarterly* 63 (2001): 464–83. Used by permission.

Chapter 14: Modal Personality— Bruce J. Malina and Jerome H. Neyrey, SJ

Chapter 14 was originally published as "Ancient Mediterranean Persons in Cultural Perspective," "Paul: Apostle and Prophet," and "Individualists and Collectivists: A Comparative Table." Pages 153–69, 202–18, and 225–31 in Bruce J. Malina and Jerome H. Neyrey, *Portraits of Paul: An Archaeology of Ancient Personality.* © 1996 Bruce J. Malina and Jerome H. Neyrey. Used by permission of Westminster John Knox Press.

The bibliographies, numbering of figures, and spellings as well as typographical errors within these articles have been modified to provide a more unified appearance suitable to their appearance as a collection.

Abbreviations

Modern Bible Versions

KJV	King James Version
NAB	New American Bible
NEB	New English Bible
NJB	New Jerusalem Bible
NRSV	New Revised Standard Version
RSV	Revised Standard Version

Old Testament Pseudepigrapha

Jub.	*Jubilees*
T. Ab.	*Testament of Abraham*
T. Benj.	*Testament of Benjamin*
T. Iss.	*Testament of Issachar*
T. Levi	*Testament of Levi*

Old Testament

Gen	Genesis
Exod	Exodus
Lev	Leviticus
Num	Numbers
Deut	Deuteronomy
Josh	Joshua
Judg	Judges
Ruth	Ruth
1 Sam	1 Samuel
2 Sam	2 Samuel
1 Kgs	1 Kings
2 Kgs	2 Kings
1 Chr	1 Chronicles
2 Chr	2 Chronicles
Neh	Nehemiah
Job	Job
Ps	Psalms
Prov	Proverbs
Isa	Isaiah
Mic	Micah
Hab	Habakkuk
Mal	Malachi

Apocrypha

Tob	Tobit
Wis	Wisdom
Sir	Sirach
1 Esd	1 Esdras
1 Macc	1 Maccabees

New Testament

Matt	Matthew
Mark	Mark
Luke	Luke
John	John
Acts	Acts
Rom	Romans
1 Cor	1 Corinthians
2 Cor	2 Corinthians
Gal	Galatians
Eph	Ephesians
Phil	Philippians
Col	Colossians
1 Thess	1 Thessalonians
2 Thess	2 Thessalonians
1 Tim	1 Timothy
2 Tim	2 Timothy
Phlm	Philemon
Heb	Hebrews
Jas	James
1 Pet	1 Peter

Rabbinic Writings

ᶜAbod. Zar.	ᶜAbodah Zarah
ʾAbot	ʾAbot
ᶜArak.	ᶜArakin
B. Bat.	Baba Batra
B. Meṣ	Baba Meṣiᶜa
Bek.	Bekorot
ᶜEd.	ᶜEduyyot
Giṭ.	Giṭṭin
Ḥal.	Ḥallah
Ḥul.	Ḥullin
Kelim	Kelim
Ketub.	Ketubbot
Neg.	Negaᶜim
Ned.	Nedarim
Peʾah	Peʾah

Pesaḥ.   *Pesahim*
Šeb.   *Šebiᶜit*
Taᶜan.   *Taᶜanit*
ᶜUq.   *ᶜUqṣin*
Yebam.   *Yebamot*

Other Ancient Sources

Aᴇꜱᴄʜɪɴᴇꜱ
Tim.   *In Timarchum*

Aʀɪꜱᴛᴏᴛʟᴇ
Eth. nic.   *Ethica nichomachea*
Pol.   *Politica*
Rhet.   *Rhetorica*

Aʀɪꜱᴛᴏᴘʜᴀɴᴇꜱ
Plut.   *Plutus*

Aᴜʟᴜꜱ Gᴇʟʟɪᴜꜱ
Noct. att.   *Noctes atticae*

Cɪᴄᴇʀᴏ
Amic.   *De amicitia*
Att.   *Epistulae ad Atticum*
Fam.   *Epistulae ad familiares*
Inv.   *De inventione rhetorica*
Off.   *De officiis*
Or. Brut.   *Orator ad M. Brutum*
Tusc.   *Tusculanae disputationes*
Verr.   *In verrem*

Dᴇᴍᴏꜱᴛʜᴇɴᴇꜱ
Timocr.   *In Timocratem*

Dɪᴏ Cʜʀʏꜱᴏꜱᴛᴏᴍ
Nicaeen.   *To the Nicaeans (Or. 39)*
1 Tars.   *Tarsica prior (Or. 33)*
2 Tars.   *Tarsica altera (Or. 34)*

Dɪᴏɴʏꜱɪᴜꜱ ᴏꜰ Hᴀʟɪᴄᴀʀɴᴀꜱꜱᴜꜱ
Ant. rom.   *Antiquitates romanae*

Eᴜꜱᴇʙɪᴜꜱ
Hist. eccl.   *Historia ecclesiastica*

Gᴀɪᴜꜱ
Inst.   *Institutiones*

Hᴏʀᴀᴄᴇ
Ep.   *Epistulae*

Jᴏꜱᴇᴘʜᴜꜱ
Ag. Ap.   *Against Apion*

Ant.	Jewish Antiquities
J.W.	Jewish War
Life	The Life

JUVENAL
| *Sat.* | Satirae |

LUCIAN
| *Nigr.* | Nigrinus |
| *Somn.* | Somnium (Vita Luciani) |

OVID
| *Fast.* | Fasti |

PAUSANIAS
| *Descr.* | Graeciae descriptio |

PHILO
Cherubim	On the Cherubim
Dreams	On Dreams
Drunkenness	On Drunkenness
Embassy	On the Embassy to Gaius
Flaccus	Against Flaccus
Heir	Who Is the Heir?
Moses	On the Life of Moses
Names	On the Change of Names
Sobriety	On Sobriety
Spec. Laws	On the Special Laws
Virtues	On the Virtues
Hypothetica	Hypothetica

PHILODEMUS
| *D.* | De diis |

PLATO
| *Leg.* | Leges |
| *Resp.* | Respublica |

PLINY THE ELDER
| *Nat.* | Naturalis historia |

PLUTARCH
Adul. amic.	Quomodo adulator ab amico internoscatur
Alex.	Alexander
Amat.	Amatorius
An seni	An seni respublica gerenda sit
Caes.	Caesar
Conj. praec.	Conjugalia praecepta
Cupid. divit.	De cupiditate divitiarum
Curios.	De curiositate
Luc.	Lucullus

Mor.	*Moralia*
Quaest. conv.	*Quaestionum convivialum libri X*
Rect. rat. aud.	*De recta ratione audiendi*
Ti. C. Gracch.	*Tiberius et Caius Gracchus*
Tranq. an.	*De tranquillitate animi*

POLYBIUS
Hist.	*Historiae*

QUINTILIAN
Inst.	*Institutio oratoria*

SENECA
Ben.	*De beneficiis*
Ep.	*Epistulae morales*

STRABO
Geogr.	*Geographica*

SUETONIUS
Aug.	*Divus Augustus*

TACITUS
Ann.	*Annales*

THEOPHRASTUS
Char.	*Characteres*

VIRGIL
Ecl.	*Eclogae*

XENOPHON
Hier.	*Hiero*
Oec.	*Oeconomicus*

Jerome H. Neyrey, SJ

Preface

In 1991 a group of scholars, convinced of the value and necessity of reading the Scriptures with models from the social sciences, published *The Social World of Luke-Acts: Models for Interpretation.* This volume was no mere collection of miscellaneous articles. From its conception, the aim of the Context Group was to introduce readers to this way of reading, not haphazardly, but using the same critical topics systematically taught in any introduction to cultural anthropology. *The Social World of Luke-Acts,* then, was intended to be a handbook of essential materials, a coherent primer of basic concepts and models, all aimed at a cultural interpretation of Luke's gospel and Acts of the Apostles.

A key foundation for this mode of interpretation relies on an adequate theory of reading. Words take their meaning from a social system, not from a lexicon. Our dictionaries translate words such as *father, mother,* and *household,* but they cannot tell us their meanings in Greco-Roman culture. Despite our temptation to take the easy road and think that those words meant then what we mean by them now, social-science reading alerts us to the fact that proper "reading" requires that we learn the ancient cultural system that filled those words with distinctive meaning. *The Social World of Luke-Acts* sought to provide appropriate cultural and social scenarios to read the ancient texts on their own terms, with full attention to cultural nuances and with recognition that this task would take great effort and perseverance. That volume, then, was unified around the interpretation of the Gospel of Luke and Acts of the Apostles, with an aim to display certain models adequately and show their utility in interpreting works from a cultural system utterly different from our own.

All contributors to *The Social World of Luke-Acts* wished that they had had twice the space for the many tasks that they knew had to be done. The contributors necessarily had to compress in that volume the kind of "fit" between social-science models and the Greco-Roman world, a strategy dear to the heart of historical critics. How can we know if modern models and concepts apply to antiquity? Filling in this gap has been the aim of subsequent work by the Context Group members. No, they were never imposing on the texts inappropriate social and cultural models, because they were continually reading Greco-Roman literature and could show how many of the modern cultural models fit well with the ancient culture and its documents.

Over fifteen years later, many of the same authors are back at it again and writing once more on their signature topics. The present volume both resembles and differs from *The Social World of Luke-Acts.* Many of the models and concepts in the first book reappear here, but now in very mature fashion. Moreover, many new models are present that greatly fill out the cultural backdrop of the ancient world: evil eye, space, gender, limited good, social location, agrarian debt, and peasant values. None of the topics within the book are trivial or incidental to learning to read the cultural world of the Scripture. Furthermore, the choice of these very models still aims to introduce novice readers to pivotal topics and models for interpretation and so to extend the education of those already reading with cultural lenses. Both vintage and new models come from the desks of scholars significantly accomplished in the use of this method.

However, this book differs from the 1991 volume in the way in which the cultural scenarios are utilized. Each chapter necessarily begins with an exposition of the model for consideration, which is then shown to be appropriate to the ancient world by means of extensive parallel materials from antiquity, which is then used to interpret a gospel or epistle. Whereas the 1991 volume focused on Luke-Acts, this book examines materials in Matthew, Mark, Luke, John, Acts, Galatians, and James. If the models serve to interpret this variety of texts, then it appears that they will be useful in interpreting other documents, biblical and secular. Finally, each chapter in this book has already been subject to peer review because all are previously published articles and chapters. It is part of the process of the Context Group for members to submit their works in progress to the assembled group for criticism in its best sense. Thus many of these chapters have received a thorough vetting by the peer group and another scrutiny by journal editors.

What makes this book and the 1991 volume distinctive is the underlying theory of knowledge. Scientists in general pride themselves on working inductively, moving from datum to datum, all of which are objectively in view. Those of us who use the social sciences to interpret the Scriptures have been accused of working deductively, a process by which a text is read through the lens of a model with scant attention to the particularities of the text. The crux of the problem lies in the presumption that any attentive person can observe data and have an "immaculate perception"—that is, know *what* things are and *how* they relate, all without making any generalizations or bringing things previously learned to bear here. The alternative mode of thinking might be called "abduction," a process in which knowledgeable persons observe, consider what is observed in light of their knowledge, and return to the observation mode—a process that entails many such cycles. Thus a person begins with some knowledge, which for the authors of this book includes social-science models; viewing with this lens surfaces data, which in turn are examined more closely in terms of the model used or other models with a prospect of relevance. The observer, then, keeps observing, surfacing data, and interpreting it in terms of a cultural system.

Wayne Meeks, a noted critic of the Context Group, said the following about this process:

> The difficulty is that without interpretation there are no facts. Every observation entails a point of view, a set of connections. The pure empiricist would drown in meaningless impressions. Even so simple a task as translating a sentence from an ancient language into our own requires some sense of the social matrices of both the original utterance and ourselves. . . . To collect facts without any theory too often means to

substitute our putative common sense. Making that substitution modernizes no less than does the scientist who follows his theory, for our common sense, too, is a cultural artifact. (Meeks 1983, 5)

The essays in this volume indeed "entail a point of view, a set of connections," which we call a social system. We seek to avoid the anachronisms and ethnocentrisms to which Meeks alerts all readers. In order to avoid ethnocentric and anachronistic readings, it is necessary to employ social-scientific models. Such models call our attention to places where our modern "common sense" understandings of ancient texts might lead us to anachronistic and ethnocentric readings. (Malina and Rohrbaugh 1998; 2003, 325–425; Malina and Pilch 2006, 331–406). These models, then, are our window into the biblical world.

The main point of Malina's essay on rhetorical criticism and social-scientific criticism is that modern readers of the New Testament, particularly in the United States, are rarely attuned to the differences between a first-century Mediterranean context and a modern U.S. context. Rohrbaugh's essay on social location introduces readers to a basic generalization of how a hearer/reader of the Gospel of Mark might be imagined. Oakman's essays on the pervasiveness of debt and Jesus' response to it and on Jesus as peasant highlight key features of the hierarchically oriented society of first-century Galilee and Judea. Patronage and benefaction were regular elements of this highly stratified society. Batten calls our attention to the distinction between patronage and benefaction in the Epistle of James. Although the contributors to this book use social-scientific generalizations about culture, they are keenly aware that no one definition of honor, for example, fits everywhere. The essays on honor and shame, purity and pollution, and male gender all represent a dominant view and a critique of that dominant view in the New Testament texts. Neyrey argues that Jesus' makarisms refer to those who specifically left their kinship group in order to follow Jesus, cutting off all social ties with their former life. Elliott argues that James's understanding of holiness relies on the concept of bodily and group wholeness. Bartchy's essay on male gender in antiquity argues that the early Christian movement in its most formative period rejected patriarchy and opted instead for a kinship-based fictive family in which all members were brothers and sisters with only God as the Father. These three essays highlight in various ways the nature of corporate personality, an idea further addressed by Malina and Neyrey in their discussion of understanding personality in an ancient Mediterranean context. It is the group that is the primary marker of identity. Corportate personality focuses on relationships, among the most important of which were those involving kinship. Hanson alerts us to kinship patterns in the first-century Mediterranean world and the key ways in which such patterns differ from kinship patterns assumed in the modern United States. Neyrey's essay on space demonstrates the social character of spaces. These too involve group identity. The study introduces the reader to the critical discussion of space divided into three types: private, public, and "private non-political, non-household space," arguing that it is this last context in which Paul was able to have voice to speak clearly to those who would listen to his message. Pilch's essay on healing discusses the fact that aggressive spirits were held to be responsible for illness in the ancient world. Jesus does battle with the evil spirits for control of the ill person, enabling people to be restored to their normal status in life. Elliott's essay on the evil eye is intimately related to the essay by Rohrbaugh and Neyrey on limited good inasmuch as the evil eye is based to a significant degree on the idea of limited good. Limited good is the basic notion that everything exists in limited supply, and the evil eye is made operative largely through envy of another's success, good fortune, or wealth. Since all things exist in limited supply, for one's share of something to increase, another's share must decrease. All of these aspects of the ancient Mediterranean context of the New Testament writings should seem foreign to modern Western people, who do not share the underlying presuppositions of the historical and cultural framework of these texts.

It should be noted that although these essays are previously published articles and chapters, the format for this book required that each of them be edited. There was necessarily some pruning or condensation of the materials as mutually agreed upon by Hendrickson Publishers, the authors, and the editors. This means that if the reader wishes to pursue a topic more fully, the original publications should be consulted.

BIBLIOGRAPHY

Malina, Bruce J., and John J. Pilch. 2006. *Social-Science Commentary on the Letters of Paul.* Minneapolis: Fortress.

Malina, Bruce J., and Richard Rohrbaugh. 1998. *Social-Science Commentary on the Gospel of John.* Minneapolis: Fortress.

————. 2003. *Social-Science Commentary on the Synoptic Gospels.* 2d ed. Minneapolis: Fortress.

Meeks, Wayne A. 1983. *The First Urban Christians: The Social World of the Apostle Paul.* New Haven: Yale University Press.

Neyrey, Jerome H., ed. 1991. *The Social World of Luke-Acts: Models for Interpretation.* Peabody, Mass.: Hendrickson.

Part
One

SOCIAL-
SCIENTIFIC
CRITICISM

Social-Scientific Criticism

1

In this essay, originally delivered at a conference in Pretoria on "Rhetoric, Scripture and Theology" in 1994, Bruce Malina addressed an audience enraptured of rhetoric. His was a strange inclusion because his thesis argues that modern concerns for rhetoric are subjective and individualistic, a foreign concept to those whose aim officially is to discover what ancient authors and their writings meant.

Malina's essay sets out the basic agenda of this book: a social understanding of an ancient author must include knowledge of the relevant institutions, culture, and typical type of modal personality. Malina (1986, 114) once compared institutions to tornadoes in that both represent ways of channeling energy in a certain direction. Institutions, then, are fixed forms of social energy meant to realize goals necessary for meaningful social human existence, such as the nature and nurture of human beings (kinship), provisioning society (economics), effecting collective action (politics), and a conception of the general order of existence that makes sense out of everything (religion). Culture looks to the meaning and affect attributed by human beings in their social settings to the objects of their experience: self, others, nature, time, space, and what/who holds it all together—that is, some All. Finally, modal personality (sometimes called "collective personality") consists of values and behavior that characterize persons as proper human beings in a given society. Abstractly, persons are all human, but we live our lives in quite different cultural ways. Some persons are group-oriented and take their clues about their identity and expected behavior from others. Identity in collectivist societies comes from the group rather than from within the individual. The primary orientation is to the group, and the individual is subordinated to the group. Their banner is "What will the neighbors think?" By contrast, most Western persons conceive of themsevles in a Freudian sense. We are ego-oriented persons whose identity comes from those core elements of our persona buried deep within the resources of our minds.

We use the three elements of social-science method noted above to identify the focus of the essays contained in the book:

1. Institutions
   Kinship (ch. 2)
   Patron and client (ch. 3)
   Economics (ch. 4)

2. Culture
    Purity (ch. 5)
    Honor and shame (ch. 6)
    Social location (chs. 7, 8)
    Gender (ch. 9)
    Space (ch. 10)
    Healing (ch. 11)
    Evil eye (ch. 12)
    Limited good (ch. 13)

3. Modal Personality
    Paul (ch. 14)

One of Malina's most significant contributions to social-scientific criticism is his acute study of language and the fundamental law of language. Words and sentences and books do not "mean" anything, such that the casual modern hearer or reader would understand. "Meaning" comes from the social system expressed in the language. He calls the modern discovery of the appropriate ancient social system a "scenario" necessary to interpret an ancient author. Each ancient author certainly had one, and the honest interpreter must strive to replicate that as closely as possible. Hence, readers, if they are considerate, must strive to learn the social system of an ancient author. One reads the statement "Honor your father and your mother," but to know its meaning, one must know what "kinship" and "honor" meant and what were the social expectations of "father" and "mother."

BIBLIOGRAPHY

Malina, Bruce J. 1986. *Christian Origins and Cultural Anthropology: Practical Models for Biblical Interpretation.* Atlanta: John Knox.

Bruce J. Malina

Rhetorical Criticism and Social-Scientific Criticism: Why Won't Romanticism Leave Us Alone?

INTRODUCTION

I AM A member of that small, literarily challenged, band of sociorational empiricists who use the social sciences to interpret New Testament writings. Like them, I had my graduate schooling and doctoral work shaped by historical criticism set within the contours of literary criticism. I should like to begin with some autobiographical information to help you situate my presentation. Under the tutelage of Luis Alonso-Schökel, Roger Le Déaut, and Wolfgang Elpidius Pax, I at least heard about the ins and outs of literary criticism applied by these talented masters to the Hebrew, Aramaic, and Greek canonical writings. However, I undertook graduate training in biblical literature while suffering from the effects of the culture shock of moving to Italy from the Philippines. Upon my return to the Philippines in 1967 and assumption of teaching duties at the Franciscan seminary there, I was led to develop a social-scientific approach to understanding the New Testament while attempting to make sense of the scenarios in the Gospels to capable and talented Filipino students.

The method was a comparative method in which U.S. social institutions and the values that they mediated were set side by side with Filipino ones, then with Mediterranean institutions and values. While considering biblical writings historically—that is, in chronological sequence and with some anti-anachronism filters—I set as my task to lay out the meanings that emerge from reading pieces of a document, with an awareness of the cultural perspective that generated those meanings. This is what the social-scientific approach is all about. Any person who seeks to bring order to a seemingly chaotic world of overlapping, interdependent, dynamic, and intricate processes is a "scientist" in our contemporary world (Knapp 1984, 32). And if the processes in question are social, then the task of deriving meaning from socially produced sources is necessarily social-scientific.

ABOUT SOCIAL-SCIENTIFIC CRITICISM

Social-scientific criticism gets its name from John H. Elliott (see Elliott 1993). He initially called it "sociological criticism" (Elliott 1981), largely due to his schooling in Düsseldorf and consequent German frame of reference. In German (and French, Italian, Spanish, etc.) there is little difference between "social" and "sociological" (just as there is no difference between "politics" and "political"). The label "sociological" was extremely misleading in a U.S. university context, where students in the department of sociology study nothing even remotely close to what Europeans called "sociology" in biblical study. Furthermore, since most so-called sociological study of the New Testament had been and still is essentially social description and social history, that label poorly represented the products of the historical approach. And since what we are about is choosing tools for an adequate job of interpreting ancient Mediterranean documents, my own preference has been for anthropology (which is essentially comparative) and comparative sociolinguistics. Subsequently, after convincing Elliott to reshape his Teutonic phraseology, we compromised by calling the enterprise by the generic "social-scientific."

The social-scientific approach to studying the New Testament has as its goal to find out what an initial audience understood when it heard some person read a given document aloud. We wish to know what the author of the document said and meant to say. Since a psychological analysis of an individual author of the past is impossible, and since psycholinguistic analysis is equally impossible to carry out without the physical presence of the speaker, the next-best approach would be to focus on the audience. Our quest is our wish to learn what the text said and meant to say. But texts really do not say anything, much less do texts mean to say anything. It is only persons who say and mean to say.

Presumably, then, the problem in biblical interpretation is to find out what persons meant as they spoke or wrote to each other at a given time and place in the past. The full set of questions involved would be: *who* said (or wrote) *what* to *whom, when, where, why,* to *whose* benefit and with *what* effect? The "when" question serves as a chronological door leading to general historical criticism rooted in chronology. However, for some adequately meaningful interpretation, it seems that answers to all the rest of the questions would be necessary. And the task of discovering those answers obviously requires *knowledge of the social system of a given group of people.* Meanings in fact are rooted in people's enculturation, socialization, interrelationships, and interactions. The reason for this is that human beings are essentially social. They do not construct reality, not even socially. Rather, they interpret all of their experiences by means of socially shared conceptions. These socially shared conceptions and the behaviors consequent upon them constitute what I am calling "the social system" (Kilby 1993).

Those biblical interpreters who use the social-science approach look for dimensions of the social system that might disclose the meaning of a given social interaction as presented in the written descriptions of social scenarios found in New Testament writings. The first and obvious question is that of the choice of social system to study. We can simply presume that all people in the whole world are indeed entirely like us and therefore follow our own social system. If they in fact do not, they should, since we are human and they too might become human if only they would behave like us. As I am sure you realize, this perspective is that of ethnocentrism. It identifies my social system with the one and only truly human social system.

The social-scientific critics of my acquaintance strive not to be ethnocentric, at least not consciously so. Hence they do not consider the social system supporting the original performances of the New Testament to have been typically American (or Norwegian or German or British). But what social system ought they choose? They wish to avoid the unhistorical quest of historical critics for the *Sitz im Leben* of New Testament documents or segments of those documents. To ascribe synoptic forms to preaching activity or church worship now seems to have derived directly from the German practice of using the Gospels in church. More specifically, consider the following for a moment.

Most of us are familiar with the academic technique known as "form criticism" and were fed a diet of the same during our days as theological students. Do you remember the work done on the Gospels, and the debate that seemed to go on endlessly between the supporters of Vincent Taylor's book on the Gospels (*The Formation of the Gospel Tradition*) and those who like the work of Rudolf Bultmann (*The History of the Synoptic Tradition*)? Apart from radically different understandings of history, one of the points of contention was the classification of the stories of Jesus' conflict with the Pharisees. Simply put, for Taylor they were "Pronouncement Stories," and for Bultmann they were *Streitgespräche* ("Arguments"). The classifications came, in fact, not from the world of first-century Palestine, but from the academic environments of Oxford and Marburg. In the first, Jesus is depicted as the typical English professor making effective witticisms or pronouncements about the world. In the second, he is a typical German professor in the intellectually agonistic world of the German university, whose very academic career and reputation depend on the ability to out-argue opponents. In most German universities there are two professors in each discipline, a structure designed to perpetuate this game of continual conflict (Hobbs 1990, 4–5).

The question is, then, whose social system ought we use as the matrix of the meanings set out in the New Testament? Of course, we have to begin with a contemporary system because we have direct access only to contemporary systems. Since our task is one of retrodiction (making predictions about the past), the contemporary system that we choose has to be stripped of any and all post-first-century accretions so as to have it work for the New Testament writings. Given the fact that those writings derive from the Eastern Mediterranean, it seems reasonable that if any social system would resonate with the New Testament writings, it would be that of the Mediterranean. For the initial task of clearing away historical accretions, it makes best sense to begin in isolated areas of the region, in regions untouched by industrialization and still controlled by administrative (not manufacturing) centers. Peasants, by definition, are people who live in small face-to-face communities under the control of administrative centers. And there are numerous peasant communities in the Eastern Mediterranean as well in the circum-Mediterranean and its outreach from Persia to Peru (Quigley 1973).

Some people have scruples about using anthropology to study the past or to retroject behaviors from the present at all. At times, anthropology is a repulsive fetish reminiscent of alien social control, to be rejected irrationally because oppressors once employed it. At other times, the problems with using anthropology are rooted in ignorance of what anthropology is, of what information is available, of how models work. At still other times, it is rooted in unawareness about how knowledge of the past is acquired at all, about how language works and about how readers actually read. All would agree that specific knowledge of the distant past is rooted in "sources" accessible solely by reading. Now the reading process requires a reader mentally outfitted with scenarios or schemes of past social systems in order to be able to use sources (Malina 1991). If a researcher insists that the scenarios employed to read sources come from the present, that is equivalent to saying that the reader of past evidence envisions the past in terms of the present. So what makes one reading better than another? How does one test one reading over against another? Those who give up the use of comparative models rooted in the present, since this is where we must necessarily start, give up any hope of socially testable models, results, and outcomes. A number of scholars seem ideologically indisposed to social-scientific criticism. What I mean is that as a rule, those who would warn us away from social-science models do so on the basis of some ideology, whether to bolster the academic boundaries of their discipline or to protect vested interests. Otherwise, why the fear?

Institutions and Values

The term *social system* refers to the set of ways in which human beings seek to realize a meaningful human social existence. In social scientific criticism we begin with serious reflection on our own social system. This makes sense for two reasons. First, in order to compare social systems, one must know one's own system both as an instance of a system and as an actual conceptual matrix for human interaction in one's own society. Second, one must know one's own social system well so as to be alert to what to look for among people with whom one wishes to compare oneself and others.

Social scientists in the United States tell us that social systems consist of institutions, culture, and modal personalities. An *institution* is a fixed form of a phase of social life. The macroinstitutions are kinship, economics, government, and religion. Institutions are considered to be means or ways to realize goals necessary for meaningful social human existence, such as the nature and nurture of human beings (kinship), provisioning society (economics), effecting collective action (politics), and a conception of the general order of existence that makes sense out of everything (religion). *Culture* is about the specific sets of meaning and affect attributed by human beings in their social settings to the objects of their experience. Culture looks to definitions of self, others, nature, time, space, and what/who holds it all together—that is, some All. Finally, *modal personality* consists of values and behavior that characterize persons as proper human beings in a given society. *Values* are general, normative orientations of action within a social system. They involve emotional commitments to pursue specific courses of action (Pilch and Malina 1998, xv–xvi).

Social Interactions

Social interactions look to the conditions of human social relations and the behaviors that follow from them. For example, a basic aspect marking the condition of human social relations is the normal mode of interaction in the group: face-to-face community, agency-controlled community (control by some agent of a central person), or disembodied-control community (control by TV, radio, and other impersonal media). Then there is the whole area covered by social psychology, such as group formation and maintenance, types of groups, group interaction in terms of labeling, deviance, conflict, violence, and the like (Morris and Mueller 1992).

Speaking is, of course, a basic form of social interaction. And in our recent nation-states, reading is likewise a form of social interaction. In fact, language, spoken and written, is basic to the whole process of social formation and maintenance. Hence some models of how the social system is realized by means of language is necessary. Such models derive from sociolinguistics.

Reading and Language

Since any access to the biblical writings is through the corridor of reading and interpreting written language, it is important to have some verifiable theory of how reading takes place (Sanford and Garrod 1981). I use a model that I call a "scenario" model, essentially because there is evidence to indicate this is how people actually read (Malina 1991). Interpreting anything indicates that some information necessary for understanding is lacking. What the interpreter does is provide this information so that the person or thing being interpreted can be readily understood. All human beings carry on an interpretative enterprise. As a rule, they carry around in their heads one or more models of society and human being. These models greatly influence what persons look for in their experiences, what they actually see, and what they eventually do with their observations by way of fitting them into a larger scheme of explanation along with other facts. In this respect, every human being is no different from any scientist in our society (Garfinkel 1967, 262–83). Each scientist, like every other human being, holds some general conception of the realm in which he or she is working, some mental picture of how it is put together, how it hangs together, how it works, and how one ought feel about it. Of course, the same is true of the biblical interpreter, professional and nonprofessional.

The scenario model is rooted in the fact that every reader has a full and verifiable grasp of how the world works. The reader brings this awareness to a document. In the linguistic interchange that follows, an author presents some distinctive sets of scenarios of how the world works that in effect rearrange the scenarios that the reader brings to the reading. The considerate author attempts to deal with the scenarios shared by his or her readers. By this standard, of course, all the biblical authors are inconsiderate. Instead, we are asked to be the considerate readers who bring a set of scenarios proper to time, place, and culture of the biblical author. Granted the considerate reader, how do the squiggles on a page become language?

The perspective that I adopt to deal with such squiggles is that of sociolinguistics, specifically that of the neo-Firthian tradition as articulated by Michael A. K. Halliday (Halliday 1978). In this tradition the purpose of language is to "mean" to another person, and the purpose of "meaning" to others is to have some social effect. Language is a three-tiered affair. Concretely, we find the sensory residue of language in soundings and/or markings. These concrete soundings and/or markings realize wordings or pattern-sets. And these wordings or pattern-sets realize meanings. And where do the meanings realized by means of wordings realized by means of soundings and/or markings come from? They come from and, in fact, constitute the social system. Since language is ultimately a realization of meanings from a social system, it is possible to sound out in any language yet still mean from some inappropriate language—for example, say Spanish "padre" yet mean U.S. "father." Most U.S. Anglo high school Spanish speakers speak U.S. English in Spanish soundings and spellings. Similarly, many biblical scholars read their native modern languages into ancient Hebrew or Greek soundings and spellings. To interpret a document, Halliday's three-tiered model of language would have the Bible reader ask, *What social system meanings are realized by means of the wordings realized by means of the spellings of biblical documents?* In this sort of sociolinguistics, "text" refers to blocks of wording that constitute a meaningful configuration of language intended to communicate. The bottom line in this sort of reasoning is to develop a set of scenarios that fit the social system realized in the language of the Bible. Such, then, are the major tools that the social-science approach has at its disposal. Where does rhetorical criticism fit into this tool chest?

Persuasion and Communication Models

I think that all would agree that the authors of the New Testament writings drew up their first-century C.E. Mediterranean documents in order to communicate with other human beings. Not all communication aims to persuade, but persuasion is an important part of communication. "Communication is a process in which participants create and share information with one another in order to reach a mutual understanding. This definition implies that communication is a process of convergence (or divergence) as two or more individuals exchange information in order to move toward each other (or apart) in the meanings they ascribe to certain events" (Rogers 1983, 5). How did New Testament authors persuade by means of their writings?

Persuasion "refers to situations where attempts are made to modify behavior by symbolic transactions (messages) that are sometimes, but not always, linked with coercive force (indirectly coercive) and that appeal to the reason and emotions of the intended persuadee(s)" (Miller 1987, 451). According to social psychologists, one modifies behavior in one of three ways: (1) by changing an existing response, (2) by reinforcing an existing response, (3) by introducing a new response. Statistically, most persuasion seeks to immunize, to induce resistance to persuasion, to shape stable response patterns where no stable patterns previously existed. By presenting their audience with witnessed information about Jesus, the New Testament communities responsible for the preservation of the New Testament writings sought at least to reinforce existing responses, to immunize the fellow group members against competing views. In the social-science perspective, information about persuasion is best derived from contemporary studies in communication and persuasion.

ABOUT RHETORICAL CRITICISM

The term *rhetorical criticism* has been used to cover a range of areas that runs from the formal rhetorical criticism of antiquity to forms of modern-language criticism. In particular, the term *rhetorical criticism* in biblical studies covers two entirely and radically distinct types of behavior. One is historical criticism, deriving from historically oriented scholars who use ancient rhetoric as a comparative matrix for understanding New Testament writings (Wuellner 1987), and the other is a modern language approach that uses modern language analysis as a comparative matrix. I believe that these are two radically different garments, even if outfitted with the same clothing labels.

Rhetorical Criticism: Rhetoric in Antiquity

Rhetorical criticism grounded in antiquity deals with the utilizing of ancient, explicit theories of rhetoric as background—that is, as sources of information about patterns and meanings of patterns in New Testament documents. This type of rhetorical criticism can be broken into two basic subsets. The first looks at how people communicated and at what they communicated. This sort of study of communication in antiquity can yield useful information for biblical interpretation. The second looks to the specific forms or patterns of communication as reported in handbooks of ancient rhetoric, which is itself an aspect of the historical-critical method called form criticism. As such, it takes ancient documentary sources quite seriously as forms of speech and writing with which to usefully compare New Testament forms of speech and writing.

Rhetorical Criticism: Modern-Language Approaches

There is a rhetorical criticism of a radically different sort that is a type of literary criticism. This type of rhetorical criticism is employed by contemporary literary critics, steeped in modern literary criticism, who apply that methodology to the New Testament. Wuellner notes two subsets of this type of modern rhetorical criticism:

> Rhetorical criticism has brought us to a crossroad where we must choose between two competing versions of rhetorical criticism: the one in which rhetorical criticism is identical with literary criticism, the other in which rhetorical criticism is identical

with practical criticism. The former is marked by a "rhetoric restrained"; the latter strives for a "rhetoric revalued," rhetoric reinvented. (Wuellner 1987, 453)

It seems that rhetorical criticism grounded in antiquity and paying attention to classical rhetoric, though important as a historical tool of comparison, has not been the focus of more recent rhetorical criticism. Rather, recent rhetorical criticism is a rhetorical criticism of literature, a branch of literary criticism. This type of literary criticism treats biblical texts as though they are English composition, essentially asserting that all texts composed in any language and in any context are subject to the same principles of rhetorical composition. I will argue that this type of literary criticism derives from the reaction to the Enlightenment known as "Romanticism" (Peckham 1965; Molnár 1987).

Roots of Literary Rhetorical Criticism

In contemporary Western universities there are two components that teach (or profess) rhetoric: modern-language departments and department(s) featuring communication. In modern-language departments, one learns rhetorical criticism of literature or literary criticism. One might call this theoretical or aesthetic rhetoric. Then there is that component, often spread around the university, that looks to rhetorical practice—that is, the type of rhetoric taught in business schools (advertising, copy writing) and schools of journalism as well as in schools of speech and communication. I call this practical rhetoric as opposed to literary, aesthetic rhetoric. Both rhetorics are interested in how people convince and persuade one another, how they influence each other, and what effects people have on one another. But the first, aesthetic literary rhetoric, has its recent roots in Romanticism, as does literary criticism in general. The second, persuasion patterns in society, has its roots in empirical social sciences, historically developed to sell products and promote people in the postindustrial world. Obviously, social-scientific criticism has much room for both ancient rhetoric and contemporary practical communication theory. Since social-scientific criticism is a development of historical-critical methods, ancient rhetoric has valuable services to perform. And given the social-system orientation of social-science criticism, pragmatically oriented rhetoric provides invaluable information because such cultural patterns of social persuasion are part and parcel of applied social sciences and social psychology. But I see little use, if any, for aesthetic, literary criticism–based rhetoric in biblical studies, since concern for texts, texture, intertexture, and the like has no impact on what an author said and meant to say to an original audience. For aesthetic, literary criticism–based rhetoric—literary rhetorical criticism, if you will—seems to be an entirely different sphere of discourse, rooted in the concerns of a time and place alien to those of social-scientific criticism. I thus end up with two questions. First, why is there aesthetic literary rhetoric at all? Second, why do some scholars think that such literary criticism is useful in biblical study? I am not sure that it is important whether novice readers recognize it when they see it.

Rise of Modern-Language Departments

In order to understand why aesthetic literary rhetoric exists at all, one will have to note the following. Since the main purveyors of modern literary criticism usually are scholars affiliated with modern-language departments, one ought ask why there are departments of modern language at all. Modern-language departments are about more than teaching modern languages. They succeeded departments of classical language in the last century (McMurtry 1985). And just as classicists in the last century dealt with more than teaching grammar and language drills to novices, so too the whole agenda pursued by classicists was taken over by modern-language scholars, largely under the influence of the worldview known as "Romanticism." By the same token, biblical study has moved from the Enlightenment, with its emphasis on objective universals ("We hold these truths to be self-evident"), to Romanticism, where truths are left up to the individual and his or her style of living out socially constructed reality, to postindustrial Realism, where perceptions are neither universal nor subjective but rather society specific, culture specific, hence relational.

Romanticism

The term *Romantic* was coined in Germany for the new outlook that emerged in Europe at the turn of the nineteenth century (Furst 1980; Garvin 1980). The word derives from the German (and French) word for a novel, *Roman*. In this perspective, a person is immersed in the world like a character in a novel. Society is like a large work of fiction, with human persons serving as so many characters in the fictional story, playing roles that radically overlay and conceal the true humanity of the self. Objects surround subjects in the novel simply so that subjects might get to know themselves better through impersonal interaction. Subjects, in turn, surround subjects in the novel simply so that subjects might get to know themselves better through personal interaction. But such subject-subject interactions really tell the self nothing about the other self, who essentially is incommunicable. It can only tell the self something about the self, condemned to uniqueness and the incommunicability that comes with it.

Romanticism as Ideology

Perhaps a better word in English to express the outlook implied by Romanticism would be *Storybookism,* or something equivalent. As an ideology, the term *Romanticism* was intended to point to the underlying perception that emerged among a range of persons concerning the quality of life in the post-Enlightenment period. The rationalist world of the Enlightenment proved to be quite inhumane, untrustworthy, disillusioning, and rather mechanistic. When the objectivity of the Enlightenment shattered, it was replaced by the conviction that any worldview told the mind nothing about the world, but merely told it something about the mind. The mind has access to nothing but to itself and uses what is not the mind to know itself. And this self was more than the roles that it played in society.

It was in fact the source of any and all rebirth, restoration, rediscovery of value. The world of human experience comes from within, from the ultimate depths of the mind, from the nature and structure of the mind. With this, subject was sundered from object, self from role.

Life in the new Romantic postrationalist world was like a story in a novel. It was apparent that the self was simply a set of roles that one played as in a story. In a novel the world is created by a novelist, hence telling us lots about the mind of the novelist but nothing about any real world. Living life, moreover, tells the mind nothing about the world, but merely reveals something about the mind. What some call "objective reality" is simply the mind viewing a reflection of itself. For example, we see dogs as animals only because we perceive a human quality in dogs, the quality of animality. It is we who have that quality, not the dog or any other creature that we call an animal. We simply learn something about ourselves by experiencing a dog.

Peckham (1965) considers the change in worldview ushered in by Romanticism as perhaps the most significant change in human history since the founding of cities. This worldview sees reality as consisting of subject and object only. The basic cognitive assumption in this worldview is that the mind has access to nothing but itself and uses what is not the mind, that is object, to know itself. Hence the world of self is made in the image and likeness of the self only because the self can know only itself. The Romantic collapse of the self into itself was triggered by the perception that the individual person had been betrayed by the promises and the ideology of the Enlightenment—the social system into which these individuals had been enculturated. The objectivity so beloved by Enlightenment thinkers is really illusory largely because what was supposed to occur in terms of prevailing social expectations simply did not happen. The Enlightenment credo of "freedom, equality, brotherhood" remained accessible only to elites. The universe is hardly a mechanism situated in space and time running on unchanging natural laws, but rather is an organic process unfolding in unpredictable and unforeseeable ways. Society does not yield self-evident truths rooted in nature as Enlightenment thinkers believed. Rather, society itself was unpredictable and unforeseeable in its ways, hence the usual discrepancies between self-evident social truths and human experience. Human beings are not unchanging animate beings endowed with reason, but rather are dynamic selves subject to personal stories, largely because prevailing social systems did not hold a social story to which all could subscribe. Human beings cannot at all be described in terms of ontology and physics, but only in terms of personal history and psychology (Peckham 1965, 15–33).

The Romantic believed that individuals demonstrated their creativity in the way they lived out the scripts or texts that society provided for them. Thus when it came to texts of the past, the Romantic, aware of living in a storybook world, was simply not interested in clear, objective, publicly verifiable, reasonable messages, since the Enlightenment messages that had been received were demonstrably false. Rather, as experience proved, all messages were really hazy, subjective, intimate, feeling-laden. One's reactions, one's impressions, one's experiences were far more significant than simple perception, objective apprehension, and stoic discernment that did not conform to personal experience. The sublime and passionate are of greater human value than the mundane and prosaic. Poets are prophets, literati have a mission to the world, artists are the truly inspired.

In like manner, the literary critics, influenced by Romanticism, sought to present gospel narrative without story, without history. Form criticism proved that the Gospels consisted of discreet passages arbitrarily set together, a sequence of pebbles that might be rearranged at will. Although each mininarrative in the sequence might make sense, the meaning of the whole was quite whimsical. Hence the best that one could do was produce a personal reading, and this alone was of value. What counted was what the subject (reader/hearer) experienced, sensed, felt, and reacted to when confronting "the text." What one experienced in reading or hearing a scriptural text-segment was the atemporal object of the reader's or listener's experience.

Socially controlled reason was questionable, for humans in fact are subject to unintelligible fate. Since reason universalizes and feeling individualizes, the self must express itself in personally experienced thoughts and feelings. Life is peopled by the pathetic and the audacious, the Bohemian and the Heroic, the Helpless and the Virtuosi, the Downtrodden and the Dandy. Nature as untouched by contemporary humans serves best to reveal the self to itself. (And a reading of the Bible uncontaminated by any interpretation best revealed the divine in the self.) The Romantic urge for personal history over generic metaphysics generated the modern sense of history. The "sense of history" here means the belief that things were once different than they are today, and that therefore things need not remain the way they are. Prior to the emergence of the sense of history in the nineteenth century, people believed that human nature was quite unchanging. History was the teacher of life, as the ancient Romans said, because it provided anecdotes from the past, normative for action in the present. One could do no better than live up to the past. The Romantics, on the other hand, did not see the past as normative, if only because it did not and could not adequately serve to explain their experiences. It was experience that counted, and experience is always present tense and personal. Consequently, the classics were really not classical for human living. It was the vernacular and actual experience that held the key. The outcome of this perspective was the formation of departments of modern language and literature. English departments, for example, emerge under the aegis of Romanticism but little more than a century ago (McMurtry 1985).

Given the Romantic orientation to life and an academic charter to deal with literature, it was but a short step to developing an approach to the Bible as literature and a literary criticism of the Bible. It is in the Romantic interest in story that the methods of literary criticism have their roots. Couple such literary criticism with a sense of history and the historical criticism of the early part of this century emerges.

The Roots of Literary Criticism in Biblical Studies

Since the nineteenth century, historians have been quite concerned with re-telling the past in terms of temporally accurate scenarios. Historical methods have grown ever more refined to guarantee authentic documents and to filter out gross anachronistic understandings of concrete details. In this sense, the historical-critical method has been applied to the Bible quite successfully. Endowed with the usual historical concerns for chronological accuracy and archaeological and geographical specificity, historically minded biblical scholars told of the distinctive ways in which persons spoke and wrote in the past, the historical settings in which such communication took place, and the concrete items referred in the writings. Although the historical method has moved biblical interpretation a long way from the impressionistic subjectivism of the anachronistic interpretations of the past, its successes leave one no less aware of its inadequacies. For the whole historical enterprise often succumbed to ethnocentrism thanks to Romantic concerns with the self, bent on transcending social limitations in its drive for meaning, order, value, and identity. The self was redeemed in the action of redeeming the world, by transcending social limits. The writings of the Romantic period are filled with schemes to save humanity, often still pursued. The hidden assumptions of any historian's cultural worldview and ideology are necessarily woven into the very fabric of the story being told. The social sciences have been introduced into the historical method specifically to surface ethnocentrism, and in the process they revealed ideological anachronism as well.

Without shaking its Romantic mantle, the historical-critical method had yet to address the question of the meaning of social realities in some objectively verifiable way—that is, in a way that might account for and filter out the ethnocentric bias of the interpreter. Witness the many interpretations of marriage and divorce in the Bible, of the poor and their poverty, and the rich and their wealth. And note the almost total absence of fundamental Mediterranean themes in biblical interpretation, such as honor and shame, challenge and riposte, faction formation and conflict. Although it is a necessary and fundamental tool for understanding the past, the historical-critical method, it seems, could not adequately deal with ideology and its abstract, symbolic referents. This is especially true in regard to religion in the Bible. What is needed are more adequate, explicit models of interpretation, validated or invalidated by a broad and large number of tests and applications.

To put it another way, in order to read and interpret the meaning of any sort of writing, whether a road sign or a restaurant check or a biblical book, the reader must share with the writer a scenario of how the world works. People who read the New Testament authors today sometimes presume that they fully share the same "religious" worldview as those authors. This fundamentalism is usually avoided by the historically minded. Yet even those persons with a sense of history often believe that the ancient world in general and Israel in particular had dominant beliefs and institutions that were explicitly religious. For example, the noted historian John Collins writes, "In the ancient world in general, and in

Israel in particular, the dominant beliefs and institutions were explicitly religious and were embodied in traditions passed on from generation to generation" (Collins 1983, 2). For such people, Paul of Tarsus and Jesus of Nazareth would have picked up and elaborated explicitly religious themes in the course of launching their respective forms of Israelite religion. What largely differentiated the two was that Jesus set a rural movement under way, while Paul had to deal with the first urban Christians.

The historical-critical method has served its purpose and continues to serve its purpose well. It alerts its users to the dangers of ethnocentrism and anachronism. However, the historical-critical method as generally used focuses largely if not exclusively on the concrete dimensions of life, present and past. People no longer confuse Gothic churches with the Jerusalem temple; ancient clothing styles are not those of today. Users of the historical-critical method are very sensitive to proper chronological sequencing, spend volumes on determining whether Bar Kokhba's revolt was in 130 or 131 c.e. In this respect, the historical-critical method has helped us to distance ourselves from the people whom we study from the past in terms of concrete and chronological dimensions of life. The problem with historical-critical method as practiced by historians is that as a rule it is both entirely insensitive to and selectively inattentive to the nonconcrete meaning, dimensions of life (institutions, culture, modal personality). From a certain perspective, it is the nonconcrete, symbolic, meaning-filled dimensions of life that take up most of human concern, energy, and activity, but the historical-critical method pays little attention to ideology, conceptions of social meaning, models of social interaction, cross-cultural psychological development of humans, and especially to these conceptions of what life was and meant.

Yet literary critics who are oriented toward the Romantic will surely find social-scientific criticism rather absurd. After all, if the group is not to be trusted, if only individual experience counts, what is the sense of anything social at all? And if the scientific approach derives from the Enlightenment, would not adopting anything scientific simply mark a return to the bankrupt objectivist worldview of the past? On the other hand, it would seem that the real problem is not that biblical interpretation of the modern literary-critical sort is asocial. The problem is that it is ideal, doctrinal, nontemporal, nonhistorical, anesthetizing, tranquilizing, fantastic, imaginary, Rohrshachian—anything but a flesh-and-blood story of flesh-and-blood persons enculturated and immersed in the nonpsychologically minded, anti-introspective, group-interactive, "sociologically" oriented society of the first-century eastern Mediterranean.

Consider the usual hidden agenda in biblical study. Since people who study the Bible are often expected to bolster, support, and clarify life for a church, it is the life of the church at present that very often determines the agenda of biblical study, perception of abstract relations such as marriage, sin, faith, and obedience, and so on. Similarly, since the State of Israel derives its ideological charter from the Hebrew Bible and from its practical "new" testament, Flavius Josephus, the agenda for the interpretation of the Hebrew Bible and Josephus has been set in terms of the setting, values, aspirations, and charter of the contemporary State of Israel.

Summary Comparison

By way of summing up the discussion to this point, I offer the following comparative table:

SOCIAL-SCIENTIFIC CRITICISM	LITERARY CRITICISM
Meaning derives from and is embedded in the social group.	Meaning derives from and is embedded in individual experience.
The world functions in the way persons are enculturated to believe that it functions.	Personal experience indicates that the world does not function in the way persons have been enculturated to believe that it functions.
There are socially rooted preexisting patterns for morality.	Just as there are no preexisting patterns for art, so too there are no preexisting patterns for morality.
Human perception of reality is simultaneously subjective, objective, and social.	Human perception of reality is essentially subjective.
The mind has access to itself, society, and objective reality.	The mind essentially has access only to itself.
Reality is socially interpreted.	Reality is socially constructed.
Objective knowledge derives from social interpretation.	Objective knowledge is an illusion.
The social must be evaluated and may be trusted.	The social is untrustworthy; only the true self is to be trusted.
Science is a way of knowing, controlling, and predicting.	Science is a way of smothering personal knowledge and experience.
Sociology and cultural anthropology consist of valid generalizations about human social behavior.	Since persons are unique, it is impossible to produce any valid generalizations about human social behavior.
Emphasis on what each individual has in common with others and in difference from others, a preoccupation with the social, socialized, and unique self.	
Emphasis on what each individual has in difference from others, a preoccupation with the unique self.	
Each work of art does not have its own aesthetic law, and each person must comply with objective moral standards.	Each work of art must have its own aesthetic law, and each person must, within obvious limits, determine his or her own moral standards.

Figure 1: Summary comparison of social-scientific criticism and literary criticism

Conclusions

Obviously, social-scientific criticism is much concerned about how persons communicated with and influenced each other in the first-century Mediterranean world. Patterns of persuasion are always rooted in patterns of social interaction. The study of classical patterns of persuasion in ancient rhetoric would provide an excellent set of data for constructing scenarios for some dimensions of New Testament documents. The problem is that so far experts in this area are not agreed about which ancient patterns are involved (Mack 1990). Furthermore, to mark off a pattern still does not yield information about the meaning of the pattern. An encomium, for example, says nothing without information of the honor/shame quality of ancient Mediterranean interaction.

With the historians, we are left with implicit models or scenarios of how the world works, usually laden with ethnocentric presuppositions.[1] And with the literary critics, we are left with the study of patterns of persuasion assessed in terms of a sampling of one (the critic) relative to a writing that has a life of its own anyway.

As is well known, the range of harmful attitudes and behaviors said to receive warrant from the Bible and chosen by selective inattentiveness is truly astounding. These include, for example, anti-Semitism, slavery, war, apartheid, sexism, and child abuse. Given such attitudes and behaviors rooted in contextualization of a text with a life of its own, social-scientific criticism seems to be the only sane (and safe) option. It is the only considerate and fair option as well.

Bibliography

Anderson, Benedict. 1983. *Imagined Communities: Reflections on the Origin and Spread of Nationalism.* London: Verso.

Collins, John J. 1983. *Between Athens and Jerusalem: Jewish Identity in the Hellenistic Diaspora.* New York: Crossroad.

---

[1] For interpreters of ancient documents, the question of literacy and illiteracy in a given culture is not simply about the prevalence of the ability or lack thereof to read and write in a social group. The question of whether a language document, to be performed or read aloud in any event, was inscribed or memorized is quite secondary to the point at issue, which is whether the document was carefully prepared or produced extemporaneously in the form in which we have it. Much that has been written on orality and literacy in the first-century Mediterranean world is rather beside the point. "[Sylvia] Scribner and [Michael] Cole's extensive research, published as *The Psychology of Literacy* (Cambridge, Mass.: Harvard University Press, 1981), reveals rather conclusively that being able to read and write has no great effect on cognition, certainly less than the experience of attending school and even less than whether or not one lives in an urban or agrarian community. Reading and writing, like any other activity, develop only those cognitive skills actually related to their use; that is, there is no reason to believe that a certain minimal mastery of literacy will result in profound changes in how people think or organize themselves" (Tuman 1983, 775).

Domeris, W. R. 1991. Sociological and Social Historical Investigations. Pages 215–33 in *Text and Interpretation: New Approaches in the Criticism of the New Testament*. Edited by P. J. Hartin and J. H. Petzer. New Testament Tools and Studies 15. Leiden: Brill.

Elliott, John H. 1981. *A Home for the Homeless: A Sociological Exegesis of 1 Peter, Its Situation and Strategy*. Philadelphia: Fortress.

————. 1993. *What Is Social-Scientific Criticism?* Guides to Biblical Scholarship: New Testament Series. Minneapolis: Fortress.

Fish, Stanley Eugene. 1980. *Is There a Text in This Class? The Authority of Interpretive Communities*. Cambridge, Mass.: Harvard University Press.

Furst, Lilian R., ed. 1980. *European Romanticism: Self Definition; An Anthology*. New York: Methuen.

Garfinkel, Harold. 1967. *Studies in Ethnomethodology*. Englewood Cliffs, N.J.: Prentice-Hall.

Garvin, Harry R., ed. 1980. *Romanticism, Modernism, Postmodernism*. Bucknell Review 25/2. Lewisburg, Pa.: Bucknell University Press.

Gay, Peter. 1986. *The Tender Passion: The Bourgeois Experience*. New York: Oxford University Press.

Halliday, Michael A. K. 1978. *Language as Social Semiotic: The Social Interpretation of Language and Meaning*. Baltimore: University Park Press.

Hobbs, T. R. 1990. Crossing Cultural Bridges: The Biblical World, *McMaster Journal of Theology* 1:1–21.

James, Paul. 1992. Forms of Abstract "Community": From Tribe and Kingdom to Nation and State. *Philosophy of the Social Sciences* 22:313–36.

Kilby, Robert Jay. 1993. Is Culture "Illusion"? A Pragmatic Response to D. W. Winnicott. *Horizons* 20:260–79.

Knapp, Mark L. 1984. *Interpersonal Communication and Human Relationships*. Boston: Allyn & Bacon.

Kroeber, A. L., and Clyde Kluckhohn. 1952. *Culture: A Critical Review of Concepts and Definitions*. Papers of the Peabody Museum of American Archaeology and Ethnology 47/1. Cambridge, Mass.: Peabody Museum of American Archaeology and Ethnology, Harvard University.

Mack, Burton. 1990. *Rhetoric and the New Testament*. Minneapolis: Fortress.

Malina, Bruce J. 1991. Reading Theory Perspective: Reading Luke-Acts. Pages 3–23 in *The Social World of Luke-Acts: Models for Interpretation*. Edited by Jerome H. Neyrey. Peabody, Mass.: Hendrickson.

McMurtry, Jo. 1985. *English Language, English Literature: The Creation of an Academic Discipline*. Hamden, Conn.: Archon Books.

Miller, Gerald R. 1987. Persuasion. Pages 446–83 in *Handbook of Communication Science*. Edited by Charles R. Berger and Steven H. Chaffee. Newbury Park, Calif.: Sage Publications.

Molnár, Géza von. 1987. *Romantic Vision, Ethical Context: Novalis and Artistic Autonomy*. Theory and History of Literature 39. Minneapolis: University of Minnesota Press.

Morris, A. D. and C. McClurg Mueller, eds. 1992. *Frontiers in teh Social Move-ment Theory*. New Haven: Yale University Press.

Peckham, Morse, ed. 1965. *Romanticism: The Culture of the Nineteenth Century*. New York: G. Braziller.

Pilch, John J. and Bruce J. Malina, eds. 1998. *Handbook of Biblical Social Values*. Peabody, Mass.: Hendrickson.

Quigley, Carroll. 1973. Mexican National Character and Circum-Mediterranean Personality Structure. *American Anthropologist* 75:319–22.

Rogers, Everett M. 1983. *Diffusion of Innovations*. 3d ed. New York: Free Press.

Rogers, Everett M., with F. Floyd Shoemaker. 1971. *Communication of Innova-tions: A Cross-Cultural Approach*. 2d ed. New York: Free Press.

Sanford, A. J., and S. C. Garrod. 1981. *Understanding Written Language: Explora-tions of Comprehension Beyond the Sentence*. New York: Wiley.

Schneiders, Sandra M. 1991. *The Revelatory Text: Interpreting the New Testament as Sacred Scripture*. San Francisco: HarperSanFrancisco.

Tuman, Myron C. 1983. Words, Tools, and Technology: A Critical Review of Walter Ong's *Orality and Literacy*. *College English* 45:769–79.

Webb, Timothy, ed. 1982. *English Romantic Hellenism, 1700–1824*. Literature in Context. Manchester: Manchester University Press; New York: Barnes & Noble.

Wuellner, Wilhelm. 1987. Where Is Rhetorical Criticism Taking Us? *Catholic Bib-lical Quarterly* 49:448–63.

Part Two

INSTITUTIONS

Kinship

2

It is often said that there were two basic institutions in antiquity: politics and kinship. Whereas modern Western democracies look to government to protect and care for their most vulnerable citizens, in antiquity the only welfare for people came from their kin. Because no welfare or social-security system was in place, individuals looked to their families to comfort, feed, nurture, and, finally, bury them. It was a tragedy to be taken from one's family or to be forced to leave. Ties of affection, identity, and support would be broken by this rupture. Modern Americans are expected eventually to leave home, make a life for themselves, pursue careers that might be utterly unlike those of their parents; in short, they are expected to become independent individuals. But individual members of ancient families were so embedded in their families that sons took up the father's trade; there never was even the possibility of a son telling his father that he wanted to be a musician rather than a farmer or craftsman. Nurtured by his family, this son was expected to reinvest all of his loyalty, resources, and energy into the maintenance of the kinship group.

It is difficult for modern Americans to imagine, much less appreciate, what kinship meant in the ancient Mediterranean world. What is needed, then, is a mental scenario of a family or of kinship relations that is acutely sensitive to the way of thinking and perceiving in antiquity. To build this scenario, one needs to learn about "gender" in antiquity, how males and females occupied different physical space, performed gender-specific tasks, and espoused gender-specific virtues. It was always an important item in any biography that the author identify the home town, family, parents, and ancestors of a person, since honor derived from geography (Athens, Corinth, Tarsus) and generation. Encoded here is a need to know and express a person's genealogy, for this may entitle that person to membership in a select group or to occupy a certain status and perform a specific role.

But it is understanding the meaning and the making of marriage that is the hardest task for modern people. Marriage in Jesus' time was not based on romantic love of two individuals that was nurtured during a courtship. On the contrary, marriages were alliances of the elders in two families who sought to strengthen their social positions by joining the two "houses" by means of the bride. And often there were elaborate rules governing who could marry, either requiring a marriage close to home or one utterly outside of the group. Since marriage joins two families for their mutual benefit, a divorce is not simply the separation of the husband from the wife; it is a breaking of the bonds of the two families. Dowry and other wealth that the bride brought must be returned to her family. More than the material difficulties here are the social ones, loss of honor and respect for the wife, who returns home, unlikely to marry again. The bride's family would lose honor as well for having a daughter seen as worthless or a shrew.

The anthropology explaining this type of kinship and marriage is ready to hand. K. C. Hanson's essay provides an example of how having an understanding of kinship can be used when reading the New Testament. He presents a detailed examination of the marriages, families, divorces, and inheritances within the family of Herod the Great, his extended kinship group, and his successors. Using cross-cultural models of kinship will enable us to understand the processes at work in this family and to recognize the motivations underlying them.

K. C. Hanson

All in the Family: Kinship in Agrarian Roman Palestine

INTRODUCTION

THE GOSPEL OF Matthew begins with a comment about Jesus' lineage record (1:1) followed by a genealogy running from Abraham to Joseph and then to Jesus (1:2–17). And in the Synoptic Gospels (Mark 3:31–35 par.) Jesus' saying seems to redefine family. Why would Matthew want to begin his narrative about Jesus with such a lineage record? What sort of society was this that valued a person's genealogy? Why are David and Abraham emphasized as Jesus' key ancestors? Can we tell whether Jesus himself was concerned with his ascribed genealogical honor? In what sense can "doing God's will" create a new kinship group? What was the traditional relationship between a mother and sons, between brothers and sisters, and between brothers in ancient Palestine?

In ancient Mediterranean societies during the first century, kinship was still the primary social domain. That is to say, virtually no social relationship, institution, or value set was untouched by the family and its concerns. But it was also no longer the only explicit domain. In these advanced agrarian societies, politics had contributed an identifiably separate set of institutions, though still heavily affected by kinship structures and relationships. The social domains (or institutional systems) addressed by cultural anthropologists (kinship, politics, economics, religion) are never discrete entities that operate in isolation from one another; they are interactive in every society. But beyond interaction, one sphere may be embedded in another. By this we mean that its definition, structures, and authority are dictated by another sphere. As Malina (1986; 1993) has demonstrated, religion in the ancient Mediterranean (specifically regarding Israelite religion) was always embedded in either politics or kinship.

Kinship in ancient Israel and Judah, as well as in first-century Palestine, was affected by the political sphere, especially in terms of law. For example, politics affected kinship framework in the areas of incest, rape, marriage, divorce, paternity, and inheritance. But kinship also affected politics, most notably in patron-client relationships and developing networks of "friends." Kinship was affected by religion in terms of purity—for example, regulating who could have sex with whom and the ethnic and religious status of one's spouse. And kinship affected religion (embedded in politics) in terms of descent, especially in the importance laid on the lineages of priests and their wives, but also by regulating membership in the political religion for the laity. Finally, kinship was interactive with the economic sphere in terms of occupations, dowry and inheritance, and land tenure.

GENDER

At the heart of understanding any set of family relations are assumptions about gender: what are the social roles and expectations for males and females in the society? These conventional configurations are the product of a society's worldview. Drawing boundaries, setting goals, and articulating fears emerge from this worldview. Some of these male/female differences may be stipulated in law, but for the most part they have to do with the assumptions operating deep in the society's structures, arrangements, and habits. Moreover, most societies assume that their gender configurations are "obvious" and simply "natural"; that is, the ways in which males and females operate in society are established in nature rather than in culture (1 Cor 11:4–16). This assumption could hardly be further from the truth, as has been established by the last century of ethnographic and cross-cultural research.

First-Century Palestine

Palestine (and the ancient Mediterranean as a whole) was patriarchal in its structures and assumptions, and this was a foundation stone of their worldview. This means that the public aspects of society were heavily controlled by males, with older males having control over the younger. In these ancient patriarchal societies, the privileged status of the male stemmed from the assumption that his "seed" was what created a child (Wis 7:1–2); in other words, the mother provided the womb for the birth of his children. This male primacy was also legitimated through the Israelite creation story: God created males first; males, therefore, have the superior position (Gen 2:7–23; 1 Cor 11:7–9). Philo (an Israelite philosopher, theologian, and diplomat who lived in Alexandria in the first century) went so far as to say that males and females have two different types of souls (*Spec. Laws* 3.178), reflecting assumptions common among Greek philosophers.

Fear of Females

But gender division is also rooted in male fears of the female. Ancient Israelites construed females not simply as different, but as potentially dangerous. A man can be overpowered by a woman simply by looking at her (Philo, *Virtues* 38–40). A daughter's chastity is described as the "weak link" in the family's shame (Sir 7:24; 42:9–11). And women are often categorized as fundamentally sinful, for example, in these proverbial statements by Ben Sira (see also Philo, *Hypothetica* 11.14–17):

Do not look upon anyone for beauty,
  and do not sit among women.
For moths emerge from garments,
  and a woman's wickedness emerges from a woman.
Better is the wickedness of a man than a woman who does good.
And it is a woman who brings shame and disgrace. (Sir 42:12–14)

These negative statements must also be put in context with positive statements made about wives and mothers. A "good wife" is grand (Prov 31:10–31), and mothers are deserving of their sons' respect, honor, and attention (Exod 20:12; Prov 1:8; 6:20). A wife or mother, a daughter or sister, is worthy of love, care, and respect, but she must also remain within the parameters set by the males and must constantly be kept in check by the adult males of the family. Males must guard the females within the family and continually be on guard against females from the outside.

Gender and Space

A clear articulation of gender roles and social space in daily practice is also provided by Philo:

> Marketplaces, and council chambers, and courts of justice, and large groups and assemblies of crowds, and a life in the open air full of arguments and actions relating to war and peace are suited to men. But taking care of the house and remaining at home are the proper duties of women; the virgins having their rooms in the center of the house within the innermost doors, and the full-grown women not going beyond the vestibule and outercourts. For there are two types of states: the larger and the smaller. The larger ones are called "cities" and the smaller ones "households."

> And the superintendence and management of these is allotted to the two genders separately: men having the governance of the larger, which is called a "polity," and women that of the smaller, which is called "economy" [household management]. Therefore, do not let a woman busy herself about those things which are beyond the province of economy; but let her cultivate solitude, and do not let her be seen going about like a woman who walks the streets in the sight of other men, except when it is necessary for her to go to the temple, if she has any proper regard for herself. And even then, do not let her go at noon when the market is full, but after the majority of the people have returned home, like a well-born woman, a real and true citizen, performing her vows and her sacrifices in tranquility, so as to avert evils and to receive blessings. (*Spec. Laws* 3.169–171 [see also *Flaccus* 89])

This is accentuated in the prohibition against women entering the inner courts of the Jerusalem temple (Josephus, *Ant.* 15.419) and such places as athletic games (Philo, *Spec. Laws* 3.178). Furthermore, garments were strictly identified as gender-specific (Deut 22:5; Josephus, *Ant.* 4.301; Philo, *Virtues* 18–21), as were hairstyles (1 Cor 11:14–15). From these passages, we can see that ancient Israelites replicated their perceptions of gender in social roles, behaviors, dress, spaces, times, and attitudes. To modern Western ears this may seem like simple male chauvinism, but our own assumptions about male and female roles are no less socially constructed and interpreted.

The results of ancient forms of gender division were heightened expectations that males and females would function differently. Household management was for females, field management for males. Public representation of the family in negotiations, making contracts, and in court was for males. Informal familial connections to other families was for females (e.g., marriage plans). Sacrificing at the temple was for males. Child-rearing was for females. In Israelite tradition, only males functioned as priests. Only females functioned as midwives. Formal education was limited to males. These are all generalizations, and they are affected by status as well as gender. Education, for example, was primarily limited to elite males; peasants had little time or need for advanced literacy. Elite females seem to have had more flexibility in their marital arrangements than did those of the rank and file.

Genealogy, Descent, and Genealogies

The particulars of ancestral background carry little practical importance within contemporary U.S. society. It is a commonplace that we are a "melting pot" culture, composed of every conceivable national, ethnic, and linguistic group (although some have suggested "mixed salad" as a better image). We may have been raised with cultural stereotypes and prejudices about groups that we consider "outsiders," whether based on race, ethnicity, regional origins, or economic status. But we seldom interpret the meaning of "insider" social status in terms of long-term family lineage. If a job applicant from Senegal, for instance, listed her tribal group, clan, and the genealogy of her family on a résumé and sent it to an American corporation, her potential employer would not know what to make of it. This information would be meaningful and clearly communicate her status only to those within the same kinship system.

A genealogy is a list of relatives arranged by generation, which may skip any number of generations for lack of information, or to achieve schematic design, or to emphasize the importance of particular members. The social setting of the genealogy is the domestic group (family, clan, or tribe) that depends upon this information. The intention of any genealogy must be assessed in terms of its institutional setting, for one's genealogy may be used to establish religious purity, rights to political leadership, inheritance rights, marriage eligibility, and ethnic connections.

Genealogies do not have one simple meaning, function, or compositional form, even when they concern actual biological links; they are always complex social constructs. They may also be composed to demonstrate social links other than biology (e.g., relationships between allied groups). These are all variables, and so how one composes a genealogy reflects one's social values, perspective, and specific goals. "All of them are accurate when their differing functions are taken into consideration" (Wilson 1977, 182); that is, they are all "accurate" within their particular construction of reality and their cultural matrix.

Regarding the social functions that a genealogy may serve, we may list several interrelated possibilities:

1. To establish the significant kinship group to which one belongs, tracing a map of social relationships and the continuity of a particular family (2 Sam 9:6)

2. To embody the honor of the family in a list of names (1 Sam 9:1)

3. To identify potential marriage partners within the family: endogamy (Josephus, *Ant.* 17.12–16)

4. To identify the actual "outsiders" who were allowed to marry into the kinship group: exogamy (Josephus, *Ant.* 18.130–141)

5. To make a political claim to leadership or office by identifying relevant ancestors (1 Kgs 13:2)

6. To assert inheritance or other family rights; thus gender, order of birth, and mother are all key issues (2 Sam 3:2–5; 5:13–16)

7. To establish membership in the religious group for which heredity is important (1 Chr 9:1; Ezra 2:59–63; 10:18–44)

8. To establish the right to hereditary offices (Exod 28:1; Lev 16:32)

MARRIAGE

Marriage is a sexual, economic, and (at times) political and religious relationship for a male and a female, contracted between families (or segments of the same family). In preindustrial traditional societies marriage is seldom (if ever) solely an arrangement between a man and woman; this is particularly true of first marriages. Herod the Great, for example, did not merely choose Marimba, the Hasmonean princess, as his wife; he made a marriage contract with her family (Josephus, *J.W.* 1.241). The parties involved act not as individuals but rather as members of households. Thus we must pursue a social, rather than an individualistic, interpretation of marriage.

Betrothal

Betrothal is utterly different from the modern U.S. custom of an engagement, a period during which a couple continue dating, deepen their knowledge of one another, make plans together, and receive counseling. In the ancient Mediterranean world betrothal (Matt 1:18) was the process prior to marriage, but its purpose was not to enhance the relationship of the couple. Rather, it was the procedure in which the male and female are promised to each other (usually by their families). During this time the families negotiate the dowry and bridewealth arrangements. It may take place shortly before the wedding or even years before children are ready for marriage.

Age at Marriage

The Mishnah's saying about the Israelite male's "times of life" indicates eighteen as the age for marriage (*m. ʾAbot* 5:21); but no early legal traditions survive that actually regulate the age of marriage. The first stage of the marriage was a betrothal, accompanied by a meal at the woman's home (*m. Pesah.* 3:7) and the groom's payment of the indirect dowry (*m. Ketub.* 5:2). The betrothal was a binding agreement, and a formal divorce was necessary to break it (Matt 1:18–19). The marriage itself was celebrated with a feast put on by the groom's father (Matt 22:2; 25:1–13; Luke 14:8–11; *m. Šeb.* 7:4; *m. Ḥal.* 2:7) that lasted seven days (*m. Neg.* 3:2) or longer (Tob 8:19–20). The basic parts of the wedding were (1) preparation of the bride, (2) transfer of the bride from her father's home to that of the groom, (3) the bride's introduction into the home of the groom, and (4) blessings and festivities within the husband's home. (Safrai 1976, 757)

The impediments to a legal marriage for Israelites were descent (near relatives as defined in Lev 18; 20) and purity (no Israelite/Gentile marriage; an adulteress could not marry her partner in adultery; a man could not remarry his former wife if she had remarried in the meantime; neither a castrated man nor an insane person could marry). (Falk 1974, 514–15)

Endogamy

Marriage between close kinship group members is known as "endogamy." In certain regions of the world (including the Middle East) marriage between the children of two brothers or two sisters (parallel cousins), or between the children of a brother and a sister (cross-cousins), ranges from 19 to 60 percent (Todd 1985, 19). This relaxation of the "incest taboo" may be the result of wanting to retain property and wealth within the kinship group, to consolidate power, to maintain cultic purity, and to protect the group from outsiders.

From antiquity to modern times, endogamy in its various forms has been one of the key characteristics of the eastern Mediterranean societies. Abraham, for example, was quite concerned that Isaac take a wife from his kinship group (Gen 24). But what evidence do we have for the Hellenistic and Roman eras? Information concerning marriages in the Herodian family comes from Josephus. It is most helpful to us in studying first-century Palestine because we can track this kinship group for more than eight generations. Thirty-nine Herodian family members entered into twenty-two endogamous marriages (accounting for multiple marriages); thirty-four of those individuals were Herodian blood relatives. Of those marriages, seventeen were between blood relatives, and five were between relatives by marriage.

Even when an endogamous strategy is held as an ideal, it cannot always be pursued; hindrances exist. A "potential mate of the correct sex or age range simply may not exist, or poor relations between siblings may prevent negotiation.... Successful negotiations depend not only upon the status of the relations between siblings, but upon those between their spouses as well" (Pastner 1981, 309).

The story of Pheroras, the brother of Herod the Great, is a telling one with regard to endogamy. Herod first arranged for his brother Pheroras to marry his wife's sister (evidently the sister of Marimba, the Hasmonean princess [Josephus, *J.W.* 1.483]). After Pheroras's wife died, Herod betrothed Pheroras to his oldest daughter by Marimba, Salampsio. But because of his affection for a slave, Pheroras reneged on the betrothal (Josephus, *J.W.* 1.484). After a period of time, Herod betrothed Pheroras to Salampsio's sister Cypros, whom Pheroras promised to marry in thirty days. But he reneged again, and these refusals were interpreted as affronts to Herod's honor (Josephus, *Ant.* 16.197). Pheroras's dishonor lay in his reneging on two promises to his brother, as well as opting for a slave-concubine over endogamous marriages. By doing so, he went against both custom and the head of his family.

Exogamy

The marriage strategy of the Herodians also included exogamy (marriage outside the kinship group): twenty-seven exogamous marriages are specifically known. For the most part, these marriages were made for the advancement of the family's honor and power by establishing network links with political and religious leaders throughout the eastern Mediterranean.

Of the twenty-seven exogamous marriages entered into by fourteen different Herodians (accounting for multiple marriages), only six were to spouses of nonelite or unknown status. The marriage between Archelaus, ethnarch of Judea, and Marimba may have been endogamous, but the record is unclear with regard to Mariamme's identity. All the others were wives of Herod the Great, some or all of whom may have been elites, but Josephus provides no clues (Hanson 1989b, 44–46). Pheroras had a child by a slave, but she was most likely a concubine rather than a wife (Josephus, *J.W.* 1.483–484; *Ant.* 16.194–199).

What functions did these exogamous marriages serve beyond the obvious kinship functions? For many of them, Josephus provides no information. But a few examples will demonstrate that more was at stake than home and hearth. The political importance of the marriages between the Herodians and the Hasmoneans (the Judean royal-priestly family that had ruled Palestine from 142 to 63 B.C.E.) can hardly be overestimated. The marriage of Herod the Great and Marimba was of central importance; important also were those of Pheroras (Herod's brother) and Mariamme's sister (whose name is unknown), as well as Herod's oldest, most powerful son, Antipater, and the daughter of Antigonus the Hasmonean. The effects of these relationships were far-reaching. This strategy was an attempt to solidify Judean legitimacy for Herod and his reign through marriage alliances to the previously reigning Hasmonean family, which was still very popular in Palestine. That this strategy was at least partially successful is spelled out by Josephus: "And Antigonus being banished, he [Herod] returned to Jerusalem where [his] success made him everyone's favorite. Even those who had not formerly been devoted, were now reconciled by his marriage into the family of Hyrcanus" (*J.W.* 1.240).

A further consequence of these three Herodian family marriages was that they tied the two competing segments of the Hasmonean family together: Marimba and her sister (the wives of Herod and Pheroras) were the granddaughters of both Aristobulus II (paternal) and Hyrcanus II (maternal); and Antipater's wife was the daughter of Antigonus, and her paternal grandfather was Aristobulus II. It would appear, then, that Pheroras's and Antipater's marriages functioned to neutralize the threat of a further Hasmonean revolt against Herodian power, for besides uniting two competing elements of the Hasmonean family, they also brought these elements into marital arrangements with the Herodian family so that the Hasmoneans' popularity did not run against the Herodian family.

The Economics of Marriage Dowry

The economic aspects of marriage are complex arrangements in all societies. In the United States, prenuptial agreements have become more important as a way to protect assets accrued before marriage or the inheritance of children from earlier marriages. Ancient Mediterranean societies also had complex "prenuptial agreements" as a means of clarifying the flow of property from one family to another, endowing the new couple, and protecting the bride's rights in case of a divorce.

Dowry

The bride's family provides her or the couple with property (usually under the control of her husband) at the time of marriage. This might be immovable property (land and buildings), movable property (such as animals, bedding, cooking utensils, jewelry), cash, or a combination of these. Dowry is mentioned in the Bible in the context of the pre-Israelite period as well as the early Israelite monarchy (e.g., Gen 30:20; 31:14–16; 1 Kgs 9:16).

Jack Goody was the first to demonstrate that dowry has broader implications than just a gift to the bride or couple. It is, in fact, a payment of a daughter's share of the family inheritance (full or partial) given to the daughter at the time of marriage (Gen 31:14–16; Josh 15:18–19; *m. Ketub.* 6:6). Since it is distributed before the death of the parents, Goody refers to it as "pre-mortem inheritance."

Women in traditional patriarchal societies shift from being "embedded in" (under the authority, legal responsibility, and care of) their fathers to a similar relationship to their husbands (*m. Ketub.* 4:4–5). Thus the groom was given the woman's property to administer (the legal term is *usufruct*), but it nonetheless belonged to her and was passed to her children, as distinct from the personal property of the husband, or his kinship group, or his children from other marriages. Israelite evidence of this appears in a fifth-century-B.C.E. document from the Elephantine papyri: Mahseiah bar Yedoniah (the bride's father) and Yezaniah bar Uriah (the groom) contract Yezaniah's marriage to Mibtachiah (the bride). Mahseiah stipulates that Mibtachiah's dowry (a house) is for the couple's joint use; it was not for them to sell or give away (the "dowryhouse" mentioned in *m. B. Bat.* 6:4). If Mibtachiah were to divorce Yezaniah, the property would be passed to their children. If Yezaniah were to divorce Mibtachiah, half the property would go to her, and half to Yezaniah (for his labor on it), until his death, when their children would inherit it.

Dowry and Honor

The dowry is not only an economic transaction; it is also an expression of the family's honor on the occasion of a daughter's wedding (Harrell and Dickey 1985). The size of the dowry demonstrates to the community how wealthy the family is and is one signal of their publicly displayed honor. This is not hoarded wealth but rather transmitted wealth, providing the daughter with her portion of the family's goods, money, and property. Still, a dowry may also be the means of acquiring honor or a client: a son-in-law of higher status increases the family's honor, or one of lower status may be enlisted with his family as clients of the family (Schlegel and Eloul 1988, 301). Marriage transactions are also "a function of the kind of property relations within the society" and are a means of adjusting "labor needs, the transmission of property, and status concerns" (Schlegel and Eloul 1988, 294, 305).

Throughout the ancient Mediterranean, dowries varied but, over the centuries, included houses, land, and slaves (Gen 24:59–61; 29:24–29; Josh 15:18–19; *m. Yebam.* 7:1). The Mishnah stipulates that a poor orphan should be given a minimum dowry of fifty *zuz* (= twenty-five shekels) from the community's fund for the poor (*m. Ketub.* 6:5). In the hypothetical case of a dowry, the Mishnah uses the amount of one thousand *denars/zuz* (*m. Ketub.* 6:3). For elites, dowries are mentioned in 1 Macc 10:54; Josephus, *Ant.* 13.82.

DIVORCE

Divorce is the severing of marital relations; it breaks the bonds of attachment and obligation instituted in marriage. Again, this is between not just two individuals, but two families. It calls for returning dowries and other disentanglements of property, as witnessed in documents from the early second-century Babatha archive.[1]

Israelite Divorce

Whereas Mark 10:2–9 indicates that divorce and remarriage were allowed under no circumstance in the early Jesus movement, Matt 5:31–32; 19:3–9 parallel the rabbinic school of Shammai in specifically restricting divorce to cases of

---

[1] The Babatha archive is a collection of contracts and deeds concerning Babatha, an elite Judean woman who lived during the period of the Bar Kochba revolt in the second century C.E. These documents were discovered by Yigdael Yadin in the "Cave of Letters" in the Judean desert.

the wife's adultery (*m. Giṭ.* 9:10). The rabbinic school of Hillel, on the other hand, seems to represent the dominant Israelite practice of allowing a man to divorce his wife for any displeasure with her (*m. Giṭ.* 9:10; Deut 24:1; Sir 25:26). Indeed, the Mishnah contains an entire tractate (section) on divorce regulations: *Giṭṭin*. In the divorce laws of the Mishnah, an Israelite wife could obtain a divorce in several instances: the husband's persistent refusal to fulfill his conjugal duties (*m. Ketub.* 7:1–5), the husband's physical impurity due to illness or vocation (*m. Ketub.* 7:10), her own impurity, her husband's impotence, her refusal to have intercourse (*m. Ned.* 11:12), or with her husband's consent (*m. ʿArak.* 5:6) (Falk 1974, 517–18). Josephus, in *Life* 414–415, narrates his own divorces.

Herodian Divorces

Josephus mentions nine divorces among the Herodians. In four cases the husband divorced his wife, and in five cases the wife divorced her husband. It becomes clear that divorce is as social an arrangement as marriage; it has immediate implications for the family, not merely for the two individuals. Furthermore, it is always tied to the value of honor. These Herodian divorces inform our views on how divorce was practiced among Israelite elites.

Herod the Great divorced both Doris and Mariamme II for reasons of honor, but the circumstances were significantly different. He divorced Doris and banished her son Antipater in order to marry Mariamme (I) the Hasmonean. Not that he was adverse to polygyny, but political considerations outweighed any devotion that he had for Doris or the heir that she had borne him. What was at stake, then, was an alliance with the Hasmonean royal-priestly family, and consequently an opportunity to increase his honor and power. In order to secure that alliance, Herod had to ensure Mariamme's honor as "queen" and clear the path of inheritance and throne-succession for any children whom she might bear him (Josephus, *J.W.* 1.431–433). Doris evidently was reinstated at some point, since Herod divorced her again and stripped her of her expensive wardrobe when a plot against Herod was exposed and she was implicated (Josephus, *Ant.* 17.68). The issue at stake between Herod and Mariamme II was loyalty. Mariamme was accused (along with Doris) of being one of the conspirators who planned the death of Herod, instigated by Doris's son Antipater and others. The result of this accusation was that he divorced her. Moreover, he expunged her son (Herod Philip) from his will and the throne-succession, and he removed her father, Simon, from the high priesthood (Josephus, *Ant.* 17.78).

It is pertinent that Josephus takes every opportunity to assert that women who divorced their husbands were acting shamefully and against Israelite tradition (*Ant.* 15.259–260; 17.341; 18.136; 20.143). In what social frame of reference can these women's actions then be placed? One might interpret their boldness in terms of their Hellenization; they did not feel bound to follow Israelite tradition in matters of kinship. But as we have noted, their marriage strategies and negotiations as well as their requirement that exogamous husbands be circumcised demonstrate that they were fully Israelite in their family system. The dissolution of marriage, like the contracting of marriage, is a social transaction that affects more than the divorcing couple. The divorces in the Herodian family demonstrate the competition for honor in marriage strategy. A spouse could be dropped when a better alliance became available, even exchanging one endogamous marriage for a superior one. Divorces may also demonstrate the expectations and breakdowns of family loyalty within the kinship group. Josephus's divorce of his third wife demonstrates that Hillel's liberal interpretation of divorce custom for men was actually practiced.

INHERITANCE

Inheritance is the distribution of the family's movable property (livestock, jewelry) and immovable property (fields, barns), most commonly at the death of the male head of the family (Sir 33:23). But, as discussed above, dowry is also a means of inheritance given to the daughters at the time of their marriage.

Inheritance in Israel

The legal paragraph in Num 27:3–4 acknowledges that sons had priority in the claim to inheritance (other than dowry). The case of Zelophehad's daughters raises the issue of inheritance when the deceased left no sons. The precedent was set in this case, and the order of inheritance was designated: daughters, brothers, father's brothers, near kin. Each successive category of relatives was included only if there was no one in the preceding categories (Num 27:8–11). Note that the wife was not included in the Numbers list or, for that matter, in most ancient lists of successors. The reason is that her portion was her dowry and indirect dowry. Deuteronomy 21:17 designates a double portion for the eldest son. This was also stipulated in the Mishnah (*m. B. Bat.* 8:3–5) as well as in other ancient Near Eastern societies (e.g., Nuzi and Babylonia).

Inheritance in the Mishnah

The Mishnah's laws of inheritance follow a sequence similar to the one articulated in Num 27:8–11, but two new factors are added. First, there is a general rule: "Whosoever has precedence in inheritance, his offspring also have precedence" (*m. B. Bat.* 8:2). In other words, if a son has died before his now deceased father, and that son had children, those children inherited ahead of the deceased father's daughters and so on. Second, the laws provided for ascendant inheritance, stipulating that the father of a deceased person would inherit ahead of that person's brothers and sisters.

The Mishnah also notes regional diversity concerning the rights of the widow in Palestine. In Jerusalem and the Galilee, the tradition was that the widow had a legal right to stay in the family home and live off her husband's property, as directed in marriage contracts (*m. Ketub.* 4:12). But in Judea the heirs were free to dispose of a widow by giving her the amount of her *ketubah,* her dowry (*m. Ketub.* 4:12) (Falk 1974, 520).

Inheritance and Herod

We possess no narrative information about Herodian inheritance except for that which followed Herod the Great's death. And it is here that Todd's point about "equality" (distribution among all the children) is demonstrated. One of the most striking things to note about Herod's distribution is that Augustus Caesar and his wife, Livia, were included as major heirs. Herod willed Augustus ten million *denarii* (= one thousand talents), silver and gold vessels, and expensive clothing (Josephus, *Ant.* 17.190). Augustus, moreover, was in charge of disposing and ratifying the terms of the will (Josephus, *J.W.* 1.669). To Livia (along with other, unnamed, Roman friends) he gave five million silver coins (= five hundred talents) (Josephus, *Ant.* 17.190). These endowments given to the emperor and the imperial family were neither whimsical nor an affront to Herod's family; they were the reciprocity of the client (Herod) to his patrons (Augustus and Livia). The Roman historian Suetonius discusses the patron-client relationship between Augustus and client-kings (*Aug.* 60). Furthermore, the relationship between patron and client was inherited from generation to generation (Elliott 1987). This explains the enduring relationship between the Herodians and the Julio-Claudians and then the Flavians over a 160-year period: Julius Caesar appointed Antipater, the father of Herod the Great, governor over all Judea in 47 B.C.E. (Josephus, *J.W.* 1.199; *Ant.* 14.143), and Trajan appointed Gaius Julius Alexander Berenicianus (a Roman senator, and a great-great-great-grandson of Herod the Great) consul of Rome in 116 C.E.

The major portion of Herod's kingdom was divided among three of his sons (all named Herod). Herod Antipas, Malthake's son, became tetrarch over Galilee and Perea (Josephus, *Ant.* 17.188, 318), with an annual revenue of two hundred talents. Herod Philip, Cleopatra's son, was made tetrarch over the northern territories: Trachonitis, Batanea, Gaulanitis, Peneas, Auranitis, and the domain of Zenodorus. This gave him an annual income of one hundred talents (Josephus, *Ant.* 17.189, 319). And Herod appointed Herod Archelaus, Malthake's oldest son, client-king, jurisdiction over Judea, Samaria, Idumea, Jerusalem, Caesarea, Sebaste, and Joppa (Josephus, *J.W.* 1.668; *Ant.* 17.188), but his position was reduced to ethnarch by Augustus (Josephus, *Ant.* 17.317). He had an annual income of six hundred talents (Josephus, *Ant.* 17.319–320). This distribution, consequently, was the same as the Israelite tradition of giving the eldest son a larger portion but including everyone. Josephus also recounts the angry response to the will from Herod Antipas and Herod Philip (*J.W.* 2.14–38, 80–100).

Inheritance, therefore, is the means of distributing the family's movable and immovable property after the death of the patriarch. It transfers the property from one generation to the next, providing the sustenance of the family, the possession of the land, and acknowledgment of patron-client obligations. The aspects often overlooked by historians have been the function of dowries as premortem inheritance, the return of the wife's dowry and indirect dowry, the contingencies of inheritance distribution, and the acknowledgment of patron-client relationships. Herod followed the Israelite tradition of inheritance distribution, while the inclusion of Salome as an heir remains unclear since the inclusion of a sister as an heir violates conventional practice.

JESUS' FAMILY IN THE GOSPELS

Matthew 1:1–17 and Elite Interests

The kinship models of genealogy and descent treated here are necessary to read biblical texts as products of the ancient Mediterranean world. In order to test these models, it is necessary to address specific passages and family groups. We begin with Jesus' genealogy in Matt 1:1–17, since this is perhaps the best known to readers of the New Testament.

The Gospel of Matthew begins with a provocative phrase: "The lineage record of Jesus Christ" (1:1). In order to tell the story of Jesus, the gospel writer chose to begin with the issue of Jesus' kinship. And a fundamental way for traditional societies to express kinship, as we have seen, is to establish an individual's lineage, his or her connection to a family group that defines the present, is rooted in the past, and expresses future potentialities. The genealogy expresses social relationships in terms of experienced, multidimensional time, which is an organically linked process (Malina 1989, 31). A résumé or formal introduction for a contemporary U.S. leader would rarely be expected to mention kinship beyond "married" or "single" but instead would likely focus on education, work experience, and financial status.

Mediterranean cultures, however, place high value upon the kinship group to which one belongs, not only one's living family but also the lineage of that family. That lineage may express the family's relative honor in contrast to other families, the trades that they have been handed, the stories out of which they live, the patron-client associations that they have made, their religious purity, the potential marriage partners that are accessible to them, and much more. Genealogies, then, by appealing to the past in terms of one's lineage, provide one avenue of understanding the present. Any individual listed in a genealogy is meant to be interpreted in light of the larger pattern of social relationships that the genealogy reflects.

Genealogy and Honor

In traditional Mediterranean societies throughout history, the fundamental and overarching social value has been honor. The type of honor that a genealogy communicates is *ascribed* honor (based upon who one is, especially in reference to one's group).

But precisely as a social value, ascribed honor, too, must continually be asserted and maintained, and it is always open to challenge. Like the Priestly writers' materials in Genesis, which introduce a set of stories about a character with a genealogy (in the case of Abraham, Gen 11:10–26 introduces Gen 12:1–25:11), Matthew introduces the story of Jesus with his genealogy. In their final redaction (both Genesis and Matthew), the stories are rooted in a preunderstanding of the kinship group from which the character comes and in the context of which he must be interpreted. That is, one must first situate the main character in terms of family honor, partially determined by descent expressed in a genealogy. Thus the literary sequence of genealogy followed by story symbolizes the social value placed on kinship and descent. If the Gospel of Mark was the primary narrative source of the Gospel of Matthew, then one can readily conclude what deficiency the Gospel of Matthew writer saw in Mark's introduction to the Jesus story: it failed to root his story in family honor.

One of the key ways that a genealogy expresses the claim to honor is by the choice of the apical ancestor—the one at the head (apex) of the list. That the gospel writer had choices is clear: Luke roots Jesus in "universal" history by tracing his genealogy to God by way of Adam (3:38), including (but placing no special emphasis on) David (3:31) and Abraham (3:34). And John introduces Jesus' story by declaring him to be the embodiment of the divine Logos—Word and Wisdom (1:1–18). Matthew could have chosen Jacob as Jesus' apical ancestor, the namesake of the people of Israel (John 4:12); or Judah, the head of his ancestral "tribe" (Heb 7:14); or Solomon, the archetypal sage-king (Matt 12:42). These all appear in Matthew's genealogy, but not at the head. The importance of Abraham as apical ancestor is as the first patriarch to have received the divine promises of children, land, and reputation. But note that primacy of place is given to "son of David" in Matt 1:1.

Forty-one Generations (Matt 1:2–16)

This prompts the audience to interpret "son of Abraham" in terms of "son of David"—in other words, to interpret Abraham in royal terms. Two passages are relevant here. In the Septuagint's rendering of Gen 23:6 the Hittites say to Abraham, "You are a king from God among us." In the *Testaments of the Twelve Patriarchs*, Levi is promised that a Judean king will arise to create a new priesthood, and that king will be a descendant of Abraham (*T. Levi* 8:14–15). The relevance of these texts is to demonstrate that in pre-Christian Israelite literature Abraham is associated with kingship. As has been noted, it is not Jesus' identification as an Israelite that is open to question in Matthew, but the claim to kingship.

The fact that Matthew wants both a genealogical connection to David and Abraham through Mary's husband, Joseph (1:16), and a virginal conception (1:18–25) does not constitute a conflict in terms of kinship. Biology is only one factor in establishing one's kinship group; the other is one's household. As Delaney makes plain, paternity is a social construct. Moreover, "dual paternity" was a well-established mode of expressing miraculous birth, royal authority, and divine power in the ancient Mediterranean.

Gordon (1977, 101; 1978, 26–27) points out that Odysseus was called "the Zeus-sired son of Laertes" (Homer, *Iliad* 10.144), and Queen Hatshepsut of Egypt was the daughter of both Pharaoh Thutmosis I and the god Amon. Besides these examples from Gordon, stories circulated to the effect that Alexander of Macedonia was the son not only of Philip II but also of the god Zeus-Ammon (Plutarch, *Alex.* 2.1–3.2); Plato was the son of Ariston and the god Apollo (Diogenes Laertius, *Lives of Eminent Philosophers* 3.1–2), and Augustus was the son of Octavius as well as the god Apollo (Suetonius, *Aug.* 94.4). The extraordinary character of these elites reputedly stemmed from both their divine origins and their kinship groups. Their kinship groups provided one form of legitimation: political right to the throne and/or social status (thus the importance of Joseph in Matthew's genealogy). Their divine procreation provided another: their honor was divinely ascribed, and their greatness as leaders derived from divine paternity.

Females in the Genealogy

Another issue involved in the composition of any genealogy is the form of descent employed. As we noted in reference to Mediterranean genealogies in general, patrilineal descent is the rule. This is clear in Matthew's genealogy of Jesus as well. The family's honor in blood and name is communicated from father to son. This must be understood in relationship to the fact that a woman was perceived as embedded in her father (or other male relatives) until she became embedded in her husband. Thus the woman became part of another family and was embedded in their honor. But as the Herodian genealogy also demonstrates, this patrilineal principle is occasionally supplemented with the cognatic principle: the tracing of heritage through maternal as well as paternal lines.

Matthew's inclusion of Tamar (1:3), Rahab (1:5a), Ruth (1:5b), Bathsheba (1:6), and Mary (1:16) calls for explanation. As Brown (1993, 71 n. 21) notes, Rahab is not connected to the Davidic lineage in the Old Testament; thus biblical genealogies were not Matthew's "direct source" for the women. He concludes that these particular women were chosen by the gospel writer for two reasons: "(a) there is something extraordinary or irregular in their union with their partners, a union which, though it may have been scandalous to outsiders, continued the blessed lineage of the Messiah; (b) the women showed initiative or played an important role in God's plan and so came to be considered the instrument of God's providence or of His Holy Spirit" (Brown 1993, 73).

I agree with Brown's conclusions, but the underlying social values of these theological formulations must be probed further. Tamar was not Judah's "wife" but rather his daughter-in-law; she had to trick Judah into providing her with children when Judah failed to fulfill his "levirate" obligations (assigning one of his sons to give her dead husband an heir). Since her initiative, rather than his, resulted in a just solution, Judah pronounced her "more righteous than I" (Gen 38:26); in other words, "Tamar acted more honorably than I." Tamar was rewarded with protection within the kinship group, as well as with children (Gen 38:27–30). Thus Matthew emphasizes the honor of the line not only as based upon the promises of God to the patriarchs (ascribed honor) but also as Tamar's acquired honor manifested in Judah's declaration.

Rahab's honor lay in her protection of the Israelite spies trying to capture Jericho, her own Canaanite city. Her service and loyalty (Josh 2:12) to Israel provide her with a grant of acquired honor, despite her occupation as a prostitute, which exposes the family to accusations of shame. The Israelites rewarded her with the deliverance of her whole kinship group and inclusion into "Israel" (Josh 6:25).

Ruth the Moabite acquired honor by virtue of her loyalty to Naomi and Naomi's kinship group. This is declared in two formal blessings on her: by Naomi (Ruth 1:8) and Boaz (Ruth 3:10). She left her own land to go, dwell, and remain embedded in Naomi's people and her God (Ruth 1:16–17). She was eventually rewarded with a new husband from Naomi's kinship group, Boaz, and a son, Obed (Ruth 4:13–22). She was a foreigner from the land of one of Israel's traditional enemies, but she acted with honor to the benefit of an Israelite family. Bathsheba's relationship to David is potentially shameful for the Davidic line, since David acquired her through a sequence of adultery, conspiracy, and murder (2 Sam 11:1–12:25). But no guilt is imputed to Bathsheba, and she subsequently bore Solomon (also named Jedidiah, meaning "Yah's beloved" [2 Sam 12:24–25]). She also acquired honor by stepping into the dispute over David's succession and promoting her son, Solomon, over Adonijah (1 Kgs 1:11–21, 28–31; 2:13–25). Solomon accorded her special honor by bowing down to her and providing her a throne at his right hand (1 Kgs 2:19). It is important that Solomon's obeisance directly follows the description of Bathsheba's actions on his behalf.

Finally, Mary acquired honor by submitting to the divine will and giving birth to Jesus (Matt 1:16) as a virgin (Matt 1:18, 23, 25). She is necessary for Matthew to include here in order to tie the genealogy to the following birth account, which emphasizes Mary's impregnation by the Holy Spirit. Her shame was exposed in terms of a pregnancy before marriage.

Thus—Brown is correct—these women "showed initiative." But this still leaves vague the fundamental issue, for all initiative is not honorable; all their initiatives specifically resulted in their acquisition of honor. For Tamar, Rahab, and Ruth this is specifically stated in the biblical stories by formal declarations and blessings; for Bathsheba and Mary it is implied. Consequently, Jesus' ascribed honor stems from the ascribed honor of his paternal lineage and the acquired honor of pivotal, exogamously related women in the lineage.

Jesus' Peasant Family

Matthew's genealogical concerns regarding Jesus, paralleled to a degree in Luke's gospel, are unknown in the other New Testament Gospels: neither Mark nor John has genealogies for Jesus. The New Testament Gospels also have different perspectives on Jesus' paternity: Mark refers to Jesus as "son of Mary" (Mark 6:3) and never once mentions Joseph; Matthew and Luke imply or refer to Jesus in passing as Joseph's son (Matt 13:55; Luke 4:22); John consistently refers to Jesus as "son of Joseph" (John 1:45; 6:42). This is an important difference in view of the general acceptance of Mark as the earliest gospel. Without a genealogy or clear statement about Joseph, Mark attests to uncertainty about Jesus' family background in the early Jesus movement. Paul's letters seem to confirm the Markan picture, likewise making relatively little of Jesus' genealogy (only Rom 1:3) or Joseph's paternity (Gal 4:4). Since later traditions are intent to show Jesus' divine origins (John 1:1–18; Heb 1–2), the general New Testament tendency is to obscure the factual origins of Jesus while "theologizing" them. Because of the historical uncertainty and the tendency to connect Jesus' origins with God, important contemporary scholarship has argued for Jesus' conception under less-flattering circumstances. One opinion makes the case that Jesus' conception happened when Mary was raped. Archaeological evidence offers some support for second-century claims by (the anti-Christian) Celsus and rabbinic traditions that Jesus was the offspring of a liaison between Mary and a Roman soldier named Pantera. The tombstone for a Roman soldier from Sidon named Pantera, found in Germany and stemming from the time of the Roman emperor Tiberius, has been known since 1859. Pantera had served forty years in the Roman army at the time of his death, so he would have been a relatively new recruit in Roman Palestine when Jesus was conceived. It is also possible that Celsus was making a hostile pun on the Greek word παρθένος ("young woman, virgin"), used of Mary in Matthew and Luke.

Similarly, the relationship of Jesus to presumed brothers and sisters is unclear (Mark 6:3). The Gospel of Mark identifies four brothers of Jesus: James (Jacob), Joses (Joseph), Judas (Judah), and Simon. These common Hebrew names perhaps reflect the great epic figures of ancient Israel (Jacob, Joseph, Judah) or one of the greatest of the Hasmonean leaders (Simon) of the second century B.C.E.; the sisters are not named. Later Christian tradition would identify them as either Assia and Lydia or Mary and Salome. These "brothers" and "sisters" have been variously understood by critical scholars as blood relatives, step-siblings, or cousins. Roman Catholic scholars especially have espoused the latter two understandings in view of the deeply held Catholic doctrine of "the perpetual virginity of Mary" (Jesus was the product of divine conception, and Mary never had sexual relations after Jesus' birth). However this issue is decided, Jesus' identification by Mark as "Mary's son," the absence of Joseph throughout most of the Synoptic Gospels, and the information about Pantera leave many questions about his family situation unclear.

Nor are the Jesus traditions united in regard to the immediate relatives' attitude toward Jesus during his lifetime. On the one hand, the family seems hostile to Jesus in Mark's narrative (Mark 3:21, 31–35, which mention Jesus' mother, brothers, and sisters only). According to John, Jesus' brothers "do not believe in him" (John 7:5–8). On the other hand, Jesus' mother sides with him in the later material of Luke-Acts and John (Luke 2:19, 51; John 2:4–5; 19:25–27). In Acts 1:14 Jesus' brothers are not said to be hostile to his cause. Paul knows an early tradition about the "conversion" of James after Jesus' death (1 Cor 15:7), a story that is more elaborately recounted in chapter 9 of the apocryphal *Gospel of the Hebrews*.

How are these divergent reports to be understood? The reader should keep in mind that people of peasant origins such as Jesus of Nazareth did not have their birthdates carefully recorded as part of an illustrious genealogy by professional scribes. Such genealogies were the prerogative only of powerful families capable of, and with an important interest in, preserving documentary archives. Most peasants had to keep their ancestry through oral traditions. There were periodic censuses by Roman officials for the purposes of taxation (every fourteen years under the principate), but the family had an interest in keeping the head count low. Besides, it is unlikely that the gospel writers had access to such census information, and, as noted, the genealogies for Jesus in Matthew 1 and Luke 3 do not agree in important respects.

It would seem, then, that the genealogies for Jesus ascribe important origins to him based upon his achievements during his adult lifetime. This was standard procedure even for notables from powerful Mediterranean families, as we noted above. Matthew, as has been seen, is intent to link Jesus to the glorious ancestors of Israel, especially Abraham and David. This accords with Matthew's interests in showing Jesus' importance in terms that Judeans everywhere could appreciate. Luke, by contrast, has a quite different list of people leading ultimately back to Adam, the progenitor of all peoples. Luke is particularly intent to show Jesus' significance for non-Israelites (Luke 2:32; Acts 1:8).

Summary

The Herodians can be traced for eight generations in four major regions: Idumea, Palestine, Armenia, Rome. Their family system affected the politics, political religion, and political economy of Palestine for a period of roughly 150 years, and the larger Roman Empire for even longer. They were thoroughly Israelite in the structure of their kinship. But, as the top level of urban elites, they employed some variations on what could be expected from urban and rural non-elites. Their family group exemplified the typical patriarchal family system of the eastern Mediterranean. They were patrilineal, patrilocal, and endogamous; they employed dowry and bridewealth and provided the eldest son with a larger share of the father's inheritance. We have clear, worked out genealogies covering eight generations for the Herodian family recounted by Josephus. They were also accountable to their Roman patrons when it came to inheritance. Far from random or individually determined, the Herodians conformed to a family system both predictable and patterned.On the other hand, a tension arises when viewing the different traditions about Jesus' family. The earliest sources (Q, Paul, *Gospel of Thomas,* Mark) make no claims for the ascribed honor of Jesus' family lineage. The Gospels of Matthew and Luke, from later in the first century, seem very interested in rooting Jesus' story in the honorable framework of great elites with highly developed genealogies. And the Gospel of John and the book of Hebrews have a thoroughly theologized view of Jesus origins.

Because all ancient Mediterranean institutions and relationships were in one way or another related to kinship arrangements, it is vital for the reader of the New Testament to have a good grasp of how different these arrangements are from modern configurations in the United States and in most western European nations. Kinship arrangements are so deeply embedded in the consciousness of the ancients that they are often left implicit.

BIBLIOGRAPHY

Brown, Raymond E. 1993. *The Birth of the Messiah*. Updated ed. New York: Doubleday

Delaney, Carol. 1986. The Meaning of Paternity and the Virgin Birth Debate. *Man* 21:494–513.

Elliott, John H. 1987. Patronage and Clientism in Early Christian Society: A Short Reading Guide. *Forum* 3:39–48.

Falk, Zeev Wilhelm. 1974. Jewish Private Law. Pages 504–34 in *The Jewish People in the First Century: Historical Geography, Political History, Social, Cultural and Religious Life and Institutions*. Vol 1. Edited by Shmuel Safrai and Menachem Stern. Compendia rerum Iudaicarum ad Novum Testamentum 1/1. Philadelphia: Fortress.

Goody, Jack. 1973. Bridewealth and Dowry in Africa and Eurasia. Pages 1–58 in Jack Goody and S. J. Tambiah, *Bridewealth and Dowry*. Cambridge Papers in Social Anthropology 7. Cambridge: Cambridge University Press.

Gordon, Cyrus H. 1977. Paternity at Two Levels. *Journal of Biblical Literature* 96:101.

———. 1978. The Double Paternity of Jesus. *Biblical Archaeology Review* 4(2):26–27.

Hanson, K. C. 1989a. The Herodians and Mediterranean Kinship, Part I: Genealogy and Descent. *Biblical Theology Bulletin* 19:75–84

———. 1989b. The Herodians and Mediterranean Kinship, Part II: Marriage and Divorce. *Biblical Theology Bulletin* 19:142–51.

———. 1990. The Herodians and Mediterranean Kinship, Part III: Economics. *Biblical Theology Bulletin* 20:10–21.

Harrell, Stevan, and Sara A. Dickey. 1985. Dowry Systems in Complex Societies. *Ethnology* 24:105–20.

Jacobs-Malina, Diane. 1993. *Beyond Patriarchy: The Images of Family in Jesus*. New York: Paulist Press.

Johnson, Marshall D. 1993. *The Purpose of the Biblical Genealogies: With Special Reference to the Setting of the Genealogies of Jesus*. Society for New Testament Studies Monograph Series 8. Cambridge: Cambridge University Press.

Keesing, Robert M. 1975. *Kin Groups and Social Structure*. New York: Holt, Rinehart & Winston.

Malina, Bruce J. 1993. *The New Testament World: Insights from Cultural Anthropology*. Rev. ed. Louisville: Westminster John Knox.

———. 1989. Christ and Time: Swiss or Mediteranean. *Catholic Biblical Quarterly* 51:1–31.

———. 1986. *Christian Origins and Cultural Anthropology: Practical Models for Biblical Interpretation*. Atlanta: John Knox.

Moxnes, Halvor, ed. 1997. *Constructing Early Christian Families: Family as Social Reality and Metaphor.* London: Routledge.

Osiek, Carolyn, and David L. Balch, eds. 1997. *Families in the New Testament World: Households and House Churches.* Louisville: Westminster John Knox.

Pastner, Carroll McC. 1981. The Negotiation of Bilateral Endogamy in the Middle Eastern Context: The Zikri Baluch Example. *Journal of Anthropological Research* 37:305–18.

Patai, Raphael. 1959. *Sex and Family in the Bible and the Middle East.* New York: Macmillan.

Pilch, John J. 1991. *Introducing the Cultural Context of the New Testament.* Vol. 2 of *Hear the Word!* New York: Paulist Press.

Richardson, Peter. 1996. *Herod: King of the Jews and Friend of the Romans.* Studies on Personalities of the New Testament. Columbia: University of South Carolina Press.

Safrai, Shmuel. 1976. Home and Family. Pages 728–92 in *The Jewish People in the First Century: Historical Geography, Political History, Social, Cultural and Religious Life and Institutions.* Vol. 2. Edited by Shmuel Safrai and Menachem Stern. Compendia rerum Iudaicarum ad Novum Testamentum 1/1. Philadelphia: Fortress.

Schlegel, Alice, and Rohn Eloul. 1988. Marriage Transactions: Labor, Property, Status. *American Anthropologist* 90:291–309.

Todd, Emmanuel. 1985. *The Explanation of Ideology: Family Structures and Social Systems.* Translated by David Garrioch. Family, Sexuality and Social Relations in Past Times. Oxford: Blackwell.

Wilson, Robert R. 1977. *Genealogy and History in the Biblical World.* Yale Near Eastern Researches 7. New Haven: Yale University Press.

The Patron-Client Institution

3

Patronage was a ubiquitous social framework in the ancient Mediterranean basin. Patrons were people with power who could provide goods and services not available to their clients. In return, clients provided loyalty and honor to the patrons. Social inequality characterized these patronal relationships, and exploitation was a common feature of such relationships. Even though the language of friendship was used to convey the idea of patronage, a number of Greek and Roman authors pointed out that true friendship involved frank speech between the parties. Patronage prevented such frank speech because the client was indebted to the patron and could not risk terminating the relationship.

Benefaction is similar to patronage, but distinct from it in that benefaction has a clear lack of self-interest on the part of the provider. Whereas the patron sought clients and an increased honor rating, the benefactor gave in order to help people without thought for the honor that it would bring. Part of the argument in the following essay is that James resists the language of patronage regarding God in favor of that of benefaction. The language of friendship is also used of benefactors, and the language of fatherhood is especially characteristic of such individuals. Benefactors, moreover, were not necessarily superiors of those to whom they gave benefactions, and they gave primarily to enhance the community. Greek and Roman descriptions of benefaction were ideal conceptions of persons who may not have actually lived up to the description of the ideal. The language of benefaction is commonly used for God in the Septuagint.

The language of benefaction shifted in the period of the Roman domination of the Greek-speaking world. Greeks attributed the title "common benefactor" to Roman emperors, and the meaning of the term *benefactor* appears to have gradually shifted to acknowledge the inferior/superior notions common to patronage. Even in this period, however, there a distinction was made between benefaction, giving without self-interested motives, and patronage, with its clearly defined structure of dependency in which obedience was expected from clients.

One way to distinguish between recipients of benefaction and clients is through the employment of the friendship *topos*. True friendship was characterized by frank speech as opposed to flattery, unity of mind, control of one's tongue and passions, and testing to determine loyalty. True friends are able to speak their minds to one another without destroying the relationship. To speak out against a patron typically would cause the end of the relationship and the cessation of the provision of goods. Benefactors, on the other hand, did not stop providing if their friends exposed their faults. True friends, rather, agreed upon their concerns and were loyal to one another without coercion.

The New Testament evinces concern for true benefaction as opposed to patronage in numerous places. Perhaps most clear in this regard is Luke 14:12–24. The introductory saying to the parable of the Great Supper makes explicit that benefaction is in view. Those who are invited are invited precisely because of their inability to repay their patron. They have nothing to offer, and their very low status in society means that even any honor that they attribute to the benefactor who is inviting them will not alter the honor status of the host.

Alicia Batten

God in the Letter of James:
Patron or Benefactor?

INTRODUCTION

THE LETTER OF James currently enjoys considerable interest from many scholars, including those who employ insights from the social sciences. In particular,
examination of the phenomenon of patronage in antiquity has fostered some rethinking as to what type of social situation lies behind this document, with several authors concluding that the short epistle challenges the audience's reliance
upon a rich patron (see Batten 1999, 364–65; Edgar 2000, 113–36; Kloppenborg
Verbin 1999; Vhymeister 1995; Wachob 2000, 178–85). Many hold the view that
James replaces the worldly and wealthy human patron, who could easily exploit
clients, with a divine patron, God, who provides generously and fairly, with no
trace of caprice.

The following discussion assumes that James challenges the practice of patronage. Through the scenarios depicted, and in the use of the vocabulary of
friendship, James criticizes the behavior that patronage could breed. Yet the
characterization of God as a substitute patron risks oversimplification and even
distortion. Although patronage was pervasive in the ancient world, and the
patron-client model is a helpful tool in understanding many dimensions of the
early Christian literature (see Malina 1988), patronage was not the only way in
which asymmetrical relationships between people or between mortals and the
divine were understood in the antiquity. Rather, evidence indicates that there
was a range of understanding connections between those of differing social rank.
The focus here is on the differences between patronage and benefaction, which
often are used interchangeably by scholars. Using the findings of Stephan Joubert
and others, I argue that during the first century C.E., patronage and benefaction
were not universally synonymous throughout the entire Roman Empire. Such
distinctions have implications for how to interpret the description of God in the
Letter of James.

PATRONAGE

There is ample consensus among historians that the phenomenon of patronage was pervasive throughout the societies of the first-century Mediterranean
basin, and a generous discussion of it can be found in several introductions to the

world of Jesus (e.g., Hanson and Oakman 1998, 63–97). Saller (1989, 54–55) has paid particular attention to North African patronal inscriptions, but evidence for patronage is found in many sites, such as Gaul, Syria (Garnsey 1988, 58–63), and Palestine, including Galilee (Schwartz 1994).

Saller (1982, 1) states that ancient patronage consisted of three chief characteristics: (1) it revolved around the reciprocal exchange of goods and services; (2) the relationship was personal and of some duration; (3) it was not an equal relationship but rather was between parties of differing status. The difficulty with patronage, at least from the clients' perspective, was that because it involved participants of unequal social and economic levels, it could "easily slide into overt exploitation" (Garnsey 1988, 58). This is because the relationship was largely determined by the more powerful person involved, a characteristic that Millett (1989, 16) tentatively deems a defining aspect of patronage.

It was common in the Greco-Roman world for patrons and clients to refer to one another as φίλος or *amicus,* despite the fact that friendship and patronage were not identical. Patron-client relationships would disguise themselves as alliances of friendship, and sometimes the boundaries between the two were not crystal clear. Moreover, it was quite possible for friendships to deteriorate into relationships based upon utility. If one friend fell down the social ladder, the relationship might functionally become that of patron-client.

The fact that friendship and patronage did become confused and that clients and patrons would call one another "friend" disturbed some writers to the extent that they composed satirical texts on the hypocrisy of this type of charade. Perhaps the most bitter attack emerges in Juvenal's fifth satire, in which the so-called friendship between Virro and Trebius is exposed as a liaison suffused with constant humiliations inflicted upon Trebius by the wealthier Virro (*Sat.* 5.170–173). Similarly, Horace counsels against seeking the "friendship" of a wealthy person, for such an alliance would result in precisely the opposite. The "weaker" friend would become dependent on the rich one, and subsequently lose the ability to speak frankly, which was a key characteristic of true friendship (*Ep.* 18). Plutarch is particularly sensitive to the misuse of the vocabulary of friendship in patron-client relationships, in which the "friend" cajoles the other "friend" through flattery. According to his *How to Tell a Flatterer from a Friend,* such a use of this language demeans and perverts friendship and the set of values upon which it is based (*Adul. amic.* 49C). Thus Plutarch and others appealed "to the nature of friendship as a means of exposing the coercive aspects of contemporary patron-client relationships" (Konstan 1995, 330).

Other ancient writers scoff at the dishonorable conduct of clients. Lucian of Samosata, for example, describes the response of Nigrinus, who jeers at both the rich and their clients after a stay in Rome. In reaction to the practice of paying court to the wealthy patrons, Nigrinus describes the clients who

> get up at midnight, run all about the city, let servants bolt the doors in their faces and suffer themselves to be called dogs, toadies and similar names. By way of reward for this galling round of visits they get the much-talked-of dinner, a vulgar thing, the

source of many evils. How much they eat there, how much they drink that they do not want, and how much they say that should not have been said! (*Nigr.* 22)

Polybius of Megara, moreover, criticizes the behavior of King Prusias of Bithynia, who visits Roman senators and generals as a client would a patron, "making it impossible for anyone after him to surpass him in unmanliness, womanishness, and servility" (*Hist.* 30.18). Plutarch scorns the conduct of clients who flatter and feign adoration for their affluent patrons. *How to Tell a Flatterer from a Friend* sharply contrasts the conduct of true friends, who speak frankly, and flatterers or clients, who sing the praises of the rich in hopes of personal gain. Plutarch calls the latter apes (*Mor.* 52B), and in another text he compares them to flies that "do not stay on after the good food is gone" (*Mor.* 94B).

BENEFACTION

These criticisms have caused some scholars to question whether patronage was identical to benefaction, a practice that reaches far back into the classical period. As Joubert (2000, 59–60, 62–63) has discussed, many authors have equated the two relationships, with little or no distinction between them, but recently he and others have questioned such an assimilation of concepts. Thus we need to examine what it meant to be a benefactor in the Greco-Roman world.

Aristotle's *Nichomachean Ethics* describes two forms of benefaction in ancient Greece. The first is the noble individual who provides important benefits for the community as a whole, and the second is the one who exchanges goods and services on an individual level with others who are status equals or near status equals. Both types are magnificent (μεγαλοπρεπής) and magnanimous (μεγαλόψυχος) people who do not stupidly spend more than they are able, nor do they spend in order to parade their wealth but rather because they are truly great people of the highest moral attributes. The benefactor is not even overly concerned with honor, although he accepts it, as he should, in Aristotle's view (*Eth. nic.* 4.3.1–11).

Seneca's *On Benefits* provides a description of the ideal conditions for benefaction. The true benefactor is not motivated by desires for repayment, but because "to help, to be of service, is the part of a noble and chivalrous soul; he who gives benefits the gods, he who seeks a return, money-lenders" (*Ben.* 3.15.4). The bestowal of benefits produces a bond between people (*Ben.* 4.41.2), making equal demands upon both. Despite the risk of ingratitude and no repayment, the ideal benefactor should give without concern for repayment, even though the ideal beneficiary will both receive and return benefits willingly (*Ben.* 1.4.3).

A key attribute of the ideal benefactor, therefore, is lack of self-interest. Benefactors, be they mortals or gods, were sometimes referred to as "father" because in some ways they embodied the selfless behavior of parents. For example, as Seneca illustrates, parents persist in raising children despite the inevitable disappointments, just as benefactors continue to provide benefactions regardless of the risk of no repayment (*Ben.* 1.1.10). Stevenson argues that this ideal picture of the selfless provider formed the backdrop against which the gods, rulers, and mortal benefactors were measured. The evidence shows, he says, "that the father analogy was used regularly of founders and saviors in the Graeco-Roman world. In Greek literary sources, 'father' appears commonly in conjunction with epithets such as σωτήρ, εὐεργέτης and κτιστής" (1992, 430). Furthermore, Stevenson states that such an image of the god or human benefactor "rests upon the recognition of the procreative/tutelary power and entails the selfless use of that power" (1996, 18). Often this picture was contrasted with that of the tyrant, who was interested only in selfish gain (Stevenson 1996, 10).

Biblical texts explicitly use the language of benefaction to describe God. The most common word for benefactor is εὐεργέτης. Danker (1992, 670) observes that of twenty-two times that the εὐεργ-word family is used relating to benefaction in the Septuagint, fourteen refer to God. Most of these references are in wisdom literature, to which James is indebted, and five of them occur in Wisdom of Solomon (3:5; 7:23; 11:5; 16:2, 11), which also refers to the idea of friendship with God. Regarding the Gospels, Danker (1982, 489–90) has argued that the author of Luke-Acts is particularly interested in presenting God as the benefactor par excellence and Jesus as a benefactor especially of the oppressed.

The language of friendship was also associated with benefaction. An Athenian inscription from 306–305 B.C.E. honors Timosthenes of Carystus, who "continues to be a friend [φίλος] to the people of Athens," and who "did not withdraw friendship [φιλία] and [who] was continually benefiting in public the people of Athens" (*Inscriptiones graecae* II 457 [translation in Harding 1985, 154]). Such a benefactor may or may not have met the ideal described later by Seneca, but in theory the inscriptional evidence reveals that for the Greeks, friendship and benefaction overlapped quite often, whereas some Greek authors objected to mixing friendship and patronage. Wisdom of Solomon is at ease in referring to God as a giver of benefits while including the notion of the possibility of friendship with God (Wis 7:27). For Seneca, friends did not need to offer benefits, as friends had all things in common (*Ben.* 7.12), but "helpfulness is traditionally the mark of a friend and services may be interpreted as a sign of good will or amicableness" (Konstan 1997, 55).

This image of the selfless benefactor who gives life, saves, and helps those in need is in contrast, some argue, with the image of the patron, the latter taking on special prominence with the triumph of Rome. Several ancient texts, as we have observed, lash out sarcastically at these patrons and the type of behavior that they incite among their clients. Moreover, Joubert (2001, 22) cites Cicero (*Verr.* 2.2.154), who describes C. Verres' expectations that his Greek dependents honor him both as a Roman patron and as a savior, as he was not satisfied with the mere Roman title. The title "savior" was often used of benefactors (Nock 1972), which suggests that the benefactor/savior concepts were not understood to be identical to that of a patron, at least not by Verres.

Joubert indicates that patronage was ultimately a Roman phenomenon, but as the Roman administration spread throughout the Greek east, the Greeks continued to use the traditional language of benefaction to honor their Roman patrons. Joubert concludes that the "Greeks in general did not understand the Roman rule over them as patrocinium (as the Romans did)" (1999, 22). Significant here is the fact that the phrase κοινὸς εὐεργέτης ("common benefactor") emerges as a new epithet once the Romans begin to take control over the Greek east. According to Erskine's studies of the inscriptions bearing this phrase, its appearance indicates that "Greek perceptions of the Romans were different from their perceptions of the Hellenistic kings" (1994, 82). Comparison of the use of κοινὸς εὐεργέτης in Egyptian papyri reveals that it was used in reference to the Egyptian king Ptolemy, who for the Egyptian peasant was all-powerful. Erskine argues that in the Greek east the phrase was not used for Hellenistic kings, as these kings had rivals. However, when Rome emerged as a power, its strength could not be challenged, and the Greek cities knew it. Thus "common benefactor" reflects the unmatched power of the Romans. For Erskine, not only did the Greeks now look to Rome as a benefactor, "they were also obedient to Rome and subordinate to it, just as the peasant was to the Ptolemies" (1994, 86). Although the language of benefaction continued to be employed in the inscriptional evidence, the precise understanding of the nature of the relationship, in this case between the Romans and their Greek subjects, appears to have shifted.

Thus the fact that many Greeks continued to honor the Romans as benefactors renders explicable why modern scholars would perceive that patronage and benefaction were one and the same. Certainly the two concepts could overlap, and many inscriptions honor the Roman patron as both patron and benefactor, for if a Roman aristocrat agreed to accept a Greek city as his client, he was also expected to be of service. However, this "need not imply that *patron* and *euergetes* were one and the same thing" (Ferrary 1997, 110). Ferrary has indicated that the Roman senate had no desire to substitute patronage for the traditional practice of benefaction; rather,

> patronage was added to the Hellenic system of services and honors, *euergesiai* and *timai*, without merging with it: every patron was necessarily a (real or virtual) *euergetes*, and received from the city honors usually paid to benefactors. But not all Roman *euergetai* were necessarily patrons . . . , because patronage was largely reserved to magistrates or senators. (1997, 112)

It seems that patronage coexisted with other forms of aid and exchange, such as benefaction and charity (Garnsey and Woolf 1989, 154).

Admittedly, there is a paradox in some writers, such as Pliny, who emphasizes that the giving of gifts should not be motivated by a desire for recognition, but who also freely advertises his generosity in his correspondence (see Dixon 1993). This could mean that by the imperial period, the concept of benefaction was still idealized in theory but less often practiced by Romans, or, that it was never fully understood by Pliny. Patronage, however, was by definition an exchange between unequal parties, and it maintained a system whereby the clients were kept obedient to, and often exploited by, their providers. In contrast, benefaction did not inevitably place the beneficiaries into a submissive role, for many honorary inscriptions clearly state how the recipients of benefits have fulfilled their obligations to the benefactor, thus indebting their benefactor to them (see Supplementum epigraphicum graecum 26.1282). Although some attributes, such as ἀρετή, ascribed to benefactors in these inscriptions indicate that the individual is of great social standing (and not just an excellent human being), such honors were a method of maintaining the benefactor's support, for if benefactors wanted to preserve their public honor, their generosity had to continue. As Danker points out, "Besides encouraging others, it is anticipated that recognition of benefits conferred will also encourage the benefactor who is being honored to continue his or her generous ways" (1982, 438). From a modern perspective, patrons and benefactors might look the same because of similar vocabulary, but from an ancient Greek point of view, these two phenomena were distinct. As Joubert (2001, 24) illustrates, one can only refer to patronage and benefaction as one and the same after the triumph of Roman ideology during the later Roman Empire.

Opposition to Patronage in the Letter of James

Several authors have identified patronage as a "problem" that the Letter of James attempts to address. The key text here is Jas 2:1–13, which begins with the exhortation to show no partiality, followed by a hypothetical situation in which a wealthy person with fine clothing and gold rings and a poor person in tatters enter the assembly; the former is treated well, while the latter is ordered around (Jas 2:2–3). The writer ends the scene with a rhetorical question, "Have you not made distinctions among yourselves, and become judges with evil thoughts?" (2:4), and then scolds the audience for dishonoring the poor person despite the fact that it is the rich who oppress them, drag them into court, and blaspheme the honorable name invoked over them (2:6–7). Moreover, James goes on to explain that such partiality violates the love commandment (2:8–9) (Stegemann and Stegemann 1999, 305).

As Kloppenborg Verbin (1999, 765) has observed, such a scene is reminiscent of Lucian's criticism of rich people who show off their clothing and rings, expecting bows and curtsies in return (*Nigr.* 21). Flattery often was associated with patronage during the Hellenistic and Roman periods, and one form of expressing it was to offer the best seat on the platform to the wealthy patron—what Plutarch refers to as "silent flattery" (*Mor.* 58B). There is no reason to believe that the author of James would not be critical of this type of activity, just as other Greek writers were (e.g., Theophrastus, *Char.* 2.2–3). Given the general bitterness that the letter displays toward the rich (e.g., Jas 1:10; 5:1–6), a denunciation of patronage and the behavior that it can produce—flattery and ill-treatment of the poor—is not surprising.

Use of the Language of Friendship in the Letter of James

When one turns to the presence of the language of friendship in the letter, the argument that the author is attempting to inveigh against the practice of patronage becomes more compelling. James uses the word φίλος twice, both times referring to the relationship between human beings and God. Abraham is designated a "friend of God" (2:23), and then James draws a clear contrast between "friendship with the world" and "enmity with God" (4:4). In his characterization of God in 1:5, James states that God gives "simply" (ἁπλῶς) and "without reproach" (μὴ ὀνειδίζοντος). Such a depiction fits well with the image of a frank friend and benefactor, for during the Hellenistic and Roman periods one of the chief attributes of true friends was that they speak with frankness (παρρησία) and simply (ἁπλῶς) to one another. Philodemus's treatise *On Frank Criticism* also states that friends must confess their faults to one another and willingly yield to the correction of others. Plutarch (*Mor.* 64B) states that the flatterer's response to favors include reproach (ἐπονείδιστον) in contrast to the friend's. Moreover, in James, God will bestow wisdom upon those who ask for it, but they must be earnest in their faith (1:5–8). A generous friend, God gives to those who show their sincerity.

James does not claim that humans are of "one mind" (μία ψυχή) with God, but he does use the word δίψυχος to characterize the "double-minded" or "double-souled" person, who is also ἀκατάστατος ("unstable") and as a result will receive nothing from God. The phrase μία ψυχή was a common description of friends among Greek writers and is especially prominent in Aristotle's discussion of friendship (*Eth. nic.* 9.8.2). The word δίψυχος is a curious one that James may well have invented (see Porter 1991). It refers to a division in one's self. Could it be that James is deliberately contrasting the "single soul" tradition of friendship, in that friends share one soul together, with someone who is so divided that it is not possible to share a "soul" with another?

It is also interesting to observe how "testing," another consistent feature of friendship, fits within this letter. Sirach 6:7–8 especially emphasizes the importance of testing to determine if one is a friend. Near the beginning of James (1:2–3), the author exhorts the audience to take joy in their trials (πειρασμός), for such trials will produce steadfastness. Then James blesses the person who bears testing (ὑπομένει πειρασμόν) and who, for having stood the test, will receive a "crown of life" from God (1:12). Finally, Abraham, the "friend of God," merits such a name because he has withstood the test and proven his faith through works (2:23).

James calls upon his audience to resist vices such as covetousness (ζῆλος [3:16]) that are inimical to friendship (see Plutarch, *Mor.* 54C), and in 3:1–4:17 he exhibits concerns for proper speech and control of the passions, also discussed by writers on friendship. For example, Sir 41:25 warns against the use of abusive words before friends, while Plutarch's *Table Talk* discusses the appropriate speech and decorum required to promote friendship at dinner parties. Qualities such as meekness (πραΰτης) (Jas 1:21; 3:13) were associated with friendship (see Aristotle, *Rhet.* 1.9.5), while envy was its opposite. James does not use the word φθόνος ("envy") here, but the use of ζῆλος πικρός ("bitter envy") and ἐριθεία ("strife") together in 3:14 strongly suggests that envy is thematic within this section of the letter (see Johnson 1983). Finally, James urges his audience to submit to God (4:7), an exhortation that echoes Philodemus's calls for openness and yielding to the instruction of the friend or teacher (D. 1.17–18). The addressees are to draw near to God, and God will draw near to them (4:8). Notably, this is the same chapter in which James refers to "friendship with the world" as being "enmity with God."

James thus draws upon some common features of this *topos* of friendship when he describes the ideal relationship between humanity and God. Although some Greek writers, such as Aristotle, objected to the notion of friendship with God (*Eth. nic.* 8.7.3–6), it seems that some Stoics accepted it, presuming a measure of equality between the two (see Philodemus, D. 1.17–18). The notion of friendship with God is present in the Septuagint (e.g., Exod 33:11; Wis 7:14, 27) and in subsequent Jewish texts (e.g., *T. Ab.* A 15:12–15; Philo, *Heir* 21; *Sobriety* 56; *Dreams* 1.193–95). Ben Sira is a notable example of an ancient Jewish writer who depicts God as a "reliable friend who is worthy of trust and will always come to the friend's aid" (Irwin 1995, 558). These observations support the claim that James is drawing from a rich and complex tradition of friendship that was flourishing by the early centuries of the Common Era.

The combination of James's criticism of the rich, the scenario of James 2, in addition to the use of language and concepts associated with friendship, and in this case friendship with God, suggests that James is deliberately contrasting patronage and the status system that it upheld with the relationship to God and the conduct that such an alliance would promote.

God as Benefactor in the Letter of James

Returning to some opening observations in this study, we note that some think that in lieu of relying upon a human patron, James urges the audience to think of God as its divine patron. For example, Edgar thinks that one of the "key persuasive themes" of the letter is the "depiction of God as the one, supremely good, unchanging creator, orderer and judge, who is thus the only fitting patron for God's chosen people" (2000, 218–19). However, it appears more likely that the image of God presented by James conforms more to the description of an ideal benefactor and friend to a community of the faithful than to a patron who forms alliances with individuals and potentially exploits power differentials.

James 1:5–8, 12–15, 16–18

James 1:2–18 opens with an emphasis upon testing and trials, features that are integral to the formation of true friendships. But it is James 1:5–8 where the description of God becomes especially relevant to the current discussion. God is described as giving "simply" (ἁπλῶς) and "without reproach" (μὴ ὀνειδίζο-ντος), bearing similarities to the friends described by Plutarch and Ben Sira. This description of God seems "unprovoked," as Kloppenborg Verbin (1999, 768) has noticed, and its purpose could be to underscore God's beneficence. It could also be the beginning of an argument against patronage, which is then more explicitly developed in James 2:1–13, as has been discussed. For Kloppenborg Verbin (1999, 784), God emerges as the divine patron upon whom the audience should depend.

The suggestion that James is preparing one for an attack upon patronage is compelling, and I would argue that James is doing so by underscoring God's beneficence in contrast to the human in chapter 2. The description of God in Jas 1:5–8 conforms more to the ideal selfless and generous benefactor who provides for the community than to a patron who delights in the honors served up by clients. Presumably, the audience would notice how different the two characters are. God, unlike the wealthy person who causes people to dishonor the poor among them, is a true friend and benefactor who advocates the opposite sorts of actions, such as caring for the poor (Jas 1:27; 2:14–17). If one asks for wisdom, God will be a reliable provider, giving simply, with no tricks up the divine sleeve and "without reproach." God will not impart the mortifying abuse that some patrons could and did deliver.

James 1:12–15 reiterates the need to endure trials and offers a promise of salvation for such endurance. Within these few verses James adamantly insists that God does not test/tempt anyone, presumably to counter those who attempted to blame their temptations on God (Jas 1:13). Many Jews resisted the notion that God could test, for they were concerned to maintain the connection between sin and human responsibility. Various texts were corrected, such as Gen 22:1, which in *Jub.* 17:16 is changed to state that it was not God who wished to test Abraham but rather the devil, Mastema (see Dibelius 1976, 90–91). Testing was important, but it comes from other sources, such as desire (Jas 1:14).

James 1:16–18 again emphasizes the need to rely upon God as a generous benefactor. These verses repeat the theme of perfection, developed in Jas 1:2–4, which some argue to be a central theme of the missive (e.g., Hartin 1999, 57–92). These verses remind the audience that God is the source of all good things, and the constancy of God "the Father of lights" is particularly stressed (Jas 1:17). Although there is complex text-critical problem in James 1:17b, all the variant readings mean the same thing: "The text opposes the steadfastness of God to the changeableness of creation" (Johnson 1995, 197). God is a loyal and unchanging provider, just as friends and true benefactors were expected to be, for no friendship could survive without this constancy (Cicero, *Amic.* 92). Again, God is the opposite of a human patron, for God will continue to provide and will not disappear or withdraw when calamity strikes (Kloppenborg Verbin 1999, 770).

James 2:14–26

James 2:14–16 expresses the author's wish that the audience attend to the needs of the poor and directly follows the scenario in which partiality shown to a wealthy person over a poor one is sharply criticized. Here the emphasis upon integrity, which demands the unification the faith and works, is continued with respect to caring for the poor.

Directly following these exhortations comes the reference to Abraham as a "friend of God" (Jas 2:23), an epithet earned from both Abraham's works of hospitality and his willingness to undergo a great test and nearly sacrifice his son (on the "works" of Abraham, see Ward 1968, 286). The theme of testing is maintained, but hospitality becomes an important dimension, especially with the reference to Rahab (Jas 2:25). James exhorts the audience to practice hospitality and, to encourage them, supplies a human example of a friend of God. Therefore, it appears that to be a friend of God is to practice caring for others. Benefaction is not solely the responsibility of God; it must be demonstrated by the community as well.

Given that early Christian communities contained people from different social strata, such complex groups experienced inner conflicts and problems similar to other associations in the ancient world. James's audience is no exception, although the letter suggests that the majority of the recipients are not rich, given the hostility displayed toward the wealthy. But certainly some members had more pressing needs than others, and these verses suggest that such people were not receiving sufficient assistance. James 2:15–17 explicitly addresses the plight of the brother or sister in shabby clothes, without enough food, who requires things "needed for the body." James insists on caring for such people. Although God is a good and bountiful provider, the author makes it clear that such beneficence must be extended among community members as well.

James 3:13–4:10

This section is unified around the central theme of true wisdom residing in humility and meekness in contrast to a life of jealousy and selfishness. An explicit mention of friendship appears in Jas 4:4, but as we noted earlier, the references to the dangers of envy and covetousness are consistent with some of Plutarch's warnings about what can destroy a friendship. God's characteristics emerge in Jas 4:6–10, in which God "gives grace" and in which a quotation from Prov 3:34 appears. This citation, almost verbatim from the Septuagint except for an exchange of θεός ("God") for κύριος ("Lord"), functions rhetorically to establish the truth of the overall statement (see *Rhetorica ad Herennium* 4.3.6). The persuasive power of citations is great "because of the universal validity of the wisdom and its unquestionable independence of the parties" (Lausberg 1998, 203). It provides proof of why one should live a good life "in the meekness of wisdom" and not according to selfish ambition, for "God opposes the proud but gives grace to the humble" (Jas 4:6 NRSV). God approves not of an envious or selfish life but rather of a humble one; the ancient texts *say so*. God's actions are polar opposite to those of an envious human spirit. God gives a "greater gift" (μείζων χάρις), a notion comparable to Jas 1:5, in which God gives ἁπλῶς. Moreover, Johnson (1995, 283) has shown how the context of Prov 3:34, which focuses on God's wisdom, walking in peace, avoiding envy, caring for the poor, and the exultation of the wise, fits remarkably well with the association of ideas in Jas 3:13–4:10.

The thing that a benefactor would typically provide, χάρις ("grace, favor, benefit"), is mentioned twice in Jas 4:6. The provision of χάρις was regularly associated with benefactors in inscriptions (see Conzelmann 1974, 374–75), and Aristotle defines it as rendering something to someone who needs it, not out of a wish for a return but rather out of care for the needy person (*Rhet.* 2.7.3). Admittedly, χάρις is a common word associated with God in early Christian literature, but here in James, given both the critique of patronage and the characterization of God that have emerged thus far, it further supports the view that James envisions God as a divine benefactor.

Conclusion

Further study needs to be done on the description of God in the Letter of James, but when we consider the distinctions between patronage and benefaction, it is apparent that in this text God is much more of a benefactor than a patron. James's overall critique of patronage, promotion of friendship with God, and insistence upon mutual aid within the community suggest that the description of God as a patron would not rest comfortably in the minds of James's audience. Rather, God is a generous benefactor, a friend, and an unwavering provider on whom these fragile Christian groups could rely, and who exhorts them to care for one another.

Although patron-client relations were deeply entrenched in the world of early Christianity, we must not assume that all ancient writers who refer either to humans and/or to the divine as providers or protectors were necessarily thinking of patronage. Attention to the complexity of the different conceptual models highlights how communities may have understood texts and decrees differently, according to their geographic, social, and cultural locations. In other words, applying the notion of patronage universally may obscure important distinctions made by ancient Mediterranean peoples. One community may have perceived their provider as a patron, while an outsider may have understood the same figure as a benefactor, or vice versa. Attempting to appreciate these different perceptions can paint a richer picture of how ancient writers perceived the divine and/or the powerful and can also shed additional light on how texts both were shaped by and contributed to religious and civic community formation in antiquity.

Moreover, how an author described God could have significant rhetorical effects upon audiences, rousing them either to resist or to conform to specific practices in their social worlds. Although no one knows what happened to the community or communities that received the Letter of James, it seems reasonable to think that the text's emphasis upon God as a benefactor of the faithful would provide more motivation to persist in mutual aid and to avoid becoming dependent upon wealthy leaders, whether inside or outside of the group.

Bibliography

Batten, Alicia. 1999. An Asceticism of Resistance in James. Pages 355–70 in *Asceticism and the New Testament*. Edited by L. E. Vaage and V. L. Wimbush. New York: Routledge.

Conzelmann, Hans. 1974. "χάρις." Pages 372–76 in vol. 9 of *Theological Diction-ary of the New Testament.* Edited by G. Kittel and G. Friedrich. Translated by G. Bromiley. 10 vols. Grand Rapids: Eerdmans, 1964–1976.

Danker, Frederick W. 1982. *Benefactor: Epigraphic Study of a Graeco-Roman and New Testament Semantic Field.* St. Louis: Clayton.

———. 1992. "Benefactor." Pages 669–71 in vol. 1 of *Anchor Bible Dictionary.* Edited by D. N. Freedman. 6 vols. New York: Doubleday.

Dibelius, Martin. 1976. *James.* Revised by H. Greeven. Edited by H. Koester. Translated by M. A. Williams. Hermeneia. Philadelphia: Fortress.

Dixon, S. 1993. The Meaning of Gift and Debt in the Roman Elite. *Echos du Monde Classique/Classical Views* 37:451–64.

Edgar, David H. 1999. *Has God Not Chosen the Poor? The Social Setting of the Epistle of James.* Journal for the Study of the New Testament: Supplement Series 206. Sheffield: Sheffield Academic Press.

Erskine, Andrew. 1994. The Romans as Common Benefactors. *Historia* 43(1):70–87.

Ferrary, J.-L. 1997. The Hellenistic World and Roman Political Patronage. Pages 105–19 in *Hellenistic Constructs: Essays in Culture, History, and Historiogra-phy.* Edited by P. Cartledge, P. Garnsey, and E. Gruen. Hellenistic Culture and Society 26. Berkeley: University of California Press.

Garnsey, P. 1988. *Famine and Food Supply in the Graeco-Roman World: Responses to Risk and Crisis.* Cambridge: Cambridge University Press.

Garnsey, P., and G. Woolf. 1989. Patronage of the Rural Poor in the Roman World. Pages 153–70 in *Patronage in Ancient Society.* Edited by A. Wallace-Hadrill. Leicester-Nottingham Studies in Ancient Society 1. London: Routledge.

Hanson, K. C., and D. E. Oakman. 1998. *Palestine in the Time of Jesus: Social Structures and Social Conflicts.* Minneapolis: Fortress.

Harding, P., ed. and trans. 1985. *From the End of the Peloponnesian War to the Battle of Ipsus.* Translated Documents of Greece and Rome 2. Cambridge: Cambridge Univsersity Press.

Hartin, P. J. 1999. *A Spirituality of Perfection: Faith in Action in the Letter of James.* Collegeville, Minn.: Liturgical Press.

Irwin, W. H. 1995. Fear of God, the Analogy of Friendship and Ben Sira's Theo-dicy. *Biblica* 76:551–59.

Johnson, L. T. 1983. James 3:13–4:10 and the *Topos* ΠΕΡΙ ΦΘΟΝΟΥ. *Novum Tes-tamentum* 25:327–47.

———. 1995. *The Letter of James.* Ancho Bible 37A. Garden City, N.Y.: Doubleday.

Joubert, S. 2000. *Paul as Benefactor: Reciprocity, Strategy and Theological Reflec-tion in Paul's Collection.* Wissenschftliche Untersuchungen zum Neuen Tes-tament 124. Tübingen: Mohr Siebeck.

———. 2001. One Form of Social Exchange or Two? "Euergetism," Patronage and Testament Studies. *Biblical Theology Bulletin* 31:17–25.

Kloppenborg Verbin, J. 1999. Patronage Avoidance in James. *Hervormde teolog-iese studies* 55:755–94.

Konstan, D. 1995. Patrons and Friends. *Classical Philogy* 90:328–42.

———. 1997. *Friendship in the Classical World.* Key Themes in Ancient History. Cambridge: Cambridge University Press.

Lausberg, H. 1998. *Handbook of Literary Rhetoric: A Foundation for Literary Study.* Edited by D. E. Orton and R. D. Anderson. Translated by M. T. Bliss, A. Jansen, and D. E. Orton. Leiden: Brill.

Malina, B. J. 1988. Patron and Client: The Analogy behind Synoptic Theology. *Forum* 4:2–32.

Millett, A. 1989. Patronage and Its Avoidance in Classical Athens. Pages 15–48 in *Patronage in Ancient Society.* Edited by A. Wallace-Hadrill. Leicester-Nottingham Studies in Ancient Society 1. London: Routledge.

Nock, A. D. 1972. *Soter* and *Euergetes.* Pages 720–35 in vol. 2 of *Essays on Religion and the Ancient World.* Edited by Z. Stewart. Cambridge, Mass.: Harvard University Press.

Porter, S. 1991. Is *dipsuchos* (James 1,18; 4,8) a "Christian" Word? *Biblica* 71:469–98.

Saller, R. 1982. *Personal Patronage under the Early Empire.* Cambridge: Cambridge University Press.

———. 1989. Patronage and Friendship in Early Imperial Rome: Drawing the Distinction. Pages 49–62 in *Patronage in Ancient Society.* Edited by A. Wallace-Hadrill. Leicester-Nottingham Studies in Ancient Society 1. London: Routledge.

Schwartz, S. 1994. Josephus in Galilee: Rural Patronage and Social Breakdown. Pages 290–306 in *Josephus and the History of the Greco-Roman Period: Essays in Memory of Morton Smith.* Edited by F. Parente and J. Sievers. Studia post-biblica 41. Leiden: Brill.

Stegemann, E. W., and W. Stegemann. 1999. *The Jesus Movement: A Social History of the First Century.* Translated by O. C. Dean Jr. Minneapolis: Fortress.

Stevenson, T. R. 1992. The Ideal Benefactor and the Father Analogy in Greek and Roman Thought. *Classical Quarterly* 42:421–36.

———. 1996. Social and Psychological Interpretations of Graeco-Roman Religion: Some Thoughts on the Ideal Benefactor. *Antichthon* 30:1–18.

Vhymeister, N. J. 1995. The Rich Man in James 2: Does Ancient Patronage Illumine the Text? *Andrews University Seminary Studies* 33:265–83.

Wachob, W. H. 2000. *The Voice of Jesus in the Social Rhetoric of James.* Society for New Testament Studies Monograph Series 106. Cambridge: Cambridge University Press.

Ward, R. B. 1968. The Works of Abraham: James 2,14–26, *Harvard Theological Review* 61:283–90.

Economics

The world in which Jesus lived was characterized by high levels of peasant indebtedness. The "factor of debt" put obligations on peasants particularly to operate in ways that benefited the elites of society. As more large landowners overtook the land of peasant farmers, indebtedness became a more real and regular experience for peasants (Oakman 1986; Hanson and Oakman 1998, 99–130; Malina 2001, 83–89). In exchange for loans, peasants were expected to produce not only repayment but also honor for their creditors. Indebtedness, in this sense, is related to the phenomenon of patronage in antiquity. To be a client of a powerful patron meant that the client received protection and some opportunity but also became somewhat emasculated, since men were supposed to be in control of their own lives.

Here Douglas Oakman presents us with a model of social stratification in which peasants continually sank further into debt whenever unfavorable circumstances, such as pestilence or low rainfall, befell them. The first century c.e. in Judea and Galilee was a time of increasing indebtedness on the part of peasants, and many found themselves unable to cope with increasing rents and taxes. A result of these combined circumstances was an increase in tenant farming and an increase in the number of formerly free peasants who were taken into slavery for failure to repay their loans.

Against this backdrop, Oakman understands the parables of Jesus to operate as a certain type of indirect critique of the mounting pressure on peasants. To mount a critique without such indirection was surely to court danger and the kind of attention that peasants did not seek. Oakman sees the parables, then, as attempts by Jesus to use common events known to his audiences in order to stress the beneficence of God's kingdom over against that of the Romans and their client kings. Jesus' vision of the kingdom of God included economic relief for those who suffered under the oppressive system of first-century Judea and Galilee.

Bibliography

Hanson, K. C., and Douglas E. Oakman. 1998. *Palestine in the Time of Jesus: Social Structures and Social Conflicts.* Minneapolis: Fortress.

Malina, Bruce J. 2001. *The New Testament World: Insights from Cultural Anthro-pology.* 3d ed., revised and expanded. Louisville: Westminster John Knox.
Oakman, Douglas E. 1986. *Jesus and the Economic Questions of His Day.* Studies in the Bible and Early Christianity 8. Lewiston, N.Y.: Mellen.

Douglas E. Oakman

Jesus and Agrarian Palestine:
The Factor of Debt

INTRODUCTION

THIS ESSAY EXPLORES, through a variety of evidence and with the help of conceptual models and comparative study, the social dynamics of debt in early Roman Palestine. It further attempts to assess whether the ministry of Jesus formulated a response to widespread indebtedness in that environment.

The value of utilizing conceptual models in the study of the past is that of allowing the known to illuminate the unknown, of testing how things were on the basis of how the modern student conceives that they might have been. The model makes explicit the assumptions and judgments of the student and helps to trace the connections between bits of evidence in the effort to eliminate unserviceable interpretations. The model also helps to build the big picture, much like a mosaic. The study of history in this way becomes a history of interpretive "successive approximations" (Carney 1981, 7–17).

In a similar way, comparative study lends precision and focus to the kinds of questions that the historian brings to this task. Employment of social-scientific studies in various ways can contribute to a more adequate interpretation of particular aspects of the past.

PRELIMINARY CONSIDERATIONS ABOUT DEBT IN ANTIQUITY

Debt was often in antiquity a formal expression of relations of dependency and (perhaps irredeemable) obligation. The ideals of reciprocity and social equality in the Graeco-Roman and Jewish traditions encouraged hopes for more "horizontal" relations in society, but more often than not imbalances of power and wealth led in fact to "vertical" relations of dominance and subjection (Gouldner 1977). Nicholas (1962, 149–53, 158ff.) offers a useful treatment of the law of obligations and debt in Roman legal tradition.

For the Greeks, the most fundamental debt was that to one's parents. So Plato writes,

> Next comes the honor of living parents, to whom, as is meet, we have to pay the first and greatest and oldest of all debts, considering that all which a man has belongs to those who gave him birth and brought him up. (*Leg.* 4.717 [see Hauck 1967, 559–66])

Aristotle also speaks of this primal debt:

> This is why it would not seem open to a man to disown his father (though a father may disown his son); being in debt, he should repay, but there is nothing by doing which a son will have done the equivalent of what he has received, so that he is always in debt. (*Eth. nic.* 8.14, 1163b19)

Aristotle further considers in the *Nichomachean Ethics* how essential reciprocity is to friendship, and whether it is better to return a favor (and thus stay out of debt) or to accept such as something that cannot be repaid (*Eth. nic.* 8.13, 1162a34–1163a23; 9.2, 1165a3 respectively).

The sociopolitical aspect of debt is expressed well by Thucydides in the mouth of Pericles:

> In generosity we [the Athenians] are equally singular, acquiring our friends by conferring, not by receiving, favours. Yet, of course, the doer of the favour is the firmer friend of the two, in order by continued kindness to keep the recipient in his debt; while the debtor feels less keenly from the very consciousness that the return he makes will be a payment, not a free gift. (*Peloponnesian War* 2.40.2)

On the Roman side, the vertical and political realities of debt were frequently evident. Cicero criticizes Sulla and Caesar for having expropriated property in order to bestow (politically useful) benefits on others. For Cicero, "liberality" in this sense is not just (Cicero, *Off.* 1.43; 2.84). Plutarch tells how Caesar ran up huge debts for the purpose of sustaining his own political position and agenda (Plutarch, *Caes.* 5 [see Finley 1973, 53f., 143, 187 nn. 47, 55]).

It is in this context that the subject of clientage needs to be mentioned. In the late republic and early empire, political networks were established, maintained, or destroyed by the bestowing of political favors, loans of money, or other social goods. This is well illustrated in, for instance, the affairs of Roman *socii* (allies) such as the Herods. For example, Antipater quickly won Caesar's friendship in Egypt by supplying a small army to support the actions of Mithridates. This gained high honors for Antipater (i.e., Caesar cancelled his obligation to Antipater and made him a client [Josephus, *J.W.* 1.187, 193–194; cf. 1.199]). Herod was unable to hide the support that he had given to Antony when he presented himself to Octavian at Rhodes (Josephus, *J.W.* 1.386ff.). With his usual boldness, Herod made a point of his former loyalty to Antony as a potential asset to the new *princeps.* To this appeal, Octavian was favorably inclined: "So staunch a champion of the claims of friendship deserves to be ruler over many subjects" (Josephus, *J.W.* 1.391).

If debt was at times the bond of friendship or the cement of political relations in Graeco-Roman antiquity, for "little people" it was more often than not brutal compulsion and oppression. The abolition of debt was frequently encountered as a revolutionary slogan of the disenfranchised, usually accompanied by a demand for the redistribution of land (Rostovtzeff 1957; Ste. Croix 1981, 298, 608–9 n. 55; Austin and Vidal-Naquet 1977; Brunt 1971, 74ff.).

In the century and a half immediately preceding the birth of Jesus, the cases of Tiberius Gracchus, Aristonicus, and Lucullus, to name just three, give evidence of attempts to reverse or escape altogether Rome's imperialistic and exploitative agrarian policies, as well as evidence of the socially disruptive effects of debt. Tiberius, witnessing the decline of a Roman peasantry long burdened by the Punic wars and many of whose lands were in the hands of the wealthy, passed an agrarian law designed to restore expropriated lands to their former owners (Plutarch, *Ti. C. Gracch.* 13 [see Brunt 1971, 78–80]). Tiberius was murdered. His aims were carried forward without ultimate success by his brother Gaius. The social order of Rome became dominated, again as of old, by a landed aristocracy.

Almost contemporaneously with the death of Tiberius (133 B.C.E.), Attalus III bequeathed his kingdom to Rome. Before a final settlement could take place, a great "slave" revolt erupted under the leadership of Aristonicus (132–129 B.C.E.). This revolt included not only slaves but also bondmen and the urban proletariat; according to Strabo and Diodorus Siculus, it had a manifestly utopian aim: the foundation of an egalitarian state (Rostovtzeff 1941, 2:757, 807–11). The Hellenistic kingdoms of Asia Minor had exploited its agricultural peoples to the hilt. Rome could be expected to follow similar policies, as was evident to the insurgents from events in Greece. The insurgents had nothing to lose and everything to gain by revolt.

Plutarch makes the agrarian aspect of this revolt plain by connecting the aims of both Aristonicus and Tiberius Gracchus with the Stoic philosopher Blossius: freedom was guaranteed only by equalitarian arrangements in property. The revolutionary actions of Mithridates several decades later apparently were modeled after those of Aristonicus, which allows more precise inference about their nature. They included remission of debts and taxes, as well as promises of land redistribution (Rostovtzeff 1941, 2:938, 943; Dickey 1928, 396–98; Tarn and Griffith 1952, 40–41, 125). A Pergamene inscription (*Orientis graeci inscriptions selectae* 338) indicates that a belated attempt was made to co-opt the insurrection by offering elevated status to the slaves involved. Although the insurrection eventually was crushed, the initial success of Aristonicus shows how powerful the hope for freedom could be for enslaved or indebted people. Several decades later, the lower classes of Asia Minor were still ready to risk all by supporting Mithridates.

After the defeat of Mithridates, the Roman general Lucullus found the population of Asia in terrible straits because of debts owed to Roman *publicani* (tax farmers). The fears of the movement associated with the name of Aristonicus were realized! Lucullus opposed the interests of these "capitalists" and implemented measures to alleviate the sufferings of the province: (1) interest was lowered to 12 percent per year, (2) interest in arrears was remitted, and (3) creditors could take annually no more than one-fourth of a debtor's income (Plutarch, *Luc.* 20.23 [see Rostovtzeff 1941, 2:953–55]). Plutarch says that these measures were successful in alleviating the crisis, but within a few short years the *publicani* and the evils associated with them were back (Rostovtzeff 1941, 2:965).

In the Graeco-Roman world, then, debt and related agrarian problems played a crucial role in historical developments. The same can be said on the Jewish side. A long biblical tradition recognized and attempted to limit, if not completely eradicate, the disruptive socioeconomic effects of debt. Prescriptions or problems related to debt are mentioned in all of the major divisions: legislative (Exod 22:25–27; Lev 25; Deut 15; 23:19–20), prophetic (Isa 5:8; Hab 2:6), historical (1 Sam 22:2; 2 Kgs 4:1; Neh 5:1–5), and wisdom writings (Prov 22:7). The tradition uniformly opposes usury and the permanent transfer of real property (Exod 22:25; Lev 25:13; see also Deut 15:2).

The basic presupposition for the biblical view of debt was the equality, with various qualifications, of each member of Israel before Yahweh. This meant equality of access to the goods of life as well. Hence comes the vociferous opposition in the tradition to disruptions of the social order from economic causes. The emergence of the monarchy and the concomitant social stratification gave fuel to the tradition of protest and legislation (Brueggemann 1979, 161–85). The interesting postexilic episode recorded in Neh 5 gives explicit detail about how the tradition might be actualized to counter agrarian problems.

Debt and a General Model of Social Stratification in Early Roman Palestine

The early Hasmonean epoch seemed to some like a return to the glorious days of Israel (1 Macc 14:4–15). The internal political struggles and agrarian unrest under Jannaeus effectively destroyed this illusion (on the agrarian aspect of this struggle, see Applebaum 1976, 635). Exorbitant exactions and suffering accompanied the Roman civil wars. There was also fratricidal strife between the factions of Hyrcanus and Aristobulus, and Antipater and Herod rose to power. This period initiated a new time of uncertain political status of the Jewish commonwealth and a new order of economic exploitation. Although peace came with Augustus, Palestine unquestionably was an occupied country. A legacy of social disruption and hardship remained. Was this situation further exacerbated by debt?

In regard to the issue of debt in the first half of the first century C.E., what actual evidence is available for assessing its historical importance? For the purposes of this essay, a distinction needs to be made between the situation in Judea and that in Galilee. Furthermore, direct and particular evidence concerning debt must be distinguished from indirect general evidence that seems to point to the existence of a debt problem. Students of this period must appeal to both types of evidence.

Two pieces of direct evidence for a debt problem in Judea are offered here (see Goodman 1982, 417–27). First, Josephus tells us that one of the initial actions of the Jewish insurgents in the war was the burning of the office where debt records were kept. A quotation of this passage is instructive: "[The rebels] next carried their combustibles to the public archives, eager to destroy the money-lenders' bonds and to prevent the recovery of debts, in order to win over a host of grateful debtors and to cause a rising of the poor against the rich" (*J.W.* 2.427).

Josephus records another such incident at Antioch, undertaken by people under pressure from debt (*J.W.* 7.61 [see Brunt 1977, 151]). The motive given by Josephus for the action of the Jerusalem insurgents parallels that of Simon ben Giora, who somewhat later offered liberation to slaves so that they would support his cause (*J.W.* 4.508). These recall similar revolutionary actions taken by Aristonicus in the late second century B.C.E. (see above).

Following the notice just cited, Josephus refers to the archives or record office as the "nerves" or "sinews" (*neura*) of the city. In another place Josephus uses this same expression to refer to stockpiles of food that the competing factions are burning up to their own destruction in the besieged city (*J.W.* 5.24). The record office, then, is seen by this former aristocrat of Jerusalem as necessary for the very sustenance of the city. Debts assure the dominance of the city over the countryside supporting it (cf. Josephus, *Life* 38).

The second piece of evidence is the Mishnah's narrative concerning Hillel's *prozbul*:

> A *prozbul* is not cancelled [in the sabbatical year]. This is one of the things which Hillel the Elder instituted; when he saw that the people refrained from giving loans to one another and transgressed what was written in the Law, "Take heed unto thyself lest there be a base thought in thy heart, etc.," Hillel established the *prozbul*. (*m. Šeb.* 10:3 [cf. Deut 15:9])

According to *m. Giṭ.* 4:3 and *b. Giṭ.* 36a, for example, Hillel implemented through the *prozbul* a humanitarian judicial proceeding to insure the availability of loans at the end of the sabbatical cycle. The talmudic tradition uniformly identifies the *prozbul* (1) as a formulaic statement (*m. Šeb.* 10:4), (2) made before a court, that (3) circumvents the usual cancellation of a debt in the sabbatical year (see further *m. Peʾah* 3:6; *m. Šeb.* 10:3–7; *m. Ketub.* 3:3; 9:9; *m. Giṭ.* 4:3; ʿ*Uq.* 3:10 is a doublet).

A number of points need to be discussed with regard to the tradition. To start with, the Hebrew text is not pointed as *prozbul,* but rather פְּרוֹזְבּוֹל. This philological detail does not support the usual interpretation of the word, as meaning "to the council" (i.e., πρὸς βουλήν). Kippenberg (following Ludwig Blau) has argued that behind the Hebrew word lies the Greek προσβολή, a word encountered in Hellenistic juristic documents. The Greek word refers to the act of distraining on the property of a defaulting debtor and disposing of it through auction (Liddell, Scott, and Jones 1968, 1504). The meaning of the word is illustrated in, for instance, Ptolemy II's instructions to the *oikonomos* of Syria and Phoenicia (Bagnall and Derow 1981, 96). *M. Šebiʿit* 10:6 supports such an interpretation of the *prozbol:* According to this mishnah, a *prozbol* can be written only on immovable property (קרקע).

The Mishnah mentions other types of debt documents, and it is useful to try to distinguish them from the *prozbol. M. Šebiʿit* 10:1 speaks of loans made with or without a "bond" (שטר). Both types of loan are cancelled by the sabbatical year. In apparent contradiction to this, *m. Šeb.* 10:2 says that loans given on pledge or bonds delivered to the court are not cancelled. In these passages the bond stands in contradistinction to pledges and perhaps to simple verbal agreements. The pledge and the third-party surety were older means of guaranteeing repayment of a loan (Barrois 1962, 809). Proverbs 6:1; 11:15; 17:18; 20:16; 22:26 suggest why the wealthy may not have wanted to stand surety for impoverished Jewish peasants.

M. Šebiᶜit 10:5, in which שטר is qualified by the noun חוב, suggests that such documents simply record a debt and the terms of repayment. The bond represents perhaps the emergence of an impersonal system of contractual or written guaranties in place of the traditional securities. Furthermore, the bond, like the *prozbol,* is not necessarily cancelled in the sabbatical year. The reference in *m. Šeb.* 10:2 to bonds conveyed to the court suggests delinquent loans that were due prior to the onset of the sabbatical year. The debts are still due.

It has been thought by D. Correns that the *prozbol* was simply a clause added to a debt document, to allow the debt to be collected in the sabbatical year (and perhaps stipulate that it is secured by real estate via a mortgage or lien [discussed in Kippenberg 1978, 139; cf. *b. Giṭ.* 37b]). Kippenberg thinks that this interpretation is mistaken because it adopts uncritically the later rabbinic view of the *prozbol.* He points out that a debt contract recovered from Wadi Murabbaʿat, Mur 18 (54–55 C.E.), does not contain any formula like the *prozbol. M. Šebiᶜit* 10:4, however, does seem to lend support to the "clause interpretation." It states that the purpose of the *prozbol* is to ensure "that every debt due me I may collect whensoever I desire." This formula (especially "whensoever") perhaps may refer to the waiving of the sabbatical year forgiveness, but it can also be understood to refer to an aspect of the aforementioned Hellenistic procedure of attaching land. The phrase "whensoever I desire" then points to the significant amount of extra-judicial power vested in the creditor. He can move against the debtor's property without further reference to the court (see *Midrash Rabbah Numbers* 19:9, where a creditor hauls away a debtor's, as well as the neighbor's, granary; on legal procedures available to Roman creditors, see Nicholas 1962, 149–53). This feature, not to speak of conveyance of land to cover a debt, was foreign to traditional Jewish law; *b. Giṭ.* 37a indicates that at a later time only the Bet Din (rabbinical court) could seize property. For this reason, the later rabbis had a difficult time assessing the meaning of the innovation attributed to Hillel. Understandably, they made their interpretation along traditional lines (see Kippenberg 1978, 138f.; *b. Giṭ.* 37a). Some authentic memory of the meaning of the *prozbol* is retained nonetheless in the talmudic material.

It is interesting to note what look like post-70-C.E. "codicils" to the *prozbol* regulations. Rabbi Huspith permitted loan arrangements to be made on a wife's or guardian's property (*m. Šeb.* 10:6), and Rabbi Eliezer (against the Sages) declared a beehive to be immovable property (*m. Šeb.* 10:7). These apparently expanded the scope of the law. Are we to infer that lands were mortgaged to the hilt after 70 C.E., and new securities needed to be found?

The direct evidence for Galilean debt, as far as I know, is found only in the Gospels. The discussion of that material is logically deferred to the next section. Turning here, then, to the general, indirect considerations, we will look at three: (1) fiscal pressure, (2) population pressure, (3) popular unrest in the pre-70-C.E. period.

Theissen (1978, 40) lists the following "socioeconomic factors" as significant in the context of Jesus' ministry: (1) natural catastrophes, (2) overpopulation, (3) concentration of possessions, (4) competing tax systems. Goodman (1982, 419), too, notes high taxation, increasing population, and bad harvests as potential explanations for the debt problem in Judea. He downplays all of these, however, and lays emphasis upon the great influx of wealth into Jerusalem after Pompey.

Over seventy-five years ago Grant (1926, 89) argued that two competing taxation systems—the Jewish and the Roman—placed an almost intolerable burden upon the agriculturalist in the early first century C.E. This has become the standard view, even though historians have not as yet achieved a comprehensive picture of Roman taxation in Palestine (Freyne 1980, 183; Theissen 1978, 44; Jones 1974, 151–85). Hamel (1990, 149) has questioned this standard view and argued that since the Romans initially depended upon the local aristocracies for tax assessment and collection (cf. Josephus, *J.W.* 2.405), it is probably better to think that each system of taxation took account of the other (see also Theissen 1978, 42f.).

Against Hamel's view, however, can be set the evidence in Josephus and Tacitus of repeated requests for relief from tax burdens. (Theissen [1978, 43], who cites Josephus, *Ant.* 15.365; 16.64; 18.90; 19.299). Goodman (1982, 419 n. 15) thinks that all such statements are "ideological" and points to the wealth of Judea. However, one must remember both who controlled most of the wealth and who dug into their pockets to pay the taxes, the latter group being those who controlled the least amount of wealth—the lower classes. If they were pressed too far, they might "bite back." The aristocracy knew this, hence the petitions for lowering the tax burden. Almost in the same breath can be mentioned the message of the embassy to Augustus (Josephus, *J.W.* 2.85–86) and the petitions to Archelaus (Josephus, *J.W.* 2.4). The latter expressly mention reduction of taxes and people imprisoned (for debt?). Tacitus (*Ann.* 2.42) reports that Tiberius received requests from the provinces of Syria and Judea for the reduction of tribute (tax on the ground). With this it is to be noted that Tiberius lengthened procuratorial tenure in order to reduce extortionate exploitation of the subject peoples (Josephus, *Ant.* 1 8.1 72ff.; [see Baron 1952, 264 n. 20]).

Population pressure in Roman Palestine at the turn of the era is easily inferred by looking at the expansion of the number of villages, towns, and cities of that time compared with other periods. One may also consider the archaeological and historical evidence for extensive and intensive farming (in Monson 1979, compare maps 11-1 and 12-1; Avi-Yonah [1977, 219–21] places the population at about 2.5 million). Hamel convincingly disputes this high number. By considering the amount of food that the country could have produced maximally, Hamel (1990, 137–40) arrives at a figure of around one million people. Numbers should not, however, obscure the fact that the population had probably risen to a level near the maximum that the land would support under ancient technological and social conditions (Applebaum 1976, 646; Hamel 1990, 138–39). Josephus speaks of both aspects—the number of villages and the intensive farming—in his description of Galilee (*J.W.* 3.42–43).

Along with such physical evidence, we should note the social evidence for population pressure: the numerous landless who are mentioned in the sources. These were excess peasant children without inheritance, expropriated smallholders, and anyone who had been deprived in one way or another of access to the land. Many of these emigrated in search of better economic opportunity (Theissen 1978, 34–41). Such elements apparently supplied the labor pool for Herod's building projects, as well as the discontents met in the pages of Josephus as bandits or messianic pretenders (Theissen 1978, 35f.). In this group are also beggars, orphans, tax collectors, prostitutes, hired laborers, petty artisans, and the like (Schottroff and Stegemann 1981, 15–28; Stegemann 1984, 13–21). Applebaum (1976, 660) has called attention to the expropriations of Jewish agriculturalists in the final years of the first century B.C.E. that swelled the ranks of these people. Lack of land led to conflict, especially in upper Galilee and Perea, between Jewish and Gentile cultivators. We also remember the hostility exhibited by the Galileans during the war toward Sepphoris and Tiberias—both with pro-Roman sentiments and at one time or another seat of the debt archives (Josephus, *Life* 38f., 123ff., 375, 384 [see Freyne 1980, 166]). It is highly probable that other social mechanisms, like persistent indebtedness, were systematically adding to this pool of the disenfranchised (Brunt 1977, 151).

Consider the model sketched in figure 2. The model is designed to show, in a general way, the pressures imposed by debt upon the lives of the lower social strata of ancient Palestine. In the lower part of the model, two continua are employed. The dependency scale marks a social continuum from a relatively independent status to a dependent status. The property scale represents an economic continuum from direct control and access to the land ("ownership") to indirect or no access to the land ("expropriation, dispossession"). The scales are oriented so that the greatest condition of dependency or lack of access to land is farthest from the upper part of the model—representing the upper social stratum (dependent labor: Finley 1973, 69; Ste. Croix 1981, 205ff.).

The dotted lines connecting the two major sections of the model display the flow of rents and taxes upward (Kippenberg 1978, 92, 114, 127). These place a heavy burden on the peasantry. In addition, "acts of God" contribute to the pressure toward debt and foreclosure. A variety of such factors can be mentioned here but, for lack of space, cannot be indicated in figure 2. Insufficient rain or drought, insects, crop diseases, and other pestilences make their contribution. The degree to which the Palestinian economy was monetized would affect the rate of insolvency. Trade and surplus funds to loan are an important ingredient in the rise of indebtedness. Opposed to "acts of God" would be "acts of men"—greed, speculation, and power struggles all play a role in the concentration of property, which is the reverse of the coin of debt and insolvency (Theissen 1978, 41; see, on Herod's

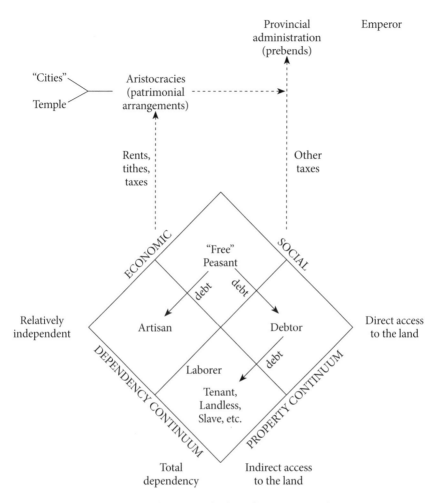

Figure 2: Social dynamics of debt in first-century Palestine

possessions, Josephus, *Ant.* 17.307, 355; 18.2). Stegemann's comment is instructive: "Herod the Great's expropriation of enormous stretches of farmland which were then sold to wealthy landowners . . . led to huge concentrations of land in the hands of a few. . . . This in turn created great numbers of dependent tenant farmers" (1984, 19).

The top of the model indicates the oligarchic structure of Roman Palestine, as it was also articulated with the centralized state of the empire. The basic "polarity" of the top part of the model is the opposition between decentralized aristocracy and centralized ruler (with bureaucratic apparatus) (Lenski 1984, 229ff.; on "patrimony" and "prebend," Weber 1978, 1:222 [prebend = benefice], 231ff.; Wolf 1966, 50ff.).

The debate surrounding Grant's thesis has already been mentioned. The model suggests that not two, but rather three, contending taxations burdened the producer in this period. In addition to the needs of the state and the old aristocracy (the priests), the needs of the new aristocracy (Herodians) and prebends for the Roman officials (procurators) must be kept in mind. These may at times, as Hamel has suggested, have complemented each other. Yet one suspects that for the most part, the old and new aristocracies competed for the same territory.

Debt probably was most thoroughly exploited by those aligned with Rome. This is basically a surmise, of course, but the previous discussion of the Hellenistic legal basis for expropriation of land certainly would point to such an alignment. It may also point to strong economic reasons for the secularization of the high priestly office and the upper priestly crust. In order for these to effectively compete, they would have had to adopt the methods of the new order. Josephus remarks about slaves of the high priests seizing produce destined for the lower orders of priests (*Ant.* 20.181, 206 [see Jeremias 1969, 181]). Consider also the role that lower orders of priests played in the Jewish revolt.

We have already given some attention to bonds and pledges as guaranties for loans. Mishnaic laws, though mostly concerned with movable or immovable securities, speak also about limited periods of debt bondage (Goodman [1982, 423 n. 40] follows E. Urbach; see *m. ʿEd.* 8:2; Kippenberg, 1978, 143). Limited debt bondage is very much in the spirit of Old Testament laws forbidding interest, prohibiting the alienation of property, and protecting any necessary of life (Deut 23:19; Exod 23:26). This type of security is to be distinguished from unlimited debt slavery—a possibility under Roman law. In fact, the Roman law of debt was extremely harsh by comparison (Finley 1973, 40, 69; Ste. Croix 1981, 165ff.).

As figure 2 shows, "free" peasant small-holders—not, of course, free of taxes and religious dues—could become dependent upon some creditor without initially losing direct access to the land. They would remain on their ancestral plot with the legal status of "debtor," which at some point crossed over into tenancy (Freyne 1980, 195).

The model suggests the following possible scenario. A bad harvest or excessive taxation, coupled with the need of the Jewish peasant to feed his family and set aside grain for animals or the next crop, led to arrears ("Indeed many tenants may have originally been owners of their own plots, but in a bad year had had to barter their land in order to pay tribute or buy grain for the following season and even feed their families" [Freyne 1980, 195]). When this was compounded with low productivity or successive bad years, default ensued (Josephus, *Ant.* 18.274). Applebaum (1976, 660 n. 3) gives some evidence for how this might have worked. When Jews after the war could not pay their taxes in kind to the imperial granary in Jamnia, they were forced to borrow the next year's food. A comparative instance from modern Puerto Rico shows how debt through the "advance system" contributed there to the concentration of land ownership (Wolf 1969, 175–76). The ancient tax collector, or a wealthy man advancing credit, might insist on securing a fiscal debt through property. The peasant, obviously, would try to secure it with the labor power of his offspring or something less valuable. Besides "legal processes," there were even dishonest machinations: *y. Ta'an.* 69a tells how the people of Beitar rejoiced over the fall of the wealthy in Jerusalem who had defrauded them out of their ancestral lands (Applebaum 1976, 663 n. 2).

The overall result of escalating debt, whether its nature was private or fiscal, was the growth of tenancy and the landless class (Rostovtzeff 1957, 2:99f., 291, 344f.). Conversely, more and more land came under the control of fewer and fewer landowners. Of both phenomena in first-century C.E. Palestinian society, there are numerous indications. The wealthy men of the immediate post-70-C.E. period—Rabbi Tarfon, Rabbi Eliezer, Rabbi Gamaliel II—did not acquire their possessions overnight (Büchler 1956, 33, 36, 37). Boethus ben Zonen acquired Jewish property through default on debt (*m. B. Meṣ.* 5:3 [see Büchler 1956, 39]). The loan contract from the Wadi Murabba'at, Mur 18 (54–55 C.E.) attests to a lien on (movable?) property in case of default. Mur 22 (131 C.E.) documents the sale of property to cover a debt (Benoit, Milik, and de Vaux 1961, 100–104, 118–21; Kippenberg 1978, 139ff.; Koffmahn 1968, 81–89, 159–162; on leases, see *m. B. Meṣ.* 9).

DEBT IN THE GOSPEL TRADITION

A number of methodological problems in dealing with the New Testament material must be acknowledged before proceeding. Is it appropriate to use the parables to consider Jesus in his sociohistorical context? Do the parables convey direct or indirect information about social conditions in first-century-C.E. Galilee? Or was Jesus' speech focused in other directions, on stock images from the Near Eastern world with little connection to actual circumstances? Was the "real world" simply a take-off point for the essential element in the parables, their alternate "narrative world"?

The hermeneutical stance adopted in this essay has two elements. First, it holds that public speech in an oppressive and conflicted political situation—like that of Jesus in Roman Palestine—cannot address any serious problem in material, social, or power relations without a certain indirection. The parables represent Jesus' attempt to publicly express critical truths in such a repressive political context. For this reason, they can always with probability be made to mean something else. This was the way Jesus protected himself. However, the basic meaning of the parables must always be assessed vis-à-vis their original audience and sociopolitical context.

Second, the hermeneutical stance of this essay stems from the recognition that if the parables are true parables (accounts of real, one-time events), their narratives will self-evidently provide source material for social history, providing that one looks for overarching themes. If the parables are similitudes (typical occurrences) or even stock images, there is nevertheless an alignment between their subject matter and the interests of Jesus, as well as a convergence with the interests of the social historian. In any case, it is believed, the parables do convey information about first-century Galilee (Smith 1937, 17; Jeremias 1972, 20).

More questions then arise. What is the nature of the concern with socio-economic realities often evidenced in the parables? Is this concern incidental or essential for understanding the ministry and message of Jesus? These questions are now taken up here in terms of the particular issue of debt.

A comparison of Matt 18:23–35 and Matt 5:25//Luke 12:58 is instructive (Kippenberg 1978, 141ff.; Ste. Croix 1981, 164). Three different situations are envisioned in which a debtor has defaulted. The two images in Matt 18 give dramatic testimony to the realities of one Hellenistic-Roman procedure for dealing with insolvency. Both are cases of "execution against the person" of the debtor (Ste. Croix 1981, 164, 240). In the one instance, however, the debtor and his whole family are going into slavery for fiscal default. In the other, the debtor is simply clapped into prison for a private debt. Sherwin-White (1978, 134ff.) sees here the stock image of a Hellenistic king, though he orients his discussion to the "little kings," including the Herods, who operated as vassals of the Romans under the early empire. Ste. Croix (1981, 164) also sees in the parable something that might happen in the family of Herod. Perhaps we are to think specifically of Herod Antipas, who exemplified such behavior in Jesus' immediate environment. Jeremias remarks about Matt 18, "The punishment of torture was not allowed in Israel. It is again evident (see vv. 25, 30) that non-Palestinian conditions are described here, unless the parable is referring to Herod the Great, who made abundant use of torture, heedless of Jewish law—but could he have been credited with the generosity of v. 27?" (1972, 212).

The picture in Matt 5:25 par. is somewhat different. Here a judicial proceeding is imminent. "Making friends" with the plaintiff thus means settling the debt out of court. This suggests that a private debt is in view. If there is no settlement, the debtor is in danger of imprisonment. What is different here over against Matt 18 is the court proceeding before imprisonment. Jeremias (1972, 180) does not believe that this is a Jewish court. Sherwin-White (1978, 133) as confidently asserts that the "judge" here is a native magistrate. Kippenberg (1978, 142–43) tries to show that imprisonment for insolvency was enforced by Jewish courts if the debtor had no real property to offset the debt (his evidence is Matt 5:25; 18; Josephus, *J.W.* 2.273 [see below]).

Whatever the historical reality, the court of Matt 5:25 par. had jurisdiction over those Jesus whom was addressing. The legal basis for its proceedings perhaps lay in part in Hellenistic-Roman jurisprudence. Whereas the transactions of the royal house in Matt 18 might have seemed remote, in Matt 5:25//Luke 12:58 the experience of Jesus' audience was directly engaged.

These three New Testament depictions suggest the model in figure 3 (similar to Kippenberg 1978, 141–42, 143). The plight of the defaulting debtor is contingent upon his landed status. If the debtor has land (assuming that it has secured the loan), then property is sold at auction or even transferred to the creditor to settle the debt. If the debtor does not have land, imprisonment or possibly slavery are in store.

Such imprisonment probably had the purpose of forcing the debtor to cough up hidden wealth or compelling his family to redeem him. Might a public auction

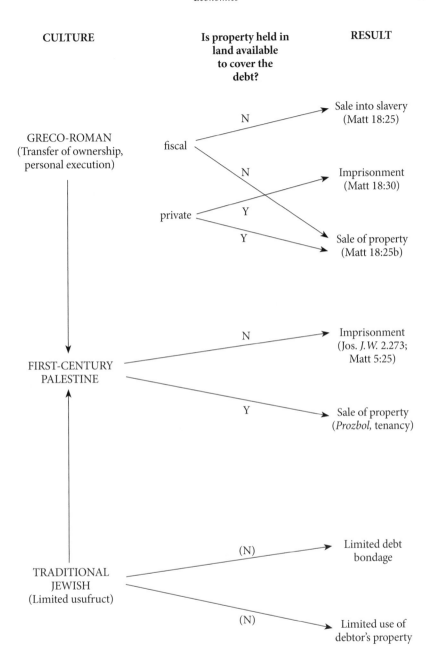

Figure 3: Procedures in case of insolvency (after Kippenberg)

of a debtor's property (i.e., the *prozbol* institution) have had a similar purpose, since Jewish families would have been under pressure to "keep land in the family"? Without property, imprisonment of the debtor was more prevalent than debt bondage, both because slaves were readily and cheaply available and because there was a large labor pool of the landless. The worth of labor thereby was debased (Kippenberg 1978; Goodman 1982, 423 n. 40; Finley 1973, 70).

We now turn to the much-discussed parable in Luke 16:1–9, and a few observations about the transactions there are in order. First, the debts are paid in kind. Second, the size of the debts is remarkable. One hundred cors of wheat would feed 150 people for a year. This figure is derived from the following calculation. About 200 kilograms of grain will keep one person alive at a subsistence level for a year (Hamel 1990, 136 n. 242). If the talmudic cor was around 400 liters in volume, equivalent to 11 bushels, and an average density of wheat today is around 27 kilograms per bushel, then $100 \times 11 \times 27 \div 200 =$ ca. 150. Similarly, the 100 *batous* ("baths," ca. 400 liters each) amounts to a very large quantity of oil. Variant readings in Codex D, of course, offer the smaller unit "qab" (= 1/6 of the bath). Jeremias (1972, 181) indicates that 100 cors = yield of 100 acres and 100 baths = yield of 146 olive trees. What is the nature of this debt?

Since there is nothing to indicate in the parable that the πλούσιος ἄνθρω-πος ("rich man") is a royal figure, it is unlikely that such large debts in kind imply arrears in taxes. These probably were paid in money under the early empire (Rostovtzeff 1941, 2:208f.). The debtors of Luke 16 may be single tenants far in arrears on their rent (normally about 10 cors a year [see *m. B. Meṣ.* 9:7; Applebaum 1976, 659]). The best assumption, however, would seem to be that the parable envisions a man who owns whole villages. These tenant villages, through representatives, pay a yearly produce rent on their agricultural lands. The rich man, then, sells these goods (oil and wheat would be negotiable) and/or provisions his own household. The debt, in any case, is a private debt. This interpretation finds support in Luke 16:4: ὅταν μετασταθῶ ἐκ τῆς οἰκονομίας δέξωνταί με εἰς τοὺς οἴκους αὐτῶν ("When I am removed from the position of manager, they will receive me into their homes"). By defrauding the master, the steward has made many "friends," whole villages in fact.

Of particular note in Matt 18:23–35, Luke 16:1–9, and also in the brief story of Luke 7:41–42 is the aspect of debt forgiveness or remission. In Matt 18 and Luke 7 a petty king or a (wealthy) money-lender supply the examples. Such things happened in the "real world," according to these similitudes. Yet as we have seen, remission of debts was a revolutionary slogan in agrarian antiquity, and such tales on the lips of a Galilean prophet probably sounded subversive.

The case of Luke 16 is somewhat different. There, an underling (cf. the contrary behavior of the underling in Matt 18) reduces the indebtedness, though not entirely. The limited nature of the reduction, nonetheless, points in the same general direction as the other two stories. The betrayal of the master's trust, along with the debt transactions, suggests an abrogation of the then-current social mores of fidelity in such relations and the rigorous exaction of debt (Cicero, *Off.* 2.84).

This point has not gone unnoticed by New Testament commentators, of course, but rarely have they drawn from it any social conclusion. One final bit of the tradition will suggest strongly the need to make more out of the concrete social implications in these parables.

The Lord's Prayer has, together with the parables, been considered the bedrock of the Jesus tradition (Perrin 1967, 47). Yet even so, the prayer comes to us in twofold form in the tradition. Which of the two presents the more authentic form? This question is not easy to decide. The Lukan form is probably closest in length to the original. However, editorial work by both evangelists can be detected. Therefore, the original form would have to be reconstructed in any case.

Fortunately, a discussion of particular points does not have to await the reconstruction of the whole. Of concern here will be only the petitions for bread and forgiveness (Matt 6:11–12//Luke 11:3–4).

First, how is the forgiveness petition to be taken? Underlying the Greek word ἀφίημι and its cognates is the notion of both debt cancellation and metaphorical forgiveness (Bultmann 1964, 509f.). Behind both ὀφειλήματα (Matt 6:12) and ἁμαρτίας (Luke 11:4) probably lies the Aramaic חַיָּב ("debt").This word had in Galilean Aramaic the meaning either "sin" or "debt" (Dalman 1930, 334f.; Perrin 1967, 151). Matthew's understanding of the petition is indicated by the supplemental condition in 6:15 (παραπτώματα) ("tresspasses"). Luke has supplied "sins" instead of "debts." Yet it is most interesting that Luke continues with a material application: "as we ourselves forgive all who are in debt [ὀφείλοντι] to us" (11:4b). The Matthean form of this comparative clause could also formally refer to actual debtors who are "forgiven" (though the above consideration argues against Matthew having so understood the clause).

Admittedly, the metaphorical use of the Aramaic word חַיָּב is well attested in the rabbinic material (Hauck 1967, 565 n. 1). So also is the petition for release from "debts" owed to ("sins" committed against) God. Here may be recalled the sixth benediction in the *Shemoneh Esreh* and especially Akiba's prayer in *b. Ta'an.* 25b: "according to thy great mercy remit [all] our promissory notes [שטרי חובותינו כל]" (Hauck 1967, 562). However, it is to be suspected that these references, like those regarding the *prozbol*, reflect concerns and socioeconomic conditions quite different from the pre-70 C.E. realities of Roman Palestine.

The basic structure of the Synoptic tradition's interpretation of this petition, apparent in both Matthew and Luke, is forgiveness requested in the context of a vertical relationship to God (in line with the later rabbinic viewpoint), as compared with forgiveness practiced in the context of a horizontal relationship to the neighbor. In the latter practice Matthew seems to metaphorize debt to cover all kinds of social obligations, while Luke retains the literal meaning. In the former practice neither Matthew nor Luke reads the petition other than as a request for forgiveness for infractions (debts = trespasses [Matthew], sins [Luke]) against God.

Is it possible to see the meaning of the prayer within the context of Jesus' ministry? I suggest here that that meaning becomes evident in the conjunction of the petition for forgiveness with the petition for daily bread.

What needs to be seen in this conjunction is the *material* link between the two petitions—a synonymous parallelism, if you will. Indebtedness threatens the availability of daily bread. Conversely, the petition for daily bread is at the same time a petition for a social order that will supply such basic human needs in a regular and consistent manner. Thus, the succeeding petition for forgiveness can be seen to address just such a social concern: indebtedness disrupts the ability of a social order to supply daily bread. Therefore, rather than release from infractions against God, Jesus primarily asked through this petition for release from the earthly shackles of indebtedness. Even if one adopts an eschatological hermeneutic framework for this prayer, as does, for instance, Jeremias, one must still see in such an eschatology this material expectation. The material link between lack of bread and debt calls into question, therefore, the "spiritualizing" interpretations of the prayer evident already in the Synoptic tradition.

The suggested interpretation urges itself on the basis of another consideration. Jesus' ministry appealed particularly to the landless—that is, those forced for one reason or another into beggary, prostitution, tax collection, or other occupations not directly linked to working the land. It may be surmised that many of these people knew the reality of indebtedness. Perhaps they had been unable to get out of debt and, for this reason, had been driven from "normal" social ties. Would such people have made no connection between their material need and the most profound expression of the aims of the Jesus movement—the Lord's Prayer?

In conclusion it must be said that if the interpretation advanced here is sustainable, Jesus' ministry takes on an explicitly revolutionary aspect according to the canons of antiquity. From one side, his ministry can be seen to have advocated the dissolution of the material mechanisms of social stratification and power. From another side, the political authorities undoubtedly would have perceived, even in the hint of a public proclamation of the abolition of debt, a subversive, revolutionary agenda. Jesus did not have to advocate armed insurrection in order to be branded as a revolutionary. In fact, he did not advocate armed insurrection. However, his vision of the liberation coming with the reign of God directly attacked a principal element of the Roman order in Palestine and attracted a following of people victimized by debt.

BIBLIOGRAPHY

Applebaum, S. 1976. Economic Life in Palestine. Pages 631–700 in vol. 2 of *The Jewish People in the First Century.* Edited by S. Safrai and M. Stern. Philadelphia: Fortress.

Austin M., and P. Vidal-Naquet. 1977. *Economic and Social History of Ancient Greece: An Introduction.* Berkeley: University of California Press.

Avi-Yonah, M. 1977. *The Holy Land, from the Persian to the Arab Conquests, 536 B.C. to A.D. 640: A Historical Geography.* Rev. ed. Grand Rapids: Baker.

Bagnall, Roger, and Peter Derow. 1981. *Greek Historical Documents: The Hellenistic Period.* Sources for Biblical Study 16. Chico, Calif.: Scholars Press.

Baron, Salo. 1952. *Ancient Times: Part I.* Vol. 1 of *A Social and Religious History of the Jews.* 2d ed. New York: Columbia University Press.

Barrois, G. A. 1962. Debt, Debtor. Pages 809–10 in vol. 1 of *Interpreter's Dictionary of the Bible.* Edited by G. A. Buttrick. 4 vols. Nashville: Abingdon, 1962.

Benoit, P., J. Milik, and R. de Vaux. 1961. *Les Grottes de Murabba'at.* Discoveries in the Judean Desert 2. Oxford: Clarendon Press.

Brueggemann, Walter. 1979. Trajectories in Old Testament Literature and the Sociology of Ancient Israel. *Journal of Biblical Literature* 98:161–85.

Brunt, P. A. 1971. *Social Conflicts in the Roman Republic.* London: Norton.

———. 1977. Josephus on Social Conflicts in Roman Judaea. *Klio* 59:149–53.

Büchler, Adolph. 1956. The Economic Conditions of Judaea after the Destruction of the Second Temple. Pages 1–23 in *Studies in Jewish History: The Adolph Büchler Memorial Volume.* Edited by I. Brodie and J. Rabbinowitz. London Jews' College Publications 1. Oxford: Oxford University Press.

Bultmann, Rudolph. 1964. "ἀφίημι κτλ." Pages 509–12 in vol. 1 of *Theological Dictionary of the New Testament.* Edited by G. Kittel and G. Friedrich. Translated by G. Bromiley. 10 vols. Grand Rapids: Eerdmans, 1964–1976.

Carney, Thomas F. 1981. *The Shape of the Past: Models and Antiquity.* Lawrence, Kans.: Coronado.

Dalman, Gustaf. 1930. *Die Worte Jesu: Mit berücksichtigung des nachkanonischen jüdischen Schrifttums und der aramäischen Sprache.* 2d ed. Leipzig: Hinrichs.

Danby, Herbert. 1933. *The Mishnah: Translated from the Hebrew, with Introduction and Brief Explanatory Notes.* Oxford: Clarendon Press.

Dickey, Samuel. 1928. Some Economic and Social Conditions of Asia Minor Affecting the Expansion of Christianity. Pages 393–418 in *Studies in Early Christianity.* Edited by S. J. Case. New York: Century.

Finley, Moses. 1973. *The Ancient Economy.* Sather Classical Lectures 43. Berkeley: University of California Press.

Freyne, Sean. 1980. *Galilee, from Alexander the Great to Hadrian, 323 B.C.E. to 135 C.E.: A Study of Second Temple Judaism.* University of Notre Dame Center for the Study of Judaism and Christianity in Antiquity 5. Wilmington, Del.: Glazier; Notre Dame, Ind.: University of Notre Dame Press.

Goodman, Martin. 1982. The First Jewish Revolt: Social Conflict and the Problem of Debt. *Journal of Jewish Studies* 33:417–27.

Gouldner, Alvin. 1977. The Norm of Reciprocity. Pages 28–42 in *Friends, Followers, and Factions: A Reader in Political Clientelism.* Edited by S. Schmidt et al. Berkeley: University of California Press.

Grant, F. C. 1926. *The Economic Background of the Gospels.* London: Oxford University Press.

Hamel, Gildas. 1990. *Poverty and Charity in Roman Palestine.* Near Eastern Studies 23. Berkeley: University of California Press.

Hauck, Friedrich. 1967. "ὀφείλω κτλ." Pages 559–66 in vol. 5 of *Theological Dictionary of the New Testament.* Edited by G. Kittel and G. Friedrich. Translated by G. Bromiley. 10 vols. Grand Rapids: Eerdmans, 1964–1976.

Jeremias, Joachim. 1969. *Jerusalem in the Time of Jesus: An Investigation into Economic and Social Conditions during the New Testament Period.* Translated by F. H. Cave and C. H. Cave. Philadelphia: Fortress.

———. 1972. *The Parables of Jesus.* Translated by S. H. Hooke. Rev. ed. New York: Scribner.

Jones, A. H. M. 1974. *The Roman Economy: Studies in Ancient Economic and Administrative History.* Edited by P. A. Brunt. Totowa, N.J.: Rowman & Littlefield.

Kippenberg, Hans. 1978. *Religion und Klassenbildung im antiken Judäa: Eine religionssoziologische Studie zum Verhältnis von Tradition und gesellschaftlicher Entwicklung.* Studien zur Umwelt des Neuen Testaments 14. Göttingen: Vandenhoeck & Ruprecht.

Koffmahn, Elisabeth. 1968. *Die Doppelurkunden aus der Wüste Juda: Recht und Praxis der judischen Papyri des 1. und 2. Jahrhunderts n. Chr., samt Übertragung der Texte und deutscher Übersetzung.* Studies of the Texts of the Desert of Judah 5. Leiden: Brill.

Lenski, Gerhard E. 1984. *Power and Privilege: A Theory of Social Stratification.* New York: McGraw-Hill, 1966. Repr., Chapel Hill: University of North Carolina Press.

Liddell, H. G., R. Scott, and H. S. Jones. 1968. *A Greek-English Lexicon: With a Supplement.* Oxford: Clarendon Press.

Monson J. 1979. *Student Map Manual: Historical Geography of the Bible Lands.* Grand Rapids: Zondervan.

Nicholas, B. 1962. *An Introduction to Roman Law.* Oxford: Oxford University Press.

Perrin, Norman. 1967. *Rediscovering the Teaching of Jesus.* New York: Harper & Row.

Rostovtzeff, Michael. 1941. *The Social and Economic History of the Hellenistic World.* 3 vols. Oxford: Clarendon Press.

————. 1957. *The Social and Economic History of the Roman Empire.* 2d ed. Revised by P. M. Fraser. 2 vols. Oxford: Oxford University Press.

Ste. Croix, G. E. M. de. 1981. *The Class Struggle in the Ancient Greek World: From the Archaic Age to the Arab Conquests.* Ithaca, N.Y.: Cornell University Press.

Schottroff, L., and W. Stegemann. 1981. *Jesus von Nazareth, Hoffnung der Armen.* Urban-Taschenbücher 639. Stuttgart: Kohlhammer.

Sherwin-White, A. N. 1978. *Roman Society and Roman Law in the New Testament.* Oxford: Clarendon Press, 1963. Repr., Grand Rapids: Baker.

Smith, B. T. D. 1937. *The Parables of the Synoptic Gospels: A Critical Study.* Cambridge: Cambridge University Press.

Stegemann, Wolfgang. 1984. *The Gospel and the Poor.* Translated by D. Elliott. Philadelphia: Fortress.

Tarn, William, and G. T. Griffith. 1952. *Hellenistic Civilization.* 3d ed. London: Arnold.

Theissen, Gerd. 1978. *Sociology of Early Palestinian Christianity.* Translated by J. Bowden. Philadelphia: Fortress.

Weber, Max. 1978. *Economy and Society.* Translated and edited by G. Roth and C. Wittich. Berkeley: University of California Press.

Wolf, Eric. 1966. *Peasants.* Foundations of Modern Anthropology. Englewood Cliffs, N.J.: Prentice-Hall.

Part Three

CULTURE

Honor and Shame

5

lassicists declare "honor" to be the most important value in the ancient world. It may be paraphrased as "fame," "reputation," "worth/worthiness," "respect," and "praise." What is honor? Why do the ancients pursue it as their greatest good? How does one get it? All ancient people were socialized to depend on what others thought of them as their source of worth and identity. Children were taught that family and friends were always evaluating them and expecting them to do what they could to bring honor to their families. "Face" is an aspect of honor: one strives not to lose face but rather to save it.

Aristotle explained where honor fits into the scheme of ancient social values. It is the greatest of external goods.

> The greatest external good we should assume to be the thing which we offer to the gods, and which is most coveted by men of high station, and the prize awarded for the noblest deeds; and such a thing is honor, for honor is clearly the greatest of external good. The great-souled man is he who has the right disposition in relation to honors and disgraces . . . since it is honor above all else which great men claim and deserve. (*Eth. nic.* 4.3.9–12)

Similarly, Xenophon claimed that those pursuing honor differ most from brute animals as well as nonambitious humans: "In this, man differs from other animals—I mean, in this craving for honor. But they in whom is implanted a passion for honor and praise, these are they who differ most from the beasts of the field, these are accounted men and not mere human beings" (*Hier.* 7.3). The ideals of honor and glory do not apply only to those in the prime of life; they are are operative from womb to tomb: birth from noble parents, prowess in schooling, military success, aesthetic awards, and even a "noble" death. Thucydides spoke about honor in old age: "The love of honor never grows old, and in the useless time of old age the greatest pleasure is not, as some say, in gaining money, but in being honored" (Plutarch, *An seni* 783F).

One either earns honor or is given it. As regards the latter, birth into a noble family brings to individuals the respect that the group enjoys. Ambassadors represent the honor of their sender. Emperors appoint procurators to certain provinces. In contrast, honor is achieved in battle, in games, in contests of drama and poetry, and in benefaction. As chapter 13 below, on "Limited Good," indicates, the world of honor is simultaneously one of agonistic conflict and envy. One envies those who gain in honor and so attacks them, mostly in a verbal manner.

The *chreia* (a brief reminiscence about a person, usually in the form of a pithy saying) learned in the *progymnasmata* ("school exercises") taught students how to structure this conflict, whereby a sage or wise man is questioned so as to cause him to lose face.

Honor and respect can be lost. Cowards flee in battle; men start projects that they cannot finish (Luke 14:28–32). A man is shamed when the females under his care are preyed upon or when his sons dishonor him. Just as men pursue renown and praise, they are crushed by failure and disgrace. Honor is also lost when families reject some members, when synagogues expel some people, and when individuals are publicly called "Fool!" by the village.

After reading this material on honor and shame, one might take the material and read further in the New Testament. A concordance will provide references to "honor," and also its conjoined twins: "bless," "praise," "glorify," "exult," "good repute," and "worthy." All titles or ranks also belong here. Since honor is related to being outstanding, one should pay attention to the indices of uniqueness pointed out in the rhetoric of praise: "We must, for example, point out that the subject of praise is the only one [μόνος], or the first [πρῶτος], or one of only a few [μετ' ὀλίγων], or the one who has most [μάλιστα] done something; for all these things are honorable" (Aristotle, *Rhet.* 1.9.38).

Jerome H. Neyrey, SJ

Loss of Wealth, Loss of Family, Loss of Honor: The Cultural Context of the Original Makarisms in Q

Introduction: Focus and Hypothesis

WE BEGIN THIS study of by bringing to the discussion of "poor" and "poverty" a cultural and social element. Stated most baldly, the word *poor* implies not simply scant economic resources—that is, little land or money—but has a decidedly cultural component as well. Most people in antiquity would qualify as poor according to economic standards. But the ancients did not automatically classify the economically deprived as poor. If peasants had what sufficed, Plutarch did not call them "poor": "In what suffices, no one is poor" (*Cupid. divit.* 523F). Seneca echoed this: "Let us return to the law of nature; for then riches are laid up for us. The things which we actually need are free for all, or else cheap; nature craves only bread and water. No one is poor according to this standard" (*Ep.* 25.4). Peasants with little of this world's goods have what is deemed "sufficient," and so are not called "poor."

But we need to distinguish two Greek terms πένης and πτωχός. Dictionaries translate πένης as "poor man," which misses the root meaning, πένομαι ("work hard"). Πένης refers to a person who does manual labor, who thus is contrasted with πλούσιος, a member of the landed class, who does not work. Considering the social status or honor rating of a "worker," Hamel writes of the πένης,

> He [the worker] was forced to work to live and had to receive some form of wage and to sell; the craftsman was dependent on others' goodwill. In this respect, he was similar to servants and slaves, free but fettered by various customs. . . . This lack of time and self-sufficiency, some philosophers argued, made the craftsman unfit to be a citizen. One had to be rich to avoid the ties of dependence usually associated with work and be able to live like a true Hellene. Work, because it meant subservience and dependence, was seen as an impediment to this ideal and was therefore contemptible. . . . The *penētes* were all those people who needed to work in shops or in the fields and were consequently without the leisure characteristic of the rich gentry, who were free to give their time to politics, education, and war. (1990, 168–69)

A πτωχός, however, is a person reduced to begging—that is, someone who is destitute of all resources. One gives alms to a πτωχός. A πένης, who has little wealth yet has "sufficiency," is not called "poor." In contrast, the πτωχός, who lacks sufficiency and most other things, such as social standing, is "poor"

(Aristophanes, *Plut.* 535–554). Of the destitute poor person (πτωχός), Hamel remarks, "The *ptōchos* was someone who had lost many or all of his family and social ties. He was a wanderer, therefore a foreigner for others, unable to tax for any length of time the resources of a group to which he could contribute very little or nothing at all" (1990, 170). If "poor" and "poverty" are not simply (or primarily) defined in economic terms, then we should ask about the cultural and social meaning of these labels in antiquity. My hypothesis about the relationship of a "poor person" (πτωχός) to the value of honor/shame may be stated thus:

1. Honor and shame are closely related to wealth and loss of wealth respectively.

2. Wealth and honor are not individual possessions, but rather are the property of the family or kinship group. When a family lost wealth, its status and honor were threatened.

3. Although most people had meager possessions and low status, some families or kinship groups could no longer maintain their inherited status in regard to marriage contracts, feasts, land tenure, and the like. Loss of wealth translated into lower status, which meant loss of honor.

Let us briefly examine the values of honor and shame and explore how wealth is linked with honor, while loss of it could be linked with shame.

What Is Honor?

Honor, considered by many to be perhaps the pivotal value in antiquity, has been brought to the attention of biblical scholars (Malina 2001, 27–57; Neyrey 1998, 14–68). Basically, honor is the value of a person in his own eyes and in the eyes of his society. It is his estimation of his own worth, his claim to pride, but it is also the acknowledgment of that claim (Pitt-Rivers 1977, 1). Honor expresses one's public standing. Although one can acquire it, normally honor is attached to social groups, especially families. All members of a certain clan, tribe, or family share in its collective worth and respect. In examing the relevant aspects of honor that constitute the background of the makarisms in the Q tradition,[1] we will focus on three aspects: (1) honor and wealth, (2) honor and the family, (3) loss of wealth and loss of honor.

Honor and Wealth

Honor is not honor unless publicly claimed, displayed, and acknowledged. Honor is displayed by the clothing worn in public, which signals status and

---

[1] "Makarism" (understood to be a state of social acknowledgement and thus best rendered, "honored," "honorable") is a transliteration of the Greek *makarismos* (Rom 4:6, 9; Gal 4:15, where it is usually translated "blessing").

wealth (see Isa 3:18, 24; 1 Kgs 10:4–10). Josephus's account of Haman's ironic advice to the king illustrates the importance of public display of wealth and clothing and honor: "If you wish to cover with glory the man whom you say you love, let him ride on horseback wearing the same dress as yourself, with a necklace of gold, and let one of your close friends precede him and proclaim throughout the whole city that this is the honor shown to him whom the king honors" (*Ant.* 11.254). All in the public would see the symbols of honor: gold necklace, elegant clothing, and proud mount. Similarly, the restored honor of the prodigal son is symbolized by the clothing that his father allows him to wear: "Bring the best robe . . . and put a ring on his finger and shoes on his feet" (Luke 15:22). Luke knows that elites are dressed in "fine linen and purple" (16:19) and that people "who wear soft raiment and are gorgeously appareled" live in king's courts (7:25). What an impression Herod made when he "put on his royal robe" to take his seat on his throne (Acts 12:21)!

Besides clothing, the elite claimed honor through the display of their table setting and the manner in which they dined. Plutarch comments about the ostentatious meals of his contemporaries, as well as the need for an adoring public to turn mere possessions into honor:

> With no one to look on, wealth becomes sightless and bereft of radiance. For when the rich man dines with his wife . . . he uses common furnishings, and his wife attends it in plain attire. But when a banquet—*that is, a spectacle and a show*—is got up, the drama of wealth is brought on: the repositories of the lamps are given no rest, the cups are changed, the cup-bearers put on new attire, nothing is left undisturbed, gold, silver, or jeweled plate, *the owners thus confessing that their wealth is for others.* (Plutarch, *Cupid. divit.* 528B [italics added])

Wedding feasts were excellent times for families to put on a public display of whatever wealth they had—clothing, coverlets, utensils, music, food, and so on (see John 2:1–11).

Thomas Carney, a student of wealth in antiquity, argues that unlike the modern industrial economy, "basically land, not capital, was of critical importance in antiquity. The vast bulk of production was agricultural. Technology was simple, and apart from slaves (used mainly in conjunction with land), inexpensive. So power and wealth went with possession of land. . . . It was land, not capital, that produced resources in antiquity" (1975, 181–82). Obviously great wealth resided in the hands of aristocrats with vast land holdings, but peasants with small plots of land also enjoyed some relative wealth because of their land. Thus honor in antiquity is related to wealth that is based on land holdings. Yet honor is a family affair, such that all members shared in the collective standing of the kinship group.

Honor and Family

In antiquity a person is primarily known as the "son of So-and-So" or the "daughter of So-and-So." Identity and honor derive in large part from membership in a family or clan. The rules for *encomia* (rhetoric designed to praise a

person, place, or thing) in the *progymnasmata* mandate that when praising or
honoring someone, writers begin their praise with mention of the ancestors and
family of the honoree, and so the importance of genealogy belongs here. The
claim that "honor resides in the blood" is illustrated widely in "biographies" as
well as speeches (Josephus, *Life* 1–6). Aristotle summarizes the expectations of
the ancients about birth and family honor: a good birth is one in which

> its members are indigenous or ancient; its earliest leaders were distinguished men,
> and from them have sprung many who were distinguished for admirable qualities.
> The good birth of an individual implies that both parents are free citizens, and that,
> in the case of the state, the founders of the line have been notable for virtue or wealth
> or something else which is highly prized. (*Rhet.* 1.5.5)

To know a person, ancient peoples thought it essential to know that person's
blood lines (see Cicero, *Inv.* 1.24.34–35; Quintilian, *Inst.* 3.7.10–11; Pelling 1990,
213–44). Hence notice of someone's genealogy, ancestors, clan, and parents contributed essential pieces of information about that person.

Peasants, moreover, have living memory of the families with whom they live.
They know which family has wealth (size of land holdings, crop yields, size of flocks).
They know the reputations of other families, their noble deeds, their chaste women,
and so on. Since arranged marriages, which are family affairs, are contracted with
social equals or betters, villagers are very careful to assess the wealth, worth, and
honor of a family with whom a marriage is contemplated.

Loss of Wealth and Loss of Honor

If honor is symbolized by family and wealth, especially land, loss of honor
can be symbolized by loss of family, land, and wealth. The ancients distinguished
between the deserving poor, whom one should help, and the undeserving poor,
who deserve their situation. This is clearest in the distinction made between those
who suffer "misfortune" and those who are poor because of their own fault. Aristotle called it virtuous for a man "to give to the right people, the right amounts,
and at the right time" (*Eth. nic.* 4.1). The virtuous person will "refrain from giving to anybody and everybody, that he may have something to give to the right
people, at the right time" (*Eth. nic.* 1120b 3–4). He does not specify exactly who
the "right" and "wrong" people are, but Cicero offers advice on whom one should
help: "The case of the man who is overwhelmed by misfortune is different from
that of the one who is seeking to better his condition, though he suffers from no
actual distress. It will be the duty of charity to incline more to the unfortunate,
unless, perchance, they deserve their misfortune" (*Off.* 2.18.61–62).

Those who experience misfortune suffer undeservedly and so warrant assistance. What, then, is a legitimate misfortune? Cicero hints at a class of misfortunes in others, for the alleviation of which a person might prove generous: "The
generous are those who employ their own means to ransom captives from brigands, or who assume their friends' debts or help in providing dowries for their
daughters, or assist them in acquiring property or increasing what they have"

(*Off.* 2.16.55–56). Put simply, some people experience misfortune through no fault of their own; they fall below the social level into which they were born, thus provoking sympathy and not contempt. Conversely, the ancients deem others as shamefully "poor" because the fault is their own. While it is no fault of a wife that her husband dies or of a farmer that drought ruins his crops, if a "fool" loses his wealth, it is shameful (Matthews and Benjamin 1991, 222–26).

Therefore, we have learned that (1) wealth is a component of honor, and both reside primarily in the family; (2) becoming "poor" (πτωχός) includes a corresponding loss of status through actual loss of wealth (loss of land) or of family (death of parents or husband); (3) such losses threaten one's honor rating as well as economic situation. It would, then, be culturally myopic to consider "poor" and "poverty" merely in terms of economic levels (Hollenbach 1987).

HONOR AND THE MATTHEAN MAKARISMS

Hanson (1994, 86–99) argues that אשׁרי and μακάριος should be translated as "esteemed," and אוי and οὐαί as "disreputable" or "shame on," because they are part of the lexical field of "honor and shame." Hanson suggests that when we approach Matthew's "beatitudes" (5:3–12) in their proper cultural perspective, we should be alert to several things. First, public honor is being accorded to certain people who fit the categories described. Μακάριος should include the cultural note of "esteemed" or "honored." Second, if "poor" means someone who cannot maintain his or her status and so suffers loss of honor as well as economic hardship, then the makarisms contain an oxymoron: "How honorable are those who suffer a loss of honor. . . ."

Loss of Family = Loss of Wealth and Honor—The Original Four Makarisms

This study of the four original makarisms builds on and challenges certain scholarly opinions. I accept the consensus that the original Q source contained only four original makarisms, and that Luke's version seems to be the more original. I do not, however, direct attention to the history of the makarisms, whether they originated separately before being gathered together in the Q tradition (see Kloppenborg 1986, 36–44). Rather, I wish to consider their cultural meaning and so suggest a plausible social and historical situation to explain them. I question the assertion that the first three makarisms deal with "the general human conditions of poverty and suffering" and the fourth makarism "is oriented toward the specific situation of persecution of the Christian community" (Kloppenborg 1987, 173). Thus, in terms of the Q document, I resist separating the fourth makarism from the other three, whatever their previous independent histories.

The four original makarisms describe someone who has lost both material wealth (poor, hungry) and social standing (loss of kin, ostracism). But do they describe four different situations—that is, the "general human condition"—or do they delineate the full extent of the crisis of one person? If they describe the full extent of one crisis, what likely scenario explains that? Evidently, in posing the question this way, I advance a new hypothesis: the original four makarisms describe the composite fate of a disciple who has been ostracized as a "rebellious son" by his family for loyalty to Jesus. This ostracism results in total loss of all economic support from the family (food, clothing, shelter) and total loss of honor and status in the eyes of the village (a good name, marriage prospects, etc.). Such persons would be "shameful" in the eyes of the family and village, but Jesus proclaims them "honorable" (μακάριοι [cf. Matt 19:30; 20:16]).

The Fourth Makarism

Let us take a closer look at the climactic fourth makarism first, for it enjoys the significant rhetorical position of being last, and it is triple the length of the others. It describes a total loss of honor. Matthew and Luke record different versions of the fourth makarism, but scholars generally credit Luke with the more original wording in this case.

LUKE 6:22	MATTHEW 5:11
Honorable are you when men	Honorable are you when men
hate you,	revile you,
exclude you,	drive you out,
revile you,	
cast out your name as evil	utter all kinds of evil against you falsely
on account of the Son of Man.	on my account.

Figure 4: Fourth makarism

According to Luke, some person is being shamefully treated; "persecuted" is infelicitous here because it is too vague and imprecise, nor does it adequately suggest either the source of the opposition or its sociocultural result. But let us examine more closely the terms that Luke uses, with an eye to their cultural meanings. This hostility is not the formal or informal excommunication from the synagogue.

μισήσωσιν, "hate," the opposite of love, has to do with group attachment; it means formal rejection and denial of loyalty (see Luke 1:71; 16:13; 19:14); it is considered virtuous to hate what is evil or disobedient.

ἀφορίσωσιν, "separating" regularly takes place between what is holy and what is unclean: unclean lepers were cast out of the camp, as was Miriam for her revolt (Num 12:14). In Matthew it means "separating" so as to judge or punish (13:49; 25:32) and has the sense of to "outlaw" from a social group.

ὀνειδίσωσιν, "reviling and reproaching" are acts of shaming another (Matt 11:20; 27:44; Rom 15:3; 1 Pet 4:14); the predominant sense is disgrace, shame, scandal, abuse, and objurgation.

ἐκβάλωσιν τὸ ὄνομα ὑμῶν ὡς πονηρόν, despite the claim by some that "the name" here is *Christianos*, I contend that an individual's personal name or reputation is at stake. Luke refers to calumny—that is, attacking the public reputation and honor of another.

The fourth makarism describes separation from one's basic social group, either being banned or expelled; it speaks of being reviled and reproached; one's honor, name, and reputation are attacked. Such a person is, thus, completely shamed in the eyes of neighbors.

The material or economic effects of this are not hard to imagine. The Tosefta describes the plight of someone banned or excommunicated: "One does not sell to them or receive from them or take from them or give to them. One does not teach their sons a trade, and does not obtain healing from them" (*t. Ḥul.* 2:20). If the person so treated is an artisan, public reproach will result in loss of employment and trade; if a peasant farmer, the result will be the loss of cooperation in planting and harvesting, a break in marriage contracts, an absence from the reciprocal feasts and weddings among villagers, and the like. Such losses entail declining material wealth for a peasant and consequent failure to maintain subsistence and previous social standing.

In the case of the fourth makarism, public shame goes hand in hand with severe loss of wealth; the person described there is "driven out" (διώξωσιν) or "outlawed" (ἀφορίσωσιν). This implies loss of property: land (if a farmer) or market stall (if an artisan). Total economic ruin, as well as corresponding collapse of social standing, quickly follow. This person will surely be a πτωχός, but is this person honorably or shamefully destitute? Whence this hostility?

Previous studies of the "forms of persecution" that befell the early disciples of Jesus focused on formal judicial acts. They describe persecution as a form of exclusion from the synagogue, not, however, the formal *niddui,* but rather the informal ban employed by every community toward those whom it despises. Although the New Testament speaks of disciples "cast out of the synagogue" (John 9:22; 12:42; 16:2) or simply "expelled" (John 9:34), there is another possibility for banning or exclusion: family sanctions against a rebellious son. I suggest that a likely scenario for the fourth makarism is the situation of a son being disinherited by his father and shunned by his family.

The Other Three Makarisms

Let us examine the other three makarisms in the light of the fourth one, for they can be understood as specifying more exactly the economic or material loss that follows the loss of honor and social standing. My strategy is to imagine them as literally and realistically as possible in the economic and cultural world of peasants and artisans.

As regards the first makarism, most peasants and artisans in antiquity possessed little material wealth; and as we saw, they were not thereby called "poor" (πτωχός) if they had what was sufficient (i.e., subsistence). Luz describes a "poor" person as one who is not simply lacking in wealth: "'Poor' means not only those who are lacking in money, but, more comprehensively, the oppressed, miserable, dependent, humiliated. . . . The basic rule is: the πένης has to work, the πτωχός has to beg" (1989, 231). In the first makarism those addressed are called πτωχοί, which I take to mean destitute beggars, not πένης or the general peasant audience of have-nots. I favor, moreover, understanding this reference to πτωχός as a general statement concerning persons who have suffered a recent and severe loss of means; more specificity is given in the subsequent makarisms.

The literal, simple meaning of "hunger" as lacking food seems warranted. Drought and famine may cause hunger in the land (Josephus, *Ant.* 15.299–316; Acts 11:28), as well as excessive taxation. Landed peasants have resources and relationships to alleviate starvation, but not so landless peasants. They have scant money with which to purchase food; even if they did, the money could hardly last for long. These "hungry" folk are promised that they will "eat their fill," but at present they are πτωχοί in regard to their daily bread (Hamel 1990, 8–52; Oakman 1986, 22–28).

Those who "mourn" might be said to be engaged in mourning for the dead (see Gen 50:3; 1 Esd 1:32; 1 Macc 12:52); they are not lamenting sins or awaiting the eschatological day. They will be "consoled." Since we find the combination of "mourning" for the dead and "comfort" in ancient literature, the mourning envisioned here most probably involves the loss of family and kin. The text gives no reason for supposing that the mourners are the ubiquitous widows and orphans of antiquity (on life expectancy in antiquity, see Carney 1975, 88). Nevertheless, someone lacks parents, family, and kin, with all the economic and social loss attendant upon this.

The Relationship of the Fourth and the Other Makarisms

The final makarism offers a plausible scenario for understanding the other three. If a son were banned or disinherited by his father, he would be "hated" by the family and "outlawed" from the family house and land. He would then truly be "poor" (πτωχός)—that is, suffering a severe loss of all resources, material as well as social. He would be said to be "mourning" the loss of kin and experiencing the loss of status that comes with being without family. Finally, if a son were driven away from the family land, he would immediately experience the loss of access to the grain, vegetables, fruits, and so forth that were the daily food of peasants; no doubt he would literally be "hungry and thirsty." The ostracism described in the last makarism, therefore, describes a situation where sufficiency and subsistence fail. Furthermore, each of the four makarisms, either individually or taken together, genuinely describes a πτωχός, someone who has suffered a loss of subsistence and so cannot maintain the social position and status into which he was born.

Moreover, this peasant would suffer a true and total loss of honor and status. His name would be reviled, his reputation held up to rebuke, and his character calumniated. Business deals and marriage arrangements with such an outcast would be unthinkable. With loss of wealth, he would hardly be in a position to maintain his social obligations and honorable status. This loss of honor, I suggest, would deprive him of all standing in the village or town. He would be looked on by his neighbors as a person reaping a deserved harvest of shame. This possible scenario is by no means the only one. What would make it probable?

Loss of Family in the Q Source

Several passages in the Q source support the probability of the scenario described above. Two describe family crises (Luke 12:51–53//Matt 10:34–36; Luke 14:25–26//Matt 10:37–39), and two deal with loss of wealth (Luke 12:22–32//Matt 6:25–32; Luke 12:33–34//Matt 6:19–21). Three of these passages are found in one continuous discourse in Luke 12, and if the general presumption of the originality of the Lukan sequence prevails here, then the materials on family crisis were originally linked with those about loss of wealth. The loss of family would be the probable context for loss of wealth and thus of honor.

Crisis in the Family

One passage records Jesus attacking the social debt of obedience owed by sons to their fathers and family.

LUKE 12:51–53	MATTHEW 10:34–36
Do you think that I have come to give peace on earth?	Do not think that I have come to bring peace on earth;
No, I tell you, but rather division.	I have not come to bring peace, but a sword.
Henceforth in one house there shall be five divided, three against two and two against three.	
They will be divided,	I have come to set
father against son,	a man against his father,
and son against father,	
mother against daughter,	
and daughter against her mother,	and a daughter against her mother,
mother-in-law against daughter-in-law,	
daughter-in-law against her mother-in-law.	and a daughter-in-law against her mother-in-law;
	and a man's foes will be those of his own household.

Figure 5: Jesus attacks social debt of obedience

Despite other sayings of Jesus in support of family (Mark 7:9–12), here he is attacking the basic solidarity and loyalty that family members owe each other. Moreover, this passage implies that the division of the family occurs precisely because of Jesus ("I have come to . . . "); it envisions members loyal to family traditions but others joining the circle of Jesus.

Linked with this is a second passage (Luke 14:25–27//Matt 10:37–39) that also has to do with family loyalty. It presents a totally divided household:

LUKE 14:26–27	MATTHEW 10:37–38
If anyone comes to me and does not hate his own father and mother and wife and children and brothers and sisters, yes, and even his own life,	He who loves father or mother more than me is not worthy of me; and he who loves son or daughter more than me
he cannot be my disciple.	is not worthy of me.
Whoever does not bear his own cross	He who does not take up his cross
and come after me	and follow me
cannot be my disciple.	is not worthy of me.

Figure 6: Jesus and the divided household

Matthew's version emphasizes "love X more than me"; it connotes a posture of respect for or acceptance of another's approval, which is the essence of honor. "Who loves X more than me" is "not worthy" of me, another term of honor. Luke's account stresses "hating" parents and family members, which results in disregard for filial obligations of obedience and respect (see Luke 9:59–60//Matt 8:21–22). This son would hardly be "honoring father and mother." Who does not hate the family group (with its social standing, land, and wealth) cannot find affiliation, status, and respect in Jesus' group. Again the issue focuses on the source of honor, either from family or Jesus. Loyalty either to family or to Jesus occasions the choice.

Both versions exhort hearers to "take up one's cross" and so become a member of Jesus' fictive-kinship group. The "cross" must surely be a metaphor for negative experiences, possibly physical sufferings (begging, hunger) and/or social ones (loss of family, shame). These sufferings are not the result of taxation, drought, or some other "misfortune," but rather are precisely the result of becoming Jesus' disciple. There would be, then, shame from the family, but honor from Jesus.

It takes little imagination to see how "hatred" of one's family would lead to a "cross." Obedience to one's parents was a paramount virtue sanctioned by custom and law, and disobedience could easily lead to social and economic ruin. A rebellious son should be banned by the family (Deut 21:18–20). If banned, he will surely take up a "cross" to be Jesus' disciple—suffering that is as physical (hunger) as it is social (mourning, begging, being an outcast). The crux of the crisis lies in honor and loyalty, either traditional loyalty to parents and family with its concomitant honor, wealth, and status, or affiliation with Jesus. Loss and gain: loyalty to Jesus entails loss of honor in the family and kinship network, because the honor code between father and son is violated; but also it entails a gain of honor, because Jesus honors those who are loyal to him (μακάριοι) and acclaims them "worthy."

Although these passages do not say that the father eventually bans the rebellious son and disinherits him, or that the son quits his father's house, they do offer an immediate and plausible scenario for the ostracism described in the fourth makarism. If any form of banning or disinheriting results from a son's loyalty to Jesus, then he will truly be "poor," as well as hungry and mourning.

Other Remarks on Loss of Wealth

Two other passages need to be examined (Luke 12:22–32//Matt 5:24–34; Luke 12:33–34//Matt 6:19–21), the correct social interpretation of which can shed light on the economic and cultural effects of families being divided over loyalty to Jesus. In the Lukan and Matthean versions both passages are linked together, an editorial clue that we respect.

Luke 12:22–32//Matt 6:25–34 explicitly treat loss of wealth and its relationship to honor. These passages begin with a topic statement:

> Do not be concerned about:
>   what to eat
>   what to wear (Luke 12:22//Matt 6:25)

The scenario envisioned here reflects the gender division of society common in antiquity: a male world (public tasks in public places) and a female world (private or household tasks in the household). The person "concerned about what to eat" is a male, whom I call the husband. When he looks at the birds of the air, he "sees" fields, which in the gender-divided world of antiquity were the male places where males did the male task of farming. Birds, however, do not perform the tasks typically done by males—that is, "sowing, reaping, gathering into barns or storehouses" (Luke 12:24//Matt 6:26). Yet God gives them subsistence food. The issue is food production, the proper concern of a male peasant (Neyrey 2003, 44–51).

Alternately, a female scenario is imagined, which builds on the commonplace that females had three duties.

> When this [agricultural produce] is stored in a covered place, someone is needed to work at the things that must be done under cover . . . the nursing of the infants, the making of the corn into bread, and likewise the manufacture of clothing from the wool. (Xenophon, *Oec.* 7.21)

Hence the female in the family is concerned about "what to wear"—that is, "clothing," which was woven and sewn in the household. The female in Matt 6:28–30 is presumably the wife of the male addressed above, so that the basic male and female tasks are in view. A basic family unit is envisioned that typically is divided into the characteristic gender-specific tasks: males, food production; females, clothing production. When this female looks at the fields with a gender-specific eye, she sees stuff for weaving. The lilies "neither spin nor toil," yet they are more gorgeous than the royal robes woven by Solomon's harem.

In light of this gender-specific reading, the exhortation exhorts a male and female about the loss of wealth—that is, insufficiency of food and clothing. The text does not say why, but the options are limited: (1) drought, which produces famine for humans and lack of fodder for wool-bearing sheep; (2) excessive taxation, which leads to peasant indebtedness, which, when foreclosed, results in lost of land; (3) family conflict, such that a son (and his wife) were disinherited, "driven away" from the family farm, and set adrift without land or animals.

Which option seems appropriate? Since the exhortation is addressed to disciples (Luke 12:22), loss of wealth is formally related to issues of group loyalty, not to "general human conditions."

The passage, moreover, links wealth with honor and status. At the very beginning, the exhortation is announced with an imperative, "Do not be anxious!" As part of that topic, a value statement is made that the soul is "more valuable" than food, and the body more important than clothing. The comparative term "more valuable" relates to the world of worth; whether it has a quantitative or qualitative note, "valuable" ranks one thing above another, thus giving respect and honor to it. After the male is told to look at the birds, he is asked (Matthew) or told (Luke) that he is "of more value" than them, another term connoting honorable status. Rhetorically, this repeats the earlier value question and explicitly bestows honor to the man who lacks food (and land). A male is worth more than mere birds. Likewise with the female, after she looks at the lilies of the field, she is told that a paternal figure values her more than them, and so she is promised honor and respect (on clothing as honor, see Neyrey 1993a, 20–22; 1993b, 120–22).

What may we say about this passage? The husband and wife are peasants who are falling below the subsistence level in regard to food and clothing. Nothing in the passage explicitly states that loss of land, especially family land, is at stake. But something is missing from the horizon: there is no family, no household, and no kinship network to catch them as they fall. In fact, the addressees are told to turn to a heavenly paternal figure rather than to the obvious kinship network (Luke 12:30; Matt 6:26, 32). Of course, the family may have all died out; but then the son should have inherited some of his father's land.

Nevertheless, the loss of wealth by this husband and wife entails a concomitant loss of honor and social standing, for a major element in the exhortation has to do with absence of "worth" and "value"—that is, honor. Therefore, this husband and wife are truly becoming "poor" in the eyes of the rest of the peasants, losing familial honor but gaining in Jesus' and God's eyes.

Family banning or disinheritance of a rebellious son would account for the loss of subsistence envisioned here, as well as the loss of honor attendant on such an economic catastrophe. This option becomes plausible and probable when we recall that this passage in Luke 12 is linked directly with other remarks about family conflict: "do not be anxious about your life" (12:22–32); "treasure in heaven" (12:33–34); "a house divided" (12:51–53).

This Lukan collection concerns itself with disinheritance (12:13) and covetousness (12:15), the former directly dealing with family conflict. The original source, then, saw a connection between loss of wealth, family conflict, and discipleship. It envisions a scenario that would make a person needy of food and clothing as described in 12:22–32, namely, loss of family through disinheritance or banning.

In an adjoining passage (Luke 12:33–34//Matt 6:19–21) disciples are instructed about "treasure." Like the previous passage, it begins with a command from Jesus: "Sell your possessions and give alms" (Luke 12:33 rsv) or "Do not lay up treasure on earth" (Matt 6:19). Since Luke regularly exhorts disciples to give alms (Luke

11:41; Acts 3:2–6; 9:36; 10:2, 4, 31), Matthew contains the more original wording here. The imperative in Matt 6:19 ("do not lay up treasure") is formally parallel in structure to that in Matt 6:25 and Luke 12:22 ("do not be anxious").

Jesus' remarks about treasure are hyperbolic, because subsistence peasants simply do not have treasure, especially in the period of ruinous Roman taxation. Peasants could have an ox (for plowing), some sheep (for wool/clothing), some goats (for milk), and some fruit trees and vines (for food). But this is hardly treasure. The moth threatens the few blankets and garments that the peasant has (on the cost and scarcity of clothing, see Hamel 1990, 64–67), and corruption rots wood (house or wooden plow) and corrodes metal (an iron plow?). Thieves abound in Galilee in this period, whose prime targets would be villages unprotected by walls.

However meager his wealth, it is a peasant's "treasure" and the key indicator of his status and honor in the village. Jesus' remark, moreover, tells the peasant not to value what all his family and neighbors value, but rather to value something else superior to "treasure on earth." At a minimum, Jesus attacks peasant covetousness (Luke 12:15) and the honor attached to wealth. Nothing explicit is said about loss of wealth here, except that moth, corruption, and thieves cause loss of something. A superior source of blessing and distinction is available to those exhorted here, surpassing any possible family wealth and honor.

From the discussion in this section, one clear theme emerges. The Q document contains a number of statements that attack family unity and loyalty. These statements, moreover, are often linked with remarks on loss of wealth and honor. Thus crisis within the family emerges as a probable cause of the disinheritance, banning, or excommunication envisioned in the fourth makarism. Such a radical action by a family against a disobedient or rebellious son would surely entail immediate, severe economic and social loss.

Summary, Conclusions, and Further Conversation

First, being "poor" (πτωχός) contains a social and cultural component as well as an economic one. "Wealth" is a component of "honor," and the loss of wealth entails a corresponding loss of honor. A person who moves from being πένης to πτωχός loses the resources to maintain social status or honor rating. Loss of honor is more serious to ancient peasants than the mere loss of wealth.

Second, the scenario envisioned by the makarisms in Q looks to both loss of honor (μακάριος = "honorable") as well as loss of wealth. But why did a person suffer loss of wealth according to the makarisms? My hypothesis has been that a son and his wife are envisioned as banned or disinherited by a father and family, and so they suffer both loss of wealth and honor.

Third, in light the above, the four makarisms are addressed to disciples, not the crowds. They do not speak of "the general human conditions of poverty and suffering" or the generic "anxiety about the basic necessities," but rather of specific consequences of discipleship.

Fourth, at least by the creation of Q, the four makarisms had come to be taken as a unit, as a comprehensive statement about the economic and social situation of certain persons. Moreover, I am persuaded that the fourth makarism functions as the appropriate climax of the makarisms and should not be separated from the other three.

Fifth, the makarisms contrast the way of Jesus with other "ways" of living (Guelich 1976, 416–19). Hence, the general situation reflected here is one of discipleship and loyalty shown to Jesus. Disciples "take up their cross" and follow him; they are willing to lose all to gain his favor and approval (Matt 19:29). As active players who make choices, they stand in contrast with mere passive victims, who suffer "misfortune" independent of their actions.

Sixth, discipleship, however, with a deviant such as Jesus is costly. Thus, the four original makarisms should been seen as Jesus' "honoring" the disciples who have paid a price and been shamed by their kinship network. They are not just typical peasants in the audience, all of whom are working poor; rather, they are begging poor (πτωχοί)—that is, people who have suffered a recent loss of wealth and status, which directly results from discipleship or loyalty to Jesus.

Seventh, what type of loss? If a village turned on man, he would still have family to fall back on, either his father's house and land or his own house and land. He would still have kin in the area, whose first loyalty would be to him. He would not necessarily be hungry or mourning. But a disciple who suffered disinheritance by his father or banning from the family land would become a πτωχός and would immediately suffer lack of subsistence, kinship, and honor.

Eighth, the Hebrew Scriptures are quite concerned with the proper obedience of sons to their fathers (see Exod 20:12; Lev 20:9; 5:16; Tob 4:3–4; Prov 1:8; 6:20; Sir 3:1–16), although less emphasis is found in early Christian writings on this theme (Mark 7:9–13//Matt 15:3–6; Eph 6:2–3). One finds the motif of "the rebellious son" in Scripture (Deut 21:18–20) and in rabbinic literature. Ancient child-rearing practices consisted of disciplining children who were perceived to be naturally rebellious (Pilch 1993, 102–7). The right relationship of sons and fathers, therefore, was a recurring, common problem throughout the male life cycle (see Mark 7:10–12; Matt 21:28–29; Luke 15:11–13). Issues of family loyalty and parental authority, not excommunication from the synagogue, emerge as the important locus of crisis in the lives of ordinary peasants. We attended to passages in the Q source where Jesus claims to have caused division in families. These divisions would not be worth mentioning if they did not result in social consequences. Luke 12:51–53//Matt 10:34–36 and Luke 14:26–27//Matt 10:37–38 envision disciples of Jesus experiencing hostility from their kinship groups, which, I maintain, results in some form of disinheritance or banning (i.e., the fourth makarism) and so loss of wealth and honor.

Ninth, the Q document contains a number of explicit remarks about the troubled relationships within families caused by discipleship with Jesus: Luke 9:59–60//Matt 8:21–22; Luke 12:51–53//Matt 10:34–36; Luke 14:26–27//Matt 10:37–39. In addition to these, there are other passages that seem to have family members in view, who suffer a crisis in the kinship network. One passage envisions the plight of a family (husband and wife) that has neither food nor clothing (Luke 12:22–32//Matt 6:25–33). Although one can imagine many reasons for this social tragedy, the persons addressed are clearly disciples to whom Jesus issues commands. But why is a disciple in such dire straits? Alternative answers such as debt foreclosure or drought do not satisfy the criterion that such a tragedy is befalling a disciple. A probable scenario seems to be the same one envisioned above in Luke 12:51–53//Matt 10:34–39: some form of kinship crisis that results in a loss of land, wealth, food, and clothing. Seen in combination with Luke 12:51–53// Matt 10:34–39, Luke 12:22–32//Matt 6:25–33 probably reflects the same situation: discipleship has caused family division and resulted in disinheritance or banning from the basic kinship network. Thus the family is seen in the Q tradition as a primary source of "persecution."

Bibliography

Carney, Thomas F. 1975. *The Shape of the Past: Models and Antiquity.* Lawrence, Kans.: Coronado.

Duling, Dennis. 1994. Matthew and Marginality. Pages 642–71 in *Society of Biblical Literature 1993 Seminar Papers.* Edited by E. H. Lovering Jr. Society of Biblical Literature Seminar Papers 32. Atlanta: Society of Biblical Literature.

Guelich, Robert A. 1976. The Matthean Beatitudes: 'Entrance-Requirements' or Eschatological Blessings? *Journal of Biblical Literature* 95:415–34.

Hamel, Gildas. 1990. *Poverty and Charity in Roman Palestine.* Near Eastern Studies 23. Berkeley: University of California Press.

Hanson, K. C. 1994. "How Honorable! How Shameful!" A Cultural Analysis of Matthew's Makarisms and Reproaches. *Semeia* 68:81–112.

Hollenbach, Paul W. 1987. Defining Rich and Poor Using Social Sciences. Pages 50–63 in *Society of Biblical Literature 1987 Seminar Papers.* Edited by K. H. Richards. Society of Biblical Literature Seminar Papers 26. Atlanta: Scholars Press.

Kloppenborg, John S. 1986. Blessing and Marginality: The "Persecution Beatitude" in Q, Thomas, and Early Christianity. *Forum* 2(3):36–56.

———. 1987. *The Formation of Q: Trajectories in Ancient Wisdom Collections.* Studies in Antiquity and Christianity. Philadelphia: Fortress.

Luz, Ulrich. 1989. *Matthew 1–7.* Translated by W. C. Linns. Hermeneia. Minneapolis: Augsburg.

Malina, Bruce J. 2001. *The New Testament World: Insights from Cultural Anthropology.* 3d ed. Louisville: Westminster John Knox.

Matthews, Victor H. and Don C. Benjamin. 1991. The Stubborn and the Fool. *Bible Today* 29:222–26.

Neyrey, Jerome H. 1993a. Clothing. Pages 20–25 in *Biblical Social Values and Their Meaning.* Edited by John J. Pilch and Bruce J. Malina. Peabody, Mass.: Hendrickson.

———. 1993b. Nudity. Pages 119–25 in *Biblical Social Values and Their Meaning.* Edited by John J. Pilch and Bruce J. Malina. Peabody, Mass.: Hendrickson.

————.1998. *Honor and Shame in the Gospel of Matthew*. Louisville: Westminster John Knox.

————. 2003. Jesus, Gender and the Gospel of Matthew. Pages 43–66 in *New Testament Masculinities*. Edited by Stephen D. Moore and Janice Capel Anderson. Society of Biblical Literature Semeia Studies 45. Atlanta: Society of Biblical Literature.

Oakman, Douglas E. 1986. *Jesus and the Economic Questions of His Day*. Studies in the Bible and Early Christianity 8. Lewiston, N.Y.: Mellen.

Pelling, Christopher. 1990. Childhood and Personality in Greek Biography. Pages 213–44 in *Characterization and Individuality in Greek Literature*. Oxford: Clarendon.

Pilch, John J. 1993. "Beat His Ribs While He Is Young" (Sir 30:12): A Window on the Mediterranean World. *Biblical Theology Bulletin* 23:101–13.

Pitt-Rivers, Julian. 1977. *The Fate of Shechem, or, The Politics of Sex: Essays in the Anthropology of the Mediterranean*. Cambridge Studies in Socila Anthropology 19. Cambridge: Cambridge University Press.

Purity

6

"Be ye holy, as I am holy" (Lev 11:44–45). Linguists remind us that the word *holy* means "separated," so that God-as-holy is enthroned above the cherubim and separated from mortals. Behind this term lies a scenario in which divisions and dichotomies are endlessly imagined. The God who is separated characteristically makes separations:

> Blessed are you, Lord our God, king of the world, who divides holy and profane, between light and darkness, between Israel and the peoples, between the seventh day and the six days of work. Blessed are you, Lord, who divides between sacred and profane. (*Havdalah*, Prayer of Benediction)

While creating the world, God commanded separation: "the waters from the waters . . . the waters under the firmament from those above it" (Gen 1:6–7) and "the night from the darkness" (Gen 1:18). But in all of those separations God was actually creating an orderly system of the world. Each thing had its proper place and its proper diet. Time was ordered by a night and a day, a week, a month, seasons marked by particular stars and a year. Thus when God "separated," he created the order of things; that is, he made maps of persons, places, times, and things. This cosmic map drafted by the Priestly writer was replicated in the temple officiated at by priests. Like creation, it was ordered according to local understandings of the proper place or relationship of persons, places, times, and things.

One distinctive aspect of this system of purity was the concern for "wholeness," which may refer to things or physical bodies or attitudes. Things that are "whole" have properly defined boundaries, lacking none of the characteristics that distinguish them according to their type. Only unblemished animals are suited for sacrifice: a pure animal for the Holy God. Human bodies defective or deficient in any part are considered unclean and must be kept separate from what is clean. This especially applies to priests whose lack of bodily purity disqualifies them for temple duty (Lev 21:16–20). Josephus relates the story of how one priest was definitively disqualified by a rival who lacerated his body:

> Hyrcanus threw himself at the feet of Antigonus, who with his own teeth lacerated his suppliant's ears, in order to disqualify him forever, under any change of circumstances, from resuming the high priesthood; since freedom from physical defect is essential to the holder of that office. (Josephus, *J.W.* 1.270 [see also *Ant.* 14.366–367])

This same evaluation is found at Qumran in the *Rule of the Congregation* (1QSa 2:3–10) and in the Mishnah in the tractate *Bekorot:*

> These same blemishes . . . render [priests] unqualified [to serve in the Temple]. Among [lay] men are added: he whose head is wedge-shaped or turnip-shaped or hammer-shaped, or whose head is sunk in or is flat at the back. (*m. Bek.* 7:1 [see also 7:2–7])

Whoever lacks wholeness is impure and should not approach his God. Conversely, sometimes the case is about something in excess or that has too much. A hunchback has too much, so too a hermaphrodite. Dropsy is judged unclean because it produces too much fluid. Leaven is removed from Judean houses before Passover because it has power to make "too much" of the flour: "People say, too, that flour rises better at the time of the full moon; indeed leavening is much the same process as putrefaction, and if the proper time limit be ignored, leavening in making dough porous and light produces the same decomposition in the end" (Plutarch, *Quaest. conv.* 659B).

Human beings, moreover, also may be of two kinds, a condition labeled "hypocrisy"—the outside does not match the inside. There should be one behavior that corresponds to a thought or desire (Matt 5:27–30; 7:21). Moreover, human beings are urged to be pure and of one kind: "The good mind has not two tongues, of blessing and of cursing, of contumely and of honor, of sorrow and of joy, of quietness and of confusion, of hypocrisy and of truth, of poverty and of wealth; but it has one disposition, uncorrupt, concerning all men" (*T. Benj.* 6:5). Double-mindedness, then, is an index of a lack of purity.

John H. Elliott

The Epistle of James in Rhetorical and Social-Scientific Perspective: Holiness-Wholeness and Patterns of Replication

Introduction

The Epistle of James, often ranked among the "junk mail" of the New Testament, deserves better press. Modern scholarship, besides echoing Martin Luther's negative verdict on this epistle's alleged theological deficiency (see, e.g., Via 1969), has frequently regarded it as a collection of diffuse parenetic elements lacking indications of conceptual coherence (for surveys of opinion, see Kümmel 1975, 403–16; Davids 1982, 22–57; 1983, xx–xxxii; 1988; Johnson 1986, 453–63; Popkes 1986; Baasland 1988). This view, popularized by Martin Dibelius's commentary on James in the 1920s, is still current. Thus Stowers, in his *Letter Writing in Greek Antiquity,* continues to find in James only "a series of seemingly disjointed hortatory topoi without any apparent unifying model or models" (1986, 97).

Where, however, attention has shifted from an earlier form-critical interest in the sources and parenetic elements in James to an appreciation of its redactional and rhetorical features, an alternative assessment of the writing has begun to emerge. In this case, analyses of both the rhetorical structure and the fundamental thematic of the letter combine to demonstrate both the formal and the material coherence of the writing.

Among sustained discussions of the writing's structure, I find the rhetorical-critical analysis by Wuellner (1978) most persuasive. What emerges from this analysis (Wuellner 1978, 37–57, with some modifications) is a carefully structured composition with three major parts: (1) an introduction (1:1–12) comprising an epistolary address and salutation (1:1–2) followed by a statement of the main theme (1:3–4) and related contrasts (1:5–12); (2) the body of the argument (1:13–5:12) comprising a series of seven contrasts of proscribed and prescribed behavior; (3) a conclusion (5:13–20) that, by echoing material of the introduction, joins 1:2–12 in providing a grand *inclusio* for the letter as a whole. (This outline varies slightly from Wuellner's proposal, which includes 5:7–12 in the conclusion, with 5:7–8 as *recapitulatio* and 5:9–20 as *peroratio.* Justification of the modification is offered below.)

Within this rhetorical structure the main theme of the letter is stated at the outset (1:3–4) and concerns the issue of completeness and wholeness and their implied opposite, division and fragmentation. This rhetorical analysis coincides with and confirms several studies that have independently identified the central theme of James as a concern about division and wholeness (Rustler 1952; Seitz 1947; 1958; 1959; Barkman 1968; Schille 1977; Zmijewski 1980; Frankemölle 1985; Popkes 1986; Tamez 1988).

In what follows I analyze aspects of the letter that further illustrate both its unified structure and its coherent thematic, its multidimensional view of incompleteness and integration, and the relation established between holiness and wholeness. My aim is to show how James, in addressing issues of fragmentation and wholeness on correlated personal, social, and cosmic levels of existence, invokes traditional distinctions of purity and pollution to press for a restoration of holiness and wholeness of the Christian community and a reinforcement of its distinctive ethos.

JAMES: STRUCTURE AND THEMATIC

Following an epistolary prescript (1:1), the letter opens with a section (1:2–12) introducing its major theme, the completeness and wholeness of the readers, of their community, and of their relation God. "Count it all joy, my brothers, when you meet various trials, for you know that the testing of your faith produces steadfastness. Let steadfastness have its full effect [ἡ δὲ ὑπομονὴ ἔργον τέλειον ἐχέτω], so that you may be complete and whole [ἵνα ἦτε τέλειοι καὶ ὁλόκλ-ηροι], lacking in nothing" (1:2–4) (for recurrences of τέλειος and paronyms, see 1:17, 25; 2:22; 3:2).

This contrast between wholeness and incompleteness, further expanded upon in 1:5–8, introduces a series of such contrasts spanning the letter from start to finish, signaling both its structure and its basic thematic. In 1:9–11 the author contrasts the reversed status of the lowly brother and the rich brother before God (anticipating the contrasts of 2:1–26; 4:1–12, 13; 5:6), and 1:12 restates the proposition concerning the endurance of trials leading to completeness and wholeness announced in 1:2–4.

Thereupon follows the body of the argument (*argumentatio*) contained in 1:13–5:12. This section consists of seven subsections characterized by a consistent pattern of exhortation contrasting negative indictments of divided or divisive attitudes and behavior with positive recommendations concerning integrity and wholeness.

1. James 1:13–27
   A. Negative: No self-deceptive attribution of trials to God but rather to human desire (1:13–16).
   B. Positive: From God come complete gifts. Worship God purely through the integration of hearing and doing (1:17–27).

2. James 2:1–13
   A. Negative: No partiality in the congregation (2:1–7).
   B. Positive: Fulfill completely the royal law (2:8–13).

3. James 2:14–26
   A. Negative: No dividing faith from action (2:14–17).
   B. Positive: Complete faith with action (2:18–26).

4. James 3:1–18
   A. Negative: No duplicitous speaking (3:1–12).
   B. Positive: Act with the pure, peaceful wisdom from above rather than with the divisive wisdom from below (3:13–18).

5. James 4:1–12
   A. Negative: No pursuit of selfish desire that leads to enmity with humans and God (4:1–4).
   B. Positive: Resist the devil and in holiness humble yourselves before God the judge (4:5–12).

6. James 4:13–5:11
   A. Negative: No arrogant planning and boasting (4:13–17); oppression of laborers and the just by the rich (5:1–6).
   B. Positive: Wait patiently for the Lord's coming and be steadfast (5:7–11).

7. James 5:12
   A. Negative: Do not secure the truth of your words with oaths (5:12a).
   B. Positive: Demonstrate your integrity with a truthful "yes" or "no" (5:12b).

In the conclusion, 5:13–20, the author returns to the introductory matters of trials and suffering (5:13a, 14a, 19–20; cf. 1:2–4, 12), prayer for what is lacking regarding wholeness (5:13b, 14–18; cf. 1:5–8), communal integration and life versus death (5:19–20; cf. 1:12). As the personal doubting of 1:6–8 is mirrored in the social defection of 5:19, so the reintegration of the doubter (1:5) is matched by the reincorporation of the errant sinner in 5:20, whose salvation from death parallels the result of endurance: completeness (1:4) and the reception of the crown of life (1:12).

Throughout the body of the argument (1:13–5:12) the author elaborates on the subject matter of his introduction and addresses specific instances of his basic theme, division and wholeness, with a series of contrasts treating the issues of doubt and vacillation versus trust/faith; separation versus integration of hearing and doing, faith and action; partiality versus impartiality; duplicity versus sincerity; uncontrolled versus controlled speech; war and discord versus harmony and peace; friendship with society and the devil versus friendship with God; arrogant boasting versus humility; instability versus steadfastness; pollution versus purity. On the whole, the writing is aptly described as a *Korrekturschreiben* (Popkes 1986, 209) in which negative assessments of fragmented and divisive behavior are countered by positive exhortations to wholeness and holiness.

In the first phase of the epistle's argument (1:13–27), a significant connection is made between wholeness and holiness, an association that is maintained throughout the writing. Concluding a contrast between (a) human desire as the source of trials, sin, and death and (b) God as the source of the word of truth and life (1:13–18), and a further contrast between (a) hearing this word but not acting on it versus (b) hearing-completed-in-action (1:19–25), is the exhortation (a) to put away "all filthiness and rank growth of wickedness" (1:21) and (b) to practice a "pure and undefiled worship [θρησκεία]" (1:27). Θρησκεία that does not include control of the tongue (and speech [1:19–22]) is ineffective, worthless, or incomplete (μάταιος [1:26]). On the other hand, θρησκεία that is "pure and undefiled [καθαρὰ καὶ ἀμίαντος] before God" is "to visit orphans and widows in their affliction and to keep oneself unstained [ἄσπιλον] from the world" (1:27)— that is, from a society regulated by the polluted values of the "world" (κόσμος). Here, holy worship of God and care for the most vulnerable in the community are declared incompatible with alliance with a polluting society and its contrary "worldly" standards of valuation (Johnson 1985, 172–77).

Later in the letter, further instances of division and wholeness are likewise discussed in terms of pollution and purity. An uncontrolled tongue is said to "stain" (σπιλοῦσα [3:6]) the entire body (3:1–12). A divisive, devilish, earthly wisdom is contrasted to a "pure" (ἁγνή) and peaceable wisdom from above (3:13–17). In 4:4–10 friendship with the world is declared to be enmity with God (4:4). To draw near to God requires resistance of the devil, "cleansing" (καθαρίσατε) one's hands, and "purifying" (ἁγνίσατε) one's heart (4:7–8).

Although the concept of pollution and purity has its roots in the cultic life of Israel, it appears to be used here, as elsewhere in Judaism and early Christianity, to define the character and responsibility of the people of God as a holy community distinct from an unholy society. Thus, for James, the wholeness of the community and its members seems to be a function of its holiness and unvacillating commitment to its holy God.

PURITY AND POLLUTION IN SOCIAL-SCIENCE PERSPECTIVE

To students of Israel, Judaism, and early Christianity, this accent on purity and its social and moral implications comes as no surprise. For the issue of cultic, moral, and social purity figures prominently in the consciousness and literature of all these communities (Douglas 1966; 1968; 1973; Buchanan 1963; Elliott 1966; 1981; 1991a; Neusner 1973; 1975; 1978; Malina 1981; Fennelly 1983; Frymer-Kensky 1983; Meeks 1983; Neyrey 1986a; 1986b; 1991). Until the exercise of social-scientific criticism by exegetes, however, attention had been directed almost exclusively to the ideational dimension of the concept of purity with little concern for its social ramifications. The tide, however, has begun to turn, owing largely to the exegetical appropriation of the work of anthropologists studying the nature and function of purity beliefs in societies both ancient and modern.

Here the research of anthropologist Mary Douglas and her colleagues has been found particularly suggestive. In her study of primitive tribal societies, Douglas (1966; 1968; 1973) has observed how concepts of purity and pollution are used to bring conceptual and social order to an otherwise chaotic world. "Dirt," Douglas has observed, is matter judged to be "out of place" (1966, 5). The concepts of "dirt" and "out-of-placeness" imply some overall system of thought according to which things, persons, times, and places are determined to be clean or unclean, sacred or secular, holy or profane, pure or polluted, life-enhancing or death-promoting. "Reflections on dirt involve reflection on the relation of order to disorder, being to non-being, form to formlessness, life to death" (Douglas 1966, 5).

Cultures variously use purity and pollution schemes in order to organize everything in its proper place, to define and demarcate what is complete or incomplete, who is damaged or whole, sick or sound, what is allowable or forbidden, who belongs to the society and who does not, what preserves the society and what endangers it. Accordingly, to call a person or a social unit impure, unclean, or unholy is to identify and evaluate the object as out-of-order, damaged, incomplete. Correlatively, a pure, clean, or holy object is one judged to be whole, complete, integral. "To be holy is to be whole, to be one; holiness is integrity, perfection of the individual and of the kind" (Douglas 1966, 54).

Social pollution, according to Douglas (1966, 122), can involve (1) danger from outside a group attacking its social boundaries; (2) danger from transgressing internal lines and norms of the system; (3) danger at the margins distinguishing inside and outside or danger from porous boundaries; (4) danger from internal contradictions where some basic postulates are contradicted by others. Purity and pollution beliefs, furthermore, serve in various ways to uphold or even substitute for a lagging moral code. As illustration, Douglas cites the following cases:

> (i) When a situation is morally ill-defined, a pollution belief can provide a rule for determining post hoc whether infraction has taken place or not; (ii) when moral principles come into conflict, a pollution rule can reduce confusion by giving a simple focus for concern; (iii) when action that is held to be morally wrong does not provoke moral indignation, belief in the harmful consequences of a pollution can have the effect of aggravating the seriousness of the offense, and so of marshaling public opinion on the side of the right; (iv) when moral indignation is not reinforced by practical sanctions, pollution beliefs can provide a deterrent to wrongdoers. (1966, 133)

In general, purity/pollution schemes are classification systems used to delineate concepts of order and reinforce codes of belonging and behavior. Underlying these schemes is the paramount concern for maintaining the wholeness and integrity of the personal and social body and relating the individual and his or her society to the all-embracing design of the cosmos. The coherence of these schemes is evident in the manner in which concepts of purity concerning the personal body and its mutilation (= pollution) or wholeness (= purity) are replicated in concepts of purity or pollution of the social body and in notions of the order or disorder of the cosmos itself. Douglas has shown this to be the case not only with primitive tribes such as the Nuer but also with Israelite society and legislation.

The analysis by Douglas (1966) of Israelite food laws and their correspondence with Israelite cosmological conceptions and depictions of the creation of the world is a case in point. Underlying Israel's conception of itself, its members, its cult, and its relation to other peoples and even the natural order is the basic command of its God: "You shall be holy as I, the LORD your God, am holy" (Lev 19:2). "You shall not defile yourself with any swarming thing that crawls upon the earth. For I am the LORD, who brought you up out of the land of Egypt, to be your God; you shall therefore be holy, for I am holy" (Lev 11:44–45 RSV). "You shall not walk in the customs of the nation which I am casting out before you [in Canaan]; for they did all these [abominable] things, and therefore I have abhorred them. . . . I am the LORD your God, who have separated you from the peoples. You shall therefore make a distinction between the clean beast and the unclean, and between the unclean bird and the clean. . . . You shall be holy to me; for I, the LORD, am holy, and have separated you from the peoples that you should be mine" (Lev 20:23–26 RSV).

Israel's pollution and purity schematization serves to conceptualize and maintain order and wholeness, distinctiveness, and union with God in the personal and social domains and in the world at large.

Attention to the pollution and purity codes of Judaism and early Christianity has taken these anthropological insights a step further. Malina (1981, 122–52) has shown how Douglas's model of purity and pollution illuminates the purity arrangements of Second Temple Judaism, its social stratification based on genealogical purity lines and its demarcation of holy and unholy space based on proximity to or distance from the holy temple. Malina likewise has shown how nascent Christianity confronted and redefined these boundaries. Eilberg-Schwartz (1990, 177–234) has illuminated the modifications of an earlier priestly definition of purity/pollution that occurred in Second Temple Judaism. He emphasizes that the classification system represented in the purity/pollution code tends to change in accord with human experience of one's place and possibilities in the order of things. A priestly conception of purity arrangements assumes that all roles and status are determined by descent and thus ascribed by "nature" (and God). Where, however, human achievement, in contrast to ascription, becomes a more influential factor in determining social roles and status, as in first-century-C.E. Judaism, there purity is conceived in terms of intention and performance rather than in terms of descent and external determinative factors. Early Christianity represents one extreme wing of Judaism conceptualizing purity in this contra-priestly manner, namely, in terms of intent and action. As we will see, the Epistle of James in particular illustrates this view. Neyrey (1986a) has demonstrated the key role that notions of pollution and purity played in Paul's conception of both the personal and social body in 1 Corinthians. In studies of the Gospel of Mark, Neyrey has also shown the coherence characterizing purity codes of places, persons, times, and actions (1988a), the difference between Pharasaic and Christian purity codes (1988a), and Mark's presentation of Jesus as agent of holiness and reorganizer of social boundaries (1986b).

The work of both Malina and Neyrey, in turn, underlies my analysis of the critique of the temple purity system contained in Luke-Acts (Elliott 1991a; 1991b; see also my comments on the social function of the holiness and election theme in 1 Peter in Elliott 1981, 118–64; 1966). Neyrey (1988b) offers an instructive introduction to a social-scientific perspective on the topic of pollution and purity in general along with some basic bibliography.

What these studies make clear is the dominant role that purity schemes played in Second Temple Judaism and early Christianity, precisely how purity conceptions and regulations formed a comprehensive and internally consistent pattern for ordering personal and social life in consonance with structures of order at the cosmological level, and how they continued to influence, in albeit modified form, early Christian conceptualizations of personal wholeness, social identity, and communal morality.

Purity and Pollution in James—A Preview

The foregoing review of the conceptual and social ramifications of pollution/purity codes in Judaism and early Christianity suggests that in James too concepts of purity and pollution may be invoked to address issues of personal, social, and cosmic disorder and order. It is thus appropriate that at the outset of James's argument (1:13–27) concepts of pollution and purity (1:21, 26–27) are used to summarize exhortation regarding incompleteness and integrity, division and wholeness. The coherence in pollution and purity codes, where the conception of order or wholeness in the personal domain is replicated at the social and cosmic levels, alerts us to the possibility that in James similar domains of existence and similar patterns of replication may be discernible. Here too concepts of pollution and purity and of division and wholeness may be merged in an effort to address the issues of distinctive Christian identity, responsibility, social cohesion, and social boundaries.

These initial observations about the structure and thematic of James, its focus on division and wholeness, and the link drawn between wholeness and holiness will now set the stage for what follows. Here we will see (1) that the author has addressed the issue of division, and its opposite, wholeness, on three interrelated levels: the personal, the social, and the cosmological; (2) that integrity or wholeness of the community and its members is portrayed as an essential feature of its holiness; (3) that this holiness has both moral and social implications.

Before considering these aspects of the author's strategy, let us first review briefly the situation presupposed by the author.

The Situation According to James: Differences, Differentiation, Discrimination, Division, and Defection

The Epistle of James is addressed to an admixture of Israelite and Gentile Christians living in the Diaspora, believers linked, according to the author, with the identity, history, and traditions of the twelve tribes of Israel (1:1). This ethnic mix is suggested by the combination of Judean and Hellenistic motifs, examples, and hortatory traditions that the author has employed to address and move a culturally mixed audience of former Judeans and Gentiles (Johnson 1986; Popkes 1986, 125–84). This cultural mix, in turn, is paralleled by a social mix of both rich and poor (1:9–11; 2:1–13, 14–26; 4:13–5:6)—teachers (3:1–18) and elders (5:14), on the one hand, and ordinary members, on the other.

Such mixture of both cultural backgrounds and social strata, as might be expected, had brought with it a plurality of perspectives and norms concerning appropriate social behavior, tension and conflict between rich and poor, trials, debilitating strife and division within the community, and serious questions regarding the interaction of Christians with non-Christian outsiders (Davids 1982, 28–34; Popkes 1986, 53–124).

The letter is written at the point when, from the author's sense of the situation, cultural plurality and social-economic disequilibrium among the believers had become the seedbed for discrimination of social classes and the currying of favor from wealthy and powerful patrons from outside the community (2:1–4 [see Coote and Wire 1979]); litigation and dishonoring of the poor (2:6–7) and their neglect (2:13, 14–16), exploitation, and oppression by the wealthy who defraud their laborers, stockpile harvests, and kill the righteous (4:13–5:6); members pursuing their own selfish interests at the cost of their fellows and social cohesion (1:14–15; 4:1–10); brothers speaking evil of and passing judgment upon brothers (4:11–12; 5:9); personal doubt and instability of commitment (1:6–8; 4:8); duplicity in speech (3:1–12); inconsistency between words and action (1:22–24; 2:1–26; 5:12); suffering leading to a loss of patience and hope (1:2, 12–15; 5:7–11); and even apostasy and defection from the community (5:19–20).

As the author describes the scene, ethnic, economic, and social differences had led to social division, and divisions to personal doubt, dissimulation, despair, and defection. Factiousness and fission within the community were accompanied by a split in the attitudes and actions of individuals themselves. The community and its members were undergoing an erosion of integrity and cohesion at both the personal and social levels of life.

Diagnosis and Prescription in Three Dimensions

What is noteworthy from a rhetorical point of view is how the structural medium of the letter—an extended series of contrasts—dramatically underscores the perceived situation of tension and conflict within and beyond the community. This pattern of contrasts likewise serves as the rhetorical mechanism for combining a description and diagnosis of the negative situation with positive teaching concerning its reversal. Moreover, it is evident that this alternation of diagnosis and remedy addresses the issue of incompleteness/completeness in its personal, social, and cosmological manifestations or dimensions. This can be illustrated as follows:

NEGATIVE CONDITION	POSITIVE RESPONSE
1. The Personal Dimension	
Lacking wisdom etc. (1:5)	Ask God (in prayer) (1:5) (cf. 4:3, 15; 5:13–17)
Doubting (1:6)	Faith/trust (1:6)
Double-mindedness (1:7–8; 4:8)	Cleanse hands, purify hearts (4:8)
Instability (1:6–8)	Be steadfast (5:11)
Temptation from desire (1:14–15; 4:1–3)	Be not deceived (1:16); benefactions from God (1:17–18, 4:3; 5:13–18)
Anger (1:19–20)	Be slow to anger (1:19); put away filthiness and wickedness and receive the implanted word with humility; purify hands and heart (1:21; 4:6–10)
Only hearers of word (1:22–24; 2:14–26)	Complete hearing with doing (1:22–27; 2:14–26)
Not bridle tongue, which stains the whole body (1:26; 3:1–12)	Bridle tongue and body and be pure and unstained from the world (1:27; 3:1–12)
Suffering, trials (1:2, 12; 5:13)	Be steadfast and whole (1:2–4) and pray (5:13)
2. The Social, Communal Dimension	
Making distinctions, showing partiality	Show no partiality (2:1) to the rich (2:1–4, 9)
Poor persons are dishonored (2:6a); rich persons oppress poor, blaspheme their honorable name (2:6b–7; 5:1–6)	Love neighbor as yourself (2:8–13)
Lack of faith-in-action toward the needy (2:14–17)	Show faith through action (2:18–26)
Teachers with unbridled tongues, boasting of great things (3:1–12)	Share wisdom with meekness (3:13)
Jealousy, selfish ambition, disorder, vile practice (3:14, 16)	Make peace and sow the harvest of righteousness (3:18)
Wars, fighting, selfish desire, killing, covetousness, friendship with society/ world (4:1–4)	Be humble before God and be friends with God; purify hands and hearts (4:7–10)
Brother speaks evil against and judges brother and law (4:11–12)	Do not speak evil against or judge a brother (4:11–12)
Desire for economic gain, unmindful of God's will, arrogant boasting (4:13)	Say "God willing" (4:15)
Rich persons have accumulated treasure (for themselves),defrauded their laborers, lived in luxury, condemned and killed the righteous man (5:1–6)	Be patient and steadfast in expectation of the Lord; do not grumble against one another (5:7–12)
Brothers (in dealing with each other) secure their words with oaths (5:12)	No oaths, but only an integral "yes" and "no" (5:12)

NEGATIVE CONDITION	POSITIVE RESPONSE
Persons are ill and (are regarded as) sinners (5:14, 16)	Pray for, anoint the ill; confess sins (5:14–16)
Some members have left the truth and the community (5:19a)	Members should restore repentant sinners to the wholeness of the community (5:19b–20)

3. The Cosmological Dimension

Endurance of trials (1:2, 12a)	Receiving from God the crown of life (1:12b)
Some lack wisdom (1:5a)	Ask God, who gives generously (1:5b)
Some say that temptation comes from God, but actually it originates with human desire, producing sin and death (1:13–15)	Every good endowment and perfect gift is from the Father above, including the gift of new life (1:17–18)
The anger of humans (1:20a)	The righteousness of God (1:20b)
Filthiness, wickedness (1:21a)	The saving word implanted by God (1:21b)
Unbridled tongue, deceived heart, vain religion (1:26)	Pure, undefiled religion before God the Father: aid to the powerless and unstained separation from society/world (1:27)
Partiality, deference to the rich and dishonoring of the poor (2:1–7)	God choose the poor as his heirs (5:5)
Partiality as transgression of the royal law (2:8–10)	God judges and shows mercy (2:11–13)
So-called faith without action is dead (2:14–26)	God justifies the active believer (2:21–26)
Teachers with unbridled tongues staining the body, full of evil and poison, blessing God but cursing people (3:1–10)	God will judge with greater strictness; made humankind in his likeness (3:1, 9b)
Earthly, unspiritual, devilish wisdom: jealousy, selfish ambition, disorder, vile practice (3:14–16)	Wisdom from above: pure, peaceable, gentle, reasonable, full of mercy and good fruits, without uncertainty or insincerity (3:17–18)
Friendship with society/world and infidelity to and enmity with God (4:4)	Humble submission to God, whose spirit dwells in believers; God opposes the proud, gives grace and exalts the humble (4:5–7a, 10)
Alliance with the devil, impurity, sin, and double-mindedness (4:7b, 8b–c)	Resist the devil, draw near to God; purity of hands and heart (4:8a–b)
Speaking evil against and judging the brother and the law (4:11, 12c)	God is the sole lawgiver and judge, who is able to save and destroy (4:12 a–b)
Selfish desire for gain, unconcern for God's will, arrogant boasting (4:13, 16–17)	God controls time and transitory human life (4:14–15)
Brother grumbling against brother (5:9)	God about to judge; is merciful to the patient (5:7, 8–9, 11)

NEGATIVE CONDITION	POSITIVE RESPONSE
Brothers using oaths (to conceal deception) (5:12a)	They fall under God's condemnation (5:12b)
Suffering believers (5:13a)	Pray to God, as the cheerful praise (God) (5:13b)
Ill, sinning believers (5:14a)	Brotherly prayer (to God) in faith and mutual confession of sins; God will raise up, forgive, and heal (5:14b–16)
Defection from the faith and the community; sin and death (5:19–20)	God will save the returning defector from sin and death (5:20)

Figure 7: Diagnosis and prescription in three dimensions

The Strategy of the Letter

As the foregoing comparison makes evident, James directs attention to three interrelated dimensions of human life in which the dilemma of incompleteness and wholeness, pollution and purity, are evident: the personal, the social, and the cosmic. This interrelationship might be visualized as three concentric circles representing the personal, the social, and the cosmic dimensions of life. Each of these dimensions of life is pervaded by the same predicament: the contrast and conflict between attitudes, values, actions, and agents representing, on the one hand, wholeness, unity, and purity, and, on the other hand, incompleteness, disunity, and pollution.

From James's perspective, these realms of purity and pollution are mutually exclusive. Double-mindedness, discrimination, disorder, and continued vacillation in allegiance between God and the devil have decimated the community and are no longer tolerable. Therefore believers must resist the devil and cleave to God (4:7–8), keep themselves unstained from society (1:27), purify their hands and hearts (4:8), and commit themselves completely to the royal law of love (2:8). Fidelity to this royal law of love is that which demarcates the pure from the polluted.

This contrast between the realms of the polluted and the pure is replicated by a further antithesis that gives this entire set of contrasts a spatial orientation: the contrast between an "earthly wisdom" and the "wisdom from above" (3:13–18). The qualities of the wisdom from below, "earthly, nonspiritual, demonic/devilish" (3:15; cf. 2:19), and the attitudes and actions that it promotes, "jealousy, selfish ambition, vile practices" (3:16) are features, like those cited in 4:1–3, linked with the devil himself, whom believers are exhorted to resist (4:7b). Contrariwise, the qualities of the wisdom from above and the actions that it promotes, "purity, peacefulness, gentleness, reasonableness, mercy, good fruits, certainty, sincerity, righteousness, and peace" (3:18), are illustrations of the "good endowments and perfect gifts" that come from God the Father above (1:17–18), to whom believers are urged to draw near with purified hands and hearts (4:8).

This distinction between divine wisdom "from above" and devilish wisdom "from below" is significant conceptually and socially. Conceptually, this distinction between above and below demarcates and contrasts two distinct and opposing realms of the cosmos in terms of a spatial perspective. Accordingly, for James, space, rather than time as in other Christian writings, becomes the dominant perspective for viewing issues of human allegiance, good and evil, purity and impurity. Attention is directed not to past or future but rather to the ongoing present as the moment of action and decision. Furthermore, the readers are hereby challenged to view the situation in which they find themselves in global terms, in terms of society, nature, and contending powers of the universe.

Socially, this distinction of realms demarcates and contrasts two societies inspired by two opposed sources and forms of wisdom: an antagonistic and divided society animated by the devilish wisdom from below, and a peaceful and integral society animated by the divine wisdom from above. From the context of the letter it is clear that the devilish wisdom from below and its wisdom characterizes the nonbelieving society in which the believers live and from which they are urged to remain unstained (1:27). Openness to this society and its alien wisdom and values (2:1–13; 4:1–4; 4:13–5:6) has resulted in the doubt and divisiveness that now plague the community and undermine its purity and wholeness. But these two realms and the contrasting allegiances they entail are mutually exclusive. Thus the contrasts made at the cosmic level have the function of validating theologically the exhortation that the believers resist the encroachments of a polluting society.

Thus James's view of the problem is a comprehensive one in which personal dichotomies relate to and replicate social and even cosmic dichotomies. By relating problems of personal integrity and social unity to cosmic polarities on a grand scale—the realm of the devil, devilish wisdom from below, and pollution, on the one hand, and the realm of God, wisdom from above, and purity, on the other—James substantiates, at the highest theological level of discourse, diagnoses and remedies of the malaise of defectiveness and division infecting both individuals and the community.

Ultimately, James proposes, it is the devil (4:4–10) and an "earthly, nonspiritual, devilish" wisdom from below (3:14–16) that pervade society (1:27), excite selfish desire (1:13–16; 3:16; 4:1–3), and foster double-mindedness, duplicity, doubt, social discrimination, division, discord, disloyalty to God, pollution, and death. Contrariwise, it is ultimately God and the divine gift of wisdom from above that are the source of purity, peace, integrity, and life (1:5, 12, 17–18; 3:17–18; 4:4–10; 5:13–18, 19–20). Individual addressees and the community as a whole are fragmented and polarized by attempts at simultaneous allegiance to these alternative realms. James faces his audience with the necessity of choice; double-mindedness, vacillation, and compromise with society are not viable options.

Failure to act in accord with the wisdom from above and the "perfect" (τέλειος) or complete law (1:25) means opting for friendship with the devil and enmity with God (4:4–10). Friendship with the devil and with a society under the sway of devilish wisdom involves adopting a code of moral standards that excludes God from consideration (4:13–17) and is hostile to God's claims over his creatures (Johnson 1985, 170–77). Subscribing to the alien values and norms of a polluted and polluting society has led to duplicity, communal divisiveness, alienation from God, and the loss of holiness and wholeness.

On the other hand, fidelity to the complete and royal law of freedom (1:25; 2:8, 12), inspired by the wisdom from above, entails an integrity of hearing-completed-in-doing (1:19–27), of seeing-completed-in doing (1:23–25), of speaking-completed-in-doing (1:13, 19, 26; 2:3, 7, 12, 14–26; 3:1–12, 14; 4:3, 11–12, 13–17; 5:9, 12, 13–18), and of faith-activated-in-love (2:1–26). Thus James calls for the integration of the three traditional zones of personal action (Malina 1981, 60–64): (1) thought (ears and eyes supplying information reflected on by mind and heart; (2) speech (expressed by mouth and tongue); (3) purposeful action (executed by hands and feet). A complete (τέλειος) law (1:25), that is, requires complete (τέλειος) persons (3:2) who are receptive to the complete (τέλειος) benefaction coming from God above (1:17), and whose words and faith are completed (τελειόω) in action (2:22).

Complete fidelity to the complete law assures personal integrity, social harmony, and union with the holy God. "Draw near to God, and he will draw near to you" (4:7–8 RSV). "Cleanse your hands, you sinners, and purify your hearts, you double-minded" (4:8 NRSV). This linking of integrity and purity echoes a similar association that we observed at the outset of James's argument in chapter 1. There integrity of word-and-deed was linked with "putting away all filthiness and rank growth of wickedness" (1:21), and purity of worship was identified as care for orphans and widows and remaining uncontaminated by society's pollution (1:27). Such holy and integral behavior involves respect for, rather than oppression of, the poor (2:1–13; 5:1–6) and thus action consistent with God's exalting the poor (1:9; 2:5).

In James's view, the believers' failure to live in accord with this complete law and their compromise with the alien values and norms of society had resulted in personal doubt, duplicity and defection, and communal factionalism and fragmentation. As a remedy for this situation, James urges his readers to sever their ties with secular pollution, humble themselves before God, live in accord with the wisdom from above, purify their hearts, and commit themselves single-mindedly to the law of brotherly love.

This entailed embracing a humble trust in God and the benefactions that God provides (1:5–8, 12, 17–18; 3:17–18; 4:2–3, 5–10; 4:13; 5:7–11, 13–18) and also a critical caution over against the wise and the rich (1:9–11; 2:1–13; 4:13–5:6), whose behavior is more consistent with external standards of conduct than with the will and action of God (1:9–11; 2:1–7), the Christian faith (1:3; 2:1, 14–26), and the requirements of the law (1:25, 2:8–13; 4:11–12; 5:9). Believers, James stresses, are bound by this law that requires integrity of faith and action (1:22–25; 2:14–26) and brotherly love (2:1–13), especially toward the poor and powerless. They are to take their lessons from God's care of the poor (1:9–11; 2:5; 5:7–12) and the behavior of Israel's heroes (2:21, 25; 5:11, 17), and to purify their hands and hearts by breaking clean from society's pollution (1:16–27; 3:6, 14–16; 4:1–4, 8).

In James's analysis, holiness and wholeness are treated as correlative concepts, as are pollution and fragmentation. To be holy, according to James, is to be whole—with respect to personal integrity, communal solidarity, and religious commitment. As correlated concepts, holiness and wholeness serve to identify the essential nature of Christian brotherhood, union with God, code of conduct, social cohesion, and distinctiveness over against society at large. What is especially noteworthy in James is the manner in which pollution and purity distinctions customarily embracing personal, social, and cosmic areas of life are also employed here to diagnose and remedy interrelated dilemmas of fragmentation, division, and instability at interrelated personal, social, and cosmic levels of existence.

Summary and Conclusion

From this study of James, the following has become evident.

1. A consistent pattern of negative assessments and positive exhortations concerning personal and communal behavior marks this composition from commencement to closure.

2. The focal theme that this series of contrasts addresses is that of incompleteness and division versus wholeness and unity, the elimination of the former and the restoration of the latter.

3. Three interrelated dimensions of this issue are treated: the personal, the social, and the cosmic.

4. In both the negative diagnoses and positive remedies proposed, notions of purity and pollution serve as an important means for conceptualizing, distinguishing, and evaluating appropriate and inappropriate attitudes, actions, and alliances with regard to the community, its members, and their relation to God and society. Like the Epistle of 1 Peter (Elliott 1981), the Epistle of James employs notions of purity and pollution to undergird an ethic of holy nonconformity.

5. The restoration and maintenance of integrity, cohesion, commitment, and justice, according to James, require both a rejection of alien values and behavior as corrupting sources of pollution and a fidelity to God and the royal law of love as the means toward holiness and wholeness.

6. In both its structural and thematic consistency, the Epistle of James exhibits a unified and coherent line of thought.

7. This letter's multidimensional focus on the problem of friction and fraction within the early Christian community offers a poignant witness to

the dilemmas confronted by the movement in its engagement and compromises with society. In its admonishment of the Christian family that "the world is too much with us," James addresses issues of integrity and solidarity, holiness and wholeness, in a manner that is both comprehensive and compelling.

PERSONAL	SOCIAL	COSMIC
Wholeness, Completeness: Holiness/Above		
Pure worship	Separation from society	Union with God
Ask, trusting	Giving to those who ask	God gives
Integration of word/deed, faith/action	Communal harmony, brotherhood	Full observance of royal law
Control of tongue	Teachers' integrity	Truth
Humility	Honoring poor	God exalts poor and humble
Complete, whole, steadfast, stable	Peace	Wisdom from above
Fragmentation, Incompleteness: Pollution/Below		
Polluted worship	Pollution by society	Union with devil
Ask, doubting, out of selfish desire	No giving to needy who ask	Desire from devil
No integration of word/deed, faith/action	Communal discord	Partial observance of law, commission of sin
No control of tongue; pollution	Cursing, judging others	Set on fire by hell; deception
Pride, arrogance	Dishonoring and exploitation of poor	Pride from devil
Lacking, vacillating unstable	Lacking cohesion, presence of strife	Wisdom from below

Figure 8: Wholeness and fragmentation: personal, social, cosmic

BIBLIOGRAPHY

Baasland, Ernst. 1988. Literarische Form, Thematik und geschichtliche Einordnung des Jakobusbriefes. Pages 3646–84 in vol. 2.25.5 of *Aufstieg und Niedergang der römischen Welt*. Edited by W. Haase and H. Temporini. New York: de Gruyter.

Barkman, P. F. 1968. *Der heile Mensch: Die Psychologie des Jakobusbriefes*. Kassel: Oncken.

Buchanan, George W. 1963. The Role of Purity in the Structure of the Essene Sect. *Revue de Qumran* 4:397–406.

Coote, Robert B., and Antoinette Wire. 1979. Alias James. *Pacific Theological Review* 12:10–14.

Davids, Peter H. 1982. *The Epistle of James: A Commentary on the Greek Text.* New International Greek Testament Commentary. Grand Rapids: Eerdmans.

———. 1983. *James.* Good News Commentary. San Francisco: Harper & Row.

———. 1988. The Epistle of James in Modern Discussion. Pages 3621–45 in vol. 2.25.5 of *Aufstieg und Niedergang der römischen Welt.* Edited by W. Haase and H. Temporini. New York: de Gruyter.

Dibelius, Martin. 1984. *Der Brief des Jakobus.* 12th ed. Expanded and revised by H. Greven and F. Hahn. Kritisch-exegetischer Kommentar über das Neue Testament 15. Göttingen: Vandenhoeck & Ruprecht.

Douglas, Mary T. 1966. *Purity and Danger: An Analysis of Concepts of Pollution and Taboo.* New York: Praeger.

———. 1968. Pollution. Pages 336–42 in vol. 12 of *International Encyclopedia of the Social Sciences.* Edited by D. L. Sills and R. K. Merton. 17 vols. New York: Macmillan, 1968.

———. 1973. *Natural Symbols: Explorations in Cosmology.* New York: Vintage Books.

Eilberg-Schwartz, Howard. 1990. *The Savage in Judaism: An Anthropology of Israelite Religion and Ancient Judaism.* Bloomington: Indiana University Press.

Elliott, John H. 1966. *The Elect and the Holy: An Exegetical Examination of 1 Peter 2:4–10 and the Phrase* basileion hierateuma. Supplements to Novum Testamentum 12. Leiden: Brill.

———. 1981. *A Home for the Homeless: A Social-Scientific Criticism of 1 Peter, Its Situation and Strategy.* Philadelphia: Fortress.

———. 1991a. Household and Temple: A Contrast in Social Institutions. Pages 211–40 in *The Social World of Luke-Acts: Models for Interpretation.* Edited by Jerome H. Neyrey. Peabody, Mass.: Hendrickson.

———. 1991b. Household and Meals vs. Temple Purity: Replication Patterns in Luke-Acts. *Biblical Theology Bulletin* 21:102–8.

Fennelly, James M. 1983. The Jerusalem Community and Kashrut Shatnes. Pages 273–88 in *Society of Biblical Literature 1983 Seminar Papers.* Edited by Kent H. Richards. Society of Biblical Literature Seminar Papers 22. Chico, Calif.: Scholars Press.

Frankemölle, H. 1985. Gespalten oder ganz: Zur Pragmatik der theologischen Anthropologie des Jakobusbriefes. Pages 160–78 in *Kommunikation und Solidarität: Beiträge zur Diskussion des handlungstheoretischen Ansatzes von Helmut Peukert in Theologie und Sozialwissenschaften.* Edited by H.-U. von Brachel and N. Mette. Münster: Edition Liberación; Freiburg: Edition Exodus.

Frymer-Kensky, Tikva. 1983. Pollution, Purification, and Purgation in Ancient Israel. Pages 399–414 in *The Word of the Lord Shall Go Forth: Essays in Honor of David Noel Freedman in Celebration of His Sixtieth Birthday.* Edited by Carol L. Meyers and M. O'Connor. American Schools of Oriental Research Special Volume 1. Winona Lake, Ind.: Eisenbrauns.

Johnson, Luke T. 1985. Friendship with the World/Friendship with God: A Study of Discipleship in James. Pages 166–83 in *Discipleship in the New Testament*. Edited by F. Segovia. Philadelphia: Fortress.

———. 1986. The Letter of James. Pages 453–63 in *The Writings of the New Testament: An Interpretation*. Philadelphia: Fortress.

Kümmel, Werner G. 1975. *Introduction to the New Testament*. Rev. ed. Nashville: Abingdon.

Laws, Sophie. 1980. *A Commentary on the Epistle of James*. Harper New Testament Commentaries. San Francisco: Harper & Row.

Malina, Bruce. J. 1981. *The World of the New Testament: Insights from Cultural Anthropology*. Atlanta: John Knox.

Maynard-Reid, Pedrito U. 1987. *Poverty and Wealth in James*. Maryknoll, N.Y.: Orbis.

Meeks, Wayne A. 1983. *The First Urban Christians: The Social World of the Apostle Paul*. New Haven: Yale University Press.

Neusner, Jacob. 1973. *The Idea of Purity in Ancient Judaism*. Studies in Judaism in Late Antiquity 1. Leiden: Brill.

———. 1975. The Idea of Purity in Ancient Judaism. *Journal of the American Academy of Religion* 43:15–26.

———. 1978. History and Purity in First-Century Judaism. *History of Religions* 18:1–17.

Neyrey, Jerome H. 1986a. Body Language in 1 Corinthians: The Use of Anthropological Models for Understanding Paul and His Opponents. Pages 129–70 in *Social-Scientific Criticism of the New Testament and Its Social World*. Edited by John H. Elliott. Semeia 35. Decatur, Ga.: Scholars Press.

———. 1986b. The Idea of Purity in Mark. Pages 91–128 in *Social-Scientific Criticism of the New Testament and Its Social World*. Edited by John H. Elliott. Semeia 35. Decatur, Ga.: Scholars Press.

———. 1988a. A Symbolic Approach to Mark 7. *Forum* 4:63–91.

———. 1988b. Unclean, Common, Polluted and Taboo: A Short Reading Guide. *Forum* 4:72–82.

———. 1991. The Symbolic Universe of Luke-Acts: "They Turned the World Upside Down." Pages 271–304 in *The Social World of Luke-Acts: Models for Interpretation*. Edited by Jerome H. Neyrey. Peabody, Mass.: Hendrickson.

Popkes, Wiard. 1986. *Adressaten, Situation und Form des Jakobusbriefes*. Stuttgarter Bibelstudien 125/126. Stuttgart: Katholisches Bibelwerk.

Rustler, M. K. 1952. *Thema und Disposition des Jakobusbriefes: Eine formkritische Studie*. Diss., Faculty of Catholic Theology, University of Vienna.

Schille, Gottfried. 1977. Wider die Gespältenheit des Glaubens—Beobachtungen am Jakobusbrief. *Theologische Versuche* 9:71–89.

Seitz, O. J. F. 1947. Antecedents and Significance of the Term δίψυχος. *Journal of Biblical Literature* 66:211–19.

———. 1958. Afterthoughts on the Term "Dipsychos." *New Testament Studies* 4:327–43.

————. 1959. Two Spirits in Man: An Essay in Biblical Exegesis. *New Testament Studies* 6:82–95.

Spencer, Aida Besançon. 1989. The Function of the Miserific and Beatific Images in the Letter of James. *Evangelical Journal* 7:3–14.

Stowers, Stanley K. 1986. *Letter Writing in Greco-Roman Antiquity.* Library of Early Christianity 5. Philadelphia: Westminster.

Tamez, Elsa. 1986. *Santiago: Lectura latinoamericana de la epístola.* Colleción Aportes. San José: Editorial Dei.

————. 1988. Elementos bíblicos que iluminan el camino de la comunidad cristiana: Un ejercicio hermenéutico de la carta de Santiago. *Revista de Interpretaciøn Biblica Latinoamericana* 1:59–66. [In German translation by R. Kessler, "Elemente der Bibel, die den Weg der christlichen Gemeinde erhellen: Eine hermeneutische Übung anhand des Jakobusbriefes," *Evangelische Theologie* 51 (1991): 92–100.]

Via, Dan O., Jr. 1969. The Right Strawy Epistle Reconsidered: A Study in Biblical Ethics and Hermeneutics. *Journal of Religion* 49:253–67.

Ward, Roy B. 1969. Partiality in the Assembly: James 2:2–4. *Harvard Theological Review* 62:87–97.

Wuellner, Wilhelm H. 1978. Der Jacobusbrief im Licht der Rhetorik und Textpragmatik. *Linguistica Biblica* 43:5–66.

Zmijewski, Josef. 1980. Christliche "Volkommenheit." Erwägungen zur Theologie des Jakobusbriefes. *Studien zum Neuen Testament und seiner Umwelt* 1:50–78.

Social Location: Jesus

7

In this chapter Douglas Oakman challenges readers to understand first the social location of Jesus so as to better understand the gospel accounts of Jesus. He examines the parable of the Good Samaritan through the light of Jesus' peasant sensibilities. Peasants, according to the definition adopted here, include both those who derive their living from the land and village artisans and those who derive their living from activities such as fishing. Peasants tend to react negatively to change, especially commercial change, since such change usually is disadvantageous to the peasantry. The peasant's negative reaction to difficult circumstances, however, tends to be aimed at local landowners and overseers rather than at more central governments.

Since Jesus' parables reflect the concerns of the peasant world (i.e., the countryside), and because his life was controlled by a few powerful others, "elites" (the Herodians and the Romans), Jesus should be identified as primarily concerned with the world of peasants. Oakman sees Jesus as a figure who mediates between the world of the elite and the world of the peasants.

When we read the story of the "good" Samaritan with the understanding that Jesus would have been trying to mediate between the elite and peasant, we unearth several overlooked elements of the parable. The traveler on the road can be understood as an elite person who is befallen by social bandits. Oakman argues that Jesus would have been sympathetic to the aims of social banditry but not necessarily to the means that it employed. Jesus' peasant audience would have sympathized with the bandits who befell the traveler, and they would have considered the Samaritan a fool.

Douglas E. Oakman

Was Jesus a Peasant? Implications for Reading the Jesus Tradition (Luke 10:30–35)

INTRODUCTION

THE MEANING OF the Jesus tradition, especially the parables of Jesus, depends upon a world of experience, values, and institutions far different from our own. Anachronistic assumptions and inadequate understanding in regard to social context and audience can mask the original meaning in authentic Jesus material. One of the methods employed for getting past socially anachronistic interpretations of the gospel tradition has been the use of the rich body of knowledge, models, and theory that the social sciences have to offer. This essay argues that the wealth of resources available through sociology and peasant studies are of particular importance for the assessment or recovery of the meaning of the Jesus tradition.

It has long been asserted that Jesus of Nazareth was a small-town artisan (e.g., Weber 1978). Such an assertion may lead to inaccurate assumptions by modern interpreters of the Gospels about Jesus' primary socialization. For instance, it may be inferred that Jesus was a "middle class" artisan or a cultured "urban man." The work of theorists on peasantry prompts a reappraisal of this definitional problem. This essay examines conceptions of peasantry currently entertained by the social sciences. I argue that Jesus is best seen as a *peasant* artisan.

What difference does appropriate social characterization—in this case, seeing Jesus as peasant—mean for reading the Jesus tradition? Although Jesus certainly looked and moved beyond the narrow horizon of the village, many of his parables reflect the concerns and values of his peasant surroundings. It is likely that Jesus had in mind at least some of the interests of his fellow peasant villagers in Roman Palestine. In an exploration of the parable of the Good Samaritan (Luke 10:30–35), I will endeavor to show this. Some of Jesus' peasant audience, if not Jesus himself, probably evaluated the Samaritan as a "fool" rather than as "good." Yet such a determination of meaning raises interesting questions: Was Jesus sympathetic with such foolishness? What could such a story have meant within the framework of Jesus' central proclamation of the kingdom of God? What did the kingdom of God imply for the majority of Palestinian peasants in Jesus' day?

What Is a Peasant? Working toward a Definition

What is a peasant? This question immerses us immediately in one of the thorny questions regularly debated by social scientists. It soon becomes evident, in the reading of studies devoted to peasantry, that peasants are neither entirely the uncultivated boors of Theophrastus's *Characters* nor the romantic stereotypes projected in the writings of Tolstoy. They are often somewhere in between. Who belongs in the category of "peasant"? Eric Wolf, Barrington Moore, and Teodor Shanin have more or less limited this appellation explicitly to those who cultivate the soil directly for their own subsistence (Landsberger 1973, 7; Mintz 1973, 93). This definition excludes, of course, village artisans, wage laborers, beggars and disabled, rural priests, and others. The definition by Wolf (1966, 3, 10) explicitly focuses on the agricultural surplus extracted from peasant cultivators that sets them apart from primitive cultivators of the soil. Mintz (1973, 98) shares some of Wolf's exclusive concerns but stresses that any treatment must take into account the internal differentiation of the peasantry and their relationships to nonpeasant groups.

Other authorities are content to leave the definition more open-ended because they are interested especially in the interrelationships of various subgroups within a broader notion of peasantry. For instance, Raymond Firth's studies of groups in the Far East extended the label "peasant" to include fishermen and craftsmen. Landsberger (1973, 8–10) is hesitant to promulgate a categorical definition and argues instead for a series of "dimensions" that help the student to identify a group as peasant. Nonetheless, Landsberger (1973, 14–15) is sympathetic to the open-ended definitional tendency, observing that landless "peasants" have played a crucial role in rural unrest in Brazil. Foster too tends toward an open-ended approach: "It is not *what* peasants produce that is significant; it is *how* and *to whom* they dispose of what they produce that counts" (1967a, 6). Foster warns that restricting the definition of peasantry to an occupational status ("cultivator of the soil") obscures vision of the common situation of a whole range of rural groups that are occupationally diversified. Members of these groups are compelled to give up a precious amount of their hard-earned sustenance to outsiders. Here we have arrived at a core of characteristics that might be said to represent a consensus of contemporary thought on what makes a peasant. Foster, following Wolf, puts it well:

> *Not the city, but the state is the decisive criterion of civilization* and it is the appearance of the state which marks the threshold of transition between food cultivators in general and peasants. . . . We believe Wolf's recognition of outside power-holders as the key variable [in determining peasantries] is correct; normally, if not always, such power is associated with the city. (1967a, 6)

In 1953 Robert Redfield made a similar point: "It required the city to bring [peasantries] into existence" (cited in Foster 1967a, 5).

Redfield, Foster, Shanin, and Hobsbawm, taking the lead of Kroeber, have remarked upon the common cultural orientation of peasantry (Landsberger

1973, 8). Peasants think of themselves as a distinctive type of humanity and have a deep distrust of those outside the village. Geertz has rightly questioned the "myth of a nearly absolute social discontinuity between the world of the ruling classes and that of the peasantry" (1968, 318). Certainly, peasant culture depends to some extent upon the great tradition of urban civilization. It is often derivative (Foster 1967a, 10). Yet what peasants and subgroups of peasants do with that culture, what Mintz, following Wolf, has referred to as "social manoeuvre" (1973, 97), is very important in their self-definition. There is, to a certain extent, a peasant counterculture that expresses the peasantry's unique sense of itself and of its situation. So Wolf has developed a typology of peasant villages that distinguishes those that are more open to the outside world from those that are relatively closed to the outside world (see Geertz 1968, 320; Roseberry 1989, 117).

To put all of this together: a peasantry is a rural population, possibly including those not directly engaged in tilling the soil, who are compelled to give up their agricultural (or other economic) surplus to an outside group of power-holders, and who usually have certain cultural characteristics setting them apart from outsiders. Generally speaking, peasants have very little control over their political and economic situation. In Mediterranean antiquity the overlords of peasants tended to be city dwellers, and a culture chasm divided the literate elite from the unlettered villager.

What Do Peasants Value?

The typical peasant's socialization and life is molded by the agricultural year. Mediterranean peasants have devoted the majority of their energies toward viticulture, arboriculture, and agriculture. Vines and orchards, as well as grain and vegetable production, provide their staples. Animals supplemented the vegetable diet. Inanimate energy sources are rarely tapped, and productivity is relatively low. Excess peasant labor may be devoted to craft specialization if agricultural opportunities dwindle and tax pressures are high. Lenski (1984, 278) has noted that surplus children of peasant households are often forced to leave the village in search of livelihood. Jewish villages in the time of Jesus knew such craft specialization—for example, the making of pottery (Klausner 1925, 177). It is important to note that peasants value self-sufficiency and generally produce for household consumption (however defined), not for commercial purposes. Yet, as emphasized in the foregoing section, peasants typically are dominated by landlords and overlords. Politics put pressure on the subsistence margin of the typical peasant household. Peasant anxieties focus around that margin. Peasants tend to see the goods of life in limited quantities, and peasant economics are traditionally "zero-sum": if someone's wealth increases, it must be at the expense someone else. For this reason, peasants are normally suspicious and envious of "windfalls" (Foster 1967b, 305, 311, 316).

What Makes Peasants Angry?

Peasants become discontented when the subsistence margin is too close or when secure access to land is denied. Peasant indebtedness is usually an indication of trouble, since indebtedness leads to less secure access to produce and to land.

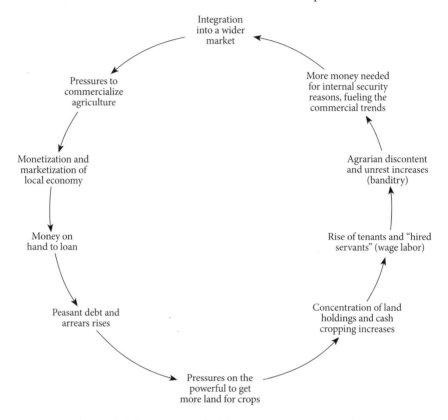

Figure 9: A dynamic model of the causes of agrarian conflict

Figure 9 presents a model of important factors that lead to rural unrest and even revolt. Landsberger has hazarded the following statement, upon which figure 9 is based:

> The economic integration of the society under consideration into a larger, possibly international market; the consequent drive to commercialise agriculture; and the subsequent encroachment on peasant lands and peasant rights and status in general; this sequence is certainly the most promising candidate for the position of "universal ultimate cause" [of agrarian discontent and revolt]. (1973, 29)

What this statement means is that the commercialization of agriculture and the encroachment of landlords on hereditary peasant landholdings consistently will be observed to go together. This generalization makes sense systemically. If there are commercial outlets for agricultural productivity, then the value of land—even marginal land—will go up. There will be the temptation for the powerful to acquire more land for the sake of gain. Usually the consumption aspirations of the powerful will rise also. One of the chief mechanisms for wresting patrimonial land from peasantry will be debt transactions. This is a rather convenient mechanism. Not only will the commercial activity of the powerful provide them with cash or commodities on hand to loan, but also the pressure on the peasantry to borrow will go up. Commercialization will bring greater monetization and marketization to the local economy in which the peasant will participate on unequal terms (Carney 1975, 146–52, 201). State taxes will doubtless rise with the expanding economic pie, adding further pressure on the local cultivator. Borrowing will be necessitated. Unpaid arrears will eventuate in the loss of the peasantry's land and the appearance of tenants and a wage labor pool. Land holdings will be concentrated in fewer hands. Agrarian unrest and discontent will cause the costs of security to rise. This will mean pressure for money to pay the troops. These developments, in turn, continue to fuel the commercial revolution. This is a neat "system," but it is extremely disadvantageous from a peasant's point of view. The peasantry comes out the loser.

Some corollaries can be arranged beside the foregoing "general theorem." Several other factors contribute to peasant disaffection and possibly revolt. Large landowners can be converted into pure rent and tax collectors, not engaged directly in farming or in any other useful function apparent to the peasantry. As such, landlords fail to perform compensatory services for the peasantry (e.g., protection); their relationship to the village becomes one of purely economic exploitation. Such situations usually imply absentee landlordism. The local aristocracy becomes weak in the face of a growing central government. Finally, there is a partial survival, through all of these changes, of peasant communities that are damaged but intact (Landsberger 1973, 17–18). These societal changes induce peasant discontent when the peasantry begins to feel status inconsistency, deprivation relative to another group, or deprivation relative to a past status, or some combination of these (Landsberger 1973, 17–18). Commercial activity, high taxation, and absentee landlordism are all mirrored in the Roman Palestine of Jesus' day (Oakman 1986; Brunt 1977; Horsley 1984; Horsley and Hanson 1985).

The political response of peasantry to such changes typically is parochial and of limited scope (Hobsbawm 1973, 12). Most peasants protest or revolt in order to "remain traditional" (Wolf 1966) or to eliminate specific evils and abuses (Huntington 1968). Most such peasant actions are aimed at local landlords and officials and rarely are self-consciously directed against a central government (Hobsbawm 1973, 13; Landsberger 1973, 36–37), nor do they typically adopt an anarchist or utopian ideology. In fact, peasant movements on a national scale are remarkably infrequent. Of significant interest concerning peasant radicalism is a comparative observation made a long time ago by Ptorokin and Zimmerman:

> Radicalism of farmers has attempted to maintain wide distribution of private property whereas radicalism among wage earners has sought to concentrate ownership

of property in the state or do away with the institution of private property. (cited in Sanders 1977, 135)

Karl Marx noted the "rural idiocy" of peasants and argued that peasants are incapable of representing themselves. Hobsbawm observed,

> A communally organised traditional peasantry, reinforced by a functionally useful slowness, imperviousness and stupidity—apparent or real—is a formidable force. The refusal to understand is a form of class struggle. (1973, 13)

When indigenous peasant leaders have arisen to lead a movement, the goals of the movement have generally mirrored what all peasants value: parochial and limited ends. Radical peasant movements typically have been organized and led by leadership from outside the peasantry itself—priests, intellectuals, and so on—although these leaders often spend their early years in peasant villages (Landsberger 1973, 40, 47–48; Hobsbawm 1973, 12).

When peasant movements or revolts have succeeded in the past, one or more of three major social components perhaps have played assisting roles. The peasants' cause might be taken up by a central power, a king, who is believed to be (or poses as) a font of justice or who is called as an ally against the peasants' real masters, the local gentry. Religion can play a major part in peasant uprisings; here social perspectives are reversed. A bishop or priest may be seen to represent a repressive and institutionalized church remote from peasant interests, while the peasants take spiritual sustenance and guidance from saints or local holy men. Finally, a "proto-nationalism" may help groups of peasants to align themselves translocally. These factors can, of course, crosscut or work against peasant aspirations as well (for a brief discussion of these components, see Hobsbawm 1973, 17).

Was Jesus a Peasant?

The social delineation of Jesus of Nazareth makes a good case in point in terms of this theoretical debate. Was Jesus fundamentally a peasant? Or does his occupation as artisan imply some other social category? Certainly, as an artisan, Jesus had access to experiences denied those who remained in the village or on the land. Yet Jesus' socialization was within a village context, as the Synoptics make plain (Mark 6:1–3; Luke 2:51), and many of the scenes of his ministry and much of the content of his teaching embrace the culture and society of rural Palestine. Occupationally, Jesus is best understood as a peasant child forced to leave the village in search of livelihood (Mark 6:3).

Jesus' parables have long been considered to reflect the mores and experiences of the countryside (see, e.g., Smith 1937). It is interesting to observe that many of the parables mirror experience upon large estates, undoubtedly including those of the Esdraelon Plain near Nazareth. Do these reflect Jesus' own experiences? It is probable that they do, at least in the typical sense. In any case, it seems certain that Jesus was a careful observer of agrarian life.

Most importantly in this connection, Jesus stood in the same structural relationship to the powerful as did other villagers and artisans of his environment. He was a peasant, because a few powerful others determined many of the important decisions of his and others' lives. It was in the cause of these weak and exploited that Jesus' own ministry was conducted, as much scholarship has demonstrated (Theissen 1978; Stegemann 1984; Oakman 1986; Borg 1987). Stegemann situates the Jesus movement this way: "The movement within Judaism in Palestine associated with the name of Jesus was a movement *of the poor for the poor*" (1984, 23).

Certainly all peasant societies are part-societies existing within more complex and complete societies, as first Kroeber and then Redfield have made clear, and people like Jesus simply underscore this fact by moving between two worlds. Yet the very existence of people like Jesus who mediate the larger world to the village and vice versa makes the interpretation of peasant realities so critically interesting and difficult. Which of those worlds is primary in the understanding of Jesus and his activities? Later Christian interpretation, beginning with the context of interpretation provided by Matthew and Luke, decided the issue in favor of the larger Mediterranean world and its dominant Greco-Roman value system. However, the historically sensitive student of the gospel tradition cannot make this unilateral decision.

I accept, therefore, that Jesus was fundamentally a peasant, qualifying the views of Weber and a long line of interpreters who have given prominence to Jesus' artisan side (see Weber [1978, 1:481], who does admit that Jesus was a "small-town" artisan). Jesus was a rural artisan working often within typical peasant contexts. His parables, focusing on rural concerns and basic subsistence, reflect these contexts. This means that although Jesus could and did move beyond the village during his life, his fundamental world of values and his fundamental interests and loyalties were shaped within and oriented toward the village. The interpretation of Jesus' parables must start with what is known typically about peasant values and expectations. Indeed, many of the parables themselves urge this starting point, assuming as they do knowledge of the Palestinian countryside under the early Roman Empire. In interpretive practice this judgment also implies the need to explore how Jesus' artisan experiences characteristically modified his typical village outlook, but that task is left for another essay.

INTERPRETING THE "GOOD" SAMARITAN STORY

A revisionary interpretation of the so-called Good Samaritan story, which takes into account the foregoing considerations, demonstrates several differences from the standard interpretations. The standard interpretations have generally done the following:

1. Allowed the Lukan framework to govern interpretation, neglecting the fact that the Lukan framework is secondary;

2. Ignored important social data in the story, such as the character of banditry in Jesus' time, the fact that the Samaritan is a trader, and the nature of public inns (πανδοχεῖα);

3. Viewed the Samaritan as self-sacrificing and "good" in contrast to the self-preoccupied priest and Levite; frequently, however, commentators note that Samaritans were hated by Jews.

The present interpretation explores the story with the following considerations in mind:

1. The Lukan framework is not original. While Bultmann (1963, 178) and Crossan (1973, 61) have seen Luke 10:36 as essential for understanding the story, a group of Jesus scholars believes that the parable ended at Luke 10:35 (Funk, Scott, and Butts 1988, 30).

2. The peasant Jesus, himself engaged in a "ministry of protest and renewal" (Theissen 1978), would likely have been in sympathy with the ends of social banditry, although not necessarily with its means.

3. Jewish peasants were hardly in sympathy with Samaritans, especially when the latter were engaged in commerce.

4. Inns had an unsavory reputation.

Jesus and Social Bandits

Horsley and Hanson (1985, 48–87) give a good orientation to the subject of social banditry in Roman Palestine. The important aspect is that bandits in Jesus' day were perceived by the Jewish peasantry as social bandits and thus were considered heroes in the villages. They stood for a justice denied by the system.

A story from Josephus well illustrates these points:

> On the public road leading up to Bethhoron some brigands attacked one Stephen, a slave of Caesar, and robbed him of his baggage. Cumanus [ca. 50 c.e.], therefore, sent troops round the neighboring villages, with orders to bring up the inhabitants to him in chains, reprimanding them for not having pursued and arrested the robbers. (*J.W.* 2.228–229)

The people in Jesus' story who were going down to Jericho from Jerusalem undoubtedly were understood as city-dwelling elite by villagers in the audience. The sympathies of the latter would have been with the bandits. Villagers probably evaluated the first part of the story in this way: "See? None of them take care of each other, and they're getting what they deserve!"

On the one hand, Jesus seems to have abhorred the violence of such bandits. So he implies that brigands are trying to force the coming of the kingdom (cf. Luke 16:16//Matt 11:12; also Mark 12:1–12). On the other hand, Jesus accepts some of the basic goals of banditry: justice and the securing of subsistence that guides peasant radicalism. Jesus promises his disciples such secure subsistence in the name of the kingdom of God (Mark 10:30; Luke 12:22–31//Matt 6:25–33). Jesus also speaks about debt forgiveness as an essential characteristic of the kingdom (Luke 7:41–42; Luke 11:4//Matt 6:12).

The Samaritan

The hatred of Jews for Samaritans was proverbial in Jesus' day (see John 4:9; see also Scott 1989, 197–98).

Luke's reading of the parable, given the framework of the lawyer's question to Jesus, has biased Christian interpreters to see the Samaritan as "good." Only the Samaritan proves to be neighbor. Yet, this reading leaves out of account the fact that the Samaritan was a merchant or a trader.

The following data in the story indicate that the Samaritan is a tradesman. He journeys (10:33) and has an animal to bear his wares (10:34). He has at his disposal "oil and wine" (10:34)—typical items of trade at the time. The Samaritan takes the injured man to a public inn, a typical stopping place for commercial people (Hug 1983, col. 527). Jeremias (1963, 204) endorses this view of the Samaritan.

As Landsberger's model above suggests, peasants would see a trader in oil and/or wine as a contributor to the social problem oppressing them. "Samaritan" would offend Jewish sensitivities; "merchant" would offend the peasant in Jesus' audience. As a matter of fact, commercial people were despised by elite groups as well. Elites felt their own honor and lineage threatened by "upstarts" and "new wealth" (see Finley 1973, 19).

Yet Jesus is not nearly so negative about traders, using them on at least one other occasion to exemplify the kingdom of God (Matt 13:45–46). Furthermore, the Samaritan's behavior toward the injured man is in line with the element of grace exhibited elsewhere in the Jesus tradition but out of line with ordinary mores. The Samaritan does not relate to the injured man as was usual in the society of Jesus. Villagers and elite alike were gracious only within the narrow confines of family. Such generosity, which Marshal Sahlins has called general reciprocity, was practiced toward nearest kin (Oakman 1986, 152; 1987, 37). Otherwise, careful accounting, balanced reciprocity, was the norm. Toward strangers and enemies, negative reciprocity was acceptable.

The Inn

Public inns were notorious in the ancient world for being "primitive, dirty and noisy" (Stählin, 1967, 19 n. 135). As Danker puts it, "Inns of that time were worse than American fifty-cent-a-night hotels. And innkeepers were not noted for their humanitarian sentiments" (1972, 132). Some short examples will illustrate these conditions.

The Greek historian, geographer, and philosopher Strabo writes,

> [Carura, a village between Phrygia and Caria] has inns. . . . Moreover, it is said that once, when a brothel-keeper had taken lodging in the inns along with a large number of women, an earthquake took place by night, and that he, together with all the women, disappeared from sight. (Strabo, *Geogr.* 12.8.17)

In the Armenian tradition of Philo, extant also in Greek fragments, the following is said:

> But he who is unlike [the wise man] does not have even his own house or a mind of his own but is confused and is treated contemptuously like those who, as it were, enter an inn [πανδοχεῖον] only to fill themselves and vomit in their passions. (cited in Royse 1981, 193)

Apocryphal Jesus tradition from the early second century C.E. has the following:

> And behold a leper drew near <to him> and said: "Master Jesus, wandering with lepers and eating with <them was I? publicans art thou?> in the inn [πανδοχεῖον]; I also <became> a le<per>." (Papyrus Egerton 2, f.1ʳ lines 34–35 [cited in Hennecke-Schneemelcher 1963–1965, 1:96–97])

Jewish tradition of the second century C.E. has equally negative things to say about inns:

> Cattle may not be left in the inns of the gentiles since they are suspected of bestiality; nor may a woman remain alone with them since they are suspected of lewdness; nor may a man remain alone with them since they are suspected of shedding blood. (*m. ʿAbod. Zar.* 2:1)

A story about Nahum of Gazmo (early second century C.E.?) is instructive:

> On the way, Nahum stopped at an inn over night. During the night the occupants of the inn got up, took out everything that was in the bags, and filled the bags with dust. (*b. Taʿan.* 21a)

MacMullen notes that "the advice of a contemporary [of Columella, mid-first century C.E.] in Palestine was, if one stopped the night at a wayside inn, to make one's will" (1974, 4 n. 13). And Bailey observes that in *Targum Jonathan* the word *prostitute* is "regularly translated 'woman who keeps an inn'" (1980, 53). Jastrow (1950, 1143 s.v. פּוּנְדָק) shows that πανδοχεῖον had become a loan word with similar connotations in both talmudic Hebrew and Aramaic.

Commentators on the "good" Samaritan story, like Danker, have regularly noted the negative image of inns but have never made much of it in terms of interpreting the story. For the Samaritan to leave the injured man at the inn seems folly in view of the evil reputations of inns. In *m. Yebam.* 16:7 we read the following:

> Once certain levites went to Zoar, the City of Palms, and one of them fell sick by the way, and they brought him to an inn. When they returned thither, they asked

the mistress of the inn, "Where is our companion?" She answered, "He is dead and I buried him."

Inns were not good places for sick people to stay. For the Samaritan to give the innkeeper a blank check (10:35) seems equally unwise. For peasant audiences, the Samaritan's "aid" has left the man in a worse condition than at first. Not only will the injured man be in danger of his life, but also he is held hostage until the Samaritan spends even more. What will the bill come to in the end?

JESUS' INTENTION IN THE STORY

How did Jesus expect his contemporaries to evaluate this story? For the ruling class in Jerusalem, the evaluation is already implied. They would endorse the actions of the priest and the Levite. Not only were purity concerns in view, but also involvement could lead to unpleasant consequences if the bandits had laid a trap. The whole story has disturbing overtones for them, since traders and public inns were despised by Greco-Roman elites (Hug 1983, cols. 522, 526–27). Tradesmen might look favorably on the Samaritan, although if the tradesmen were Jewish, this would be difficult. Yet tradesmen might also ask whether the Samaritan was a complete fool to endanger any shipment or commercial activity to help a stranger.

Jewish peasants would have multiple reasons for being unsympathetic. For them, the Samaritan is a cultural enemy, an evil man, and a fool: an enemy because he is a Samaritan, evil because he is a trader, a fool because he treats a stranger like family and is unsavvy about the situation at the inn. Conversely, the bandits are probably viewed as "good" in the eyes of villagers in Jesus' audience. The innkeeper is one of their own. In peasant eyes, only such negative reciprocity will bring about secure subsistence (someday). Would not peasants have laughed all the way through Jesus' story?

Very likely Jesus counted on this kind of response. He counted on positive reactions to the victimization of the Jerusalemite and the activities of the bandits; he counted on knowing nods to the behaviors of the priest and Levite; he anticipated visceral responses to the coming of the Samaritan; he "upped the ante" in showing general reciprocity and leaving the audience hanging, probably laughing, with the Samaritan's final words. How then did Jesus understand the story? Does he embrace the view of the village?

Was the story originally intended to function in a social-critical fashion (as perhaps did Mark 12:1–12 and Matt 20:1–20)? If so, the story exemplifies all of the evils of the age that will see the kingdom arrive: Israelite no longer cares for Israelite; exploitation has led to endemic banditry; and the commercial activities of Samaritans make the situation all the worse. This interpretation, however, is not entirely satisfying, for it does not bear the surprising or radical stamp of other parables of Jesus. A deeper reading might be gained by rethinking the kingdom connection with the story of the Samaritan.

THE STORY OF THE SAMARITAN IN JESUS' MESSAGE
OF THE KINGDOM

For Jesus, the question of most parables was not a general moral question about neighborliness, but rather what the kingdom is like. Luke or pre-Lukan tradition has biased the reading of the story of the Samaritan toward the development of the "example story" view (the Samaritan is simply a model of good behavior). Such a development does not take into account all of the data of the parable, especially the negative connotations of inns and the apparent foolishness of the Samaritan at the end of the story. How might this data be incorporated into a reading closer to the intention of Jesus?

Several features of the story stand out. (1) The Samaritan, practicing general reciprocity toward the injured man, shows generosity out of line with cultural expectations. (2) Inns and innkeepers had very low moral reputations. (3) The Samaritan—carelessly, dangerously, and foolishly?—indebts himself to, and gives himself and the injured Jerusalemite over into the power of, the innkeeper. Suppose, then, that Jesus concluded his narrative not with a question about neighborliness but rather with an implied "And the kingdom of God is like this." Similar comparisons can be found in the Jesus tradition—for instance, in the parables of the Pearl (Matt 13:45–46; *Gospel of Thomas* 76) and of the Great Supper (Luke 14:15–24//Matt 22:1–10; *Gospel of Thomas* 64).

God's reign, then, is strikingly compared to the actions of a hated foreigner of despised social occupation and is revealed literally in the wilds of bandits and inns. The generosity of God is portrayed as enormous (general reciprocity toward enemies). Even more so, the generosity of God reaches the point, in the human terms of Jesus' day, of danger and folly. God, like the Samaritan, is indebted to pay whatever may be required. The innkeeper has incentive to keep the injured man alive as security. The Samaritan offers a blank check.

And so the story ends. That is *what* God's grace is like. The parable also implies *where* the kingdom is found: in the most unlikely, even immoral, places! In consequence, the story of the Samaritan, which I will finally call the parable of the Foolish Samaritan, is in fact not an example story but does function as a parable of reversal, as Crossan sees:

> When the north pole becomes the south pole, and the south the north, a world is reversed and overturned and we find ourselves standing firmly on utter uncertainty. The parables of reversal intend to do precisely this to our security because such is the advent of the Kingdom. (1973, 55)

Crossan (1973, 56) also correctly analyzes the process by which such parables are turned into example stories, especially in Luke. Such a process domesticates the "immoral" danger of the kingdom. Likewise, Crossan classifies the parable of the Great Supper with that of the Foolish Samaritan. Crossan accomplished his classification with insufficient attention given to the sociocultural framework of Jesus' parables.

In Jesus' world peasants always existed with a threat from outside; that threat is what constituted their world. In the parable of the Foolish Samaritan the threat is manifest in the bandits, in commerce, and in the hostile environment of the inn. Jesus characteristically turns that outside threat into a positive metaphor for the kingdom of God. For some, the kingdom is critical opportunity; for others, perhaps judgment. Jesus is like his peasant acquaintances and neighbors in promising that the kingdom brings what all peasants want: secure access to subsistence. He moves beyond the village in seeing that those on the margins or in the interstices of society are more reflective of the coming kingdom than conventional expectations. Jesus does not endorse violent means to the end of the kingdom. Yet the kingdom will more effectively turn the world upside down than could all social bandits combined.

Conclusion

Reading the Jesus tradition against the background of peasant typicalities highlights aspects hitherto ignored. Jesus, though himself of peasant origins and upholding important peasant values, found promise where most peasants would have seen challenge. In the reading of the parable of the Foolish Samaritan developed in this essay, Jesus has counted on typical peasant valuations but has not simply identified with all peasant interests. A tension is evident. Peasant villagers may have to overcome some of their own prejudices and interests in order to see the kingdom that Jesus proclaims come near. But so also, and even more so, will the governing elites. The kingdom is total social challenge and transformation.

A certain indeterminacy in the reading remains, of course. No interpretation of a parable from Jesus can ever be established with absolute certainty, due to the ambiguous nature of parables and to the recontextualizing nature of the tradition. It is clear, however, that there is more to the story of the Samaritan than has met the eye of traditional Christian readings (beginning with Luke).

Retrojecting the hermeneutical investigation of Jesus' parables into the social setting of early Roman Palestine promises to bring new insights into Jesus' overall message. This methodology also apparently will raise many new questions, not all of which may prove answerable. Every new development in biblical studies brings its own set of problems. The employment of social-scientific perspectives will be no different. Let us hope that the results will outweigh in importance the problems and unanswered questions generated.

Bibliography

Bailey, Kenneth. 1976. *Poet and Peasant: A Literary Cultural Approach to the Parables in Luke.* Grand Rapids: Eerdmans.

———. 1980. *Through Peasant Eyes: More Lucan Parables, Their Culture and Style.* Grand Rapids: Eerdmans.

Balz, Horst, and Gerhard Schneider, eds. 1983. *Exegetisches Wörterbuch zum Neuen Testament.* Vol. 3. Stuttgart: Kohlhammer.

Bauer, Walter. 1988. *Griechisch-deutsches Wörterbuch zu den Schriften des Neuen Testaments und der frühchristlichen Literatur.* Edited by Kurt Aland and Barbara Aland. Berlin: de Gruyter.

Borg, Marcus. 1987. *Jesus: A New Vision; Spirit, Culture, and the Life of Discipleship.* San Francisco: Harper & Row.

Brunt, Peter. 1977. Josephus on Social Conflicts in Roman Judaea. *Klio* 59:149–53.

Bultmann, Rudolf. 1963. *History of the Synoptic Tradition.* Translated by John Marsh. San Francisco: Harper & Row.

Carney, Thomas F. 1975. *The Shape of the Past: Models and Antiquity.* Lawrence, Kans.: Coronado.

Crossan, John Dominic. 1973. *In Parables: The Challenge of the Historical Jesus.* San Francisco: Harper & Row.

———. 1986. *Sayings Parallels: A Workbook for the Jesus Tradition.* Foundations and Facets. Philadelphia: Fortress.

Danker, F. W. 1972. *Jesus and the New Age, according to St. Luke: A Commentry on the Third Gospel.* St. Louis: Clayton Publishing House.

———. 1976. *Luke.* Proclamation Commentaries. Philadelphia: Fortress.

Finley, Moses. 1973. *The Ancient Economy.* Sather Classical Lectures 43. Berkeley: University of California.

Fitzmyer, Joseph. 1981–1985. *The Gospel According to Luke.* 2 vols. Anchor Bible 28, 28A. Garden City, N.Y.: Doubleday.

Foster, George. 1967a. Introduction: What Is a Peasant? Pages 2–14 in *Peasant Society: A Reader.* Edited by Jack Potter, May Diaz, and George Foster. Little, Brown Series in Anthropology. Boston: Little, Brown.

———. 1967b. Peasant Society and the Image of Limited Good. Pages 300–323 in *Peasant Society: A Reader.* Edited by Jack Potter, May Diaz, and George Foster. Little, Brown Series in Anthropology. Boston: Little, Brown.

Funk, Robert. 1986. Poll on the Parables. *Forum* 2:54–80.

Funk, Robert, Bernard B. Scott, and James Butts, eds. 1988. *The Parables of Jesus: Red Letter Edition.* Sonoma, Calif.: Polebridge.

Geertz, Clifford. 1968. Village. Pages 318–22 in vol. 16 of *International Encyclopedia of the Social Sciences.* Edited by D. L. Sills and R. K. Merton. 17 vols. New York: Macmillan, 1968.

Goodman, Martin. 1983. *State and Society in Roman Galilee.* Totowa, N.J.: Rowman & Allanheld.

Hennecke, Edgar, and Wilhelm Schneemelcher. 1963–1965. *New Testament Apocrypha.* Translated by A. J. B. Higgins. Edited by R. McL. Wilson. 2 vols. Philadelphia: Westminster.

Hobsbawm, Eric. 1973. Peasants and Politics. *Journal of Peasant Studies* 1:3–22.

Horsley, Richard. 1984. Popular Messianic Movements around the Time of Jesus. *Catholic Biblical Quarterly* 46: 471–95.

Horsley, Richard, and John S. Hanson. 1985. *Bandits, Prophets, and Messiahs: Popular Movements in the Time of Jesus.* New Voices in Biblical Studies. Minneapolis: Winston.

Hug, August. 1983. Pandocheion. Cols. 520–29 in vol. 18 of *Paulys Realency-clopädie der classischen Altertumswissenschaft.* Edited by K. Ziegler. 2d ed. Munich: Druckenmüller.

Huntington, Samuel P. 1968. *Political Order in Changing Societies.* New Haven: Yale University Press.

Jastrow, Marcus. 1950. *Dictionary of the Targumim, the Talmud Babli and Ye-rushalmi, and the Midrashic Literature.* 2 vols. New York: Putnam: London: Luzac, 1903. Repr., Brooklyn: International Hebrew Book.

Jeremias, Joachim. 1963. *The Parables of Jesus.* Translated by S. H. Hooke. Rev. ed. New York: Scribner.

Kaplan, David, and Robert Manners. 1972. *Culture Theory.* Englewood Cliffs, N.J.: Prentice-Hall.

Klausner, Joseph. 1925. *Jesus of Nazareth: His Life, Times, and Teaching.* Trans-lated by H. Danby. New York: Macmillan.

Landsberger, Henry. 1973. Peasant Unrest: Themes and Variations. Pages 1–64 in *Rural Protest: Peasant Movements and Social Change.* Edited by H. Lands-berger. Publications of the International Institute for Labour Studies. New York: Barnes & Noble.

Lenski, Gerhard. 1984. *Power and Privilege: A Theory of Social Stratification.* Chapel Hill: University of North Carolina Press.

Lewis, Naphtali, and Meyer Rheinhold. 1955. *Roman Civilization: Selected Read-ings.* Vol. 2. New York: Columbia University Press.

MacMullen, Ramsay. 1966. *Enemies of the Roman Order: Treason, Unrest, and Alienation in the Empire.* Cambridge, Mass.: Harvard University Press.

———. 1974. *Roman Social Relations: 50 B.C. to A.D. 284.* New Haven: Yale Uni-versity Press.

Malina, Bruce. 1981. *The New Testament World: Insights from Cultural Anthro-pology.* Atlanta: John Knox.

Marshall, I. Howard. 1978. *The Gospel of Luke.* New International Greek Testa-ment Commentary. Grand Rapids: Eerdmans.

Mintz, Sidney. 1973. A Note on the Definition of Peasantries. *Journal of Peasant Studies* 1:91–106.

Oakman, Douglas E. 1986. *Jesus and the Economic Questions of His Day.* Studies in the Bible and Early Christianity 8. Lewiston, N.Y.: Mellen.

———. 1987. The Buying Power of Two Denarii: A Comment on Luke 10:35. *Forum* 3:33–38.

———. 1991. The Countryside in Luke-Acts. Pages 151–79 in *The Social World of Luke-Acts: Models for Interpretation.* Edited by Jerome Neyrey. Peabody, Mass.: Hendrickson.

Rohrbaugh, Richard. 1987. Models and Muddles. *Forum* 3:23–33.

Roseberry, William. 1989. Peasants and the World. Pages 108–26 in *Economic Anthropology.* Edited by Stuart Plattner. Stanford: Stanford University Press.

Rostovtzeff, Michael. 1941. *The Social and Economic History of the Hellenistic World*. 3 vols. Oxford: Clarendon Press.

————. 1957. *The Social and Economic History of the Roman Empire*. 2d ed. Revised by P. M. Fraser. 2 vols. Oxford: Oxford University Press.

Royse, James R. 1981. A Philonic Use of πανδοχεῖον (Luke x 34). *Novum Testamentum* 23:193–94.

Sanders, Irwin T. 1977. *Rural Sociology*. Englewood Cliffs, N.J.: Prentice-Hall.

Scott, Bernard Brandon. 1986. Essaying the Rock: The Authenticity of the Jesus Parable Tradition. *Forum* 2:3–53.

————. 1989. *Hear Then the Parable: A Commentary on the Parables of Jesus*. Philadelphia: Fortress.

Smith, B. T. D. 1937. *The Parables of the Synoptic Gospels: A Critical Study*. Cambridge: Cambridge University Press.

Stählin, Gustav. 1967. "πανδοχεῖον κτλ." Pages 1–36 in vol. 5 of *Theological Dictionary of the New Testament*. Edited by G. Kittel and G. Friedrich. Translated by G. Bromiley. 10 vols. Grand Rapids: Eerdmans, 1964–1976.

Ste. Croix, G. E. M. de. 1981. *The Class Struggle in the Ancient Greek World: From the Archaic Age to the Arab Conquests*. Ithaca, N.Y.: Cornell University Press.

Stegemann, Wolfgang. 1984. *The Gospel and the Poor*. Translated by Dietlinde Elliott. Philadelphia: Fortress.

Theissen, Gerd. 1978. *Sociology of Early Palestinian Christianity*. Translated by John Bowden. Philadelphia: Fortress.

Thorner, Daniel. 1968. Peasantry. Pages 503–11 in vol. 11 of *International Encyclopedia of the Social Sciences*. Edited by D. L. Sills and R. K. Merton. 17 vols. New York: Macmillan, 1968.

Weber, Max. 1978. *Economy and Society*. 2 vols. Berkeley: University of California Press.

White, K. D. 1977. *Country Life in Classical Times*. Ithica, N.Y.: Cornell University Press.

Wolf, Eric. 1966. *Peasants*. Foundations of Modern Anthropology. Englewood Cliffs, N.J.: Prentice-Hall.

Social Location: Jesus' World

8

This chapter, like chapter 7, examines the social location of a New Testament text. Ancient society was stratified with a small minority ruling over the vast majority of people. Numerous classicists and social theorists have understood clearly that this fact also applies to the period during which the New Testament was written and assembled. What is seemingly less clear, however, are the full implications for understanding a text such as Mark's gospel. In the first place, it seems that most of the early audience for this gospel would have been illiterate people who heard it read aloud. Most scholars contend that there were generally low literacy among the original audience of Mark's gospel. Data on education in the Greco-Roman world, though significant for understanding the composition of such documents as Mark's gospel, cannot be assumed to apply to this audience. That means that it cannot be assumed that this audience would have undestood Mark's gospel as a sophisticated rhetorical document (even though it may very well be that) with which they were invited to interact. Mark's hearers/readers were not modern churchgoers or academics who possessed their own copies of the text that they read over and over again. Their relationship to the text came through an aural avenue.

There are other significant aspects of the original social location of the Gospels that are often overlooked by modern people. Ancient society was highly stratified and divided along several lines. The elites, not representing more than 2–3 percent of the population, controlled the lives of most other persons. Often this control was exercised through a retainer class that served at the behest of the elites and operated to preserve the status quo. Most of the elites resided in cities (though most often also possessing significant lands on which often they had villas), and their retainers frequently resided in cities as well, although they also operated in village contexts. In this chapter Richard Rohrbaugh argues that all of Jesus' opponents come from the urban elite or retainer class in the Gospel of Mark. Further, borrowing on the work of others on this gospel, he notes that the disciples, who are low-status persons in this society, represent the hearers of this gospel. The Gospel of Mark continually presents these characters as positive respondents to Jesus' message.

The Gospel of Mark, according to Rohrbaugh, represents a clash between the "Great Tradition" and the "Little Tradition." Peasants and outcasts, burdened by the financial difficulties of observing ritual purity laws, especially concerning foodstuffs, observing the Sabbath, and contact with diseases and with the dead and the infirm, lived in a state of perpetual uncleanness, according to the Great Tradition. Jesus, however, constantly violates the purity laws throughout the Gospel of Mark and is declared clean and pure by its author. Jesus, then, becomes an archetype for how to relate to divine power (i.e., the kingdom of God) even in a state of ritual uncleanness.

Richard L. Rohrbaugh

The Social Location of the Markan Audience

INTRODUCTION

ATTEMPTS TO DESCRIBE the social location of the Markan audience are faced with a formidable obstacle right from the start: scholars have been unable to agree on its place of origin. The view of many scholars, perhaps a majority, has been that Mark's gospel was written for people in Rome (Hengel 1984; Senior 1987). If that is correct, and if Mark is thus to be understood as an urban gospel, we must locate his audience among the nonelite of the preindustrial city. But in previous decades an increasing number of scholars locate Mark's readers/hearers in the rural areas of southern Syria, Transjordan, or upper Galilee (Kee 1977; Myers 1988; Waetjen 1989; Lührmann 1987; Theissen 1991; Marcus 1992). Obviously, if this location is correct, then the Markan audience must be located among largely nonliterate peasants in a village or small town context.

In a short essay such as this on the social location of Mark's audience I cannot hope to argue this question of geographical locale adequately. Moreover, since our interest is in the social level of Mark's audience rather than its physical location, geography is only incidental to our purposes; it simply points us toward the alternatives of city or village. Following the studies noted above, therefore, I simply will presume that Mark's gospel was written in a village or small town context in southern Syria or Transjordan or upper Galilee, at a date very close to the events of 70 C.E. Thus my task will be to provide a map of the various social groups present in or impacting village life in those areas and at the same time to specify at least a few ways in which the Gospel of Mark is plausible to readers or hearers in that kind of setting. Before we begin, however, a few preliminary matters are of critical importance.

LITERACY/SCHOOLS

In any attempt to estimate the social level of Mark's audience it is essential to consider the extent of reading and writing in the type of village in which this gospel may have been produced. How widespread was literacy in rural Syria-Palestine? Are we to imagine the recipients of Mark reading privately to themselves as any modern American might do? Should we picture a literate community, perhaps even a scholastic one, in which the Scriptures were studied by an educated audience? Or did one of the literate members of the community read this gospel aloud for the majority who could not read for themselves? In answering these questions, I will take a view that differs substantially from some studies of Mark.

Among both classicists and New Testament scholars there has been a long-standing tendency to imagine widespread literacy during the Roman period. It has been claimed, for example, that schools were common, and that at least elementary education was broadly available. Yet there is noteworthy research that suggests that both literacy and the scope of the Hellenistic school system have been sharply overestimated (Harris 1989, 241–44, 329). Probably no more than 2–4 percent of the population in agrarian societies could read, or both read and write, and the majority of these lived in the cities. Especially important for our understanding of Mark's audience is the lack of evidence that significant schooling existed at the village level (Hezser 2001, 39–109).

Literacy rates (of at least a minimal sort) among elite males were indeed very high, even a distinguishing mark of such status. In addition, officials, bureaucrats, servants of the elite, and high-ranking military officers were mostly literate, as were many Italian legionnaires. But in spite of the fond wishes of scholars to the contrary, the fact is that rural people, artisans, slaves, and women were mostly nonliterate. Not only could very few village people read or write, but also many could not use numbers either (Hanson 1991). The cost of written materials and their relative scarcity at the village level insured that (Hezser 2001, 118–25). Equally important is the degree to which writing played a role in the control of the nonliterate. Fear of writing and of those who could write was widespread among peasants, who often resisted it as a tool of elitist deception. That was especially true where the literate group was small and the nonliterate group large— exactly the situation in rural Syria-Palestine in the first century C.E.

THE AUTHOR/AUDIENCE OF MARK'S GOSPEL

A number of studies have tried to locate the author of Mark's gospel among the educationally sophisticated, usually by comparing its literary structure to the rhetorical models of the Hellenistic schools. A commonly held view is articulated by Beavis, who asserts that "since the evangelist was literate, we can assume that he was educated in a Graeco-Roman school. His reader/audience would thus have brought certain skills and interests to the composition and reading of the text which can be illumined by data on education in the Roman empire" (1989, 21). Beavis (1989, 42–44) imagines "competent" first-century Markan readers "trained to make connections between parts of a narrative" and able to catch sophisticated literary allusions the author might have used. Because of the difficulty of catching such things during oral performances, however, Beavis hypothesizes a scholastic Markan community in which Mark's rhetoric might have been studied closely and therefore properly appreciated.

Perhaps Beavis is correct. But if it is true that Mark originated in a Christian community that in any significant measure reflected the social profile of a typical peasant village, and if Mark nonetheless expected his village readers to appreciate such rhetorical matters as literary allusion, style, and structure, then one thing should be abundantly clear: he had precious little company. In fact, if Mark's gospel embodies the plot, structure, and novelistic and dramatic features that would have been "attractive and instructive to Graeco-Roman audiences," as Beavis and some others claim, then we are in a literary world that would have been lost on 98 percent of the people in rural Syria.

But for our purposes it is enough to assert that there is no need for the social level of audience and author to match, especially since Mark's gospel almost certainly was written to be read aloud or recited from memory. It is perfectly plausible that a few literate people such as Beavis imagines could have been in Mark's audience, and it is likely that one such person read this gospel aloud for nonliterates. In fact, given the widespread fear of writing among nonliterates, it is highly unlikely that a gospel such as Mark could have gained broad acceptance in a village without being read aloud with great frequency (note that frequent reading aloud in public was a key test of canonicity for Eusebius, *Hist. eccl.* 3.3.6). In what follows, therefore, I will presume a mixed audience more nearly like the profile of an ancient village and will try to determine if the evidence in Mark's gospel supports such a view.

STRATIFICATION IN MARK'S STORY

Given the fundamental importance of social stratification in agrarian societies, we must begin by describing key social groups that would have been present in or had an impact on life in the villages and small towns of upper Galilee, southern Syria, or Transjordan. To structure these comments, I will refer to the following diagrammatic description of social relationships in the Herodian period, which is typical of advanced agrarian societies. We will look at each group in turn and then specify its presence in the story world of Mark.

As represented in figure 10 (see next page), the urban elite made up about 2 percent of the total population. At its upper levels, the urban elite included the highest-ranking military officers, ranking priestly families, and the Herodians and other ranking aristocratic families. They lived in the heavily fortified central areas of the cities, usually enclosed in separate walls; hence they were physically and socially isolated from the rest of the society. Since the elite were the only group with disposable income, they constituted the only real "market" in the ancient economy. The literacy rate among them was high, in some areas even among women, and along with their retainers they maintained control of writing, coinage, taxation, and the military and judicial systems. Their control was powerfully legitimated by the religious and educational bureaucracy, which typically became the keepers of the so-called Great Tradition (the "official" version of the religious tradition, which only the elite could afford to practice, contrasted

Urban Elite

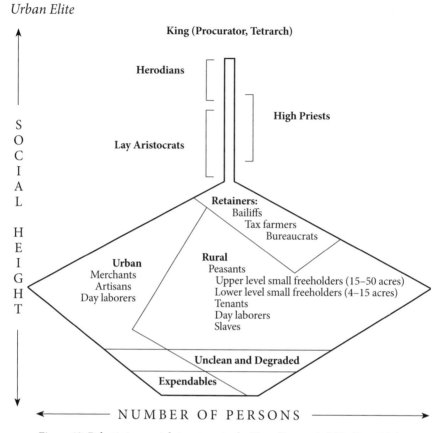

Figure 10: Palestinian social structure in the Herodian period (Duling 1994)

with the so-called Little Tradition, common among the lower classes). Although birth rates were high in all segments of the society, survival rates meant that large extended families were characteristic only of this urban elite. In fact, socially, culturally, and politically, they had little in common with the lower classes of the society. Since they maintained their own mannerisms, vocabulary, speech patterns, and dress, they could easily be spotted on sight.

The wealth of the elite was based primarily on land ownership and taxation, which effectively drained the resources of the rural areas. This "redistributive" economic system, as it is called in economic anthropology, served to expropriate peasant surplus and redistribute it among those in control. As in most agrarian societies, between 1 and 3 percent of the population owned the majority of the arable land in Galilee, southern Syria, and Transjordan at the time Mark wrote. There are significant studies that indicate large-scale latifundialization there during the first century c.e. as large estates came under control of the Herodians and other powerful families. Fiensy (1991, 60) describes large estates varying from roughly fifty acres to the very large one at Qawarat Bene-

Hassan that covered 2,500 acres. Especially important in lower Galilee was the land controlled by the Herodian family, which included tens of thousands of acres. By contrast, Fiensy (1991, 93–94) estimates the average peasant plot at six acres or less.

Those members of the urban elite that we can identify in Mark are listed in figure 11.

URBAN ELITE

Caesar (12:14, 17)	Strong man (3:27)
Pontius Pilate (15:2, 8, 15)	Those who have (4:25)
Rulers of the Gentiles (10:42)	Elders (8:31; 11:27; 14:43, 53; 15:1)
Herod (6:14; 8:15)	Rich man (10:22)
Herodias (6:17)	Wealthy (10:23, 25)
Herodias's daughter (6:22)	Vineyard owner and son (12:1, 6)
Philip (6:17)	Sadducees (12:18)
Governors (13:9; 15:16)	Family of seven brothers (12:20)
High Priest (2:26; 14:47, 53, 54, 60, 61, 63, 66)	Rich people (12:41)
	Kings (13:9)
Chief priests (8:31; 10:33; 11:18, 27; 14:1, 10, 43, 53, 55; 15:1, 3, 10, 11, 31)	Man going on a journey (13:34)
Scribes (1:22; 2:6, 16; 3:22; 7:1, 5; 8:31; 9:11, 14; 10:33; 11:18, 27; 12:28,35, 38; 14:1, 43, 53; 15:1, 31)	Owner of upper room (14:14)
	Joseph of Arimathea (15:43)
	Jairus and his family (5:22, 23, 40)

Figure 11: Urban elite mentioned in Mark

Given the prominent role of social conflict in Mark's narrative, we are not surprised to find that all of Jesus' opponents come from this group or its retainers. There is no need here to repeat the details of the controversies in Mark, since they have been studied often. but recognition that Jesus' opponents come from a single social strata and act in genuine solidarity with each other is sufficient to demonstrate that the conflict is social as well as theological.

Prominent in figure 11 are the scribes. Since the social level of scribes could vary considerably, it is difficult to know whether they should be placed here among the urban elite or, as is common, moved down one rank among the various retainers (see below). But Orton (1989, 111–18) has demonstrated at least that urban scribes were more than mere copyists and frequently functioned as respected sages of considerable influence. On that basis, I have chosen to place them here. We should note, however, that evidence from the Tebtunis Papyri suggests that village scribes are a different matter. They should be understood as retainers beholden to the urban aristocracy for their rural appointments (Hunt and Edgar 1934, ix.339: 393).

Mark's readers are warned to "beware of the scribes, who like to go about in long robes, and to have salutations in the market places and the best seats in the synagogues and the places of honor at feasts, who devour widow's houses and for a pretense make long prayers" (12:38–40). Together with the Pharisees they engage Jesus in the controversy over ritual cleanliness in 2:13–17, and again at 7:1–23, where Mark explains for his audience that Pharisees and Judeans (usually translated, incorrectly, "Jews") wash themselves and their eating vessels in keeping with the "tradition of the elders." This latter, of course, is the Great Tradition of the literate aristocracy, which few peasants could afford to maintain. And in Mark's story Jesus' disciples are clearly identified with this peasant inability (7:5). There also the scribes show a typical aristocratic incomprehension of peasant attitudes or capabilities ("why do your disciples . . . ?"). In his retort Jesus not only defends the peasant attitude but also offers another example (7:9–13), in which peasant family solidarity is legitimated in the "commandment of God" as opposed to the practices of the elite ("your" tradition), from which Jesus distances himself (7:9, 13).

In Mark's Passion Narrative the conflict intensifies as scribes and Pharisees link up with both the elders (probably nonpriestly aristocrats) and the chief priests in opposition to Jesus. The latter clearly are the most powerful members of the Jewish aristocracy, and their struggle with Jesus is primarily one for political influence over the nonelite (11:18). Mark predicts that this group not only will reject Jesus but also will destroy him in the end (10:33). Pilate, another member of the (Roman) elite, clearly understands this struggle (15:10). So also do the Herodians and Sadducees, whom Mark describes as joining other elite groups in their solid opposition to Jesus (12:13–17, 18–27; 3:1–6).

Three exceptions stand out in this list: the scribe who is "not far from the kingdom" (12:34), Joseph of Arimathea (15:43), and Jairus (5:21–43). The first two clearly are urbanites, though the latter more probably was part of the village leadership. As Malbon (1989, 275–76) has pointed out, these examples prevent us from excluding members of the elite From Jesus' community and may indicate that some such were in the community of Mark as well.

Retainers

In a continuum from the lower echelons of this elite and ranging downward toward nonelite levels were those whom social scientists call "retainers." This included lower-level military officers, officials and bureaucrats such as clerks and bailiffs, personal retainers, household servants, scholars, legal experts, and lower-level lay aristocracy. They worked primarily in the service of the elite and served to mediate both governmental and religious functions to the lower classes and to village areas. This group did not wield much power independently, however, but rather depended for its position on its relation to the urban elite.

RETAINERS

Pharisees (2:16, 18, 24; 3:6; 7:1, 3, 5; 8:11, 15; 10:2; 12:13)

People from Jairus' house (5:35)

Men arresting John the Baptizer (6:17)

Soldier of the guard (6:27)

Levi (2:14)

Those selling in the temple (11:15)

Servant-girl of High Priest (14:66)

Crowd sent from chief priests, scribes, and elders (14:43)

Physicians (2:17; 5:26)

Galilean priest (1:44)

Courtiers, officers (6:21)

Judas Iscariot (14:11)

Tax collectors (2:15, 16)

Moneychangers (11:15)

Doorkeeper (13:34)

Soldiers (15:16)

Centurion (15:39)

Slave/servant (1:20; 9:35; 10:43, 44; 12:2, 4; 13:34; 14:47)

Figure 12: Retainers mentioned in Mark

Such functionaries play key roles in Mark's story. Significantly, we see more people here who are followers of Jesus (the people from Jairus' house, Levi, tax collectors, and the centurion) than we found in the elite group. Of course, the key actors in this group are the Pharisees, and they are opponents.

Saldarini (1988) has correctly characterized the Pharisees (of Mark's day) as a group of retainers competing with the Jesus groups for influence among the nonelite. As a group, they lacked "independent wealth or power" but obviously could not have "developed their own interpretation of Judaism and propagated it among the people if they were full-time lower-class peasants" (Saldarini 1988, 71). They are associated with the scribes (2:13–17; 7:1–23) and with the Herodians (3:1–6; 8:15; 12:13–17) as Jesus' opponents, but they are not the dominant group as the conflict escalates later in the story. They were most likely literate local village leaders (in Mark, *contra* Josephus, the Pharisees are in Jerusalem only in 12:13) who depended on the urban elite for their livelihood. From that position they formed a united front with all of Jesus' elite opponents.

Before leaving these two dominant groups, we should note the sheer number of references to them in Mark's story. This is not because much of Mark's story takes place in an urban environment where these groups lived, but rather because their control extended into the rural areas in a pervasive way (see above on the appointment of village scribes). Conflict between them and the rural populations was a constant of agrarian village life.

Urban Nonelite

A third group playing a role in Mark's story is the nonelite of the cities. It included merchants, artisans, day laborers, and service workers of various kinds.

In most agrarian societies this group represented about 8 percent of the total population. Given the extremely high death rates among the urban poor, cities were able to absorb a constant stream of such persons from the rural areas with little or no gain in total population. Their economic situation could vary from extreme poverty among day laborers and certain artisan groups to considerable wealth among successful merchants. Yet even the rich among them bore little social or cultural influence.

Most of the urban poor lived in segregated areas at the outer edges of the cities where neighborhood or craft associations were a common means of creating the social networks that meant survival in agrarian societies. These urban neighborhoods often had internal walls that could be used to separate elite and nonelite as well as occupational or ethnic groups. Both internal and external gates were locked at night and guards posted on the walls. Among the urban poor health and nutrition often were worse than in the villages, and life expectancies were shorter. A child born among the lower classes in the city of Rome during the first century C.E. had a life expectancy of only twenty years (Lenski and Lenski 1974, 249).

URBAN NONELITE

Those buying in the temple (likely includes peasants) (11:15)	Crowd/People (1:5; 11:18, 32; 12:12, 37, 41, 14:2, 43; 15:8, 11, 15)
Widow (12:42)	

Figure 13: Urban nonelite mentioned in Mark

It is not surprising that this group plays a very small role in Mark's gospel, simply because aside from the Passion Narrative, very little of Mark's story takes place in an urban environment. Where sentiments can be identified, the crowd here is with Jesus until they are stirred against him by the authorities in 15:11. The one person in this group who is clearly identified, the widow in 12:42, is being unwittingly victimized by the redistributive economic system of the temple (Wright 1982).

Degraded, Unclean, and Expendables

Outside the walls of every preindustrial city lived the degraded, unclean, and expendables: beggars, prostitutes, the poorest day laborers, tanners (forced to live outside the cities because of their odor), peddlers, bandits, sailors, gamblers, ass drivers, usurers, dung collectors, and even some merchants. They were present in both villages and cities, though much more numerous in the latter. All such persons were forced out of the cities at night when gates were locked but frequented the cities during the daytime to beg or find work. The poorest lived the along hedgerows of adjacent fields. Although they were not a large portion of the total population, the living conditions and life chances of most of these people were appalling.

EXPENDABLES

Man with an unclean spirit (1:23)	Syro-Phonecian woman and daughter (7:25–26)
The sick and demon possessed (1:32–34, 39; 6:9, 13, 55; 9:38)	Deaf man with speech impediment (7:32)
Leper (1:40)	Blind man (8:22)
Paralytic (2:3)	Boy with an unclean spirit (9:14)
Man with withered hand (3:1)	Blind Bartimaeus (10:46)
Those who have nothing (4:25)	Simon the leper (14:3)
Demoniac (5:2)	Swineherds (5:14)
Hemorrhaging woman (5:25)	Man carrying a jar (14:13)

Figure 14: Unclean, degraded, and expendables mentioned in Mark

Given the fact that they were a relatively small percentage of the total population, the striking thing about this group is the sheer number of them in Mark's story and the frequency with which Mark gives us summaries of Jesus' interaction with them (1:28, 32–34, 45; 3:7–10; 6:31–34, 54–56; 7:36–37). In fact, Mark wants us to know early on in his story that Jesus' healing activity among this group of people is a major reason for the reputation that he develops (1:28). Note that two of those listed above are there by virtue of occupation: swineherd and porter were among the most degraded employments. Another, the Syro-Phonecian woman, may originally have been a person of higher status, though with a daughter afflicted by an unclean spirit, she and her daughter probably would have been understood by villagers as marginalized or ostracized persons (see Theissen 1984; Corley 1994).

Rural Peasants and Other Villagers

In agrarian societies such as that of the New Testament era, the cities dominated culturally, economically, and politically. Yet 90 percent of the population lived in villages and engaged in what social scientists call "primary" industries: farming and extracting raw materials. We must look briefly at several groups in these rural areas who play a role in Mark's story: freeholding peasants, tenant farmers, day laborers, slaves, and the various landless groups that included fishermen, artisans, and other craftsmen.

Freeholders

A substantial debate exists over the percentage of land held by Galilean freeholders in the late first century C.E., but nearly all agree that if it was a majority, it was a slim one (Fiensy 1991, 60). Since land was the basis of most wealth, and since yields were both low and unstable (Oakman 1986, 26), peasant debt leading to loss of land was epidemic (Oakman 1986, 57; Horsley 1989, 88–90;

PEASANTS

Those from the Judean countryside (1:5)	Little ones (9:42)
Peter, Andrew (1:16)	Children (10:13)
James, John, Zebedee (1:19–20)	Bystanders in Bethphage (11:5)
Simon's mother-in-law (1:30)	Those buying in the temple (likely included urban poor as well) (11:15)
Jesus (6:3)	
Mary (6:3)	Tenants (12:1)
James, Joses, Judas, Simon, and Jesus' sisters (6:3)	Sower (4:3)
	Simon of Cyrene (15:21)
Seed scatterer (4:26)	Crowd (2:4, 13; 3:9, 20, 32; 4:1, 36; 5:21, 24, 27, 30, 31; 6:14, 17, 34, 39, 45; 7:14, 17, 33; 8:1; 2, 6, 34; 9:14, 15, 17, 25; 10:1, 46)
Mary Magdalene, Mary the mother of James, Joses, Salome (15:40)	

Figure 15: Rural peasants and other villagers mentioned in Mark

Fiensy 1991, 93; Goodman 1982). Estimating standards of living for freeholding peasants has proven a difficult task, however, especially given the variability of soil and rainfall from area to area. Nonetheless, there is little doubt that minimal survival levels were common. In most of Syria-Palestine approximately 20 percent came off the top of each crop for the next year's seed. Fodder for animals and products to trade for what a family did not produce consumed about as much, though local conditions varied greatly. In addition, the burdens of supporting the temple, priesthood, Herodian regime, and Roman tribute were crushing. Evidence for total taxation is difficult to compile (estimates vary from 15 percent to as high as 35–40 percent), but combined with other needs, taxation took peasant economic viability to the brink (Oakman 1986, 57–72; see Josephus, *J.W.* 5.405).

Isolated farms on which peasant families lived separately from their neighbors gradually disappeared prior to the New Testament period, and the majority of peasants came to live in villages or small towns, going out to the fields daily. Lands adjacent to (and often owned by) cities were farmed in similar fashion. The family rather than the individual was the unit of both production and consumption. Barter sufficed for the majority of needs, and few peasants participated heavily in the spreading monetarization of the economy. The peasant ideal of self-sufficiency meant that most of what was consumed or used was produced in an extended kinship group, though evidence suggests that by New Testament times the extended families of an earlier period were being replaced by nuclear families living in close proximity around courtyards or clustered along narrow alleys (Fiensy 1991, 123–33).

Tenants, Day Laborers, and Slaves

Evidence for aristocratic control of major portions of the arable land is most abundant for the period following the revolt of 66 c.e. There we get a clear picture of large estates employing tenant farmers, landless laborers, and slaves in producing crops for absentee landowners.

In ever increasing numbers during the first century c.e. landless peasants worked the lands of the wealthy, to whom they paid significant portions of the produce for the opportunity (Fiensy 1991, 75–85). Tenancy contracts usually were written rather than oral and could cover one year, five years (the most frequent), seven years, or even a lifetime. Some tenants paid fixed rents in kind, others in money, and still others paid a percentage of the crop. Rents for tenants could go as high as two-thirds of a crop, though rabbinic sources more commonly mention figures ranging from one-fourth to one-half. Many tenants, particularly those with fragmented extended families, fell hopelessly in debt and abandoned their ancestral lands altogether. In some extreme cases—Qawarat Bene Hassan, for example—an entire village worked as tenants for a single landlord (Fiensy 1991, 84).

In addition to tenant farmers there were both day laborers and slaves. Many did seasonal work during harvests, though often they were employed as "barbers, bath-house attendants, cooks, messengers, scribes, manure gatherers, thorn gatherers, or workers with building skills" (Fiensy 1991, 86). Although day laborers were not necessarily landless people (small freeholders often worked out to supplement farming income), those who were indeed without land were near the bottom of the socioeconomic scale. Commonly they were either peasants who had lost land through indebtedness or noninheriting sons whom small peasant plots could not support. Our sources indicate that they worked by the hour, day, month, year, three years, or seven years (Fiensy 1991, 85). Many such landless people drifted to the cities and towns, which were in frequent need of new labor, not because of expanding economic opportunity but rather because of extremely high death rates among the urban nonelite.

Other Rural Groups

In addition to peasant farmers, most village and rural areas contained at least several other groups. Lower-level retainers and lay aristocrats often provided village leadership, and most villages of any size had a council to govern local affairs. Artisans, craftsmen, fishermen, and herders were common as well, though few artisans or craftsmen could make a living in the smaller villages and thereby had to work in several locations. Since villagers considered people who traveled around socially deviant, itinerant workers were very low on the social scale. Shepherds were especially despised, being stereotyped as thieves without honor because their grazing sheep wandered onto the fields of others.

Peasant Health

Before leaving our description of rural groups, we should note something of peasant health. Such comment is appropriate in light of the prominent role healing stories play in Mark's narrative and should support my thesis that Mark is particularly plausible in a peasant/village setting.

Birth rates in the first century C.E. were approximately forty per thousand per year, twice that in the United States today, though death rates were even higher (Although U.S. birth rates are much lower than those of antiquity, our death rates have dropped even further than our birth rates. We thus have the curious phenomenon of far fewer births and rapidly rising population). Infant mortality rates have been estimated at 30 percent in many peasant societies, and that may well have been the case in first-century C.E. Palestine. Evidence suggests that life expectancies were extremely short by modern U.S. standards. Children were the first to suffer from disease, malnutrition, and poverty, and many never made it to adulthood before their parents were sick or dead. About 60 percent of those who survived their first year of life were dead by age sixteen, and in few families would both parents still be living when the youngest child reached puberty (Carney 1975, 88).

Obviously disease and high death rates were not evenly spread across all elements of the population but rather fell disproportionately upon the lower classes of both city and village. For most lower-class people who did make it to adulthood, health would have been atrocious. By age thirty, the majority suffered from internal parasites, rotting teeth, and bad eyesight. Most had lived with the debilitating results of protein deficiency since childhood. Parasites were especially prevalent, being carried to humans by sheep, goats, and dogs. Fifty percent of the hair combs from Qumran, Masada, and Murabbat were infected with lice and lice eggs, probably reflecting conditions elsewhere (Zias 1991, 148). If infant mortality rates, the age structure of the population, and pathological evidence from skeletal remains can be taken as indicators, malnutrition was a constant threat as well (Fiensy 1991, 98).

Infectious disease was the most serious threat to life and undoubtedly accounted for much of the high mortality rate among children (Zias 1991, 149). Few peasants could afford professional physicians and so frequented folk healers of various kinds. As in virtually every known society that was economically dependent on animal husbandry (especially large domestic animals such as camels, sheep, and goats) for a portion of its livelihood, there was widespread belief in spirit-aggression as an important cause of illness (Pilch 1991, 196).

Finally, as Oakman has shown in a study of Luke, violence was also a "regular part of village experience" (1991, 168). Fraud, robbery, forced imprisonment or labor, beatings, inheritance disputes, and forcible removal of rents are all reflected in the village life in the Mark's gospel (1:14, 45; 3:6, 27; 5:3; 6:16–28; 10:33–34; 12:1–8, 40, 41–44; 13:9–13; 14:1, 43–48; 15:7, 15–20). Widows, aged parents without children or parents of abnormal children, the very young, the very old, those with diseases or deformities, and those without land were the most common victims. Suspicion of outsiders, fear and distrust of officials, and hatred of anyone who threatened subsistence were the social constants of ancient village life. In sum, given poor housing, nonexistent sanitation, constant violence, economically inaccessible medical care, and bad diet—as much as one-fourth of a male Palestinian peasant's calorie intake came from alcohol (Broshi 1989)—one begins to revise the somewhat romanticized picture that modern readers might be tempted to conjure up for Mark's peasant audience.

As one might expect, these various groups of rural persons, which comprised the overwhelming bulk of the population in ancient societies, are prominent throughout the story world of Mark.

An especially important group here is the crowd (ὄχλος, used 38 times in Mark, translated variously in the RSV). Byung-mu (1981, 139ff.) has demonstrated both Mark's use of ὄχλος as both a term for the poor (the equivalent of עַם הארץ, those poor, uneducated peasants outside the law) and an indicator of the social location of his own audience (see also Myers 1988, 156). The rabbis, of course, taught that observant Jews should neither eat nor travel with the עַם הארץ, although the Jesus of Mark did both (e.g., 2:13ff.; 8:1ff.).

Another important group is the disciples. Mark tells us much about their fears, emotions, immaturity, stupidity, disloyalty, and eventual failure (Tannehill 1977; Malbon 1986). We cannot revisit here the many studies of the disciples as the prime indicators of Mark's audience, but it is especially important to note that since flaws are things that one talks about inside a Mediterranean family but never outside it, we can only construe Mark's talk about the disciples' failures as "insider" (read: surrogate family) talk. In taking the reader into confidence on such family matters, Mark obviously indicates that he is writing for members of the Christian family.

Our primary interest, of course, is in a social characterization of the Markan disciples, though social information is obvious for only four of the twelve. Peter, Andrew, James, and John were fishermen. Fishing is a despised occupation as Cicero sees it, since fishermen "cater to sensual pleasures" (*Off.* 1.150–151). In Mark's gospel, Peter and Andrew appear to have been net casters (1:16–18), while James and John obviously fished from a boat (1:19)

Increasing demand for fish as a luxury item in the first century C.E. led to two basic systems of commercialization. In the first, fishermen contracted with either royal concerns or large landholders for a specified amount of fish to be delivered at a designated time. Records indicate that this system was highly profitable for estate managers or royal coffers, while the fishermen themselves got little. The second system made fishing part of the taxation network in which fishermen leased fishing rights from toll collectors for a percentage (as high as 40 percent) of the catch. Such tax fishermen often worked with "partners" (μέτοχοι), the term used in Luke 5:7, hence the fishing done by Peter, Andrew, James, and John may have been of this second type. Mark, however, specifies that the latter two left their father with the hired hands (1:20). This does not necessarily imply that this family was better off than most, since tax farmers often hired day laborers to work with contract fishermen. In any case, the four disciples whom we can locate socially are clearly members of the exploited lower class. Socially and economically, they were below even peasant farmers and had less long-term security.

Those from the Judean countryside (1:5), the sower (4:5), the tenants (12:1), the crowd (passim), and the other rural persons listed above were mostly likely peasant farmers. Jesus and his family, however, were artisans. Though Mark does not mention the Bethlehem tradition, if Jesus' family was originally Judean, we can assume that a predecessor there lost the land; otherwise, they would not be trying to make a living in a tiny Galilean village. As figure 10 above shows, most artisans were below peasants on the socioeconomic scale. Moreover, the small minority who were village artisans would have been especially marginalized.

The Social Level of Mark's Audience

There have been many attempts to characterize the Markan audience (Beavis 1989; Malbon 1986; Kee 1977; Theissen 1991; Hengel 1984; Tannehill 1977), but the majority of these have concentrated on various ethnic, geographical, or religious aspects of the group's identity. Our interest, however, is in locating Mark's hearers/readers on the social map of rural Syria-Palestine that I have been describing. To what social level or social groups has Mark addressed his work?

In looking over the five lists of characters in Mark cited above, we can safely say that the narrative world that the author has produced accurately re-creates the sharply stratified peasant society. Of course, we must acknowledge that in the gospel we are not in the real world but rather are in a story world created by an author. At some points it corresponds with the real world of Jesus, while at others it certainly does not. Perhaps the same is true in relation to the real world of Mark, though the simple requirements of verisimilitude and relevance in literature that is designed to persuade make substantial overlap between Mark's story world and Mark's real world probable. In fact, it is safe to say that there is no real alternative. The "truth" of a text would be self-evident in large measure from the way it overlapped (or contravened) the real world. Trying to find contraventions or correspondences between the real world of social antagonisms described above and the story world of Mark is thus the only real choice we have for finding the social location of Mark's audience. Basically, of course, it will come down to a question of how high or low on the social scale we might imagine it to be. Space permits only the following observations.

Group Boundaries and Self-Definition

A good place to begin is with studies of boundary language that Mark uses to clarify the lines of demarcation between his own community and those outside (Neyrey 1991, 91–128). As Neyrey has suggested, the prevalent conflict between Jesus and the temple authorities and their representatives belies a certain defensiveness on Mark's part about both Jesus and his own community. Mark reports that Jesus is affirmed as the "Holy One of God" (1:24), but this view is not shared by his elite opponents. The standards by which they defined themselves as Israelite were disregarded by Jesus in every important respect. He repeatedly violated the purity rules regarding persons (1:41; 2:13–14; 4:35–42; 5:24–28; 5:41; 7:24–30; 7:31) by coming in contact with the diseased, the dead, the malformed,

and the possessed. He violated rules about the body (7:33; 8:23), about meal practice (6:37–44; 8:1–10), about times (2:24; 3:1–6), and about places (11:15–16; 12:33).
We are not surprised that in the controversy about the source of Jesus' power in
3:22–27 his opponents claim that his rule-breaking has its origin in Satan.

Mark's defense of Jesus is a spirited one, however, and one that simultaneously
functions as a form of self-definition for Mark's group. Mark asserts that appearances notwithstanding, Jesus' purity is affirmed by God in both his baptism (1:10–
11) and his transfiguration (9:2–8). He claims that the Scriptures offer justification
(2:25–26; 7:6; 10:5; 11:17) for Jesus' actions even though others judge them to be
purity violations. Mark's Jesus can therefore legitimately offer new purity rules
that imply that holiness is an internal matter of the heart rather than an external
one of protecting body surfaces and orifices (7:18–23). Confession of Jesus as the
Christ is the key (8:27–30). Moreover, as Neyrey (1991, 123) reminds us, membership criteria in the Jesus group differ from those of the synagogue, where blood,
physical, or genealogical concerns are paramount. Jesus' surrogate family is non-
biological and made up of believers: "Whoever does the will of God is my brother,
and sister, and mother" (3:35 RSV). By contrast, objection to Jesus' teachings or
practices (2:7; 7:1–4) or lack of belief in him (6:3–6) makes one an outsider.

The key point that Neyrey (1991, 122–23) makes in all this, however, is that
in constructing his defense for Jesus, Mark is engaged in defending his own community as well. "When Jesus crosses boundaries and when he allows unclean
people to contact him, this polluting activity functions in Mark vis-à-vis the in-
clusive membership of Mark's church. Marginal and unclean Israelites as well as
Gentiles are welcome in God's new covenant group" (Neyrey 1991, 124). It is a
group that includes all those unholy types with whom Jesus interacted and who
in their own communities can be defended as a part of the people of God in the
same way that Jesus himself is defended in the narrative (Myers 1988, 35–36).

Focus on boundary definition is important in one additional way. As White
(1991, 221–28) has shown in a study of Matthew, boundary definition is especially important for communities caught in conflict or crisis. Definition draws
the lines between insiders and outsiders, loyalists and opponents. Thus Myers has
argued that in the crisis of the impending Jewish-Roman war, groups in the bor-
der areas of upper Galilee and southern Syria were being forced to define and declare themselves in the emerging dispute. The thesis by Myers (1988, 323–28) that
Mark 13 describes the situation just prior to the war when Christians might be
handed over to councils and beaten in synagogues in an attempt to force them to
declare for one side or the other is perhaps open to scholarly debate (see also Marcus 1992, 453). But surely he is correct that the Markan community was caught in
a crisis that required struggling on two fronts. Reconciliation of Jew and Gentile
was opposed by Pharisees on purity grounds and encouraged by Romans on imperialistic grounds. Christians choosing reconciliation, but on pointedly nonim-
perialistic grounds, understandably engaged the wrath of both sides (Myers 1988,
224, 226, 228–30). Thus, as Myers suggests, something like the dilemma posed
over taxes to Caesar in 12:13–17 may have been precisely the crisis facing the

community for which Mark wrote. Were they on the side of Caesar or the side of God? To many Jews or Romans, those seemed to be the only two alternatives.

Important as these studies of purity and boundaries are, however, they tend to miss a critical fact of peasant life. Jesus may have been seen as unholy and unwashed by the religious elite, and his behavior may have seemed to them iconoclastic or even perverse. To a peasant, however, it would have been nothing out of the ordinary at all. Very few peasants could maintain the Great Tradition even if they wanted to. They came in constant contact with bodily secretions, dead animals, and unwashed food. They could not always afford to keep the Sabbaths and holy days, for in dry-land farming with marginal or uneven rainfall, each day that passes between the first rains and plowing reduces the final yields. Nor could they always afford the prescribed sacrifices or guarantee the cleanliness of meal companions. We must note, therefore, that the rules that the Markan Jesus breaks having to do with dietary laws, washing, Sabbath observance, and temple sacrifice are precisely those that peasants had the most difficulty keeping. Jesus' lifestyle would thus have been familiar to them in every respect. His defense of an internal purity that could be maintained without heavy expense or the disruption of necessary peasant farming practices would have surprised them indeed, but his lifestyle as such would not. Thus if Mark's Jesus is also defending Mark's community, what is really being provided is a statement that purity before God is possible within the limits of a peasant way of life.

Character of the Folkloric Tradition

The social level of Mark's audience can be inferred in yet another way. Attempting to correlate Mark's audience (as opposed to the author himself) with the social elite of his story world would make it extremely difficult to explain the characteristics of the folkloric tradition in the way Mark has chosen to perpetuate it. We may take for granted that Mark is not simply a passive purveyor of what has come down to him. He is a creative author. Nonetheless, as Robbins (1984, 8) has shown, the so-called minor forms (much studied by form critics) received by Mark are folkloric in character, and as a form of oft-repeated tradition, they functioned to create social cohesion in the Markan community. They did so by articulating conflicts and antagonisms felt by members of the group who still perceived themselves to be victims of the adversaries in the story. By portraying the attitudes of the elite toward Jesus as defeats and the responses of the degraded as victories, Mark creates a story that could be used to perpetuate identity, to educate children and new members, and to ensure conformity to the group's own norms in contrast to those of their opponents.

It could be objected, of course, that the negative examples of the elite in the story world and the contrasting actions of Jesus to rescue the weak are being held up as a form of social criticism aimed at elite members of Mark's audience. That is certainly possible, though a narrative plotted to achieve that effect is much more evident in Luke than in Mark. Indeed, Luke's reshaping of the Markan tradition makes such a shift in social location (and thus audience) quite clear (Rohrbaugh

1991). Thus we are left to conclude that Mark's particular way of telling this story implies a group of readers who will celebrate the victories of the weak and the defeats of the strong, who find mirrored in the characters of the story and the events that engulf them the dramas of their own lives.

We have already noted the widespread agreement that this is true in at least one important respect: Mark's disciples are representative of Mark's audience (Tannehill 1977; Dewey 1989; Malbon 1986). As we have seen above, this group is low on the social scale indeed. Yet focus on the disciples alone would be a bit narrow from our point of view since other characters play such important roles in the social drama as well. Malbon (1986) has shown, for example, that the "crowd" in Mark shares many of the same responses to Jesus as are identified for the disciples. In fact, all characters are important, as Weeden (1971, 13–19) has demonstrated in collecting evidence on the centrality of characterization as the basis for moral instruction in first-century C.E. literary creations. Thus the drama being played out by the characters in Mark's story mirrors what the author is commending or condemning for his own audience and thereby signals their social location indirectly.

Studies of both the implied reader and the omniscient narrator of Mark confirm this same judgement (Rhoads and Michie 1982, 35–43). The disciple outside the story (reader/hearer) is invited to respond to the interactions of Jesus and his upper-class antagonists in ways commended by the story, though of course with the benefit of considerably more insight provided by the narrator than is available to the disciples inside the story. As the plot line returns again and again to the disturbing inability of the disciples and others to grasp what Jesus was doing and saying, it evokes a similar disturbance for the reader (Waetjen 1989, 16–26). "Insider" explanations offered to the disciples inside the story (4:10–34; 8:16–21) are only partially successful, and the disciples abandon Jesus in the end. Will the disciple/reader outside the story do the same?

Perhaps. But Mark's gospel also celebrates the many victories of faith on the part of peasants, the degraded, the unclean, and expendables. There are so many of these people that they crowd Jesus repeatedly. They are key actors on Mark's stage. And as the narrator often points out (e.g., 5:20; 6:2; 7:37; 12:34), they are frequently astonished by two things: Jesus' healing power, of which they are the principal beneficiaries, and his ability to defeat his elite adversaries at every turn in the story. Such developments in the social drama of the narrative engender expectations and promises in the life of the real reader as well. In fact, given the numbers of such low-class and degraded people who were inevitably a part of Mark's real world, if high expectations and promise for just that kind of people were not essence of the story, it could hardly have been termed "good news."

BIBLIOGRAPHY

Beavis, Mary Ann. 1989. *Mark's Audience: The Literary and Social Setting of Mark 4:11–12.* Journal for the Study of the New Testament: Supplement Series 33. Sheffield: Sheffield Academic Press.

Botha, P. J. J. 1991. Mark's Story as Oral Literature: Rethinking the Transmission of Some Traditions about Jesus. *Hervormde teologiese studies* 47:304–31.

Broshi, Magen. 1989. The Diet of Palestine in the Roman Period—Introductory Notes. *The Israel Museum Journal* 5:41–56.

Brunt, Peter. 1977. Josephus on Social Conflicts in Roman Judea. *Klio* 59:149–53.

Byung-mu, Ahn. 1981. Jesus and the Minjung in the Gospel of Mark. Pages 138–152 in *Minjung Theology: People as the Subjects of History.* Maryknoll, N.Y.: Orbis.

Carney, Thomas F. 1975. *The Shape of the Past: Models and Antiquity.* Lawrence, Kans.: Coronado.

Corley, Kathleen. 1994. *Private Women, Public Meals: Social Conflict and Women in the Synoptic Tradition.* Peabody, Mass.: Hendrickson.

Dewey, Joanna. 1989. Oral Methods of Structuring Narrative in Mark. *Interpretation* 43:32–44.

Duling, Dennis. 1994. *The New Testament: An Introduction.* New York: Harcourt, Brace, Jovanovich.

Fiensy, David A. 1991. *The Social History of Palestine in the Herodian Period: The Land Is Mine.* Studies in the Bible and Early Christianity 20. Lewiston, N.Y.: Mellen.

Goodman, Martin. 1982. The First Jewish Revolt: Social Conflict and the Problem of Debt. *Journal of Jewish Studies* 33:417–27.

Hanson, Ann E. 1991. Ancient Illiteracy. Pages 159–71 in *Literacy in the Roman World.* Edited by J. H. Humphrey. Journal of Roman Archaeology: Supplementary Series 3. Ann Arbor: Department of Classical Studies, University of Michigan.

Harris, William V. 1989. *Ancient Literacy.* Cambridge, Mass.: Harvard University Press.

Hengel, Martin. 1984. Entstehungzeit und Situation des Markusevangeliums. Pages 1–45 in *Markus-Philologie: Historische, literargeschichtliche und stilistische Untersuchungen zum zweiten Evangelium.* Edited by H. Cancik. Wissenschaftliche Untersuchungen zum Neuen Testament 33. Tübingen: Mohr Siebeck.

Hezser, Catherine. 2001. *Jewish Literacy in Roman Palestine.* Texte und Studien zum antiken Judentum 81. Tübingen: Mohr Siebeck.

Horsfall, Nicholas. 1991. Statistics or States of Mind? Pages 59–76 in *Literacy in the Roman World.* Edited by J. H. Humphrey. Journal of Roman Archaeology: Supplementary Series 3. Ann Arbor: Department of Classical Studies, University of Michigan.

Horsley, Richard. 1989. *Sociology and the Jesus Movement.* New York: Crossroad.

Horsley, Richard, and John Hanson. 1985. *Bandits, Prophets, and Messiahs: Popular Movements in the Time of Jesus.* Minneapolis: Winston.

Hunt, A. S., and C. C. Edgar. 1934. *Non-literary Papyri: Public Documents.* Vol. 2 of *Select Papyri.* Loeb Classical Library. London: Heinemann.

Kee, Howard C. 1977. *Community of the New Age: Studies in Mark's Gospel.* Philadelphia: Westminster.

Lenski, Gerhard, and Jean Lenski. 1974. *Human Societies: An Introduction to Macrosociology*. New York: McGraw-Hill.

Lührmann, D. 1987. *Das Markusevangelium*. Handbuch zum Neuen Testament 3. Tübingen: Mohr-Siebeck.

Malbon, Elizabeth Struthers. 1986. Disciples/Crowds/Whoever: Markan Characters and Readers. *Novum Testamentum* 28:104–30.

———. 1989. The Jewish Leaders in the Gospel of Mark: A Literary Study of Marcan Characterization. *Journal of Biblical Literature* 108:259–81.

Marcus, Joel. 1992. The Jewish War and the *Sitz im Leben* of Mark. *Journal of Biblical Literature* 3:441–62.

Myers, Ched. 1988. *Binding the Strong Man: A Political Reading of Mark's Story of Jesus*. Maryknoll, N.Y.: Orbis.

Neyrey, Jerome. 1991. The Idea of Purity in Mark's Gospel. Pages 91–128 in *Social-Scientific Criticism of the New Testament and Its Social World*. Edited by John H. Elliott. Semeia 35. Decatur, Ga.: Scholars Press.

Oakman, Douglas E. 1986. *Jesus and the Economic Questions of His Day*. Studies in the Bible and Early Christianity 8. Lewiston, N.Y.: Mellen.

———. 1991. The Countryside in Luke-Acts. Pages 151–79 in *The Social World of Luke-Acts: Models for Interpretation*. Edited by Jerome Neyrey. Peabody, Mass.: Hendrickson.

Orton, David E. 1989. *The Understanding Scribe: Matthew and the Apocalyptic Ideal*. Journal for the Study of the New Testament: Supplement Series 25. Sheffield: Sheffield Academic Press.

Pilch, John J. 1991. Sickness and Healing in Luke-Acts. Pages 181–209 in *The Social World of Luke-Acts: Models for Interpretation*. Edited by Jerome Neyrey. Peabody, Mass.: Hendrickson.

Rhoads, David, and Donald Michie. 1982. *Mark as Story: An Introduction to the Narrative of a Gospel*. Philadelphia: Fortress.

Robbins,Vernon K. 1984. *Jesus the Teacher: A Socio-Rhetorical Interpretation of Mark*. Philadelphia: Fortress.

Rohrbaugh, Richard L. 1987. "Social Location of Thought" as a Heuristic Construct in New Testament Study. *Journal for the Study of the New Testament* 30:103–19.

———. 1991. The Preindustrial City in Luke-Acts: Urban Social Relations. Pages 125–50 in *The Social World of Luke-Acts: Models for Interpretation*. Edited by Jerome H. Neyrey, SJ. Peabody, Mass.: Hendrickson.

Saldarini, Anthony J. 1988. The Social Class of the Pharisees in Mark. Pages 69–77 in *The Social World of Formative Christianity and Judaism: Essays in Tribute to Howard Clark Kee*. Edited by Jacob Neusner et al. Philadelphia: Fortress.

Senior, Donald. 1987. "With Swords and Clubs . . ."—The Setting of Mark's Community and His Critique of Abusive Power. *Biblical Theology Bulletin* 17:10–20.

Tannehill, Robert. 1977. The Disciples in Mark: The Function of a Narrative Role. *Journal of Religion* 57:386–405.

Theissen, Gerd. 1984. Lokal-und Sozialkolorit in der Geschichte von der sy-
     rophönikischen Frau (Mk 7:24–30). *Zeitschrift für die neutestamentliche
     Wissenschaft* 75:202–25.
——. 1991. *The Gospels in Context: Social and Political History in the Synoptic
     Tradition.* Translated by Linda M. Maloney. Minneapolis: Fortress.
Waetjen, Herman C. 1989. A Reordering of Power: A Sociopolitical Reading of
     Mark's Gospel. Minneapolis: Fortress.
Weeden, Theodore. 1971. *Mark: Traditions in Conflict.* Philadelphia: Fortress.
White, L. Michael. 1991. Crisis Management and Boundary Maintenance. Pages
     211–47 in *Social History of the Matthean Community: Cross-Disciplinary Ap-
     proaches.* Edited by David L. Balch. Minneapolis: Fortress.
Wright, A. 1982. The Widow's Mite: Praise or Lament? A Matter of Context.
     Catholic Biblical Quarterly 44:256–65.
Zias, Joseph. 1991. Death and Disease in Ancient Israel. *Biblical Archaeologist*
     54(3):146–59.

Gender

9

Gender everywhere is culturally defined; that is, it is socially constructed. Every culture, in every time, has a distinct concept of what sorts of behaviors and attitudes should be expressed by males and by females. These cultural mores and expectatations are taught to children and enforced by adults.

The world behind the New Testament was highly gender-divided. We possess many examples from ancient sources (see Neyrey 2003, 44–45). Here we look at one, from the Greek historian and philosopher Xenophon (ca. 431–355 B.C.E.):

> Human beings live not in open air but need shelter. To fill the covered place, persons are needed to work at the open-air occupations (plowing, sowing, planting and grazing) which supply the needed food. When this is stored in the covered place, there is need for someone to keep it and to work at what must be done under cover. Cover is needed for the nursing of infants, the making of corn into bread, and the manufacture of clothing from wool. . . . God from the first adapted the woman's nature to the indoor and man's to the outdoor tasks and cares. (*Oec.* 7.19–22)

This description helps us understand that in this ancient worldview (1) *space* is gender-divided (male = open air, outdoor, fields and pasture; female = covered, indoor, places for household duties); (2) *tasks* are gender divided (male = plowing, sowing, planting; female = nurturing of children, food preparation, clothing production); Xenophon does not say this, but it follows that (3) *tools* and *animals* are also gender-specific (male = plows, pruning and harvesting cycles, plow animals and sheep; female = loom, pots and pans, milking goats). Similar traditions can be found in Philo's *Spec. Laws* 3.169 and Clement's *Misc.* 2.23.146.

In addition to the physical division, the New Testament world had a clear gender division on the attributes of men and women. Males were socialized to procreate, to be courageous, obedient, protective, and eager to increase the family's reputation or wealth. Females, on the other hand, were virtuous if they remained sexually exclusive, submissive to their fathers and then their husbands, defensive of their own and their family's reputation. This social world has a sexual double standard: males gain respect for sexual aggression, whereas females' virtue resides in sexual exclusivity.

This chapter leads the reader more closely into the social construction of the male gender—the world of fathers, sons, and brothers. Only after understanding the socialization of males, and so the cultural expectation of them, can we fully appreciate what Jesus means when he says, "Call no man 'father,'" when he seems to reject patriarchal authority, and when he advocates a world were honor comes from giving, not taking.

S. Scott Bartchy

Who Should Be Called "Father"? Paul of Tarsus between the Jesus Tradition and Patria Potestas

INTRODUCTION

WHO SHOULD BE called "father"? What an odd question. Does not everyone in every culture grow up calling the male who begot them their linguistic equivalent of "father"? In the world of Jesus and Paul the term *father* included reference not only to one's male blood progenitors, and perhaps to one's fathers' fathers, but also to the emperor at Rome, the *pater patriae,* the "father of the fatherland." This title, as Purcell observes, "was eloquently suggestive of the protecting but coercive authority of the *paterfamilias*" (1996, 1121).

In Roman culture this nearly absolute, coercive authority was called *patria potestas,* which in its range included the father's power of life and death over his children, beginning in infancy when a father chose to acknowledge and rear a child or "expose" it—that is, throw the child away. The second-century-C.E. Roman jurist Gaius noted, "There are virtually no other peoples who have such power over their children as we have" (*Inst.* 1.55). From ancient republican times Roman fathers had been permitted by law to sell their sons into slavery, as many as three times. Yet during the empire, paternal monopoly on the control of property probably influenced the behavior of sons and daughters more than their fathers' legal right to execute them. Nevertheless, paternal moderation, even toward serious filial misbehavior, was praised as a virtue. And family affection and genuine respect could motivate the obedience of children, as Hallett (1984) has especially documented for Roman daughters. However the children were motivated, their father was to be obeyed absolutely; and the deeply felt appropriateness of this demand was rooted in Roman male ideology, according to which children, slaves, and women lacked full powers of judgment.

Thus grown daughters and sons usually were bound by their father's authority until he died. Until then, they could own no property, and any of their earnings or gifts that they received belonged by law to their father. His consent was necessary for the marriage of both sons and daughters, and he could coerce a divorce. In the *sine manu* form of marriage that prevailed from the late republic on into the empire, the wife remained under the authority of her father. Ovid (*Fast.* 6.219ff.) called attention to the importance Roman fathers placed on obtaining husbands for their daughters. Yet once such fathers were successful in this regard, legislation by Augustus guaranteed that these fathers retained considerably more authority over their married daughters than their husbands could have. This fact will be particularly relevant later when I invite you to reconsider Paul's words in 1 Cor 7. Who should be called "father"? What a silly question!

FILIAL PIETY AND THE AUTHORITY OF FATHERS

Patriarchy is frequently but inadequately defined solely as male domination of females. Yet patriarchal social codes are enforced beyond the household by the actions of men who seek to acquire more honor by dominating as many other *men* as possible. Men were brought up to gain honor for themselves precisely by dominating as many others as they can, both men and women. And the lessons in such domination began in the home. Sons raised to be absolutely obedient to their fathers grew up anticipating that they, in turn, would become patriarchs who would appropriately demand such obedience from everyone in their own families. Thus a boy was raised to be aggressive, to demonstrate self-mastery, and not only to look forward to being served by his wife, children, and slaves, but also to expect deference from other males.

Boys trained to be obedient sons became loyal political subjects who were indeed subject to the ruling powers. For such sons, calling the Roman emperor "father" fit well with their common sense of how the world worked. Thus any in-depth understanding of patriarchy in the Roman Empire or any society must begin with an analysis of male socialization and the power arrangements valued among men. Across all social classes, traditional male socialization programmed males to pursue a never-ending quest for honor and influence, including fathers arranging their children's marriages, so that the honor of their families would be enhanced. Hence most descriptions of ancient patriarchy are incomplete because they disregard this systemic quest for honor by competition among men and the resulting domination of males by other males. By ignoring this, scholars blind themselves to one of the most interesting countercultural challenges on which Paul agreed with Jesus.

JUDEAN PATRIARCHY

In all the cultures around the ancient Mediterranean, including the one in which Jesus grew up, a father's honor depended on the unquestioning, faithful filial piety of his sons and daughters. Thus in Proverbs, a father exhorts his son, "Let your heart hold fast my words; keep my commandments, and live" (4:4 RSV). Israelite tradition included draconian warnings for sons whose behavior shamed their fathers:

> If someone has a stubborn and rebellious son who will not obey his father and mother, who does not heed them when they discipline him, then his father and his mother

shall take hold of him and bring him out to the elders of his town at the gate of that place. They shall say to the elders of his town, "This son of ours is stubborn and rebellious. He will not obey us. He is a glutton and a drunkard." Then all the men of the town shall stone him to death. So you shall purge the evil from your midst; and all Israel will hear, and be afraid. (Deut 21:18–21 NRSV)

In the rhetoric of this passage this son is called "stubborn and rebellious" not because he was a literal glutton and a drunkard but rather because his behavior demonstrated lack of filial piety shamed his parents. In Israel's wisdom tradition children were taught that "a wise child loves the discipline of his father" (Prov 13:1) and "those who respect their father will have long life . . . they will serve their parents as their masters" (Sir 3:6 NRSV). Reciprocally, parents were taught that "when the father dies, he will not seem to be dead, for he has left behind him one like himself" [namely, his obedient son] (Sir 30:4 NRSV).

In striking contrast to the positive emphasis on family loyalty and obedience that has persisted in most if not all cultures throughout millennia, Jesus of Nazareth, in the name of Israel's God, called for an absolute break with such filial piety and initiated potential conflict between a son and his father. Jesus' sharp challenge to the authority of earthly fathers was an essential first step toward implementing his redefinition of three related concepts: power, honor, and family.

According to the historical Jesus, the aspect of God's power that human beings should imitate must result in empowerment of others, which stands in striking contrast to the understanding of power on which every patriarchal system is based: domination. In astonishing contradiction to the values that they had been taught since childhood, men should seek to acquire honor by giving honor to others rather than seeking endlessly to take it away from others. The family has been restructured as a human group living as brothers and sisters without an earthly father, bound together by their common commitment to doing the will of God as revealed by Jesus.

Jesus' Challenge to Filial Piety and the Authority of Fathers

Consider briefly what are arguably the most offensive, the most misinterpreted, the most subtle, and the most antipatriarchal passages in the gospel traditions: "I have come to set a man against his father" (Matt 10:35 NRSV). To modern ears, perhaps the most offensive, antifamily Jesus tradition is this statement: "Whoever comes to me and does not hate father and mother, wife and children, brothers and sisters, yes, and even life itself, cannot be my disciple" (Luke 14:26 NRSV). Even the less strident version in Matt 10:37 sounds disturbingly opposed to traditional family values: "Whoever loves father or mother more than me is not worthy of me; and whoever loves son or daughter more than me is not worthy of me" (NRSV). Indeed, according to Matthew, Jesus introduced this challenge with this assertion: "Do not think that I have come to bring peace to the earth; I have not come to bring peace, but a sword. For I have come to set a man against his father, and a daughter against her mother, and a daughter-in-law against her mother-in-law; and one's foes will be members of one's own household" (10:34– 36 NRSV). The *Gospel of Thomas* attests to this tradition in two passages in almost identical words: "Whoever does not hate father and mother cannot be my disciple" (55:1; 101:1). The first passage continues, "Whoever does not hate brothers and sisters, and carry the cross as I do, will not be worthy of me" (55:2). Is there a stronger challenge to blood-family ties?

Scholars insist that here the Greek verb μισέω ("hate") does not mean what it seems to mean. Jesus is not cultivating a negative emotion among his followers but rather is challenging them to make a hard choice. "In this context, hate is not primarily an affective quality but a disavowal of primary allegiance to ones kin, a courageous distancing themselves from the high cultural value placed on their family network" (Green 1997, 565). "Hate" means a rejection of filial piety.

The Greatest Offense to Filial Piety?

The most misinterpreted sentence on Jesus' lips in this connection is his response to a would-be follower who temporized Jesus' challenge to join his group with the plea that he first be permitted to go home and bury his father. According to both Matthew (8:22) and Luke (9:60), Jesus replied with one of the most breathtaking rejections of traditional family values coming to us from antiquity: "Let the dead bury their own dead" (NRSV)! In the judgment of Hengel (1981, 14) there is hardly one logion from Jesus that more sharply runs counter to law, piety, and custom.

The argument by McCane (1990) that this saying refers not to the initial burial but rather to the reburial of the person's bones in an ossuary is unpersuasive. In view of the solemn obligation in filial piety for the son to assure that his father receive a dignified burial, it is much more likely that this would-be disciple of Jesus was saying, "I need to go home and serve and support my father until he dies, and I have buried him. Then I will return to follow you." Only years after reaching this conclusion did I discover that Kenneth Bailey, one of the first scholars to stress the importance of Mediterranean cultural values for understanding the Gospels, had also observed that the potential disciple's request to bury his father expressed the son's duty to obey his father until his father's death and fitting interment (Bailey 1980, 26–27).

The young man had been taught that the fifth commandment, "Honor your father and mother," obligated him at the minimum to support his father materially in his old age and to give him an honorable burial. Jesus seemed to be aware that this young man would never be able to escape the family obligations that would be heaped upon him if he returned to his father's house. His father was a patriarch; the young man had been socialized to become a patriarch himself. And after his father's death and proper burial, all those around the young man would expect him to act like a patriarch—otherwise, he would risk being dishonored and bringing shame upon his family.

No Traditional Fathers Needed When God's Will Is Done

The most subtle and easily overlooked elimination of earthly fathers from the ideal society in which God alone is ruling is found in this exchange between Peter and Jesus in Mark 10:28–31: "Peter began to say to him, 'Look, we have left everything and followed you.' Jesus said, 'Truly I tell you, there is no one who has left house or brothers or sisters or mother or father or children or fields . . . who will not receive a hundredfold now in this age—houses, brothers and sisters, mothers and children, and fields with persecutions—and in the age to come eternal life'" (NRSV). Notice that fathers are not included in the second half of the parallel-constructed saying by Jesus. Is this an oversight?

Lohfink comments, "The question would have to be left unanswered if other texts did not show that the absence of any reference to fathers is anything but coincidence or forgetfulness. Fathers are deliberately not mentioned . . . they are too symbolic of patriarchal domination" (1982, 45 [see also Dewey 1994, 478–79]). Part of the good news is that there are no fathers but God in Jesus' vision. And Mark emphasizes that these "fatherless" families are gifts of God that are given now, already in the present time, not some indefinite future. With the absence of "fathers" goes the transcendence of domination: "But many who are first will be last, and the last will be first" (Mark 10:31). Similarly, Schüssler Fiorenza (1983, 148) comments that Jesus' paradoxical exhortation in Mark 10:15 to "receive the rule of God like a child" (or "slave") is not an invitation to childlike innocence and naïveté but rather a challenge to relinquish all claims of power and domination over others.

Now Only God Is "Father"

Jesus' most startling challenge to patriarchal authority is found in Matthew: "Call no man 'father' on earth, for you have one Father—the one in heaven" (Matt 23:9). The context for this saying is provided by Matthew, who may have especially prized it because of its reference to God as Father, a favorite theme in his gospel. But there is little question that the core of the saying came from the historical Jesus. Schüssler Fiorenza (1983, 150) suggests that the original form of the saying may have read, "Call no one father, for you have one father (and you are all siblings)." By it, Jesus declared that his followers should not and need not address anyone but the God of Israel as "father." Neyrey comments that there is a stream of material in Matthew that "replaces the sense of loyalty and faithfulness owed parents with that owed God-Father"; however unjust this appeared to outsiders, "Matthew portrays Jesus pursuing a different kind of justice, placing the interests of his heavenly Father over those of earthly parents" (1998, 114).

After challenging all to reject the authority and protection of their blood fathers, Jesus invited his followers to join him in a sense of intimacy with God as their only true "father." Jesus addressed the God of Israel as his αββα, thereby employing the common way children were taught to address their fathers with respect throughout their lives. Now only God is addressed as αββα, stripping the legitimation from existing patriarchal institutions and implicitly undermining all relationships of domination. No one, male or female, among Jesus' followers could then claim the authority of a father in the Jesus movement, because such authority now belonged to God alone. But by reserving the title "father" for God alone, Jesus did not at all intend for God to be conceived as a dominating patriarch; rather, as Jesus' words and actions made clear, God's fatherly care was quite motherly when measured by Mediterranean cultural stereotypes.

Paul's Challenge to Filial Piety and the Authority of Fathers

Anyone alarmed by Jesus' exhortation to "call no man 'father' on earth" would have found scant comfort in the writings and actions of his messenger Paul of Tarsus, who sought in a variety of ways to put into effect Jesus' strategy of undermining the authority of the patriarchal family. For both Jesus and Paul, rejecting both the obligations of blood ties and the venerable traditions that reinforced those relationships was the first step toward their creating a new kind of family: faith-related brothers and sisters, without a traditional father.

Paul wrote in direct continuity with the historical Jesus' focus on God as father, frequently referring to God as "our father" and "the father." For example, the greeting "Peace from God our Father" appears in almost all Paul's letters. In 1 Cor 8:6 God is identified as "the Father": "For us there is one God, the Father, from whom are all things and for whom we exist." And Paul's use of the phrase "Abba! Father!" in Gal 4:6 and Rom 8:15 provides another striking connection to the Jesus tradition, since the Aramaic term almost certainly was a characteristic prayer form used by Jesus himself.

To be sure, no pithy statement like "call no man 'father'" appears in Paul's writings. Yet there is much evidence that he could take for granted that his early audiences had indeed rejected filial piety and no longer thought of themselves as living under the authority of their fathers—or of their husbands, or of their owners. Paul assumed that they could and should make important decisions without consideration of family traditions, filial piety, and the constraints of patriarchal authority. And by acting on this assumption, Paul followed Jesus' innovative and controversial strategy of rejecting the obligations of filial piety.

1 Corinthians 7

Paul's line of argument in 1 Corinthians assumes that adult children without their parents, wives without their husbands, and slaves without their owners have become members of the house churches in Corinth. Throughout the letter Paul addressed all the "holy ones" in Corinth as if they no longer had any obligations of filial piety. Chapter 7 begins with a striking subversion of traditional patriarchal authority in marriage.

Paul urged followers of Christ who are married to understand that the husband belongs to the wife in exactly the same way as the wife belongs to the husband, with the consequence that decisions regarding their sexual life together are to be made by mutual agreement rather than by patriarchal fiat. In his words, "The husband should give to his wife her conjugal rights, and likewise the wife to her husband. For the wife does not have authority over her own body, but the husband does; likewise (ὁμοίως ['in the very same way']) the husband does not have authority over his own body, but the wife does. Do not deprive one another except perhaps by agreement (ἐκ συμφώνου ['with one voice together'])" (1 Cor 7:3–5 NRSV). Some modern readers wish that Paul had gone even further and completely avoided using the language of "authority over." What is truly striking is that he showed no respect for one of the primary codes of first-century-C.E. life, taken for granted by both men and women: a woman's body belonged to her husband, period.

More directly to the point regarding respect for a father's authority, all the advice that Paul gave regarding marriage assumes that his readers would respond with decisions made without respect to their blood family's interests or wishes. How truly astonishing in light of the cultural values of the ancient Mediterranean world, where, in the words of Hanson, marriage was "a social contract negotiated between families, with economic, religious, and (occasionally) political implications that went far beyond the interests of sexuality, relationship, and reproduction" (1996, 69). Marriage rarely was arranged by individuals apart from their fathers' interests and authority.

In the world of both Jesus and Paul, when a woman married, her status changed from being embedded in her blood-family's honor and living under the authority, legal responsibility, and care of her father to being similarly embedded in her husband's honor, even if not also in his authority. Yet throughout 1 Cor 7 Paul wrote to the unmarried, male and female, as if each of them would make decisions independently about refraining from marriage or entering into it. Note carefully that Paul gave this advice to both women and men, assuming here and throughout this chapter their equality in moral responsibility and decision-making. Instead of directing his words primarily or exclusively to the men, twelve times Paul strikingly alternates between the men and the women, his "brothers and sisters" (7:15). As Fee correctly concludes, "in every case there is complete mutuality between the two sexes" (1987, 270). Furthermore, in every case Paul addresses both the men and the women as moral agents who are free to act apart from the authority of their fathers or concerns of their blood families.

When Paul then addressed the case of a woman in Corinth who had left her husband, he neither chided her for having rejected the authority of her husband nor advised her to return to the authority of her father (7:11), both of whom surely were shamed by her actions. Not even Paul's awareness of a command from Jesus opposing divorce led him to suggest in her case that family piety was more important than her freedom in Christ. The only condition that he mentioned was that she should be reconciled to her husband, if she chose again to live a married life. With such advice, Paul risked provoking the resentment and retaliation of non-Christian husbands and fathers.

Roman men, in particular, were hostile to non-Roman religious groups by which their wives and daughters were drawn away from the family religion, bringing shame upon their blood kin. Thus the late first-century moralist Plutarch (45–125 C.E.) gave this advice to married couples:

> A wife ought not to make friends of her own, but to enjoy her husband's friends in common with him. The gods are the first and most important friends. Wherefore it is becoming for a wife to worship and to know only the gods that her husband believes in, and to shut the front door tight upon all queer rituals and outlandish superstitions. (*Conj. praec.* 140D)

In this strongly male-oriented context, in which a wife was expected to worship only the gods her husband honored, Paul's advice for women who had become "sisters in Christ" without their husbands must have shocked and often angered these as-yet pagan husbands. Furthermore, in 1 Cor 7:12–16 Paul not only confirmed these married "sisters" in their own, independent religious status but also turned traditional cultural values upside down by asserting the power of these women to determine the spiritual ambiance of their marriages (see 7:13–15). All aspects of his advice are based on a truly astonishing rejection of the expectations that every male brought to his marriage; it directly challenged the religious dominance that every husband assumed would be his throughout his marriage. David Daube, a distinguished Jewish scholar of Roman and biblical law, refers to Paul's counsel here as "a momentous *novum*" and suggests that Paul revealed his clear awareness of his own radicality when he painstakingly stated everything that he had to say twice, once for the man, and once for the woman (Daube 1971, 240).

At the end of 1 Cor 7 Paul then advised widows that they were free to marry anyone they wished as long as they chose a partner who was "in the Lord" (7:31). Paul made no reference to the widow's obligation under the law of guardianship, *tutela mulierum*, to consult blood kin, to consider their interests, or to obey the family's wishes regarding remarriage. More than a few women may well have felt encouraged by Paul's counsel to ignore the continuing authority and interests of their fathers, or of their other kin if their father had already died. Consistent with Paul's advice throughout chapter 7, filial piety and patriarchal authority were once again simply ignored as relevant cultural values for those who were following Jesus.

Questioning Our Assumptions

When warning the Corinthians against being "mismatched with unbelievers" (2 Cor 6:14), Paul assumed that they could and would respond without reference to the obligations of filial piety. Here, as in 1 Corinthians, Paul addressed each follower of Christ, without respect to sex or social status, as individual moral agents, as decision-makers, no longer imbedded in the honor of their blood families, no longer restrained by the social codes rooted in traditional family values.

Largely overlooked is the fact that Paul's encouragement of sexual celibacy for both men and women in 1 Cor 7 seriously challenged the authority of parents, in particular of fathers, to arrange their children's marriages. Giving such counsel to marriageable women would have been regarded as scandalous, especially by their fathers, whose reputations were at stake when planning a "good marriage" for their daughters. Was not a major value of a daughter her potential for bringing honor to her father and the entire family by joyfully entering the marriage that her father arranged? Yet Paul took no notice of a father's interest, rights, or honor when he wrote to those daughters who had become followers of Christ in Corinth. In Paul's eyes, they had become empowered to marry or not, as they chose. And he urged women as well as men to join him in his own celibate state, if they were so "gifted" (see 7:7), for the purpose of joining with him in undistracted service in Christ (see 7:32–35).

But Was Paul Himself Called "Father"?

Joubert argued that Paul saw himself as the *paterfamilias* of the Christian household group in Corinth: "Even when Paul did not make explicit use of familial concepts, he acted out typical role expectations associated with that of a *paterfamilias* and at the same time also conferred the role of 'children' upon the Corinthians" (1995, 218). Joubert concludes that "Paul's interaction with the Corinthians was to a large extent focused on their recognition and acceptance of his patriarchal authority" (1995, 222). Observe, however, that in the context of the patriarchal culture in which Paul was raised and then worked as an adult, it surely is remarkable that he avoided using the term *father* for any of the leaders in house churches that he founded. Never did he refer to members of his communities, even mature ones, as "mothers" or "fathers" of the faithful. In almost every case, Paul echoed the historical Jesus in reserving the term *father* for Israel's God alone. And in tune with the Jesus tradition, God's authority takes clear precedence over any biological father.

Paul's personal example provided a striking contrast. He wrote, "When reviled, we bless; when persecuted, we endure; when slandered, we speak kindly. We have become like the rubbish of the world, the dregs of all things, to this very day" (1 Cor 4:12–13 NRSV). In 1 Cor 4:15–16 he implored these "kings": "In Christ Jesus I became your father through the gospel. I appeal to you, then, be imitators of me" (NRSV). The behavior to which he directly referred for emulation focused on his nonauthoritarian, nonretaliatory response to these many experiences of humiliation and dishonor in his life as a "servant of Christ and steward of God's mysteries" (4:1). This is neither the attitude nor the behavior of a person inclined to perpetuate patriarchal privileges and values!

"With a Stick"?

So what are we to make of his words in 1 Cor 4:21: "What would you prefer? Am I to come to you with a stick, or with love in a spirit of gentleness?" (NRSV). First we should keep the immediate context in mind, remembering that he was still seeking somehow to persuade the "spiritual kings" in Corinth to repent of their arrogance. And this sentence reveals Paul's ongoing dilemma as he sought to resocialize his converts, especially the males among them. To speak without the domineering tone that they had been brought up to respect invited disdain for Paul's person and dismissal of his radical message of God's reversal of patriarchal values. His attempts to appeal to them "by the meekness and gentleness of Christ" (2 Cor 10:1 NRSV) had often fallen on deaf ears, as his line of argument in 2 Cor 10–13 amply verifies. Those competitors for influence among the Corinthians, whom Paul designated "super-apostles," "false apostles and deceitful workers," operated according to long-familiar social codes. They boasted of their personal accomplishments (10:12–11:18), sought to take advantage of their hearers by creating dependency relationships, and demanded to be given honor.

In direct and astonishing contrast, Paul had previously urged his readers to become "imitators of me, as I am of Christ" (1 Cor 11:1 NRSV)—that is, in "not seeking my own advantage but that of many, so that they may be saved" (1 Cor 10:33 NRSV). Paul sought to persuade the Corinthians who were "wise, powerful, and of noble birth" (as he refers to them in 1 Cor 1:26) to surrender their traditional, status-linked privileges in favor of functioning as God's community, in which "the members may have the same care for one another," with particular attention to "giving the greater honor to the inferior member" (1 Cor 12:24–25 NRSV). In Paul's new understanding of reality the God of Israel measures the strength of the "strong" by their capacities and willingness to empower the "weak."

Paul sought to be strong in just this paradoxical way. As he wrote, "Whenever I am weak [in terms of conventional patriarchal expectations], then I am strong [in terms of serving others 'for the sake of Christ']" (2 Cor 12:10 NRSV). But how was he to gain the attention again of those who either were reverting to long familiar ways of treating others, probably under pressure from their friends and neighbors, or who were making indiscernible progress in the process of their conversions to Christ and his ways? For example, had not some of them sought to gain advantage over others within the group by bringing lawsuits against them (1 Cor 6:1–7)? Their behavior in general provoked him to use exaggerated rhetoric and to express himself in ways that he regarded as "foolish."

Consider Paul's Letter to Philemon, in which Paul did not let this slaveholder "off the hook." First note that Paul referred to himself as the one who "begot" Onesimus, not at all to suggest his authority over Onesimus but rather to emphasize to Philemon as Onesimus's owner the deep bond that had resulted from Paul's spiritual "begetting" of Onesimus as his "offspring" (τέκνον) in Christ. In Paul's rhetorical jousting with Philemon, Paul apparently sought to argue like this: On the one hand, Onesimus was Philemon's slave, but on the other hand, he had recently become Paul's surrogate "son." Yet more importantly, Onesimus had also become Paul's surrogate "brother" in Christ. Therefore Philemon should also recognize Onesimus as his brother—indeed, as "a beloved brother" (v. 16). Paul, then, sincerely addressed Philemon as one brother speaking to another, in the hope that he could persuade him to start regarding Onesimus as a brother too. At the same time, Paul backed this rhetoric with his own example of surrendering patronal control over both Onesimus and Philemon.

The same spirit pervades the passage in 1 Thess 2:11–12: "As you know, we dealt with each one of you like a father with his children [τέκνα], urging and encouraging you and pleading that you lead a life worthy of God, who calls you into his own kingdom and glory" (NRSV). Here the emphasis is on "urging, encouraging, pleading," not on "demanding, commanding, and dominating," the latter actions and attitudes being more readily associated with the fathers in Paul's world. Concerning Paul's paternal role, Bossman observes, "Paul's role of father is one of instruction, encouragement, and reinforcement rather than one that is authoritative, powerful, or punitive as one might assume from true patriarchy" (1996, 165). Paul's preferred manner of addressing the Thessalonians, already in 1 Thess 1:4, is as his "brothers and sisters," not as his offspring. He noted their emulation of his service among them (1:6). And he described his demeanor among them as "gentle . . . like a nurse tenderly caring for her own children" (2:7 NRSV). Paul's converts may well have regarded his behavior toward them as that of a maternal uncle, an *avunculus*, who had no recognized authority but who was admired when he offered nurture and teaching to his nephews and nieces (Malina 1978, 99).

Paul's Personal Example

In support of this claim, note carefully the radically antipatriarchal, personal model for the surrender of privileges that Paul himself had demonstrated to the Corinthians. Judge has called attention to Paul's "pursuit of radical self-humiliation" which Judge finds running through all Paul's work "in theology and ethics alike, and on into his practical relations with both followers and rivals" (1972, 36). Judge comments that Paul's attitude was "in violent reaction to much that was central to the classical way of life" (1972, 36). In short, Paul's behavior demonstrated that his understanding of the gospel had undermined in his own life the patriarchal assumptions that were "central to the classical way of life" with which he had grown up. Judge focuses attention on Paul's constant use of status terms and his voluntary assumption of a lower social status than that to which his education and background gave him a justifiable claim, and then he concludes that "the conflicts between St Paul and his converts in Corinth were affected by the growing sense of his cultural non-conformity" (1982, 18). As we have already observed, twice in 1 Corinthians Paul urged them to "be imitators of me," and in each case he was challenging behavior that he regarded as spiritually arrogant (4:8–21) and divisive (11:1).

Three Barriers to Understanding

Why, then, has it been so easy to misread Paul's words as if he intentionally or inadvertently reinforced the prevailing patriarchal system of his world? Three suggestions occur to me.

First, with regard to fantasies about Paul's authority, many misinterpretations are based on the assumption that Paul already enjoyed during his lifetime a high degree of institutional authority. To the contrary, his letters gained widespread authority only many decades after his death. As his own letters clearly reveal, his mission and his message were sharply challenged by other teachers and "apostles"; and by no means was his ongoing influence secure within the diversity of the early Christian movement, even among the house churches that he himself had planted. In the first century C.E. there simply was no central teaching authority for Christians, neither that of Paul, nor Peter, or anyone else. And in those areas where Paul was breaking ground for the gospel, his claims about a divine reversal of major cultural values must have been regarded both as life-giving and as the greatest foolishness. As he wrote, the gospel is "foolishness to the Gentiles, but . . . God's foolishness is wiser than human wisdom, and God's weakness is stronger than human strength" (1 Cor 1:22–25 NRSV).

Second, with regard to roles and goals of leadership, I maintain that we need to construct a culturally sensitive reframing of our perception of Paul's role and goal as a leader. Here Malina (1986, 109) helpfully distinguishes between the roles of managers and leaders in social networks. For example, managers include kings, priests, fathers, lords, bank presidents, and all others whose rights and authority are rooted in law, tradition, and ascribed social position. In contrast, leaders are those who have achieved their influence by what they have actually done for their followers. In Malina's words, "Normally the following is due to some generalized reciprocity initiative," such as generosity or freely offering vital information "that serves as a starter mechanism building up a following in generalized reciprocity" (1986, 109). None of Paul's roles—such as scribe (among the Judeans), itinerant philosopher (among the Gentiles), and prophet/apostle (among his house-based groups)—fit well in the managerial category. Rather, his power and influence in all these roles were based on the trust that he had generated as a person who knew what he was talking and writing about and whose personal behavior modeled his message. That is, Paul did not seek to exploit the managerial role of a father. To be sure, Paul used strong words of rebuke and blame when writing to those he experienced as arrogant, as "'recalcitrant students' difficult to cure and in need of a dose of stringent medicine," as Glad quite helpfully concludes (1995, 311). Glad fruitfully compares the pedagogy and psychagogy ("leadership of souls") of Paul and the Epicurean Philodemus. He contends that "Paul's use of blame lodges him squarely within the tradition that valued therapeutic harshness" (1995, 310). Further, Glad observes that Paul presents himself in the roles of a "frank friend and a loving but stern father who attempts by means of more stringent forms of persuasion to change the self-deceptive and arrogant wise in Corinth" (1995, 325). Glad (1995, 236–332) argues forcefully that Paul's gentleness or harshness was specifically calculated to influence the distinctive views and behaviors of his hearers: gentleness for the insecure students, and rough, even sarcastic, rhetoric for those whom he regarded as arrogant. In both cases Paul spoke frankly as a considerate friend and brother.

Third, egalitarianism is not the opposite of patriarchy. Scholars have largely ignored the fact that patriarchal systems in general and the ancient Mediterranean system in particular socialized men not only to dominate women but also to gain the upper hand over as many other men as possible. They have also mistakenly assumed that the terms *egalitarianism* and *patriarchy* describe opposite ends of the same sociopolitical spectrum. Inadvertently, they have blurred the distinctions between two ancient social institutions: politics and kinship. These two missteps lead inevitably away from comprehension of Paul's implicit and explicit critique of the patriarchy of his day (see Bartchy 1999).

In the Greco-Roman world kinship and politics provided the key metaphors for a wide variety of human relationships. On the one hand, the term *patriarchy* belongs to the semantic field of kinship, the realm of the family. On the other hand, the term *egalitarian* belongs to the semantic field of politics and refers to such things as equal access to the vote, to positions of public leadership, and to ownership of property. Thus the opposite of patriarchal dominance is not egalitarian anarchy (or cooperation), as interpreters have commonly inferred, but instead something else—something for which we may not yet have a better term than *nonpatriarchy*.

Likewise, the opposite of egalitarianism is not patriarchy as such but rather monarchy, oligarchy, or despotism. To be sure, part of our confusion in this area has been abetted by those Roman emperors who sought to disguise their monarchy by selling it as a higher and public form of patriarchy. After five hundred years of the Roman republic and the Romans' pride in not having to obey a king, by no means could the emperor be thought to be a king or a dictator. Julius Caesar came to a nasty end because he was so perceived. So his successful successor, Octavius (Caesar Augustus), headed off the charges that led to the assassination of his predecessor by asserting that he was not a king. Rather, in 2 B.C.E. the Roman community conferred on Caesar Augustus the less politically charged title *pater patriae,* the "father of the fatherland." Who could object to such beneficent-sounding epithet? Yet the followers of Jesus, who were taught to "call no man 'father' on earth," inevitably clashed with such a blatant political co-opting of kinship rhetoric. And by the fourth century C.E., thousands of Christians had paid with their lives for their refusal to honor the emperor as their "father."

Any confusion about the metaphors taken from kinship and politics is understandable, but certainly regrettable, for having obscured the primary thrust of Paul's challenges to the patriarchal system of his world. Paul's vision of a society of siblings in which only God is called "father" would not have led him or his followers to think of egalitarian political relations. Rather, he exhorted his readers and hearers to join him in undermining patriarchal ideology and those whom it privileged and to practice "general reciprocity"—that is, generous mutual support and sharing without keeping score (see, e.g., 1 Cor 13). Paul envisioned the followers of Jesus respecting and giving honor to each other in the ways that characterized the relations among siblings at their best.

CONCLUSION

By no means are these profound challenges to any patriarchal arrangement of society the last word on the ancient family in either the Jesus tradition or Paul's letters. Rather, they present the *first* word, apparently intended to dismantle conventional patrilineal blood ties in preparation for the creation of an alternative, surrogate family structure in which no person would function as a patriarch. No person, including blood-kin fathers, would be expected to dominate, or have permission to dominate, the others in the family. Indeed, in Paul's new understanding of reality the God of Israel measures the strength of the "strong" by their capacities and willingness to empower the "weak."

The historical-Jesus traditions and the writings of Paul share and emphasize the same radical reversals of core traditional cultural values, including (1) the rejection of patriarchal authority and domination and of the traditional obligations of filial piety; (2) the invitation to become members of a surrogate family not based on blood ties yet expressive of the interpersonal values of sibling kinship; (3) the redefinition of the basis for attaining honor: serving rather than competing; (4) the demonstration of authentic power that now was characterized by empowerment rather than by control of others.

Paul continued the historical Jesus' vision of the surrogate kinship of "brothers and sisters" according to which kinship based on blood ties was rejected in favor of relationships rooted in the personally chosen, intentionally embraced and shared commitment to the will of God the compassionate. Paul's basic model for his communities was a family of such "brothers and sisters"—his favorite designation for his readers—without an earthly father. For Paul, almost without exception, only God was to be the father of each community (cf. 1 Pet 2:17).

What, then, did Paul have to say to the fathers who became members of his house-based groups? In light of my argument, I suggest that he would have expressed the first-century-C.E. Greek equivalent of "Get over yourself, my brother! For in our group we are all brothers and sisters. If your son or daughter is in the group, meet your new brother and sister 'in the Lord.' For among us, only God is called 'Father.'"

Bibliography

Bailey, Kenneth E. 1980. *Through Peasant Eyes: More Lucan Parables, Their Culture and Style.* Grand Rapids: Eerdmans.

Bartchy, S. Scott. 1999. Undermining Ancient Patriarchy: Paul's Vision of a Society of Siblings. *Biblical Theology Bulletin* 29:68–78.

Bossman, David. 1996. Paul's Fictive Kinship Movement. *Biblical Theology Bulletin* 26:163–71.

Daube, David. 1971. Pauline Contributions to a Pluralistic Culture: Recreation and Beyond. Pages 223–37 in vol. 2 of *Jesus and Man's Hope: Papers Presented at the Pittsburgh Festival on the Gospels.* Edited by D. G. Miller and D. K. Hadidian. Pittsburgh: Pittsburgh Theological Seminary.

Dewey, Joanna. 1994. The Gospel of Mark. Pages 470–509 in vol. 2 of *Searching the Scriptures.* Edited by Elisabeth Schüssler Fiorenza. New York: Crossroad.

Elliott, John H. 1993. *What Is Social Scientific Criticism?* Minneapolis: Fortress.

Fee, Gordon D. 1987. *The First Epistle to the Corinthians.* New International Commentary on the New Testament. Grand Rapids: Eerdmans.

Glad, Clarence E. 1995. *Paul and Philodemus: Adaptability in Epicurean and Early Christian Psychagogy.* Supplements to Novum Testamentum 81. Leiden: Brill.

Green, Joel. 1997. *The Gospel of Luke.* New International Commentary on the New Testament. Grand Rapids: Eerdmans.

Hallett, Judith P. 1984. *Fathers and Daughters in Roman Society: Women and the Elite Family.* Princeton, N.J.: Princeton University Press.

Hanson, K. C. 1996. Kinship. Pages 62–79 in *The Social Sciences and New Testament Interpretation.* Edited by Richard Rohrbaugh. Peabody, Mass.: Hendrickson.

Hengel, Martin. 1981. *The Charismatic Leader and His Followers.* Translated by James Greig. New York: Crossroad.

Joubert, Stephan J. 1995. Managing the Household: Paul as *paterfamilias* of the Christian Household Group in Corinth. Pages 213–23 in *Modelling Early Christianity: Social-Scientific Studies of the New Testament in Its Context.* Edited by Philip F. Esler. London: Routledge.

Judge, Edwin A. 1972. St Paul and Classical Society. *Jahrbuch für Antike und Christentum* 15:19–36. Repr. Judge, Edwin A. St Paul and Classical Society. Pages 73–97 in *Social Distinctives of the Christians in the First Century: Pivotal Essays by E. A. Judge.* Edited by David M. Scholer. Peabody, Mass.: Hendrickson, 2008.

————. 1982. *Rank and Status in the World of the Caesars and St Paul.* University of Canterbury Publications 29. Christchurch: University of Canterbury Press. Repr. Judge, Edwin A. Rank and Status in the World of the Caesars and St Paul. Pages 137–56 in *Social Distinctives of the Christians in the First Century: Pivotal Essays by E. A. Judge.* Edited by David M. Scholer. Peabody, Mass.: Hendrickson, 2008.

Lohfink, Gerhard. 1982. *Jesus and Community: The Social Dimension of Christian Faith.* Minneapolis: Fortress.

Malina, Bruce J. 1978. The Social World Implied in the Letters of the Christian Bishop-Martyr (Named Ignatius of Antioch). Pages 71–119 in vol. 2 of *Society of Biblical Literature 1978 Seminar Papers.* Edited by Paul J. Achtemeier. Society of Biblical Literature Seminar Papers 14. Missoula, Mont.: Scholars Press.

————. 1986. *Christian Origins and Cultural Anthropology: Practical Models for Biblical Interpretation.* Atlanta: John Knox.

McCane, Brian R. 1990. Let the Dead Bury Their Own Dead: Secondary Burial and Matt 8:21–22. *Harvard Theological Review* 83:31–43.

Neyrey, Jerome H. 1998. *Honor and Shame in the Gospel of Matthew.* Louisville: Westminster John Knox.

————. 2003. Jesus, Gender, and the Gospel of Matthew. Pages 43–66 in *New Testament Masculinities.* Edited by Stephen D. Moore and Janice Capel Anderson. Society of Biblical Literature Semeia Studies 45. Atlanta: Society of Biblical Literature.

Purcell, Nicholas. 1996. Pater Patriae. *Oxford Classical Dictionary.* Edited by S. Hornblower and A. Spawforth. 3d ed. New York: Oxford University Press.

Saller, Richard P. 1994. *Patriarchy, Property and Death in the Roman Family.* Cambridge Studies in Population, Economy, and Society in Past Time 25. Cambridge: Cambridge University Press.

Schüssler Fiorenza, Elisabeth. 1983. *In Memory of Her: A Feminist Theological Reconstruction of Christian Origins.* New York: Crossroad.

Space

10

Bird watchers can distinguish the communication in different calls from a single bird. One signals that the bird is present, another that a space is the bird's own territory, and still another invites a mate into the controlled space. Hedges and bushes are empty or neutral spaces until birds begin classifying and controlling them. But when the male cardinal decides which bush would make a great nest, for instance, he stakes a territorial claim by his new song. Now he will fight others who encroach on "his turf." The same has been observed in canines and felines, who mark their territory with scent to ward off intruders. They classify space, communicate that classification, and exert control over it. This chapter presents a cross-cultural model about how empty space becomes "your" or "my" space—that is, how it becomes "territory."

Satellite geopositioning systems can locate where we are; geography can inform us of large- and small-scale features. But they cannot tell us what the space means, for meaning is only in the minds of interpreters who give space its significance. Classification of space, the key to the model, takes many forms, such as "mine" versus "yours," in the example of the male cardinal. But the ancient world developed many such binary opposites for thinking about space: (1) sacred/profane, (2) center/periphery, (3) pure/impure, (4) male/female, (5) honorable/nonhonorable, and (6) public/private. This chapter examines the last two classifications in detail, but first let us look briefly at some others.

Philo provides a summary of gender-division in the ancient world that introduces us to a male/female classification in regard to space:

> Markets, council-halls and law-courts where a large number of people are assembled, and open-air life with full scope for discussion and action—these are suitable to men. The women are best suited to the indoor life which never strays from the house, within which the middle door is taken by the maidens as their boundary and the outer door by those who have reached full manhood. (*Spec. Laws* 3.169)

Male space is "public" because the persons congregating there conduct civic business (or work at open-air tasks, such as agriculture). Female space is "private" because household business is done there; for nonelite females this included trips to the well and foraging for fuel for cooking. Males in public act and speak boldly to rule or wage war and make peace. Females in households attend to their duties, such as child rearing, food preparation, and clothing production.

Classification as "public" or "private" in turn govern and control who goes where and does what.

The Mishnah provides an excellent example of the classification of "sacred/profane."

> There are ten degrees of holiness: the Land of Israel is holier than any other land. . . . The walled cities [of the Land of Israel] are still more holy. . . . Within the wall [of Jerusalem] is still more holy. . . . The Temple Mount is still more holy. . . . The Rampart is still more holy. . . . The Court of the Women is still more holy. . . . The Court of the Israelites is still more holy. . . . The Court of the Priests is still more holy. . . . Between the Porch and the Altar is still more holy. . . . The Sanctuary is still more holy. . . . The Holy of Holies is still more holy. (*m. Kelim* 1:6–9)

The key to this classification is proximity to Jerusalem's temple, which gives content to the word "holy." Holiness (i.e., purity) increases as one moves from periphery (land, cities) to center (temple mount, courts, sanctuary, and holy of holies). Since "holiness" indicates being dedicated to God (or sacred) and separation from uncleanness (or pure), the holy spaces also correlate with persons who have differing degrees of holiness: females stand behind the court of the adult male Israelites (they are potentially unclean because of menstruation), and men are separated from priests, who alone stand "between the porch and the altar," with the high priest alone entering the holy of holies. Thus persons are classified according to various degrees of holiness, and control is exercised over the spaces that they may and may not occupy.

Jerome H. Neyrey, SJ

"Teaching You in Public and from House to House" (Acts 20:20): Unpacking a Cultural Stereotype

Introduction: Focus, Status Quaestionis, Model, and Plan

In Paul's farewell address he claimed, "I did not shrink from declaring to you anything that was profitable and teaching you in public [δημοσίᾳ] and from house to house [κατ᾽ οἴκους]" (Acts 20:20). Two things are contained in this remark: (1) space, classified as public or private; (2) speech, regarding who may speak what, when, where, to whom, and for what purpose. Commentators give Acts 20:20 minimal attention, perhaps because the expression about "public and private" seems too obvious for comment. Although Stanley Stowers did not directly treat Acts 20:20, he focused on where the historical Paul[1] likely taught. He dismissed the conventional view that Paul spoke in public in the manner of Cynics. Stowers shifted attention from public venues to private ones, such as houses and the "hall of Tyrannus" (19:9), which, he argues, were regularly used by philosophers for their discourse. Stowers concludes,

> The private home was a center of intellectual activity and the customary place for many types of speakers and teachers to do their work. Occasional lectures, declamations and readings of various sorts of philosophical, rhetorical and literary works often took place in homes. The speaker might use his own house or be invited to speak or teach in another home. These were private affairs and audiences came by invitation. (1982, 65–66)

Stowers provides no further discussion about this classification of space. He leaves unexamined the true nature of private space, gender aspects of space, and the distinction between "common" parts of a house and "private" ones. Here I take up these issues by bringing into the conversation an anthropological model on space to interpret "in public and from house to house."

What is meant in Paul's claim that he spoke both in public and in private. What is meant by "public" and by "private"? Since this is a social/cultural question, the method for researching and interpreting this classification of space turns to the social sciences for appropriate concepts and models. The argument

---

[1] The "historical Paul" refers to Paul as he actually existed in his lifetime as opposed to Paul as narrated in the book of Acts.

here consists of four parts. First, I will present the model of "territoriality" developed by the social sciences as the appropriate way for interpreting the classification of space as public/private. Second, I will survey the various emic reports on public/private in Greco-Roman literature and interpret those data in the light of territoriality. Third, I will address the matter of who has voice in this or that space—that is, of who is allowed to speak. Finally, I will bring these three blocks of data to bear on the correct cultural interpretation of Acts 20:20.

BASIC MODEL: TERRITORIALITY

"Territoriality," the chief cultural model for interpreting space, is defined as "the attempt by an individual or group to affect, influence, or control people, phenomena, and relationships, by delimiting and asserting control over a geographic area. . . . Territories require constant effort to establish and maintain" (Sack 1986, 19). This model contains three foci: (1) classification of place, (2) communication of this classification, (3) control of the place so classified. Like others, Sack emphasizes the attempt to control some place or some persons. Control presumes that the controlling group has in some way labeled or classified space in relationship unto itself so as to "affect, influence or control" places, as well as "people, phenomena, relationships."

Classification Systems

The classification system, the key to the model, refers to the ways in which humans invest space with meaning or label it for some purpose. For example, people declare this space "ours" and that space "yours," thus making "our" space sacred and set apart from other, profane spaces. Parents classify their bedrooms as "off limits" for their children, thus distinguishing adult from family space. Muslims and Israelis both claim Jerusalem's temple mount as their own sacred space and thus see the presence of the other as profaning it.

Anthropologists surface many patterns of classification of territory, which contain binary opposites that set apart certain spaces as restricted/unrestricted, ours/yours, holy/profane, and the like. Those who label space intend their labels to have dramatic impact on how people think about and behave in regard to a certain space. A sample inventory of classifications includes (1) public/private, (2) honorable/nonhonorable, (3) sacred/profane, (4) clean/unclean, (5) fixed/fluid sacred space, (6) center/periphery, (7) civilization/nature. In regard to Acts 20:20, only the first two pairs seem relevant here.

Communication and Control

Communication of these classifications is relatively simple. All that a prosperous city needs do to claim that it is an honorable or civilized space is to build a wall around itself with a well-guarded gate (e.g., Josh 2:1–21). The same applies to sections within cities where various occupations or ethnic groups were separated from each other and from the elites by interior walls and gates (e.g., Acts 19:23–25). Nonelites are thus separated from urban elites as well as from others with whom there might be rivalry or conflict. Similarly, the purpose of a city's walls and gates is replicated by the doors of houses, palaces and temples, sometimes manned by guards (see John 18:15–17; Acts 28:16). A dramatic example of communication and control is the inscription in the Jerusalem temple prohibiting Gentile access to the court of the Israelites: "No foreigner is to enter within the forecourt and the balustrade around the sanctuary. Whoever is caught will have himself to blame for his subsequent death" (see Segal 1989, 82–84; Philo, *Embassy* 212; Josephus, *Ant.* 12.145). Control takes many forms.

Native Classification Systems

Native classifications of space were widespread in the ancient world. Of the seven noted above, by far the most important for this study is "public/private," which is also the one most commonly used in the Greco-Roman and Israelite worlds. The classification of public/private deserves careful examination because our survey of data about it identifies differing linguistic expressions of it and meanings for it. We proceed now to examine (1) the variations of the classification system public/private, (2) its relationship to male/female space and to honorable/shameful space.

Public and Private Space

Nine variations of the classification "public/private" are found in Greco-Roman literature, which require careful analysis.

1. κοινός/ἴδιος. Aristotle: "Both those who give advice in private [ἰδίᾳ] and those who speak in the assembly [κοινῇ] invariably either exhort or dissuade" (*Rhet.* 1.3.3). "Public" refers to politics, whereas "private" looks to social circles of male friends, not to households.

2. δημόσιος/ἴδιος. Plato: "What a widespread corruption of the young in private families [ἰδίοις οἴκοις] as well as publicly in the State [δημοσίᾳ]" (*Leg.* 10 890B). "Private" now refers to kinship or household, and "public" to politics.

3. ξυνός/ἴδιος. Plutarch: "Now he who said, 'The man who would be tranquil in his mind must not engage in many affairs, either private [ἰδίη] or public [ξυνῇ],' first of all makes our tranquility very expensive" (*Tranq. an.* 465C).

4. ῥήτορες/ἴδιοι. Aeschines: "They legislated for the other age-groups in succession, including in their provision, not only private citizens [περὶ τῶν ἰδιωτῶν], but also the public men [περὶ τῶν ῥητόρων]" (*Tim.* 7). "Private" means nonpolitical, male associations, whereas "public" refers to politics.

5. πρεσβεία/ἴδια. Josephus : "When any Athenians come to him [Hyrcanus] either on an embassy or on a private matter [ἢ κατὰ πρεσβείαν ἢ κατ' ἰδίαν πρόφασιν] . . ." (*Ant.* 14.151). Embassies are political/public; "private," refers to patronage on a one-to-one basis.

6. δημόσιος/κατοικίδιος. Dionysus of Halicarnassus: "Secret political councils [πολιτευμάτων] were meeting in private houses [ἐν ἰδίαις οἰκίαις]" (*Ant. rom.* 11.57.3). "Private," not household, refers to the rooms in houses where males hosted their friends.

7. πόλις/οἰκία. Aristotle: "The city-state is prior in nature to the household" (*Politics* 1.1.11). Philo: "Organized communities are of two sorts, the greater we call cities [πόλεων] and the smaller we call households [οἰκίαι]" (*Spec. Laws* 3.171).

8. *publice/privatim*. Romans too make distinctions between public and private. According to Aulus Gellius, the philosopher Taurus received as guests a governor of the province and his father. A single chair was brought, to which Taurus directed the father. But he deferred to his son "since he is a magistrate of the Roman people." The ensuing debate concluded,

> In public places, functions and acts, the rights of fathers, compared with the authority of sons who are magistrates, give way and are eclipsed; but when they are sitting together unofficially in the intimacy of home life, or walking about, or even reclining at a dinner party of intimate friends, then the official distinctions between a son who is a magistrate and a father who is a private citizen are at an end. (*Noct. att.* 2.2.1–10)

As regards space, the magistrate is considered to be in public space, for he acts like a political official; alternately he enjoys private space when at home with his father. The father, however, who is not a public official, has no public space; all he has is private space such as (1) house/residence ("in the intimacy of home life"), (2) dining rooms ("a dinner party of intimate friends"), (3) outdoor walking space ("walking about"). This example makes salient the interplay of status and role (magistrate/citizen; father/son) and space (*polis*/residence/outdoors).

9. *communus/privatus*. Vitruvius: "In private [*privatis*] buildings, the rooms belonging to the family and those shared with visitors should be planned thus. Into private rooms no one can come uninvited, such as bedrooms, dining-rooms, baths. The common rooms [*communia*] are those into which though uninvited, people can come by right, such as vestibules, courtyards, peristyles" (*Architecture* 6.5.1). Elite houses, then, have private parts, which are restricted to members of the household, and public or common spaces open to nonhousehold persons. From the nine classifications for "public/private," we may draw the following conclusions.

Private: Nonpolitical but Nonhousehold Space

The ancients recognized a middle space that is neither public/political nor private/household. Greeks and Romans distinguished male participation in the public or political life in the city from the private social relations of an ordinary citizen. Demosthenes states,

> There are two problems with which the laws of all nations are concerned. First, what are the principles under which we associate with one another, have dealings with one another, define the obligations of private life [περὶ τῶν ἰδίων]? Secondly, what are the duties that every man owes to the commonwealth, if he chooses to take part in public life [τῷ κοινῷ]? Now it is to the advantage of the common people that laws of the former category, laws of private intercourse [περὶ τῶν ἰδίων], be distinguished by clemency and humanity. On the other hand it is to your common advantage that laws of the second class, the laws that govern our relations to the State [πρὸς τὸ δη- μόσιον], shall be trenchant and peremptory, because politicians will not do so much harm to the commonalty. (*Timocr.* 192–193)

Males, then, may associate with other males in public/political life (πρὸς τὸ δημόσιον) or restrict themselves to private life (περὶ τῶν ἰδίων), which is not synonymous with staying within one's household. Different expectations characterize male public behavior and male private behavior: laws governing public activity should be "trenchant and peremptory" versus "clement and humane" in private intercourse.

Private: Household Space, Roles, and Concerns

Male public figures, of course, had private household roles and duties. Male duties in this private world of the household include (1) control of children, (2) procurement of dowries (Isaeus, *On the Estate of Cleonymus* 39–40), (3) proper use of patrimony (Aeschines, *Tim.* 154), (4) funeral rites for parents (Isaeus, *On the Estate of Menecles* 36–37; see Matt 8:21–22), (5) concern for the virtue and reputation of wives and other females (see Lysias, *On the Murder of Eratosthenes* 15–26), (6) ruling over slaves and servants. Only males who exhibit private governance of their own households are suitable for public leadership of the church (1 Tim 3:4–5, 12).

Lysias provides an excellent example of distinction of three types of male public and private space (*In Defense of Mantitheus* 16.9–12). He first recounts honorable behavior in regard to the private world of the household:

> Although little property had been bequeathed to me, I bestowed two sisters in marriage, with a dowry of thirty *minae* apiece; to my brother I allowed such a portion as made him acknowledge that he had got a larger share of patrimony than I had; and towards all else my behaviour has been such that never to this day has a single person shown any grievance against me. So much for the tenor of my private life [τὰ ἴδια]. (16.10–11)

As eldest male, he fulfilled his duty with regard to the marriages of the family's daughters; as patron, he distributed the father's patrimony to his siblings and the family's clients. In regard to the second, or public, world outside the private household, he says,

> With regard to public matters [περὶ δὲ τῶν κοινῶν], I hold that the strongest proof I can give of my decorous conduct is the fact that all the younger set who are found to take their diversion in dice or drink or the like dissipations are at feud with me, and are most prolific in lying tales about me. It is obvious that if we were at one in our desires they would not regard me with such feelings. (16.11)

This is neither the public/political world nor the private/household world. Rather, in view here is the nonhousehold world where males entertain themselves in the company of other males via symposia, games, gambling, and the like. Finally, he turns to the public/political world, where the affairs of the city are in view—in this case, the city's army and its defense of its allies:

> As regards campaigns in face of the enemy, observe how I discharged my duty to the State. First, when you made your alliance with the Boeotians, and we had to go to the relief of Hilartus, I had been enrolled by Orthobulus for service in the cavalry. (16.12–13)

Mantitheus goes on to say how he volunteered for the more difficult military role of an infantryman, attesting to his courage and solidarity with that part of the army. Because of his military service, he claims that he has been a model public (i.e., political) person who has "discharged his duty to the State." Thus, Mantitheus serves as an excellent emic informer on the triple spaces that make up the male world that was both public and private.

Honorable/Nonhonorable Places

This second classification of space does not have the hard linguistic data that "public/private" has, but it is nevertheless a key evaluation by the ancients that has bearing on our interpretation of space in Acts 20:20. In virtue of the gender-division of ancient society, space, roles, and tasks were likewise divided: males performing male roles and tasks in male space were separated from females performing corresponding female roles and tasks in female space (Neyrey 2003a, 44–58). It would be shameful for a male to be excessively at home when other males are either in the *agora* or the fields, and the same would be true for females. Gender, then, is part of the classification of "honorable/shameful" space.

Furthermore, it was axiomatic for ancient writers to celebrate the place of birth of characters in their writings. The principle is simple and clear: persons in antiquity were known in terms of geography and generation. Honorable persons come from honorable places. Nathanael impugns Jesus' honor, remarking that he comes from a statusless village: "What good can come from Nazareth?" (John 1:46). In contrast, Paul claimed honor by birth in an honorable place: "Tarsus in Cilicia, a no low-status city" (Acts 21:39). The honor rating of a place, then, constituted part of the stereotypical knowledge of it. It was inevitable that a person from an honorable place would have its honorable characteristics. Places of origin, then, were classified as honorable or nonhonorable.

"Honorable/nonhonorable" represents a spectrum of classification of spaces. Villages lack honor because they are crude; towns, while nobler than villages, lack the sophistication of major cities. Pausanias describes the honorable city, classifying it in opposition to nonhonorable places: ". . . if indeed one can give the name of city to those who possess no public buildings, no gymnasium, no theatre, no marketplace, no water descending to a fountain, but live in bare shelters just like mountain huts on the edges of ravines" (*Descr.* 10.4.1). Honorable cities, then, have honorable public spaces where elites gather, speak, and enjoy a vibrant civic life and a sophisticated cultural ambiance. Honorable spaces serve the honorable urban elite. Apart from death, the worst punishment that a Roman citizen could suffer was banishment from Rome to an obscure island or region. "Public," then, should include "honorable" urban places and cities.

TERRITORIALITY AND ACTS 20:20

With our appreciation of the key classifications of space, we can begin to interpret Acts 20:20. No doubt, Luke expresses some classification in the phrase "in public and from house to house"; but what is meant here? (1) Does "public" refer to the political arena or to outdoors or to nonhousehold space? (2) Does "house to house" mean household space—that is, house churches and indoor space? Could it refer to noncivic, nonpublic space? We know that Acts 20:18–35 is Paul's farewell address, a genre suggestive of broad generalizations about his behavior and scope of his labors (Malherbe 1985). Hence, we read "in public and from house to house" as the broadest classification of space—that is, (1) political-civic space as well as (2) male private space, such as the synagogue, and (3) household-private space. It is time to read Acts closely to learn where Paul appears. In what typical spaces does Luke locate Paul? We will look at (1) civic/political space, (2) private space, such as synagogues or riverside groves, (3) kinship houses, (4) *aulē*, such as the hall of Tyrannus, (5) the Jerusalem temple. In considering each venue, we will also examine how it is classified, how this classification is communicated, and how it may serve as a mechanism of control of this space.

Public Space as Political, Civic

Paul frequently appeared in the *agora,* the civic center of significant cities. According to Acts, in Athens Paul spoke daily there (17:17). Because Paul is not restricted from this space, we infer that those present acknowledge his role and status as a person worthy of public voice. All other instances of public space tell of Paul "brought to the magistrates" (16:20) in the marketplace. Sometimes, no space is mentioned, only the remark that "they dragged them . . . before the city authorities" (17:6) or that "they brought Paul before the tribunal" (18:12).

Acts tells us, moreover, that Paul regularly spoke in the presence of elites. For example, the proconsul Sergius Paulus "summoned Barnabas and Saul and sought to hear the word of God" (13:7). They entered political/public space, probably where the proconsul's βῆμα (judicial court) was located. We imagine a space filled with Sergius's retainers and maybe some other dignitaries. Far from restricting Paul, the proconsul gave him license to speak, thus acknowledging his role and status. Felix, the Judean governor, even though he kept Paul in confinement, "sent for him very often and conversed with him" (24:26 NRSV) over the course of the next two years. To be sure, their conversations took place not in Paul's confined space but rather in Felix's official space, which is the political/public space where Felix held meetings and heard reports. Although Felix did not release Paul, he did not restrict his speech, thus giving some acknowledgment to Paul's role and status. The next governor, Festus, brought Paul before King Agrippa and his queen, Bernice, to hear his side of the case. Again, the space envisioned here is the most important place in the political space of the governor's fortress, a space befitting Roman governors, Judean royalty, and Paul. Here he has public voice to state his case. Finally, Paul found refuge from shipwreck in the house of Publius, the chief man of the island (28:7). Again, Paul is in elite space, which is both public/political space ("chief man of the island") and private (nonkinship males together) space where Paul was entertained hospitably for three days (28:8). Luke does not say that Paul spoke boldly here, but that others classified Paul as god-favored and that he was given freedom of movement despite being a prisoner. Paul, then, is at ease in the presence of certain political elite, where he enjoys voice.

Private but Not Household Space

According to the classification system that we have seen, the synagogue is private, nonpublic space where males gathered outdoors in association. The synagogue, though neither political/public nor household space, is nevertheless private. The members of the synagogue classify Paul as a corruption and act to control his speech.

TEXT IN ACTS	LOCATION	CONTROL
13:5	Salamis	no restriction of speaking mentioned
13:15–50	Antioch of Pisidia	restrictions on speech (13:45); expulsion (13:50)
14:1–7	Iconium	attempted stoning (14:5), then flight (14:6)
17:1–8	Thessalonica	restriction on speech and violence (17:5), accusation of treason before a magistrate (17:6–7)
17:10	Beroea	restriction on speech, flight by Paul (17:13–14)
18:5–18	Corinth	restriction of speech (18:6), yet open speaking for a year and a half (18:11); accusation before Gallio (18:16); violence (18:17), then flight (18:18)
19:8–10	Corinth	restricted from synagogue, but free speech in "the hall of Tyrannus" (19:9)

Figure 16: Restrictions on Paul's speech by the leaders of local synagogues

In terms of classification, synagogues are private (versus public/political space). Although synagogues provided informal settings, it is unclear who had voice in them, but surely local synagogue rulers (13:15; 18:8, 17) and males with learning to read and to exhort the group. Paul belongs to this second class. He appears to be a messenger of significant news. But a second classification of synagogue also seems operative: "pure/polluted." Speakers who speak a word in keeping with traditional understanding of Scripture and Judean practice are pure and have voice in the synagogue. But speakers bringing strange or blasphemous words are a pollution to the synagogue. The guardians of tradition, then, rise up to control this voice, usually by expelling the speaker. They also hale such speakers before the political court or chase them from the city. Here the model of territoriality shows its worth, for it allows us to grasp the classification of the local synagogue in gender terms as male space that is private, but not in the sense that household is private. Moreover, it indicates how space, when classified, can be controlled. For when Paul is perceived as polluting the synagogue by his speech, the congregation rises up to silence him and expel him from their midst. At stake here is the social issue of who has public voice.

House as Two Types of Private Space

A house may be classified as private in two senses: (1) private space for unrelated males to assemble for symposia and the like; (2) private as household residence for kinship-related males and females. It seems that Luke makes exactly this distinction when he narrates the reasons for Paul's presence in private houses: either (1) hospitality or (2) invitation to speak.

In the first category, certain Acts narratives locate Paul in private houses under the rubric of hospitality. For example, when Paul lodged in "the house of Judas" (9:11, 17), he appears to be his guest, although no details are given about how Paul came to this place. After Ananias correctly classified him as God's elect, he found his voice in the synagogue (9:20–22). Similarly, under the rubric of hospitality, Lydia invites Paul to lodge at her house (16:15), with implicit permission to continue speaking about God. At Caesarea Paul "entered the house of Philip the deacon . . . and stayed with him" (21:8), which house became the locus of dire prophecies. We classify these houses as private/household space, which extends hospitality to those of the household of God. Although surely Paul spoke in them, they do not appear as the formal venue of his bold public speaking. No control is exercised on his speech.

In the second category, a different scenario is appropriate for other houses, which are private both as residences for kinship-related persons and as forums for nonkinship-related folk. It is not hospitality that characterizes them so much as a new venue for Paul to speak. For example, chased from the synagogue in Corinth, Paul left there "and went to the house of a man named Titius Justus" (18:7 NRSV). Thus the house of Titius Justus replaces the synagogue as the place where Paul has voice; the former is less a residence for Paul than a forum for his speech. Similarly, the third-story room where Paul preached through the night (20:8–9) probably was someone's residence in an *insula* (hence, private as household), but with non-kinship-related people assembled there, it became private as place of assembly. Finally, at Rome Paul "was allowed to stay by himself" (28:16), which place, although it was his private household, became the space where Paul received Judeans and spoke with them (28:17, 23). His private household space became private space for males to assemble. And Paul, of course, enjoyed public voice there. In none of these house settings does Paul ever experience control of his speech and message.

The Hall of Tyrannus: Private Space

Acts reports that when Paul was excluded from the Corinthian synagogue, he withdrew with his new disciples to the hall of Tyrannus. As regards the size and shape of this hall, we can only guess whether the σχολή is an independent building or a room of a building, and Luke does not say if there was any cost incurred to argue daily in the hall of Tyrannus for two years (19:9–10). Nevertheless, it should be classified as private space where males assemble. Moreover, not all in the hall have voice; surely Paul did, as he likely was considered to be a philosopher, but probably no one else. Moderate control was exercised over this space: only some people were invited to enter and listen.

The Jerusalem Temple: Public Space

Paul's only appearance in the Jerusalem temple, the unique shrine of the political religion of Israel, occurs on his return to Jerusalem in Acts 21:17. Because his presence in Greco-Roman synagogues has been vigorously controlled by the Israelites, the elders at Jerusalem urge Paul and company to undergo public rites of purification and so provide Judeans with a classification of Paul different from that of the non-Judean synagogues. The chart below indicates how territoriality, when applied to Jerusalem's temple, shows a high degree of classification and especially control (i.e., walls, gates, temple police). The temple, so rigorously controlled in the case of Peter and Stephen, continues to be so with Paul.

TEXT IN ACTS	CLASSIFICATION	COMMUNICATION	CONTROL
Acts 3:2	"Gate of the temple which is called 'Beautiful'"—unclean beggar is excluded from the holy temple	The very "temple system" communicates by means of gates, walls, restricted entrance ways, etc. that only the holy/whole may enter	Strong: gates, walls, restricted entrance ways; yet no restriction on voice
Acts 3:11	Solomon's Portico—a large stoa on southern end of complex; a meeting place	Place of assembly; a likely gathering place out of sun or rain; usual gender restrictions	None, once one is past the perimeter scrutiny; voice unrestricted

TEXT IN ACTS	CLASSIFICATION	COMMUNICATION	CONTROL
Acts 4:1	Solomon's Portico	Priest, captain of the temple, and Sadducees confront and arrest them	Very strong: their voice about Jesus is deviance (4:17–18), and so they are removed from Solomon's Portico
Acts 21:26	"Paul took the men, and the next day he purified himself with them and went into the temple to give notice when their days of purification would be fulfilled and the offering presented for every one of them"	By virtue of purification and offerings, Paul accepts (much of) the classification of the temple as a place of prayer and even sacrifice (i.e., thanksgiving offerings)	Strong: the usual gates, walls, internal demarcations; in the perception of some, Paul has violated these (21:27–30); having declared Paul a deviant, "they dragged him out of the temple, and at once the gates were shut" (21:30)

Figure 17: Territoriality applied to the Jerusalem temple

In Acts 21 those who classify Paul as a pollutant of the temple start a public process to label him as such. They charge him with total corruption of the Judean way of life: "Men of Israel, help! This is the man who is teaching men everywhere against the people and the law and this place; moreover he also brought Greeks into the temple, and he has defiled this holy place" (21:28 RSV). Whether in private synagogue or house, the speech of Paul corrupts because it is "against this place," and Paul's behavior in the public space of the temple likewise corrupts because he has brought Greeks into the temple and "defiled this holy place." Because certain people classify Paul as utterly unacceptable in sacred space, they act to control the access: "The people ran together; they seized Paul and dragged him out of the temple, and at once the gates were shut" (21:30). According to our model of territoriality, the three basic elements are clearly in view: (1) classification: the temple is for holy, observant Israelites only; (2) communication: accusations of deviance in 21:27–29; (3) control: expulsion of Paul from temple and attempts to kill him (21:30–31). Thus whereas Paul has voice in public Greco-Roman space, he is denied it in Israelite public (temple) space and private (synagogue) space.

Territoriality, Honorable Public Space, and Acts

The classification of space as honorable/nonhonorable can add much to our interpretation of Paul's remark in Acts 20:20: "in public and from house to house." I suggest that public space translates as honorable space. Many public spaces that Paul refers to are political spaces—the residences of proconsuls (13:7), the chief man of the island (28:7), and Roman procurators (24:1–26:32), which are in and of themselves honorable spaces because of the elites who occupy them. Thus honor accrues to Paul by his appearance in these venues and especially by the fact that he enjoys voice there. Also, Paul is portrayed as speaking in the *agora,* likewise a public and honorable space.

Agora, usually translated as "marketplace," represents a special kind of space (Hoenig 1979). Hellenistic *agorai* were especially public meeting places, the social and political centers of a *polis* (city or town), and the places where elites gathered to gossip, debate, and conduct court. As the center of public life, the *agora* was adorned with statues and colonnades and was surrounded by temples and other public buildings, which reflected the wealth, power, and sophistication of the elite, by whom and for whom such facilities existed. But the Hellenistic *agora* was honorable space, frequented by honorable persons who signaled this by the quality of their dress and adornment, special seating arrangements, retinue of servants and clients, and presumption to speak.

As we saw, Acts relates only two appearances of Paul in the *agora.* At Philippi he is dragged before the magistrate (16:19–20). Public trials are invariably shaming, as the ancients inform us. Hence, Paul gains no honor from appearing in this honorable space. But in Athens he spoke with whomever came to the *agora* (17:17). Athens, not a low-status city, accords him voice, and so Paul gains honor from speaking in the Athenian *agora.* But by far the more noble Athenian space was the Areopagus, a place of colonnades that housed philosophers such as Stoics and Epicureans. Males assembling here would be of the elite or retainer class, with philosophical education, and of respected roles and statuses to have public voice. Thus Paul, who speaks there, is accorded honor from discoursing with worthy people in an honorable location—at least in Luke's eyes. Public space in Acts, then, refers to political and civic space; those who appear there and speak there are considered honorable. "Public," then, includes "honorable."

Paul in No Low-status Cities

"Public" also refers to the cities in which Paul resides, as well as to civic and political spaces within them. But not all cities are honorable. In Acts, Luke comments on the status of various cities—for example, "Tarsus, a no low-status city" (21:39), and Philippi, "the leading city of the district of Macedonia" (16:12). But what makes a city honorable? In general, certain cities were renowned as major centers of learning and commerce, such as Antioch, Ephesus, and Tarsus. Archeological data concerning them indicate that they had public buildings, gymnasia, theaters, marketplaces, and so on—that is, Pausanius's criteria for noble cities. Although specific information may or may not have been available to general audience of Acts, Luke presumes some common lore or fame for various cities mentioned, such as the following material.

As regards honor, cities were characterized by intense "vanity and rivalry of cities in the matter of rank and titles" (Magie 1950, 2:1496). They regularly made honor claims to titles such as "metropolis" (μητρόπολις), "first and greatest" (πρώτη καὶ μεγιστή), "warden of the (imperial) temple" (νεωκόρη) "inviolable" (ἀσυλή), and "friend of Rome" (φίλη or συμμάχη Ῥωμαίων) (Neyrey 1996). Dio Chrysostom said of Nicea that it is

> noble and worthy of renown . . . both as to its power and grandeur, for it is inferior to no city of distinction anywhere, whether in nobility of lineage or in composition of population, comprising as it does, the most illustrious families, not small groups of sorry specimens who came together from this place and from that, but the leaders among both Greeks and Macedonians, and, what is most significant, having had as founders both heroes and gods. (*Nicaeen.* 1)

These titles mattered to the ancients, who drew much of their personal honor from the renown of the city in which they lived. And they were highly jealous of sharing this honor with a neighboring city. Public space, when referring to cities, then, might be honorable. Let us briefly examine three cities that Paul visited, with a view to their honor rating and the importance of this for Paul.

Tarsus. Luke records Paul's birthplace was a "no low-status city" (Acts 21:39). Climaxing a glorious history, Tarsus became the capital of the Roman province of Cilicia. Cicero, when proconsul of the province, resided there (*Att.* 5.20.3; *Fam.* 2.17.1). Augustus exempted it from taxes and fostered its development as a center of philosophy and rhetoric. Dio Chrysostom spoke of its rank as a "metropolis" from the start and as "the greatest of all the cities of Cilicia" (*1 Tars.* 17; *2 Tars.* 7). Strabo praised it as a premier center of learning, surpassing Athens and Alexandria (*Geogr.* 14.5.13). Excavations identify a typical theater, gymnasia, marketplaces, and fountains.

Antioch. Josephus said of Antioch that it is "a city which, for extent and opulence, unquestionably ranks third among the cities of the Roman world" (*J.W.* 3.29). It was famous for elegance ("Antioch the Great," "Antioch the Beautiful"), size, wealth, and importance (Dio Chrysostom, *1 Tars.* 18). Coins from it record "Antioch, metropolis, sacred, and inviolable, and autonomous, and sovereign, and capital of the East." With the Roman conquest, it maintained its importance as a major city, becoming the capital of Roman Syria. As befitted a major city, it was encircled with great walls and enjoyed the typical public buildings of a noble city: a great colonnaded street, circus, theater, forum, *agora,* palace, baths, and the like.

Ephesus. Strabo (*Geogr.* 641) called it the largest commercial center in Asia Minor west of the Taurus. It contained extensive public buildings: the temple of Artemis (Acts 19:24, 27–28), a splendid theater (Acts 19:29), several market places, gymnasia, and fountains. Since Augustus, it was honored as the capital of the Roman province of Asia, and was acclaimed as "First and Greatest Metropolis of Asia." The encomium on Ephesus by Strabo (*Geogr.* 14.1.22–25) lauded the city for its famous temple, its environment, harbor, and famous citizens.

What does this tell us about Paul's claim in Acts 20:20? First, throughout Acts Luke portrays Paul as traveling to and residing in provincial capitals, "no low-status" cities. Paul is a citizen of the world, at home in the important cities of the empire. Luke's positioning of Paul in the empire's major cities constitutes a rhetorical strategy that would have his readers accept Paul as a sophisticated person, at home in honorable cities and so an honorable person. Honorable people come from and belong in honorable cities. Thus, Luke also knows of the classification "honorable/non-honorable."

Voice and Territorial Control

Thus far we have examined classifications of space. But the purpose of this is to take into account the control exercised by various classifications. The precise question is this: Who may speak to whom, when, and in what context? Who has voice? In Acts 20:20–21 Paul states that his activity in "public and from house to house" was speech: "I did not shrink from declaring to you anything that was profitable, and teaching you in public and from house to house, testifying both to Jews and Greeks of repentance to God" (RSV). A guarantee of freedom of speech to everyone, such as that promised in our context by the U.S. Constitution, by no means applied in antiquity. Plutarch implies this: "Nature has given us two ears and one tongue, because we ought to do less talking than listening" (*Rect. rat. aud.* 39B). Not everyone had voice in the *agora,* the synagogue, or the house where the messianic assembly gathered. First of all, in the ancient world, with its hierarchy of gender division, males in private space outside the household had varying degrees of voice, depending on age, honor, social role, and status, but females did not—a distinction all the more true of the public/political world. Thus space is controlled in terms of who has voice. Who, then, "did the talking"?

Factors such as age, status, and the classification of space serve as indicators of who has voice and may speak. Age, for example, was a chief factor in determining who had voice. Young males generally do not have voice, as Lysias states: "Some people are annoyed at me merely for attempting at too early an age to speak before the people" (*Defense of Mantitheus* 16.20). How arrogant and unseemly for youths to lecture elders! Luke could have had this cultural criterion in mind when he stated that Jesus, en route to the Jordan to begin his ministry, was "about thirty years of age" (Luke 3:23), which some see as a claim that Jesus was sufficiently mature to be considered an elder. Likewise, social status factored into who had voice. Elite citizens had public voice, but not male peasants. In general, then, male elders, not young males, not females, had voice.

Certain threads of the territoriality model can be woven together to clarify who has voice. Both public and private space accord voice to someone with sufficient honor. The worthiness and standing of a potential speaker are recognized by those in such spaces, and so he is accorded voice. When the venue is classified as honorable public/political space and the would-be speaker is of a certain status and role, then no control is exercised over him; he has voice. But when the speaker is classified as lacking honor or even corrupting the assembly, then control is exercised over him; he loses voice. He is then unsuited for that space. In terms of Acts, Luke correlates place, voice, and control for Paul (it is unclear in Acts who else enjoys voice).

1. *Public/political space:* in the residences of proconsul (13:7), governors (25–26), and the chief man of the island (28:7–8), Paul has voice: no control of space; his role and status are honored.

2. *Private/nonhousehold space:* in the hall of Tyrannus (19:9) and places where Christians assembled, Paul has voice: no control of space; his role and status are respected. But in synagogues, Paul is eventually denied voice and expelled from the place: control of space enters; his role and status are rejected.

3. *Private/households:* although few households are mentioned as Paul's residence, there he may speak: no control of space; he has respect and honor.

Several patterns emerge in Acts that relate directly to the control or non-control of Paul's speaking. In certain public spaces, elites summon Paul to speak (13:7; 24:24) or invite him to address them (17:18–20). Paul thus is acknowledged as having sufficient elite standing to have voice there. In the private space of synagogues, moreover, Paul, either invited "to give a word of exhortation" (13:15) or more frequently simply standing up on his own, speaks, exhorts, and argues with the audience (14:1; 17:2; 19:8). Although initially granted voice in this setting by virtue of his status, Paul loses his voice when control is exercised over synagogal space. He is silenced and expelled. In general, Paul has voice in many public venues as well as in private households, but he lacks voice in the private space of the synagogue.

Summary and Conclusions

What have we learned?

First, the interpretative model of territoriality proves to be a reliable and productive tool for examining space in Acts. It does what no amount of linguistic sifting or archaeological recovery can provide: patterns of the social perception of space—classification, communication, control of space.

Second, of the many classifications of space listed early in this study, two proved most useful: public/private and honorable/nonhonorable.

Third, examination of many ways of expressing "public"/"private" in the Greco-Roman world provides solid data for interpreting how Luke and other New Testament authors might be using these terms. And the key to their proper interpretation requires awareness of the two chief ancient institutions (*polis,* household) and social patterns of interaction.

Fourth, we now have a nuanced understanding of the classification of "public"/"private." We can distinguish three spaces for males: public/political, private/nonhousehold, private/household. Embedded here are gender classification of male/female.

Fifth, when in Acts 20:20 Paul says that he spoke in "public and from house to house," the narrative of Acts indicates that "public" refers to the residences of governors and kings and to city centers, and that "house to house" refers primarily to space used for assembly. Paul may receive hospitality in the houses of Judas,

Lydia, and Philip, which are private household spaces. Paul, however, "declares, teaches, testifies" in other private locations, possibly even houses now classified as suitable for nonkinship members.

Sixth, Luke's strategy is to tell the reader that Paul is treated like an honorable person who resides and speaks in the most honorable cities of the Greek East. Thus "honor/nonhonor," another native classification of space, confirms Paul as a citizen of a "no low-status city" and even a citizen of Rome (22:25–27).

Seventh, when in public, Paul enjoys voice and no control is exercised to silence him; on the other hand, he is both silenced and controlled in the private synagogue. As a boost to Paul's role and status, Luke portrays him enjoying voice before governors, proconsuls, and kings. Not everyone had voice in public or in private.

BIBLIOGRAPHY

Carpenter, C. R. 1958. Territoriality: A Review of Concepts and Problems. Pages 224–50 in *Behavior and Evolution*. Edited by Anne Roe and George Simpson. New Haven: Yale University Press.

Casimir, Michael J., and Aparna Rao, eds. 1992. *Mobility and Territoriality: Social and Spatial Boundaries among Foragers, Fishers, Pastoralists, and Peripatetics*. Oxford: Berg.

Hoenig, Sydney B. 1979. The Ancient City-Square: The Forerunner of the Synagogue. *ANRW* 2.19.1:448–79.

Humphreys, S. C. 1993. Oikos and Polis. Pages 1–21 in *The Family, Women and Death: Comparative Studies*. 2d ed. Ann Arbor: University of Michigan Press.

Magie, David. 1950. *Roman Rule in Asia Minor, to the End of the Third Century after Christ*. 2 vols. Princeton, N.J.: Princeton University Press.

Malherbe, Abraham J. 1985. "Not in a Corner": Early Christian Apologetic in Acts 26:26. *Second Century* 5:193–210.

Neyrey, Jerome H. 1996. Luke's Social Location of Paul: Cultural Anthropology and the Status of Paul in Acts. Pages 251–79 in *History, Literature, and Society in the Book of Acts*. Edited by Ben Witherington III. Cambridge: Cambridge University Press.

———. 2002. Spaces and Places, Whence and Whither, Homes and Rooms: "Territoriality" in the Fourth Gospel. *Biblical Theology Bulletin* 32:60–74.

———. 2003a. Jesus, Gender and the Gospel of Matthew. Pages 43–66 in *New Testament Masculinities*. Edited by Stephen D. Moore and Janice Capel Anderson. Society of Biblical Literature Semeia Studies 45. Atlanta: Society of Biblical Literature.

———. 2003b. "Teaching You in Public and from House to House" (Acts 20:20): Unpacking a Cultural Stereotype. *Journal for the Study of the New Testament* 26:69–102

Roy, J. 1999. *Polis* and *Oikos* in Classical Athens. *Greece and Rome* 46:1–17.

Sack, Robert D. 1986. *Human Territoriality: Its Theory and History.* Cambridge Studies in Historical Geography 7. Cambridge: Cambridge University Press.

Segal, Peretz. 1989. The Penalty of the Warning Inscription from the Temple of Jerusalem. *Israel Exploration Journal* 39:79–84.

Smith, Jonathan. 1987. *To Take Place: Toward Theory in Ritual.* Chicago: University of Chicago Press.

Stowers, Stanley K. 1982. Social Status, Public Speaking and Private Teaching: The Circumstances of Paul's Preaching Activity. *Novum Testamentum* 26:59–82.

Healing

How hard it is for modern Western readers to study the healings of Jesus without the distorting lens of ethnocentrism. Surely, we say, the affliction of the boy in Mark 9:20–22 is epilepsy, and the stooped posture of the woman in Luke 13:11 is some form of arthritis. Moreover, those enlightened by the Enlightenment might even question the very historicity of miracles. Thus modern readers tend to think about and examine the stories of illness and healing in Luke-Acts in anachronistic and ethnocentric terms. That is, we tend to suppose that the ways we understand and diagnose sickness and disease adequately explain and interpret the accounts of illness in the New Testament. Is there another way? How can we learn it? What good will it do us?

If one wishes to study sicknesses and healings in the New Testament, Luke-Acts is indeed a worthy document for examination, because it narrates many sicknesses and healings. Take, for example, the accounts of blindness. The evangelist narrates the traditional story of how Jesus healed a blind man (Luke 18:35–43//Matt 9:27–31//Matt 20:29–34//Mark 10:46–52). In Acts, however, we have the curious phenomenon of the temporary blindness of Paul, from which he is quickly healed (9:18; 22:13). Along with this, we find the story of Paul cursing Elymas the magician with blindness; this blindness, says Paul, is due to "the hand of the Lord" and will last "for a time" (13:6–11). Blindness, then, may be long-standing, perhaps signaling a genuine disease, or temporary, as in the cases of Paul and Elymas. Blindness befell Paul, who was a sinner (Gal 1:13; 1 Cor 15:9), and Elymas, who opposed the gospel, thus suggesting a symbolic dimension to it. Yet how are we to understand these varying examples of sickness and healing?

What is needed is a way to imagine Luke's language of sickness and healing in terms of his own culture. Thus, it is imperative to design a new reading scenario to do this (Malina 1996). A vaccine for anachronism and ethnocentrism is available to us by the use of cross-cultural investigation and comparison that call for a reader to utilize appropriate social-science methods and concepts. For example, how should we understand health and well-being? In terms of the culture of the first century C.E., health or well-being is but an example of good fortune (Worsley 1982, 330). Alternately, sickness is but one example of a wide range of misfortunes. The key lies in understanding the relation of sickness and healing to fortune and misfortune—not a very modern idea, but one quite common in and more appropriate to other cultures. In terms that modern social scientists use to understand healing and sickness cross-culturally, purity and spirit-possession both provide taxonomies through which to examine the Gospel of Luke and Acts. Illness in these texts is caused by aggressive spirits and renders persons unclean. Healing, however, restores people to wholeness and a state of purity. To understand sickness in a given society, one needs also to know the cultural values and social norms of that society.

To vaccinate ourselves against ethnocentrism, we call upon cultural and social-science methods to aid in interpretation. Accordingly, this chapter devises and employs social-science models for a cultural interpretation of illness and healing in Luke-Acts that help us to surface previously undetected data in the narrative and to interpret with greater accuracy the abundant healing stories therein.

BIBLIOGRAPHY

Malina, Bruce J. 1996. Reading Theory Perspectives. Pages 3–31 in *The Social World of Luke-Acts: Models for Interpretation*. Edited by Jerome H. Neyrey, SJ. Peabody, Mass.: Hendrickson.

John J. Pilch

Healing in Luke-Acts

INTRODUCTION

SICKNESS AND HEALING, though common features in Luke-Acts, are by no means easy to understand. Social-science methods and concepts are tools of retrieval as well as aids to interpretation. This essay, then, calls upon and constructs several social-science models for reading the stories about illness and healing in Luke-Acts: (1) cross-cultural concepts of sickness and healing, (2) the health care system in Luke-Acts, (3) a taxonomy of illnesses in the story line of Luke-Acts. In the light of cross-culturally appropriate methods, models, and concepts, many hitherto undetected data in Luke-Acts emerge as significant.

DEFINING HEALTH AND HEALING IN LUKE-ACTS

How hard but how necessary it is for us to learn this lesson: "It is no longer possible to assume that generalizations based on observations of one culture have a universal applicability" (Papajohn and Spiegel 1975, 19). Bible interpreters need to be wary of imposing observations drawn from Western culture upon Mediterranean culture. Scientifically based Western understandings of health and sickness, sight and blindness, and healing and curing cannot be imposed upon information from the biblical period. Medical anthropology identifies this erroneous methodology as "medicocentrism," which is a belief that scientific Western medicine is the only truth relative to questions of health and sickness. Outside this medical framework, it is argued, there is no truth, and it is highly doubtful that any authentic cures may take place. "Apparent" cures can be explained by subsequent advances in scientific knowledge or perhaps as a form of "mind over matter." The appropriate scenario rejects medicocentrism for understanding sickness and healing, but we must deal dramatically with the issue posed by a culture foreign to ours.

THE HEALTH CARE SYSTEM IN LUKE-ACTS

From the beginning we must be as clear as possible on the terms that we use to describe and classify the sickness mentioned in Luke-Acts. Fortunately, we are not the first readers to grapple with this problem, and we can borrow from the field of medical anthropology the standard terms used there. In this way, we can tap into the valuable work done there, even as we gain a necessary precision in our professional language.

In medical anthropology the word *sickness* is considered a blanket term describing a reality, whereas the words *disease* and *illness* are considered explanatory concepts and terms useful in exploring different facets of that single reality. Think of *sickness* as genus, and *disease* and *illness* as species. We note that these English words have been so designated in modern times by medical anthropologists to describe more accurately the human experience of misfortune in the realm of health and well-being. They do not seem to have any one-to-one counterpart in Classical or New Testament Greek. In other words, Greek or Hebrew words that are translated as "disease" or "illness" or even "sickness" in the Bible reflect the interpretation of the translator and should not be interpreted with the medical-anthropological precision just indicated. In this regard, the caution issued by Hemer (1986, 52) about drawing conclusions based on the "uncertain terminology of literary sources" such as New Testament Greek vocabulary is quite appropriate. The modern interpreter needs to ask this question of each instance in the biblical literature: Can this emic (native) report be fairly interpreted by the etic (outsider [in this case, medical-anthropological]) term *disease* or *illness*?

Disease

The concept and word *disease* reflects a biomedical perspective that sees abnormalities in the structure or function of organ systems. Whether or not they are culturally recognized, these pathological states do exist (Kleinman 1980, 72). As such, a disease affects individuals, and only individuals are treated. To think in terms of individuals and individual disease is a perspective quite foreign to Luke's first-century-c.e. world, which was radically group-oriented, has been noted in earlier chapters of this book. In such a world, persons were collectivistic personalities, dyadic individuals rather than rugged individualists.

Considering that this kind of knowledge of disease hinges on the identification of pathogens, germs, viruses, and other microscopic entities, it is clear that biblical people would be entirely ignorant of a disease. They might be experiencing one but would not have the necessary concepts or terminology to know and express it. Evidently, if we are interested in Luke's narrative and his cultural world, we will not use the term *disease* much if at all, for it is a term foreign to Luke's culture. Instead, we will employ the term *illness*.

Illness

The concept and word *illness* reflect a sociocultural perspective that depends entirely upon social and personal perception of certain socially disvalued states, including but not necessarily restricted to what modern Western science would recognize as a disease. Let us take a classic example. Leprosy as described in the Lev 13–14 is simply not the modern Hansen's disease (*mycobacterium leprae*);

rather, it is some kind of repulsive skin condition. Yet the sociocultural concern over and consequences of this condition are very real. In other words, biblical leprosy is definitely not a disease, but it is an illness (Pilch 1981, 108–9).

Curing and Healing

Technically speaking, when therapy can affect a disease so as to check or remove it, that activity is called *curing*. As a matter of actual fact, cures are relatively rare even in modern Western scientific medicine. When an intervention affects an illness, that activity is called *healing*. The rule of thumb is this: curing :: disease as healing :: illness. Since healing essentially involves the provision of personal and social meaning for the life problems that accompany human health misfortunes, all illnesses are healed, always and infallibly, since all human beings ultimately find some meaning in a life situation including disvalued states.

In biblical reports evidence for the incidence, identification, and management of disease is difficult if not impossible to discover with certitude. Thus it cannot be known with certainty whether in modern terms anyone ever cured an afflicted person. And so, modern readers of the Gospels might be taking a hopeless and even misguided approach if they concentrate on issues of disease and curing. On the other hand, in modern terminology the obvious social concern that accompanies the reports of human health-related misfortunes in the New Testament is evidence that the discussion of them in the Gospels centers on illness, and these are almost always healed. This suggests that all of Jesus' dealings with the sick in Luke's gospel are truly healed, although they may not be cured in the technical sense.

Health

From an anthropological perspective, health should be defined as a state of complete well-being, not the restoration of individual activity or performance that the values of the Western world, in general, would require.

The Health Care System

Although no one is certain whether health care now or ever was delivered in a systematic fashion, the health care system is a conceptual model with three constituent and overlapping parts: a professional sector, a popular sector, and a folk sector. It would actually be more accurate to call this a *sickness care system* because that is the primary focus, but *health care system* is the recognized term, and it is a good heuristic tool for analyzing the way sickness is identified, labeled (i.e., placed into a taxonomy or proper category), and managed in all cultures.

The Professional Sector

The professional sector of a health care system includes the professional, trained and credentialed healers. If the Greek word ἰατρός (usually translated as "physician") can be assumed to identify a professional healer, there are two, perhaps three, relevant passages to review: Luke 4:23; 5:31; 8:43.

The proverb that Jesus cites in 4:23, "'Physician, heal yourself'; what we have heard you did at Capernaum, do here also in your own country," is common in antiquity (Noland 1979). It always depends on context for its meaning, and the word *physician* is almost always applied figuratively. An analogous contemporary proverb, "Every dog has its day," almost never refers to dogs, but humans are never offended when this proverb is applied to situations of human misfortune or bad luck.

The Lukan context (4:21–44) suggests that Jesus identifies himself as a prophet (4:24) who exorcizes and heals. The identity is repeated and confirmed in 13:32–33: "I cast out demons and perform cures. . . . I must go on my way for it cannot be that a prophet should perish away from Jerusalem" (RSV). Others acknowledge and reinforce the identity (Luke 7:16; 9:8, 19; 24:19). Being a prophet who exorcizes and heals is very likely part of Jesus' specific identity as a folk healer.

In 5:31 Luke's Jesus once more quotes a proverb: "Those who are well have no need of a physician, but those who are sick" (RSV). In all three Synoptics it is cited as an explanation for his socializing with tax collectors and sinners, but only in Luke does Jesus specify that he has come to call sinners "to repentance" (5:32).

Once again, the context of the word *physician* adds a further piece of information useful for understanding the kind of illness that a healer in Luke's community would be expected to address. Tax collecting and the condition of a sinner entailed a distortion of social life as it should properly be lived in Israel. In order to refocus one's personal meaning in life, repentance is required. That, in fact, is a consistent subject of preaching (see, e.g., Luke 3:3, 8; 10:13; 11:32; Acts 2:38; 3:19; 11:18; 13:24). From a medical-anthropological perspective, Mark, who notes the failure of physicians to heal the woman who had a flow of blood (5:26), highlights the failure of the professional sector of the health care system in this instance. Luke, on the other hand, whether or not he has willfully expunged the criticism of physicians, quite clearly points to the failure of all sectors of the health care system in his statement that she "could not be healed by anyone" (8:43 RSV).

In the Gospel of Luke Jesus adopts the image of a healing prophet, or prophet-healer. A central function of his healing ministry is to lead those whose lives have lost cultural meaning back to the proper purpose and direction in life. That is, the prophet-healer preaches repentance, change of heart, transformation of horizons, broadening of perspectives.

The Popular Sector

The principal concern of the lay, nonprofessional, nonspecialist popular culture is health and health maintenance, not sickness and cure. Obviously, however, this focus on health sensitizes people to notice deviance from the culturally defined norm known as "health." Therefore, it is in this, the popular sector, that the deviant condition known as "sickness" is first observed, defined, and treated. There are four levels in the popular sector of the health care system: (1) individual,

(2) family, (3) social network, (4) community beliefs and activities. Each level yields additional information about the entire system.

First, at the level of individual dyadic persons, Luke-Acts reports twenty-three cases involving men and eight involving women. In Luke's gospel men are afflicted in three symbolic body zones (Malina 1979; 1993): mouth-ears (1:20, 64; 11:14–23; 22:47–54a), hands-feet (5:17–26; 6:6–11), heart-eyes (7:21; 18:35–43). People with skin problems (lepers [see Pilch 1981) are cleansed (5:12–16; 17:11–19), possessed individuals are freed (4:31–37; 8:26–34; 9:37–43a; 11:14–23), and dead or near dead are raised (7:1–10; 7:11–16).

The cases in Acts involving men reflect only two of the symbolic three body zones: hands-feet (3:1–10; 9:32–35; 14:8–18; 28:1–6) and heart-eyes (9:18//22:13; 13:1–12). Spirit-induced ills afflict Herod (12:23 [stricken by an angel of Lord, eaten by worms]) and the sons of Sceva (19:14–16). There is one raising from the dead (20:7–12).

Women in Luke's gospel reflect some distinctively feminine experiences, such as difficulty in conception (1:24; 1:35) and menstrual irregularity (8:42b–48). One woman is raised from the dead (8:40–42a, 49–56); one released from a fever (4:38–39); one is freed from a spirit of infirmity (13:10–17) and others from evil spirits (8:2). In Acts only two cases involving women are reported: Tabitha is raised from the dead (9:36–43), and a slave girl is released from bondage to an evil spirit (16:16–24).

At this point, what does the health care system model reveal? Men and women are reported to suffer a variety of ills, some that are experienced by both groups (death; possession of a spirit), and others that are experienced by each group singly: only men are reported with skin problems/leprosy, only women suffer from difficulty in conception and menstrual irregularity, distinctively female problems. Further, only men's ills seem to fit into one of the three identified symbolic body zones. Curiously, in Luke's gospel all three zones are affected, while in Acts only two are affected. (We will need another model to interpret the significance of this observation, and it will be presented and explained below in the discussions of taxonomies of illness.) For women, what emerges from a bird's-eye view of Luke-Acts at this level of the health care system model is that specifically feminine ailments recorded in the Gospels no longer plague women in Acts, although, as is true also for men, evil/unclean spirits still pose problems, as also does death. We will return to this consideration below in the fuller discussion of the symbolic body-zone model.

Second, kinship is one of the two formal institutions in the biblical world, so it is no surprise that the family, including fictive kin, is involved and affected in many of the instances reported in Luke-Acts. For instance, the death of a son is tragic enough, but for a widow that is double jeopardy (Luke 7:11–16) because she relies on that male next-of-kin for her livelihood. Jesus, by restoring life to the widow's son, effectively saved her life as well. Conversely, when Paul healed a slave girl who had a spirit of divination (Acts 16:24), her masters felt adversely affected by her good fortune. This level of the health care system model reminds us to keep in mind that in the Mediterranean world, even more so than in the modern Western world, illness affects and involves everyone in the kinship group. The consequences of healing affect this wider group as well.

Third, still another pathway for seeking help in an illness episode is the social network—that is, the set of contacts with relatives, friends, neighbors, and so forth through which individuals maintain a social identity, receive emotional support, material aid, services, and information, and develop new social contacts.

One way in which health status is maintained and continually checked among the personalities who populate the pages of the Bible follows the normal pattern of dyadic relationships. Malina (1979) notes that in the Middle East persons are viewed not as individuals but rather as dyadic personalities; the same is true in the Far East (Ohnuki-Tierney 1981, 67). Such a person lives in a continual dependence upon the opinions of others, including the judgment of whether or not one is ill.

Social scientists classify networks into two major categories: (a) according to structure or morphology, or (b) according to the type or quality of interaction. For example, consider the healing of the paralytic by Peter and John in Acts 3:1–4:22. The paralytic, who was more than forty years old, was carried to the temple gate daily by "them," probably family, friends, or neighbors. This cripple from birth who begged here was known by many, some of whom may have been daily benefactors. Thus, in the crippled man's network those who carried him maintained one kind or quality of interaction probably rooted in lovingkindness ḥesed (a kinship virtue), whereas those who saw him begging and gave alms had another quality of interaction with him probably rooted in צדקה (Isa 56:1; Sir 3:29–4:10).

Finally, the popular sector of the health care system is characterized by a distinctive set of community beliefs and practices. For example, belief in spirits and spirit-aggression, including possession, is found in all the Gospels but seems especially prominent in Luke. Murdock (1980, 73) observes that such a belief is virtually universal and shows no tendency to cluster in a particular ideational region as do, for example, witchcraft theories. Evidence indicates that every society that depends primarily on animal husbandry for its economic livelihood regards spirit-aggression as either the predominant or definitely an important secondary cause of illness. This is especially true where large domestic animals are the focus: camels, sheep, and goats.

As mentioned above, Luke's worldview lies heavily under the influences of spirits, demons, and the like. Luke's gospel reports that Jesus is conceived by the power of the Holy Spirit (1:35), and at his baptism the Holy Spirit descends upon him in the form of a dove (3:21). Still full of the Holy Spirit and under his impulse, Jesus goes to the desert to do battle with the devil, a malicious spirit whom he bests (4:1–13). Then Jesus returns in the power of the Spirit to Galilee, teaches in synagogues, and one day reads the text of Isaiah that says, "The Spirit of the Lord is upon me" (4:14–18 RSV). In the very next episodes Jesus, while teaching in the Capernaum synagogue, frees a man from the unclean spirit that had possessed him (4:31–37), and then, according to the interpretation by Hull (1974, 102–3), Jesus frees Simon's mother-in-law from the demon "Fever" that had possessed her

(4:38–39). The section ends with a summary statement that Jesus healed people sick with a variety of diseases and "demons also came out of many" (4:40–41 RSV). Finally, in a passage unique to in Luke, Jesus asserts, "Behold, I cast out demons and perform cures today and tomorrow" (13:32 RSV). He thus proclaims his identity as an exorcist. Recall the aforementioned evidence from the professional sector in which Jesus is presented as a prophet who heals and exorcizes.

In addition to spirit-related illness episodes also reported by other evangelists (4:33–37; 8:26–39; 9:37–43a; 9:49; 11:14–15; 11:24–26), Luke adds these reports: in the gospel, 10:17 (disciples against demons); 22:3 (Satan entered Judas); 22:31–34 (Satan wants to sift Simon); in Acts, 8:7 (deacon Philip casts out unclean spirits); 12:23 (Herod is afflicted by an angel of the Lord); 19:12 (Paul's power through handkerchiefs and cloths against evil spirits); 19:14–16 (exorcist sons of Sceva overpowered by a man with an evil spirit).

And in Luke's gospel the descriptions of ailments afflicting women give prominent place to spirits: Peter's mother-in-law is afflicted by a spirit named "Fever" (4:38); among the women who follow Jesus, some were freed from evil spirits and infirmities (8:2–3); in the raising of Jairus's daughter, Luke notes that "her spirit returned, and she got up at once" (8:55 RSV); the stooped-over woman had a spirit of infirmity (13:10) and was bound by Satan for eighteen years (13:16). And in Acts Paul liberates a woman possessed by a spirit of divination (16:16).

In summary, in Luke's understanding and reports spirit-possession looms large, and healers such as Jesus, Peter, Philip the deacon, and Paul must be able to address this human ailment with some measure of success. Furthermore, the four levels operative in the popular sector of the health care system surface much information about illness (including the results of spirit-aggression) in the world of Luke-Acts as well as about those who are afflicted by and involved with the illness (men and women, families, social networks). The heuristic value of this part of the model seems apparent. But its inability to interpret all the information surfaced makes the investigator impatient to move on to another model: taxonomies of illness. However, one more sector of the health care system model, the folk sector, awaits exploration before we can make that move.

The Folk Sector

In Luke's gospel Jesus identifies himself as an authorized, spirit-filled prophet who vanquishes unclean spirits and illnesses associated with them. His constituency accepts and affirms this identity (Luke 7:16; 9:8, 19; 14:19). In addition, Jesus heals illnesses not associated with any spirit. As such, then, Luke's Jesus is a folk healer, and his "license to practice" is tacitly granted and acknowledged by each individual sick person and the local community. Luke's report that some of the crowd doubted Jesus' abilities as a folk healer and questioned the source of his power (Luke 11:15; cf. Matt 9:34; 12:24, which specify the Pharisees as the ones who challenged Jesus on this matter) only highlights the limitations of a folk healer's abilities. Indeed, some communities prefer that the folk healer not practice in their midst (see Luke 8:37).

The power of Jesus relative to evil spirits and demons, however, is noteworthy. Except for exorcisms, Jesus generally has no power at all in his social world. Power is the capacity to produce conformity based on what is necessary for the good of the group. And politics deals in part with how members of a group achieve and use power to implement public goals. Jesus' exorcisms, the instances in which he does have access to power, can, from the definition of politics just given, be identified as political actions performed for the purpose of restoring correct order to society. Since kinship and politics were the only two formal (i.e., distinct and free-standing) social institutions that existed in the first-century-c.e. Mediterranean world, the political dimensions of Jesus' healing activity would be self-evident to all witnesses, friendly and hostile alike.

Contemporary medical anthropology supports this insight. It views a theory of disease as a sign or emblem that marks what a group values, disvalues, and preoccupies itself with (Fabrega 1984, 274). Certainly, in Jesus' world spirit-possession was a disvalued state, and the relationship of spirits to this world preoccupied him and his contemporaries. Within this scheme the healing enterprise is concerned with diagnosing the problem, prognosticating outcomes, and applying suitable therapies. Another way of viewing this process is that the healing enterprise seeks to explain, predict, and control reality. In the Beelzebul episode (Luke 11:14–26) the problem diagnosed is a case of spirit-possession. The prognosis or predicted outcome is that the cast-out spirit might return with seven more powerful demons to repossess the person. The therapy Jesus applied or the reality that he seeks to control is "He who is not with me is against me, and he who does not gather with me scatters" (11:23). Since Jesus has effective power against demons, he has the power to maintain order in society as it should be. By keeping demons in their place, Jesus maintains good order in society. He also controls reality as he and his contemporaries understood it. Anyone who would stand in the way of that power, challenge it, or obstruct it stands in the way of the order that belongs in society.

The healers in Acts (Peter and John, Paul, Ananias, Stephen, and Philip) are presented as continuing the healing activity of Jesus, much like Elisha is deliberately presented by the author of 1–2 Kings as continuing the work of his master, Elijah. Peter's and John's healing of the crippled man in Acts 3:1–4:22 is an explicit example.

In conclusion, Luke's portrayal of Jesus as an anointed, spirit-filled, exorcising-and-healing prophet and the community's general acknowledgment and acceptance of him as such set Jesus clearly in the folk sector of the health care system reflected in Luke-Acts. Thus, the health care system model, with its three intersecting sectors, not only helps us to mine more information from the text than does a cursory reading but also describes the context in which healers would function. Insights from the professional and the popular sectors flesh out the picture of Jesus' activity that is properly situated in the folk sector of that system. It is now time to focus more specifically on the misfortunes that Jesus healed and try to build a taxonomy that will best account for those reported in Luke-Acts.

Taxonomies of Illnesses in Luke-Acts

The identification, classification, and clustering of illnesses into culturally meaningful categories is called a taxonomy. In the modern scientific Western practice of medicine a very complete taxonomy of physical and mental health problems can be found in exhaustive manuals of differential diagnosis. Your physician may have consulted such a book after listening to your report of a recent physical experience or set of experiences. The modern physician's challenge is to translate your "lay" report into appropriate professional jargon and then seek to locate your "real" problem on a grid or map of respiratory, circulatory, or other systemic problems.

Historians of ancient medicine classify the works of some ancient writers as comparable to these modern manuals because they list, describe, and discuss the "health" problems known to them in their own culture. Some writings of Hippocrates and Galen are often categorized in this way. Critics of this approach believe it to be medicocentric; that is, contemporary historians of medicine too often unwittingly impose modern scientific Western interpretations on these ancient texts.

Furthermore, some interpreters of biblical literature sometimes seek to utilize such ancient Latin or Greek resources in analyzing biblical texts. This strategy produces mixed results precisely because of the potential interpretative hazards just mentioned. Biblical authors themselves do not appear to have had at hand any of these ancient resources, nor do they use the terminology utilized by those authors. In fact, such ancient volumes may represent an elite understanding of human health misfortunes.

Biblical interpreters, therefore, fare better by taking seriously the reports of biblical authors and then resorting to both Mediterranean and medical anthropology for fresh insights to make sense of the admittedly meager data in biblical literature. Utilizing the tools of Mediterranean and medical anthropology, a biblical interpreter can construct a few different illness taxonomies from the data in Luke-Acts. The process involves designing an imposed etic view in the hopes of refining this until it becomes an etic perspective that is clearly derived from the etic data (Pilch 1996, 133–36).

A Taxonomy Based on Spirit Involvement

The first taxonomy embraces illnesses in which a spirit is involved. Modern Western readers of the Bible are struck by the frequent reports of spirit-possession and illness associated with spirits. Recall that Murdock (1980, 73) noted that belief in spirits is practically universal and shows no tendency to emerge in a particular ideational region as do witchcraft theories. Foster (1976, 773–80) proposes a twofold taxonomy for illnesses in non-Western medical systems based on whether or not spirits are involved. The insights of Murdock and Foster suggest that a spirit-focused taxonomy would fittingly address the New Testament data but with a major modification for "believers." The New Testament associates some misfortunes with malevolent (unclean, evil, etc.) spirits. Since in this culture every event must have a personal cause, and no human or malevolent spirit has caused it, one might presume that the other misfortunes should be ascribed to God. Thus Foster's twofold taxonomy could be more appropriately modified to include illness in which a malevolent spirit is involved and illness in which no malevolent spirit is involved (though God is or might be so perceived).

Several times we have noted that illness is understood in terms of "misfortune." Such a concept is important here, because "fortune" or "misfortune" in the world of Luke-Acts comes not from personal human activity but rather from the operation on humans by gods or spirits. This is a world in which the first question to be asked in the case of fortune or misfortune is "Who did this to me?" Hence, when we investigate a taxonomy of illness based on spirit involvement, we are tapping into a basic conception of the way the world works: a "spirit" (or god) has acted upon a mortal.

The Taxonomy of Spirit Involvement Applied to Luke-Acts

As observed above, Luke's worldview is heavily influenced by the perception of the activity of spirits, demons, and the like. In fact, this feature is more prominent in Luke-Acts than in Matthew, Mark, and John. The activity of the spirits and demons is especially linked to sickness, and Jesus "cures" those who are ill by means of the powerful, healing spirit of God. To grasp the importance of this for our study of illness and healing in Luke, we turn to a text found only in the Gospel of Luke. Jesus asserts, "Behold, I cast out demons and perform cures today and tomorrow" (13:32 RSV). Casting out demons is itself not just another instance of healing; it is also a way of describing the illness itself. By this association of the relationship of evil spirits and healing, Luke thus proclaims Jesus' identity as an exorcist. But *exorcist* is our term, an imposed etic concept; Luke considers Jesus' exorcisms to be the healing of illnesses. Let us not understate the amount or importance of spirit-related illness in Luke-Acts. Luke, of course, received many such stories from other gospel traditions. For example, the other evangelists also report episodes of spirit-related illness found in Luke (Luke 4:33–37; 8:26–39; 9:37–43a; 11:14–15, 24–26).

In addition to these, Luke adds his own reports of the presence and activity of spirits, demons, and Satan: (1) in the gospel, 10:17 (disciples against demons); 22:3 (Satan entered Judas); 22:31–34 (Satan wants to sift Simon); and in Acts, 8:7 (deacon Philip casts out unclean spirits); 12:23 (Herod afflicted by an angel of the Lord); 19:12 (Paul's power exerted through handkerchiefs and cloths against evil spirits); 19:14–16 (exorcist sons of Sceva overpowered by a man with an evil spirit). The malevolent presence of demons and unclean spirits in Luke-Acts is considerable.

As we noted above, in Luke's gospel the descriptions of ailments afflicting women give prominent place to spirits: Peter's mother-in-law is afflicted by a spirit named "Fever" (4:38); among the women who follow Jesus, some were freed from evil spirits and infirmities (8:2–3); in the raising of Jairus's daughter, Luke notes that "her spirit returned, and she got up at once" (8:55 RSV); the stooped-over woman had a spirit of infirmity (13:10) and was bound by Satan for eighteen years (13:16). And in Acts Paul liberates a woman possessed by a spirit of divination (16:16). Again, it is obvious that in Luke's understanding and reports spirit-possession looms large, and healers such as Jesus, Peter, Philip the deacon, and Paul are able to address this human ailment with some measure of success. Therefore, a review of the summary statements in Luke-Acts detailing illnesses and summarizing healings does indeed reveal that possessions or spirit-caused maladies are one category of illness: Luke 4:40–41; 5:17; 7:21, 22–23; 8:2–3; 9:1, 10–11; 10:9, 17–20; 13:32; Acts 5:15–16 (Peter); 8:6–7 (Philip); 10:38 (Peter about Jesus); 19:11–12 (Paul).

A Taxonomy Based on Symbolic Body Zones Affected

In our quest to learn how Luke and other inhabitants of his world perceived illnesses, we inquired above about the parts of the body that tend to be afflicted with illness. Again, let us not impose our modern scientific Western viewpoint of how the body is perceived; let us instead strive to learn how ancients understand and describe the body. Malina (1979, 133–38; 1993, 73–81) formulated and developed a pattern of personality perception quite easily discernible among the largely Semitic biblical authors. Human beings are perceived as socially embedded and interacting personalities reacting to persons and things outside themselves; in other words, they are not Western individualists. Biblical personalities, moreover, are not introspective and find it quite difficult, if not impossible, to know what goes on inside themselves and others. "For the Lord sees not as human beings see; human beings look on the outward appearance, but the LORD looks on the heart" (1 Sam 16:7).

This is a world where "hypocrisy" is a constant plague (Pilch 1994), with the consequence that people are actually deceiving others by hiding their inner, evil thoughts behind a facade of orthopraxis (Luke 6:42; 12:1, 56; 13:15). They are like actors (the literal meaning of the Greek word *hypokritēs*) who refuse to be their authentic selves and instead play another role. Yet some powerful prophetic figures, such as Jesus, penetrate this facade. Consider the significance of Jesus' comment in Luke 5:22: "Why do you question in your hearts?" (RSV). He could read human hearts; he was not deceived by appearances. This has implications for Jesus' healings, for he can discern what illness is within, and he can read hearts to know what spirit is present. Healing, then, may require a "physician" who can discern spirits and inner states as well as apply correct healing technique.

More to the point, however, people in the ancient Semitic world simply had a different perception from ours of which bodily organs human activity related to. Nor did they perceive the human body in the same way we do. In that culture the individual person and the outside world with which that person interacts are described metaphorically by using parts of the human body as metaphors. In fact, this body is divided into three zones of organs and behavior.

> Zone 1: Westerners associate thought with the brain, but not so the people in Luke's world. There, humans have hearts for thinking together with eyes that collect data for the heart.

Zone 2: Humans have mouths for communicating along with ears that collect the communications of others. This activity is very important in biblical culture and receives a considerable amount of attention (see Jas 3:1–12).

Zone 3: Humans have hands and feet for acting or behaving.

To state this in another way, human beings consist of three mutually inter-penetrating yet distinguishable symbolic zones for interacting with various environments: (1) the zone of emotion-fused thought (heart-eyes), (2) the zone of self-expressive speech (mouth-ears), (3) the zone of purposeful action (hands-feet), digrammed thus:

ZONE	BODILY PARTS	FUNCTIONS
1	heart-eyes	emotion-fused thought
2	mouth-ears	self-expressive speech
3	hands-feet	purposeful action

Figure 18: Human zones for interacting with various environments

According to Malina (1993, 74–75), these three zones describe human behavior throughout the Bible from Genesis to Revelation. He presents a rather comprehensive list of the vocabulary that pertains to or reflects each zone. It will be of considerable importance to us as we read the narrative of illness and healing in Luke-Acts to attend to which bodily parts are ill, because correct understanding of the symbolic significance of eyes, ears, or hands-feet may signal misfortune in regard to thought, speech, or action. This second taxonomy of illness based on symbolic body zones is able to cluster those reports in which specific parts of the body or their distinct activities are mentioned. Interpretation of the reports then hinges on noticing which zones are omitted, or which are healed, and so forth. Let us now apply this taxonomy to Luke's narrative.

The Taxonomy of Symbolic Body Zones Affected Applied to Luke-Acts

Our author reports thirty-one episodes of sick individuals involving twenty-three men and eight women who are afflicted differently in terms of bodily zones. In the gospel, men are afflicted in all three symbolic body-zones. (1) Heart-eyes: of Jesus it is reported that "on many that were blind he bestowed sight" (7:21 RSV); a blind man near Jericho regains sight (18:35–43). (2) Mouth-ears: Zechariah, father of John the Baptizer, is stricken dumb and then regains his speech (1:20, 64); Jesus casts out a demon who was dumb (11:14–23); the ear of the high priest's slave is amputated and then healed (22:47–54a). (3) Hands-feet: A paralytic is able to walk away healed in his feet and legs (5:17–26); a man in a synagogue with a withered right hand is restored to wholeness (6:6–11); the dead or near dead are restored to life; they who could do no activity whatsoever are given back that potential (7:1–10, 11–16). Affected in all three zones, men are totally unhealthy.

The cases in Acts involving men reflect only two of the three symbolic zones. (1) Heart-eyes: Ananias heals Paul's temporary blindness (9:18//22:13); Bar-Jesus, known also as Elymas, is made temporarily blind by Paul (13:1–12). (2) Hands-feet: Peter heals the man lame from birth at Beautiful Gate of the temple (3:1–10); Peter heals the eight-year bedridden paralytic Aeneas (9:32–35); Paul heals the born-paralytic at Lystra (14:8–18); Paul survives a lethal snake bite on the hand (28:1–6 [cf. Luke 10:19]).

Women in the gospel reflect some distinctively feminine experiences such as difficulty in conception (1:24 [Elizabeth]; 1:34 [Mary]) and menstrual irregularity (8:42b–48). This would pertain to the hands-feet zone, the zone of purposeful activity, since child-bearing and child-rearing are activities (a hands-feet function in this schema) committed to women in this culture. One woman, Jairus's daughter, is raised from the dead (8:40–42a, 49–56), which also pertains to the hands-feet zone. The dead can perform no purposeful activity; only the living can do that. Peter's mother-in-law is freed from a demon named "Fever" (4:38–39), and immediately begins to serve them; this suggests that she too was affected in the hands-feet zone: lying in bed is to be deprived of foot and hand activity, being up and around as a woman ought. The bent women is freed from a spirit of infirmity (13:10–17) and is able to stand up straight again, suggesting yet another healing in the hands-feet zone. All of the women healed in Luke's gospel, then, were healed in the symbolic bodily zone of hands-feet, the zone of purposeful activity. According to the model of Kluckhohn and Strodtbeck (1961), the primary value orientation for women in ancient Mediterranean culture is purposeful activity. Illness impeded these women from pursuing their dominant cultural orientation. Healing restores them to that capacity. There are but two healings of women in Acts, and they give no significantly different picture. Tabitha is raised from the dead (9:36–43 [the hands-feet zone]), and a slave girl who was a soothsayer is purged of the evil spirit who prompts her to speak in this way (16:16–24 [the mouth-ears zone]).

From this taxonomic description we might draw some conclusions. The overall picture for men is that whereas in the gospel they are ailing in all three symbolic zones, in Acts the mouth-ears (consider all those speeches!) are problem-free, but heart-eyes (understanding) and hands-feet (actually doing) are still in the process of being healed. For women, what emerges from a bird's-eye view of Luke-Acts is that specifically feminine ailments no longer plague women in Acts as they did in the gospel. But the symbolic zone of purposeful activity (hands-feet) continues to require healing or empowering. Recall how in the gospel Elizabeth and Mary composed canticles of praise and gratitude, and other women in search of healing were able to approach and dialogue with Jesus. The mouth-ears zone, which appeared "healthy" in the gospel, needs healing in Acts 16 because it has fallen under the domination of an evil spirit and is being exploited by men.

Where do lepers fit? Lepers or those afflicted with skin problems could also be considered as afflicted with a hands-feet illness because their malady excludes them from participating in the holy community, particularly at worship. Their "purposeful activity," which is what the hands-feet symbolic body zone highlights, is severely limited. Indeed, the skin problem condition that they called "leprosy" prevented them from performing the most purposeful activity known in their culture: joining the group in publicly acknowledging God, who has control over their existence.

A Taxonomy Based on Purity and Impurity

Considering the difficulty that accompanies imagining skin problems (leprosy) as part of a taxonomy based on symbolic body zones, it is alternatively possible to construct a taxonomy of illnesses mentioned in the Gospels based on degrees of impurity (Pilch 1981). Skin problems called "leprosy" affect the body's boundary and thus symbolize threats to purity or wholeness. People with skin problems are considered impure (Lev 13–14) because their body's boundary has been invaded and their presence in the community obviously violates the community's boundary. The presence of people with skin problems in the community makes it unclean, impure, and lacking in wholeness and holiness.

Men and women with uncontrolled or uncontrollable bodily effluvia (Lev 15) are also impure, as are people who come into contact with them. The woman with the uncontrollable hemorrhage (Luke 8:42b–48) who touched Jesus' garment in hope of healing was herself considered impure, and by touching Jesus, she rendered him impure as well. Jesus remedied her condition and restored her to purity, wholeness, and holiness, but obviously he did not consider himself adversely affected by her touch. Similarly, people afflicted in one or another of the symbolic body zones can also be considered unwhole or impure because of their perceived lack of symbolic bodily integrity, which also points to a deficiency in purity, wholeness, and holiness. The same could be said for those possessed or affected in some way by a malevolent spirit. Thus, a taxonomy based on impurity could be still another all-encompassing category for explaining the illnesses listed in the Gospels. In each instance Jesus' therapeutic activity restores such afflicted individuals to purity, to wholeness. The practical outcome is that such healed individuals are also restored to full and active membership in the holy community, the people of God. Certainly this taxonomy could be developed in greater detail in another essay.

A Summary of the Taxonomies

At least three different taxonomies can be constructed that would facilitate the understanding of health misfortunes reported in the Gospels to guide the interpretation of healing narratives. Foster's taxonomy of illnesses based on the influence of a spirit or lack of such influence can be refined for interpreting biblical texts to include illness associated with a malevolent spirit and illnesses presumably attributable to God's will, since God is ultimately responsible for everything that happens. Another taxonomy reflects the symbolic understanding of body zones (hands-feet, heart-eyes, mouth-ears) that permeates the Bible from beginning to end. Many of the illnesses reported fit into such a taxonomy, and significant interpretations emerge, as noted above, by observing which zones remain unaffected and which zones seem amenable to therapeutic activity. Finally, perhaps the most comprehensive taxonomy is the one based on different kinds of impurity. Given the penchant of first-century-C.E. Mediterranean people to judge one another on the basis of externals, a pure or whole person is one quite visibly clean, pure, whole. Anyone with a skin lesion ("leprosy") is visibly unclean, unwhole, impure.

Conclusion

Drawing upon models and concepts from Mediterranean and medical anthropology helps an interpreter to be a respectful reader of biblical material such as Luke-Acts. The Mediterranean cultural preference for being or being-in-becoming recommends a definition of health that emphasizes a state of wholesomeness. The biblical culture's acceptance of spirits as operative and interfering in human affairs validates a division of human ailments into those involving malevolent spirits and those attributable to the spirit known as God.

Biblical culture's view of the healthy and wholesome human being as being composed of three balanced symbolic body zones helps us to identify and categorize the ailments suffered that were presented for healing. Another look at the same material from the perspective of purity, wholeness, cleanness and its opposites (impurity, uncleanness, unwholeness) suggests perhaps the most comprehensive taxonomy of all, one based on purity concerns.

From the perspective of symbolic body zones, Luke appears to have singled out the heart-eyes zone as a leitmotif in Luke-Acts, although the other dimensions also are present. To my knowledge, these insights are unique contributions from the application of social-science models and concepts to the interpretation of biblical texts.

Bibliography

Caplan, Arthur L., H. Tristram Engelhardt Jr., and James J. McCartney, eds. 1981. *Concepts of Health and Disease: Interdisciplinary Perspectives*. Reading, Mass.: Addison-Wesley.

Cassell, Eric J. 1976. Illness and Disease. *Hastings Center Report* 6:27–37.

Chrisman, Noel J., and T. W. Maretzki, eds. 1982. *Clinically Applied Anthropology: Apologists in Health Science Settings*. Culture, Illness, and Healing 5. Dordrecht: Reidel.

Eisenberg, Leon. 1977. Disease and Illness: Distinctions between Professional and Popular Ideas of Sickness. *Culture, Medicine, and Psychiatry* 1:9–23.

Englehardt, H. Tristram. 1986. The Social Meanings of Illness. *Second Opinion* 1:26–39.

Fabrega, Horacio. 1974. *Disease and Social Behavior: An Interdisciplinary Perspective*. Cambridge, Mass.: MIT Press.

————. 1984. Lay Concepts of Illness. Pages 11–31 in *The Experience of Illness*. Edited by Ray Fitzpatrick et al. Social Science Paperbacks 272. London: Tavistock.

Foster, George M. 1976. Disease Etiologies in Non-Western Medical Systems. *American Anthropologist* 78:773–82.

Geertz, Clifford, 1976. "From the Native's Point of View": On the Nature of Anthropological Understanding. Pages 221–37 in *Meaning in Anthropology*. Edited by Keith H. Basso and Henry A. Selby. School of American Research Advanced Seminar Series. Albuquerque: University of New Mexico Press.

Gilmore, David D. 1982. Anthropology of the Mediterranean Area. *Annual Reviews in Anthropology* 11:175–205.

Hemer, Colin J. 1986. Medicine in the New Testament World. Pages 43–83 in *Medicine and the Bible*. Edited by Bernard Palmer. Exeter: Paternoster.

Hull, John M. 1974. *Hellenistic Magic and the Synoptic Tradition*. Studies in Biblical Theology 2/28. Naperville, Ill.: Allenson.

Kleinman, Arthur. 1980. *Patients and Healers in the Context of Culture: An Exploration of the Borderland between Anthropology, Medicine, and Psychiatry*. Comparative Studies of Health Systems and Medical Care 3. Berkeley: University of California Press.

Kluckhohn, Florence R., and Fred L. Strodtbeck. 1961. *Variations in Value Orientations*. Evanston, Ill.: Row, Peterson.

Malina, Bruce J. 1979. The Individual and the Community—Personality in the Social World of Early Christianity. *Biblical Theology Bulletin* 9:126–38.

———. 1993. *The New Testament World: Insights from Cultural Anthropology*. 3d ed. Louisville: Westminster John Knox.

McGoldrick, Monica, John K. Pearce, and Joseph Giordano, eds. 1982. *Ethnicity and Family Therapy*. New York: Guilford Press.

Murdock, George Peter. 1980. *Theories of Illness: A World Survey*. Pittsburgh: University of Pittsburgh Press.

Noland, John. 1979. Classical and Rabbinical Parallels to "Physician, Heal Yourself" (Lk. IV 23). *Novum Testamentum* 21:193–209.

Ohnuki-Tierney, Emiko. 1981. *Illness and Healing among the Sakhalin Ainu: A Symbolic Interpretation*. Cambridge: Cambridge University Press.

———. 1984. *Illness and Culture in Contemporary Japan: An Anthropological View*. Cambridge: Cambridge University Press.

Papajohn, John, and John Spiegel. 1975. *Transactions in Families*. San Francisco: Jossey-Bass.

Pilch, John J. 1981. Biblical Leprosy and Body Symbolism. *Biblical Theology Bulletin* 11:108–13.

———. 1985. Healing in Mark: A Social Science Analysis. *Biblical Theology Bulletin* 15:142–50.

———. 1986. The Health Care System in Matthew: A Social Science Analysis. *Biblical Theology Bulletin* 16:102–6.

———. 1988. Understanding Biblical Healing: Selecting the Appropriate Model. *Biblical Theology Bulletin* 18:60–66.

———. 1994. Secrecy in the Mediterranean World: An Anthropological Perspective. *Biblical Theology Bulletin* 24:151–57.

————. 1996. Altered States of Consciousness: A "Kitbashed" Model. *Biblical Theology Bulletin* 26:133–38.

Pilisuk, Marc, and Susan Hillier Parks. 1986. *The Healing Web: Social Networks and Human Survival.* Hanover, N.H.: University of New England Press.

Worsley, Peter. 1982. Non-Western Medical Systems. *Annual Review of Anthropology* 11:315–48.

Young, Allan. 1982. The Anthropology of Illness and Sickness. *Annual Review of Anthropology* 11:257–85.

Evil Eye

12

The modern Mediterranean world still has a widespread belief in the "evil eye," the idea that certain persons, animals, or spirits are able, through their gaze, to impact negatively other people. In the following essay John Elliott argues that there is ample evidence for such a belief in the ancient Mediterranean world as well. As a test case, he turns to Galatians, a text in which Paul instructs his readers/hearers how to react when someone casts the evil eye upon them.

The evil eye is part of a larger system of belief in which the world is assumed to be inhabited by all kinds of spirits, some helpful and some inimical. The evil eye is part of the phenomenon of witchcraft, and due diligence must be taken to avoid its affects. Amulets and numerous rituals protect against the evil eye. The possessor of the evil eye, by gazing, can cast a curse upon the victim. Since the eyes are the window to and from the heart (the locus of thought in ancient biological conceptions), the evil thoughts and desires of a person's heart are projected through the eyes onto enemies.

Evil eye is quite closely related to envy. Envy, moreover, is related to the idea of limited good, which is the idea that all things (including honor) exist in finite quantities. For one person to gain more than what he or she has, another person must lose something. (For a further discussion of limited good, see chapter 13.) When someone casts the evil eye upon someone else, he or she is expressing envy, attempting to prevent the victim from acquiring or maintaining something in order that the possessor of the evil might preserve or gain some advantage over the victim.

Elliott demonstrates that Paul uses the idea of evil eye in discussing the situation of the Galatians. More significantly, he argues that it is not Paul who introduced the language and concept of the evil eye into the discussion at Galatia, but rather that Paul himself had been accused of bearing the evil eye. Paul's strategy is to remind the Galatians that they did not "spit" at him upon encountering him (a common defense strategy against possessors of the evil eye), but rather that they received him joyfully.

Elliott maintains that when Paul twice mentions his physical infirmities, it is further evidence that Paul is himself attempting to ward off the accusation of being a possessor of the evil eye. Both Paul's weak physical stature and his status as an outsider would mark him as a likely possessor of the evil eye. Paul contends, however, that he does not have the evil eye, but instead that his opponents introduce the evil eye (envy) into the community of Galatian followers of Christ.

John H. Elliott

Paul, Galatians, and the Evil Eye

INTRODUCTION

PAUL'S CELEBRATED LETTER to the Galatians has remained an inexhaustible source of inspiration and fascination through the centuries. For historians it provides not only information that is basic for a reconstruction of Paul's early career and the early course of Christian history, but also a graphic insight into the practical struggles of the Judean messianic movement as it sought to gain not only Judean but also Gentile adherents to its gospel of universal salvation. For theologians it has represented a revolutionary "Magna Carta of Christian freedom" in which Paul contrasts the favor of God available to all who are one with Jesus Christ in faith and life in the Spirit with the exclusionary and ineffective observance of the Mosaic law.

This letter, however, is valuable for another reason. It provides revealing evidence of the social and cultural world that Paul and his contemporaries inhabited. This was an environment marked by constant competition and conflict, a world viewed as inhabited by demons and humans with extraordinary powers who played a regular and threatening role in human affairs, a world in which the mysterious forces of magic, witchcraft, and the evil eye were everywhere at work.

My intention in this essay is to focus on one aspect of that magical world that receives particular expression in Paul's Letter to the Galatians: the omnipresent conviction in Mediterranean antiquity concerning the malignant power of the evil eye and the destructive powers of its various possessors.

In the opening words of chapter 3 of Galatians Paul makes direct reference to this belief when he states, "O foolish Galatians, who has afflicted you with the evil eye?" (3:1). The verb that he employs here, βασκαίνω, as Bauer et al. (1979) indicate, is the conventional term used throughout the Hellenistic world for injury and bewitchment with the evil eye. Its occurrence here, together with several other allusions to features of evil-eye belief and practice, makes it clear that accusation and counteraccusation concerning the evil eye play a greater role in the Galatian conflict than is generally realized.

EVIL-EYE BELIEF IN THE ANCIENT WORLD

Throughout the Mediterranean and Near Eastern regions of antiquity fear of the evil eye and its pernicious effects was pervasive (Jahn 1855; Elworthy 1895;

1912; Blau 1898; 1907; Kuhnert 1909; Park 1912; Levi 1941; Koetting 1954; Noy 1971; Engemann 1975; Budge 1978; Johns 1982; Russell 1982; Dunbabin and Dickie 1983; Bernidaki-Aldous 1988). From its ancient circum-Mediterranean origins, evil-eye belief eventually traveled across the centuries and around the globe (Elsworthy 1895; MacLagan 1902; Seligmann 1910; 1922; 1927; Trachten-burg 1939; Gifford 1958; DiStasio 1981; Dundes 1981; Siebers 1983). It has been studied most extensively by anthropologists and is considered to be one of the most widespread and enduring instances of magical thought and behavior (Foster 1972; Maloney 1976; Lykiardopoulos 1981; Gilmore 1982).

Evil-eye belief and practice, of course, can be understood and analyzed only as particular components of an entire worldview and cultural system. A full treatment of the subject would require consideration of a constellation of factors that can only be mentioned here and left undiscussed. This would include issues such as the system of beliefs of which the evil-eye concept is one instance—belief in spirits, demons, witches, and extraordinary human and superhuman agencies thought to affect or control human welfare and destiny; the cosmologies, world-views, and plausibility structures that lend these beliefs credibility and power; the ecological, economic, and social conditions in which these cosmologies and beliefs emerge and thrive; the specific social and cultural scripts according to which these beliefs are enacted—in the case of evil eye and witchcraft accusations, for example, the social dynamics of the interaction, the expectations aroused, and the consequences anticipated; and how such a concept, in the case of the biblical communities, was considered compatible with a monotheistic belief system.

To such issues historians, exegetes, and theologians have been turning their attention. In regard to the cultural and conceptual framework for analyzing the magical world of early Christianity, the *Forschungsbericht* by Aune (1980) surveys steps in this direction (see also Derrett 1973, 114–28; Brox 1974; Engemann 1975). Malina and Neyrey (1988) illuminate the witchcraft accusations in the Gospels through comparative use of anthropological studies of other witchcraft societies. In two further studies on 2 Corinthians and Galatians, Neyrey (1986; 1988) also shows how demonic belief, witchcraft, and evil-eye accusations are part and parcel of the world of Paul.

SALIENT FEATURES OF EVIL EYE BELIEF AND PRACTICE

Turning now to the evil-eye phenomenon in particular, let us first consider some salient features of this belief and its accompanying practices. Basic to this belief is the conviction that certain individuals, animals, demons, or gods have the power of casting an evil spell or causing some malignant effect on every object, animate or inanimate, upon which their eye or glance may fall. Through the power of their eyes, which may operate involuntarily as well as intentionally, such evil-eye possessors were thought to be capable of injuring or destroying the life and health of others, their means of sustenance and livelihood, their honor and personal fortune. The eye was considered to be the window to and of the heart and the physical channel of one's innermost attitudes, desires, and intentions, and so an evil eye was linked with the negative moral attitudes of envy and greed, stinginess and covetousness, and was considered to be directed against objects of the possessor's displeasure or envy.

In Greek culture this association of evil eye and envy is evident in the combination of ὀφθαλμός ("eye") or βάσκανος ("evil-eye possessor") and paronyms with φθόνος ("envy"), φθονερός ("envious") (e.g., Sir 14:10: ὀφθαλμὸς πονηρὸς φθονερός; Tob 4:7, 16: φθονεσάτω σου ὁ ὀφθαλμός; *T. Iss.* 3:3: φθονερὸς καὶ βάσκανος; and frequently in Philo [*Cherubim* 33; *Names* 112; *Dreams* 1.107; *Moses* 1.246; *Virtues* 170; *Flaccus* 29]). Plutarch, in his *Table Talk* on the evil eye (*Quaest. conv.* 680C–683B, esp. 681D–682A) expatiates at length on its connection with envy.

In Latin the Greek terms βασκαίνω, βάσκανον, βάσκανος, and βασκανία are taken over directly (*f* for *b*, *c* for *k*, etc.) and Latinized as *fascino, fascinus, fascinator,* and *fascinatio.* Thus to "fascinate" is actually to injure with the evil eye. Moreover, in Latin the same association of evil eye and envy is expressed linguistically in the very word for *envy,* which is *invidia,* a composite of *in* + *videre*—literally, to "over-look." Thus *invidia* involves the notion of "looking over" something or someone with the desire to possess or destroy it.

The enormity of the danger posed by the evil eye, coupled with the fear that its possessors lurked everywhere, led the ancients to maintain constant vigilance against potential fascinators and to employ a vast array of protective devices and strategies to ward off attack. Although all objects were thought to be susceptible of injury, children and persons enjoying good fortune or social prestige were regarded as particularly vulnerable.

Likewise important was the detection of potential evil eye possessors. Here strangers, outsiders, or social deviants and the physically deformed, disabled, or blind (Bernidaki-Aldous 1988) were judged to be prime candidates as fascinators. To protect themselves and their homes, shops, and public places, the ancients wore or exhibited a host of apotropaic amulets. In the presence of an epileptic, lame person, or stranger, Pliny (*Nat.* 28.36, 39) notes that persons would also defend themselves against possible evil-eye injury by spitting (a strategy to which Paul also alludes in Gal 4:14). Beyond spitting, the ancients employed a veritable arsenal of devices and methods for warding off the dreaded evil eye. The underlying principle was that of homeopathic magic and *similia similibus,* the use of "like against like." Such practices, attested in art, artifacts, and architecture as well as literature, included the hanging of *bullae* around the necks of children; the wearing of *fascina* (replicas of phalluses), engraved amulets, and cloth of red or blue color; the manual gestures of the *digitus infamis* (extended middle finger of a fisted hand—the American "high sign"), the *mano cornuta* (extended first and fourth fingers of a fisted hand), and *mano fica* (the thumb inserted between first and second fingers of a fisted hand); and an array of similar designs and devices on public monuments and private homes, thresholds, shops, and graves— all for the purpose of distracting, deflecting, or counteracting the omnipresent threat of the evil eye.

Such information on the particulars of evil-eye belief and practice is derived from the literary sources and numerous authors, including Plato, Aristotle, Pliny, and Plutarch, who in his *Moralia* devoted an entire section of the *Table Talk* (*Quaest. conv.* 680C–683B) to the subject of the evil eye. There is a continuous record of evidence of this belief and its accompanying practices from Sumerian civilization onward through Egyptian, Hebrew, Greek, Roman, Judean, and Christian cultures down through and beyond late antiquity. In the immediate environment of the biblical communities this includes not only information from secular Greek and Roman literary sources (Jahn 1855) but also much material from the Hebrew and Christian Scriptures (Blau 1898; Elliott 1988), the Mishnah, the Talmud, and Judean tradition (Blau 1907; Trachtenburg 1939; Schrire 1982; Noy 1971) and the church fathers (Koetting 1954) as well as evidence from private letters preserved on papyri, from inscriptions and epigrapha, and from art, artifacts, and monuments (Kuhnert 1909; Dobschuetz 1910; Lafaye 1877–1919; Levi 1941; Delling 1962; Engemann 1975; Russell 1982; Johns 1982; Mountfield 1982; Dunbabin and Dickie 1983).

In sum, in the world of the biblical communities fear of the evil eye was pervasive, and the specific features of the belief were remarkably consistent. Hebrew, Judean, and Christian communities shared with their contemporaries a firm conviction of the power of the evil eye, a constant fear of its possessors, and conventional strategies for neutralizing its suspected malice.

THE MAGICAL WORLD OF PAUL AND THE CONFLICT AT GALATIA

Paul and the Galatians were inhabitants of this same world. In a study of the apostle's Letter to the Galatians and the magical thought-world that it presumes, Neyrey (1988) has analyzed salient features of the cosmology of this world, described by anthropologists as that of a witchcraft society. In such societies where humans saw themselves as subject to the powers of demons and malicious forces lurking everywhere and often operating through human agents, belief in witches and evil-eye possessors played a powerful role in the regulation of behavior and social interaction. Neyrey has advanced a more accurate reading of the Galatian letter by situating it in its actual cultural context and pointing out aspects of the cultural script heretofore unconsidered by modern interpreters. This sets the stage for now examining how evil-eye belief and practice in particular come into play here, especially the strategy of evil-eye accusation and counteraccusation.

Anthropologists have observed that in evil-eye cultures, where competition and conflict are constant and formal means of adjudicating disputes are unavailable, evil-eye accusations are employed in issues concerning the marking of social boundaries, the maintenance of social well-being, and the control of social deviance (see Maloney 1976). Among these close-knit communities, defined primarily by geographical proximity and group loyalty, the stranger or outsider is generally perceived as a threat to the common weal and thus a likely evil-eye fascinator with malicious or envious designs. Within such communities, subject more to custom than a centralized and effective system of law, accusations of evil-eye possession and injury are frequent means employed by rival factions for discrediting and disabling their opponents. Labeling an opponent a fascinator or evil-eye possessor serves as an informal but effective social mechanism for marshaling public opinion against that person, discrediting his honor and credibility, censuring his behavior, and ostracizing him as a social deviant.

A close reading of Galatians indicates that such a strategy of evil-eye accusation played a prominent role in Paul's confrontation with his opponents in Galatia. Here rival Judean-Christian and Gentile-Christian factions of the messianic movements had clashed over the social and moral implications of a gospel and a household of faith founded not on fidelity to the Mosaic law but rather on solidarity with a crucified Messiah. In his initial visit to Galatia Paul had preached a gospel proclaiming a universal salvation, offered as a divine gift of the Spirit and accepted by trust/faith in a divine promise rather than by submission to the Mosaic law. After his departure from Galatia this teaching was challenged by rival Judean Christians demanding continued observance of the Mosaic law, kosher food laws, circumcision, and the traditional Judean calendar. In addition, they challenged Paul's apostolic authority and tried to discredit him with a variety of ad hominem arguments. Their attack had produced debilitating cleavages within the Galatian churches and had seriously undermined Paul's credibility.

Responding to this situation by letter, Paul attempted to repair the damage, restore order, and regain the upper hand and the moral high ground. This response includes a historical retrospective of his own career and previous friendly reception by the Galatians, a further elaboration of his gospel, a defense of his own person, actions, and motives coupled with a counterattack on his opponents, and a concluding appeal for faith active in love, communal solidarity, and cooperation within the "household of faith" (6:10) and the "Israel of God" (6:16).

In this process of attack and counterattack evil-eye belief and practice are invoked, and evil-eye accusations are hurled back and forth. Familiarity with salient features of evil-eye belief and practice now makes it possible for us to see its role in this bitter exchange of accusation and counteraccusation.

Elements of the evil-eye repertoire in Galatians include the following. First, Paul's explicitly refers to evil-eye injury in 3:1: "O foolish Galatians, who has injured you with the evil eye [τίς ὑμᾶς ἐβάσκανεν], you before whose very eyes [ὀφθαλμοὺς] Jesus Christ was proclaimed as justified?" Here Paul employs the specific verb for evil-eye injury (βασκαίνω), a fact generally overlooked or obscured by modern translations. Renditions such as "who has bewitched you" (KJV, RSV, NEB, and most other versions) or "who has put/cast a spell on/over you" (NJB, NAB) fail to convey to modern readers the ancient association of spells, bewitchment, and the evil eye. Among modern commentators, the translation by J. B. Lightfoot (1905), "who has fascinated you," is directly on target, and his commentary on the evil-eye phenomenon, though limited, is more informative than most. Ancient Christian commentators, of course, including Jerome (PL 26, 372–73) and John Chrysostom (PG 61, 648), were still familiar with the term, the evil eye concept in general, and the danger that fascination was thought to pose to children in particular.

Many centuries later the phenomenon was still known to Martin Luther, who in his commentary on Gal 3:1 devotes extensive attention to the subject (1963, 189–98; 1964, 243–45). "'To bewitch,'" states Luther, "means to do harm with an evil look . . . the Greek word [ἐβάσκανεν], as Jerome attests, means not only to bewitch but also to envy" (1964, 244).

In accord with Jerome, Luther repeats the citation of Virgil, "I do not know what eye is bewitching my tender lambs" (*Ecl.* 3.103), and notes the threat that the evil eye poses to children, including the Galatians, "who were like new-born infants in Christ" (cf. 4:19; 3:23–4:7). In contrast to Jerome, however, who questioned whether Paul actually believed in such witchcraft, Luther affirmed its reality, for both the apostle and himself. "Paul does not deny that witchcraft exists and is possible; for later on, in the fifth chapter (v. 20) he also lists 'sorcery,' which is the same as witchcraft, among the works of the flesh. Thereby he proves that witchcraft and sorcery exist and are possible" (1963, 190).

Luther too envisioned witchcraft and the evil eye as operative in his own day. "As I have said, I believe that with God's permission those witches, with the aid of devils, are really able to harm little infants for the punishment of unbelievers and the testing of believers, since, as is evident from experience, they also work many other kinds of harm in the bodies of men as well as of cattle and everything. And I believe that the apostle was not unaware of this" (1964, 245). Citing experiences from his own time, Luther observes, "This [evil eye bewitchment], I believe, is the ailment of little infants that our womenfolk commonly call *Die Elbe* or *Das Hertzgespan,* in which we see infants wasting away, growing thin, and being miserably tormented, sometimes wailing and crying incessantly. The women, in turn, try to counter this ailment with I know not what charms and superstition; for it is believed that such things are caused by those jealous and spiteful old hags if they envy some mother her beautiful baby" (1964, 244).

With respect to Galatians, Luther (1963, 194, 197) sees Paul accusing the false apostles of the law as bewitchers in league with Satan. Regarding his own time, Luther (1963, 195–96) cites as a further example of satanic bewitchment the tragic suicide of his contemporary, Dr. Krause of Halle.

A second indication of the evil-eye repertoire in Galatians involves Paul's repeated reference to "eyes" (ὀφθαλμοί) and ocular aversion as evil-eye defense. Twice Paul mentions the "eyes" of the Galatians, which they not only did not avert from Paul when he first proclaimed Christ to them (3:1) but which they also were actually ready to pluck out and offer to him in gratitude (4:15).

Third (and fourth), in this rehearsal of their first encounter (4:12–15) Paul refers to two further elements of evil-eye belief and behavior. When the Galatians first met him, Paul notes, despite his off-putting physical appearance (4:13–14a), they did not "spit" (ἐξεπτύσατε [4:14]) when they met him (as was the custom when encountering a suspected evil-eye possessor with tell-tale physical markings of physical deformity or bodily ailment). Rather, he recalls, they received him "as an angel of God, as Christ Jesus" (4:14b RSV).

Fifth, as already noted by Luther and ancient commentators, another aspect of evil-eye belief here is the particular vulnerability of the Galatians as newborn "children" in Christ (4:19; 3:23–4:7) to the attack of evil eye possessors.

Sixth, the repeated stress on "envy" here (ζηλόω [4:17–18]) and elsewhere in the letter (ζῆλος [5:20]; φθόνοι [5:21]; φθονοῦντες [5:26])—the moral disposition most frequently associated with the evil eye—is yet another indication of the evil-eye repertoire.

Finally, all these related features of the evil eye phenomenon, taken together with still further indications of Paul's conceptual world and strategy, such as his censure of "sorcery" or "magic" (φαρμακεία [5:20]) and his invocation of a curse upon his opponents (1:8, 9), make clear the magical dimensions of the universe presumed here as well as the role that evil-eye belief in particular played in the Galatian conflict.

Although it could be inferred from 3:1 that Paul himself first introduced the issue of the evil eye, a closer examination of the letter suggests a different scenario, in which Paul is in fact parrying an evil-eye accusation directed against him with a counteraccusation leveled against his opponents. This scenario may be reconstructed as follows.

Paul's opponents, beside challenging his gospel and its novel social implications, sought to discredit him personally by stressing his unusual physical appearance and its negative moral implications. Two references by Paul to his physical condition appear to deal with this tactic of his rivals. (1) When reminding the Galatians of their first encounter (4:12–15), Paul concedes that he appeared with a "bodily ailment" (ἀσθένεια τῆς σαρκός) that was a "trial" (πειρασμός) to them (4:13–14). This was most likely the physical condition that he described elsewhere in a letter to the Corinthians (2 Cor 12:7) as a "thorn in the flesh" (σκόλοψ τῇ σαρκί). (2) Again at the very end of the Galatian letter he abruptly returns to this subject and defends his physical appearance with this warning: "Henceforth let no [one] trouble me, for I bear on my body the marks of Jesus [τὰ στίγματα τοῦ Ἰησοῦ]" (6:17). This repeated attention to his physical condition and the defensive tone of both passages indicate that Paul is countering a charge of utmost gravity involving conclusions drawn concerning his physical condition.

In evil-eye cultures, as is documented profusely in the anthropological and historical evidence, unusual physical features, disfigurement such as a humped back, epilepsy, lameness, or strange ocular features, including blindness and joined eyebrows, have signaled their bearers as potential possessors of the evil eye. To protect themselves against such suspected fascinators, as already noted, persons spit in their presence. This same combination of evil-eye elements occurs in Gal 4:14–15, where Paul states, "Although my physical condition was a trial to you, you did not despise [me] or spit [ἐξεπτύσατε]."

In connection with this issue of Paul's strange physical appearance, it is interesting to recall other early Christian tradition according to which Paul was once afflicted with blindness (Acts 9:1–19). Also relevant is the first description of Paul's physical appearance in the *Acts of Paul and Thecla* (3:3), where attention is called to unusual aspects of Paul's anatomy, including, of all things, his knitted eyebrows. Paul was, the description notes, "a man of small stature with a bald head and crooked legs, in a good state of body, with eyebrows meeting and a nose somewhat crooked." Here too we meet precisely those features conventionally associated with evil-eye possessors.

Paul's acknowledgment and defense of his strange physical appearance, coupled with a specific mention of the Galatians not spitting, put us once again in the arena of evil-eye belief and practice. This fact, when combined with further contextual references to the Galatians as "children" (especially vulnerable to the evil eye) (4:19), who yet were willing even to "pluck out their eyes" on Paul's behalf (4:15) and who did not divert their eyes at Paul's public announcement of his gospel (3:1), together with Paul's censure of the envy of his opponents (4:17–18; cf. 5:20, 21, 26), indicates that in 4:12–20 and elsewhere in the letter Paul is attempting to refute an evil-eye accusation leveled against him by his rivals. His physical features, they had asserted, betray this stranger with his strange gospel as an evil-eye possessor who aimed to injure the Galatians, and therefore his gospel deserves no credence.

Paul's response to this accusation was two-pronged. It involved both a defensive and an offensive maneuver in line with his strategy in general (1:6–2:14; 5:7–12; 6:11–17). To repel the charge of evil-eye aggression, he reminds the Galatians of his fatherly love for them (4:19) and their cordial reception of him at their first encounter (4:12–15). Despite his physical appearance and status as a stranger, he states, they did not treat him as a hostile fascinator and spit (to protect themselves from his supposedly injurious glance). On the contrary, they received him as an angel of God, as Christ Jesus, and "you would have plucked out your [own] eyes and given them to me" (4:15 RSV), he notes. Returning to this point at the conclusion of his letter, he warns, "Let no man trouble me; for I bear on my body the marks of Jesus" (6:17 RSV). These are the marks not of an evil-eye possessor, as might be inferred, but rather of a suffering apostle of the suffering Christ.

The other prong of Paul's response involved his taking the offensive by countering the accusation of his opponents with an evil-eye accusation of his own. It is not he but rather they, Paul asserts, who have afflicted the Galatians with the evil eye. This is the sense in which we may take 3:1. Implied in the rhetorical question "Who has afflicted you with the evil eye?" is Paul's answer: it is not he who did so, but rather his opponents. He develops this accusation further in 4:17 and what follows. It is they who have taken advantage of the Galatians' childlike condition in the faith (4:19; cf. 3:23–4:6). It is they who envy the Galatians' liberty, exploit them for self-seeking purposes, and injure them by attempting to exclude them from the household of faith (4:17; 6:12–13). It is they whose sorcery and envy engender envy and dissension in the community (5:19–21, 26) in contrast to Paul's gospel of freedom and love in the Spirit (5:1–6:16). It is they who, by their preoccupation with aspects of the physical body, circumcised converts (5:2–3, 6, 11; 6:12–13; cf. 2:3, 7–9, 12), and Paul's stigmata (6:17), reveal themselves to be slaves of the flesh rather than children of the Spirit (5:1–6:10). It is they and their supposed gospel that are accursed (1:6–9; 3:10).

Thus behind the angry question of 3:1 looms this implication: it is Paul's opponents, not he, who have injured the Galatians with the evil eye. To substantiate this, Paul asks that the Galatians recall their own experience, which only validates the truth of his gospel and his integrity, the bond of friendship between apostle and Galatians, and the malicious and destructive actions of his adversaries.

CONCLUSION

In this factional struggle for the faith and commitment of the Galatians, Paul and his rivals confront each other with equal claims to authority: apostolic credentials and the word of God. In this situation, where a superior legal authority for adjudicating conflicts is absent, both contending parties are subject finally to the court of public opinion. Consequently, his opponents resort to evil-eye accusation, and Paul parries with curse (1:8–9; cf. 3:10) and counteraccusation (3:1; 4:17; cf. 1:6–7; 5:7–12; 6:12–14). The experience of the Galatians (3:1–4; 4:8–20; 5:1–6:10, 12–13) and public opinion are Paul's court of final appeal. Their experience, he argues, makes it clear that it is his opponents, not he, who are the malicious agents of evil and strife infecting the community. Evil-eye accusation is countered by evil-eye accusation, and Paul seeks to hoist his opponents on their own evil-eye petard.

Although resort to evil-eye accusations as attempts to marshal and move public opinion played a noteworthy role in the struggle at Galatia, its importance should not be exaggerated out of proportion. Although the reputation and credibility of rival factions was at stake, the issues over which they contended—Christ versus Torah as basis and norm for righteousness and membership in the Israel of God, the incompatibility of exclusivist Torah observance and the inclusiveness of divine favor and salvation proffered in a crucified Christ, infantile subjection to the law versus adult freedom in the Spirit of Christ, promise and trust versus command and obedience as contrary modes of the divine-human relationship—overshadow by far in importance the social mechanisms employed by the proponents of these opposing positions to mutually discredit their rivals. In Paul's thought the notion of the evil eye plays as minor a role as in that of Jesus and the evangelists (Matt 6:22–23; 20:1–15; Mark 7:22; Luke 11:33–36). But play a role it did. The examination of this role enables us to grasp more concretely the social as well as theological strategies at work in the bitter conflict at Galatia. Familiarity with this fascinating feature of ancient belief and practice, moreover, brings us one step closer to that foreign, magical world of the biblical communities, their conceptual horizons, and the cultural scripts according to which they thought and acted.

Anxiety about the present evil age (1:4), enslavement to the elemental spirits of the universe (4:3), and magic (φαρμακεία [5:20]), and resort to curses (1:8–9; 3:10), solemn warning (6:17), and charges of evil-eye possession—all these are vivid features of the witchcraft society in which Paul, the Galatians, and the early church were at home. Such societies may strike the modern reader as distressingly strange and uncomfortably alien in their "primitive" beliefs and "superstitious" practices. Modern biblical translators and commentators with a worthy concern for the Bible's contemporary relevance may even resort to minimizing or domesticating its alien features for modern consumption. But for those committed to understanding the word of God in all its historical and cultural particularity, the only course possible is to study and comprehend these texts as products of and witnesses to their own historical, social, and cultural contexts, including their characteristic perceptions of the world, constellations of beliefs, and patterns of behavior. The role of evil-eye belief and practice in Galatians and in numerous other biblical documents should serve as an important reminder to exegetes and theologians often preoccupied exclusively with lofty theological concepts and arguments always to keep at least one good eye also on the popular culture that informed the biblical authors and provided the cultural scripts according to which they thought, acted, and communicated.

BIBLIOGRAPHY

Aune, David. E. 1980. Magic in Early Christianity. Pages 1507–57 in vol. 2.23.2 of *Aufstieg und Niedergang der römischen Welt*. Edited by H. Temporini and W. Haase. New York: de Gruyter.

Bernidaki-Aldous, Eleftheria. 1988. The Power of the Evil Eye in the Blind: Oedipus Tyrannus 1306 and Oedipus at Colonus 149–156. Pages 39–48 in *Text and Presentation*. Edited by Karelisa Hartigan. University of Florida Department of Classics Comparative Drama Conference Papers 8. Lanham, Md.: University Press of America.

Blau, Ludwig. 1898. *Das altjüdische Zauberwesen*. Jahresbericht der Landes-Rabbinerschule in Budapest für das Schuljahr 1897–98. Strassburg: Trübner.

―――. 1907. Evil Eye. Pages 280–81 in vol. 5 of *The Jewish Encyclopedia*. Edited by Cyrus Adler et al. 12 vols. New York: Funk & Wagnalls, 1901–1907.

Brox, Norbert. 1974. Magie und Aberglaube an den Anfaengen des Christentums. *Trierer theologische Zeitschrift* 83:157–80.

Budge, E. A. Wallis. 1978. *Amulets and Superstitions: The Original Texts with Translations and Descriptions of a Long Series of Egyptian, Sumerian, Assyrian, Hebrew, Christian, Gnostic, and Muslim Amulets and Talismans and Magical Figures, with Chapters on the Evil Eye, the Origin of the Amulet, the Pentagon, the Swastika, the Cross (Pagan and Christian), the Properties of Stones, Rings, Divination, Numbers, the Kabbalah, Ancient Astrology, etc.* London: Oxford University Press, 1930. Repr., New York: Dover.

Danker, F. W., W. Bauer, W. F. Arndt, and F. W. Gingrich. 2000. *Greek-English Lexicon of the New Testament and Other Early Christian Literature*. 3d ed. Chicago: University of Chicago Press.

Delling, Gerhard. 1962. *Worship in the New Testament*. Translated by Percy Scott. Philadelphia: Westminster.

Derrett, J. Duncan M. 1973. *Jesus's Audience: The Social and Psychological Environment in Which He Worked; Prolegomena to a Restatement of the Teaching of Jesus.* New York: Seabury.

DiStasio, Lawrence. 1981. *Mal occhio (Evil Eye): The Underside of Vision*. San Francisco: North Point Press.

Dobschuetz, Ernst von. 1924. Charms and Amulets (Christian). Pages 413–30 in vol. 3 of *Encyclopedia of Religion and Ethics*. Edited by J. Hastings and J. A. Selbie. 13 vols. Edinburgh: T&T Clark, 1908–1927.

Dunbabin, Katherine M. D., and M. W. Dickie. 1983. Invidia Rumpantur Pectora: The Iconography of Phthonos/Invidia in Graeco-Roman Art. *Jahrbuch für Antike und Christentum* 26:7–37, and plates 1–8.

Dundes, Alan, ed. 1981. *The Evil Eye: A Folklore Casebook*. Garland Folklore Casebooks 2. New York: Garland.

Elliott, John H. 1988. The Fear of the Leer: The Evil Eye from the Bible to Li'l Abner. *Forum* 4:42–71.

Elworthy, Frederick Thomas. 1895. *The Evil Eye: An Account of This Ancient and Widespread Superstition*. London: Murray.

———. 1912. The Evil Eye. Pages 608–15 in vol. 5 of *Encyclopedia of Religion and Ethics*. Edited by James Hastings. 13 vols. Edinburgh: T&T Clark, 1908–1927.

Engemann, Josef. 1975. Zur Verbreitung magischer Übelabwehr in der nicht-christlichen und Christlichen Spätantike. *Jahrbuch für Antike und Christentum* 18:22–48, and plates 8–15.

Foster, George M. 1972. The Anatomy of Envy: A Study in Symbolic Behavior. *Current Anthropology* 13:165–202.

Gifford, Edward S. 1958. *The Evil Eye: Studies in the Folklore of Vision*. New York: Macmillan.

Gilmore, David D. 1982. Anthropology of the Mediterranean Area. *Annual Review of Anthropology* 11:175–205.

Jahn, Otto. 1855. *Über den Aberglauben des bösen Blicks bei den Alten*. Leipzig: Hirzel.

Johns, Catherine. 1982. *Sex or Symbol? Erotic Images of Greece and Rome*. Austin: University of Texas Press.

Kittel, Gerhard, and Gerhard Friedrich, eds. 1964–1976. *Theological Dictionary of the New Testament*. Translated by Geoffrey W. Bromiley. 10 vols. Grand Rapids: Eerdmans.

Koetting, Bernhard. 1954. Böser Blick. Pages 474–82 in vol. 2 of *Reallexikon für Antike und Christentum: Sachwörterbuch zur Auseinandersetzung des Christentums mit der antiken Welt*. Edited by Theodor Klauser. 12 vols. Stuttgart: Hiersemann, 1950–1985.

Kuhnert, Ernst. 1909. Fascinum. Cols. 2009–14 in vol. 6.2 of *Paulys Real-Encyclopaedie der classischen Altertumswissenschaft*. Edited by A. Pauly et al. Munich: Druckenmüller.

Lafaye, G. 1877–1919. Fascinum, fascinus. Pages 983–87 in vol. 2 of *Dictionnaire des antiquités grecques et romaines*. Edited by C. Daremberg and M. E. Saglio. 5 vols. in 10. Paris: Hachette.

Levi, Doro. 1941. The Evil Eye and the Lucky Hunchback. Pages 220–32 in vol. 3 of *Antioch-on-the-Orontes*. Edited by Richard Stillwell. 4 vols. in 5. Publications of the Committee for the Excavation of Antioch and Its Vicinity. Princeton, N.J.: Department of Art and Archaeology, Princeton University, 1934–1972.

Lightfoot, J. B. 1905. *Saint Paul's Epistle to the Galatians: A Revised Text with Introduction, Notes and Dissertations.* 10th ed. London: Macmillan.

Luther, Martin. 1963. *Lectures on Galatians, 1535, Chapters 1–4.* Edited by Jaroslav Pelikan. Luther's Works 26. St. Louis: Concordia.

———. 1964. *Lectures on Galatians, 1535, Chapters 5–6; Lectures on Galatians, 1519, Chapters 1–6.* Edited by Jaroslav Pelikan. Luther's Works 27. St. Louis: Concordia.

Lykiardopoulos, Amica. 1981. The Evil Eye: Towards an Exhaustive Study. *Folklore* 92(2):221–30.

MacLagan, R. C. 1902. *Evil Eye in the Western Highlands.* London: David Nutt.

Malina, Bruce J., and Jerome H. Neyrey. 1988. *Calling Jesus Names: The Social Value of Labels in Matthew.* Foundation and Facets: Social Facets. Sonoma, Calif.: Polebridge Press.

Maloney, Clarence, ed. 1976. *The Evil Eye.* New York: Columbia University Press.

Mountfield, David. 1982. *Greek and Roman Erotica.* New York: Crescent Books.

Neyrey, Jerome H. 1986. Witchcraft Accusations in 2 Cor 10–13: Paul in Social Science Perspective. *Listening* 21(2):160–70.

———. 1988. Bewitched in Galatia: Paul and Cultural Anthropology. *Catholic Bibilical Quarterly* 50:72–100.

Noy, D. 1971. Evil Eye. Pages 997–1000 in vol. 6 of *Encyclopaedia Judaica.* 16 vols. Jerusalem: Keter, 1971–1972.

Park, Roswell. 1912. *The Evil Eye, Thanatology, and Other Essays.* Boston: R. G. Badger.

Russell, James. 1982. The Evil Eye in Early Byzantine Society. *Jahrbuch der österreichischen Byzantinistik* 32.3: 539–48.

Schrire, Theodore. 1982. *Hebrew Magic Amulets: Their Decipherment and Interpretation.* New York: Behrman House.

Seligmann, S. 1910. *Der böse Blick und Verwandtes: Ein Beitrag zur Geschichte des Aberglaubens aller Zeiten und Völker.* 2 vols. Berlin: Hermann Barsdorf.

———. 1922. *Die Zauberkraft des Auges und das Berufen: Ein Kapital aus der Geschichte des Aberglaubens.* Hamburg: Hermann Barsdorf.

———. 1927. *Die magischen Heil-und Schutzmittel aus der unbelebten Natur, mit besonderer Berücksichtigung der Mittel gegen den bösen Blick: Eine Geschichte des Amulettwesens.* Stuttgart: Strecker & Schröder.

Siebers, Tobin. 1983. *The Mirror of Medusa.* Berkeley: University of California Press.

Trachtenburg, Joshua. 1939. *Jewish Magic and Superstition: A Study in Folk Religion.* New York: Behrman's Jewish Book House.

Walcot, Peter. 1978. *Envy and the Greeks: A Study of Human Behavior.* Warminster: Aris & Phillips.

Limited Good

13

A ll people do not view the world similarly. The industrialized West considers the world to be a limitless source of resources for an ever-expanding economy that benefits all. A rising tide lifts all boats. But anthropologists who study other cultures, modern and ancient, inform us that other people see the world as a fixed and limited source of just so much grain, water, fertility, and honor. For them, this supply will never expand, and the benefits must be divided out between all people. Thus, one person or group's share increases only because it is being taken away from others. When people operating under the presumption that everyone is born into a family with only so much wealth, grain, siblings, and respect perceive others apparently getting more of the limited goods, the scene is set for conflict.

Many of the essays in this book deal with stable values and institutions. But conflict was and is a large element in social life. George Foster, who is our guide in observing the "prevalence of conflict" in peasant relationships, described it thus: "All the families quarrel with each other. Always the same squabbles, endless squabbles, passed down from generation to generation in endless lawsuits" (1960, 174–78). David Cohen reveals the intense combative character of Athens' courts that exemplified ancient Greek society. He describes that society as highly agonistic: it truly loves fighting (φιλόμαχος) and celebrates rivalry and combat (φιλόνεικος), and so is in love with victory or rivalry (φιλονεικία). A contentious society, it is always competing (ἀμιλλάομαι). In fact, it rejoices in making enemies (φιλαπεχθήμων) (Cohen 1991, 183–98). Christopher Faraone, in his study of spells in the Hellenistic world, classified them in terms of four "agonistic contexts": conflict relative to commerce, athletes and public performers, rival lovers and judicial proceedings (1991, 10–17).

To appreciate the pervasiveness of conflict in the agonistic world of antiquity, we must consider the prevalence and function of envy. In his catalogue of emotions to which an orator might appeal, Aristotle defines envy this way: "It is equally clear for what reason, and of whom, and in what frame of mind, men are envious, if envy is a kind of pain at the sight of good fortune in regard to the goods mentioned; in the case of those like themselves; and not for the sake of a man getting anything, but because of others possessing it" (*Rhet.* 2.10.1). Aristotle's definition remained constant in the ancient world, as reference to Cicero and Basil indicates: for Cicero, envy is "distress incurred by reason of a neighbor's prosperity" (*Tusc.* 4.8.17); for Basil, it is "pain caused by our neighbor's prosperity" ("Concerning Envy" [PG 31.377]). Envy basically consists of pain or distress caused by another's success. Furthermore, Aristotle (*Rhet.* 2.11.1) distinguishes envy (φθόνος) from emulation (ζῆλος). Although both are "distress" at the success of another, an envious person attacks a successful person without being spurred on to achieve anything on his or her own.

If one sees the world in terms of limited good, it becomes an agonistic world. Someone in the village seems to be gaining, so others must be losing. Enter envy: the success that one sees fuels a desire to put that person down and to maintain the status quo. How does one envy? Various forms of conflict, such as ostracism, gossip and slander, feuding, litigation, the evil eye, and homicide (Hagedorn and Neyrey 1998, 32–34). Athenians ostracized prominent citizens from the city in order to strip them of public respect. Gossip, like fog, spread on little cat feet. Philosophical schools battle, as do Israelite religious groups. These are only the obvious ways in which combat is choreographed in antiquity.

Where might a reader find further evidence of limited good and envy in the Bible? The intense rivalry of brothers in the Bible illustrates limited good and envy: Cain and Abel, Isaac and Ishmael, Jacob and Esau. In addition to the materials in this chapter, see, in the preceding chapter, John Ellott's essay on the "evil eye." See also Matt 20:1–15; Mark 15:10; James 3:13–4:10. The conflict between the disciples and the chief priests in Acts 3–5 welcomes interpretation in the key of envy. The *chreia* found in the *progymnasmata* ("school exercises") describes a conflict situation whereby a wise man is attacked by a questioner to destroy his reputation.

Bibliography

Foster, George M. 1960. Interpersonal Relations in Peasant Society. *Human Organization* 19: 174–78.

Jerome H. Neyrey, SJ,
and Richard L. Rohrbaugh

"He Must Increase, I Must Decrease" (John 3:30): A Cultural and Social Interpretation

THE EPISODE IN John 3:22–30 regularly gets short shrift from commentators. That is especially true of the Baptizer's striking remark in 3:30, which is often praised but rarely interpreted. Nor has anyone taken notice of how foreign to Mediterranean culture that remark really is; hence, to our knowledge, no one has ever felt the need for or found suitable ancient, nonbiblical parallels that might be brought to bear on its interpretation. In the discussion that follows, however, we examine relevant parallel material that is indeed illuminating. Yet we do not do so as just another history-of-religions investigation. Instead, we bring to the task models from comparative anthropology that enable us to assess John 3:30 in its proper cultural and social context.

It is also true that this passage is rarely compared with other materials in the Fourth Gospel that might offer clarification. Monographs and commentaries typically investigate the links between John and Jesus in chapter 1 and indicate their continuance in 3:22–30. Yet we will argue that at least in 11:45–52 we find an important but unnoticed contrast to 3:22–30. Whereas John the Baptizer did not suffer envy at Jesus' success, the Jerusalem elite did. The interpretive key to that contrast, we argue, lies in the sociology of perception ("limited good") and the anthropology of envy.

Our thesis is that in this story John's disciples are on the verge of envying Jesus and his disciples. Like most people in antiquity, they appear to share the view that all goods are limited in quantity and are already all distributed. There is only so much land, gold, fame, and praise existing in the world. Thus if someone seems to be gaining any of these, inevitably others must be losing—possibly I or one of my friends. In other words, the world is a zero-sum game: for some to increase, others must decrease. The Baptizer himself steps apart from the game, but not so his disciples. For them, Jesus' success appears to be a gain that implies their loss. It is this cultural concept of "limited good" and relevant ancient instances of it that we bring to our interpretation of John 3:30.

PRELIMINARY READING OF JOHN 3:22–30

The scene begins with notice that both Jesus and John are baptizing in the Judean territory. That sets the stage for the controversy that follows. The disciples of John engage in a "controversy" with someone over purification. The key term here, ζήτησις, can have neutral meanings such as "philosophical inquiry or investigation," but it can also have a much more highly charged meaning such as "controversy or legal investigation." The sense in 3:25 is that of controversy and even of envy. These disciples then go to John to voice their interpretation of the ζήτησις· "Rabbi, he who was with you beyond the Jordan, to whom you bore witness, here he is, baptizing and all are going to him" (3:26 RSV). Their complaint clarifies the subject of the ζήτησις· a rivalry between Jesus (and his disciples) and John (and his disciples).

The nub of the ζήτησις resides in the perception that Jesus' growth in fame and reputation comes at the expense of John and his disciples. In many ways, John's disciples voice the same kind of remark as do Jesus' enemies in 11:47 at the growth of Jesus' fame because of his raising of Lazarus: "this man performs many signs. If we let him go on like this, everyone will believe in him" (RSV). In both stories some people perceive that their own worth diminishes precisely as Jesus gains greater respect and honor. In fact, Jesus' increase indeed causes their decrease.

The audience of the Fourth Gospel has been carefully prepared how to assess remarks such as those of John's disciples. No less than three times John announced Jesus' superiority to himself, indicating that he and Jesus are not in competition but rather that John's career is precisely to herald Jesus.

"He who comes after me ranks before me, for he was before me." (1:15 RSV)

"among you stands one whom you do not know, even he who comes after me, the thong of whose sandal I am not worthy to untie." (1:26–27 RSV)

"This is he of whom I said, 'After me comes a man who ranks before me, for he was before me.'" (1:30 RSV)

John, then, has already declared his position on the success of Jesus; he himself does not see the situation in terms of limited good, nor will he engage in envy.

However, John steps apart from this typical game of envy by making several critical remarks. First, he declares that Jesus has not achieved anything on his own. No one, including Jesus, has anything except "what is given from above" (3:27). Thus, in the jargon of honor and shame, the honor that Jesus enjoys is honor ascribed by God, with which mortals may not disagree (cf. Acts 5:39). In this way, John states that he himself does not share his disciples' perception of a controversy, since it is God who gives Jesus' status and fame. Second, John reminds his disciples of his own earlier testimony to Jesus (3:28; cf. 1:19–23), indicating that his major role has been to herald and acknowledge Jesus' honorable precedence and status before all. John has always promoted Jesus; it is his mission to see Jesus increase. Third, he describes his relationship to Jesus as the "friend" (φίλος) who stands close by and "rejoices greatly at the groom's voice" (3:29 RSV). Surely, groom and friend are not rivals; nor does the friend lose anything if the groom is happy. In fact, as John immediately says, "This joy of mine is now full"; that is, in no way has it diminished because of Jesus' success. Thus John disputes his own disciples' interpretation of the situation. Whereas they see only loss in

Jesus' growing success, John sees "fullness of joy" at Jesus' fame, just as the φίλος revels in the voice of the groom.

Finally, John makes one of the most countercultural statements in the New Testament: "He [Jesus] must increase, but I must decrease" (3:30 RSV). Why countercultural? What is taking place between the characters of the story and the reader and the audience? How would readers know that John has made a remark so unusual as to turn their world upside down? To answer this, we must borrow from cultural anthropology a model for assessing social perceptions of gain and loss in honor/shame (agonistic) societies.

CULTURAL MODEL OF "LIMITED GOOD"

Several decades ago, the anthropologist George Foster described how peasants perceive that all good things in the world exist in limited supply:

> By "Image of Limited Good" I mean that broad areas of peasant behavior are patterned in such a fashion as to suggest that peasants view their social, economic, and natural universes—their total environment—as one in which all of the desired things in life such as land, wealth, health, friendship and love, manliness and honor, respect and status, power and influence, security and safety, exist in finite quantity and are always in short supply, as far as the peasant is concerned. Not only do these and all other "good things" exist in finite and limited quantities, but in addition there is no way directly within peasant power to increase the available quantities. (Foster 1965a, 296)

For peasants, ancient as well as modern, the world exists as a zero-sum game in which land provides the basic analogy for understanding the world. There is only so much arable land in the world, and it is already all distributed. If one person gets more, someone else has to get less. Moreover, the same is true of all other good things in the world, including water, food, and wealth, as well as respect and fame. Thus Foster argues that "any advantage achieved by one individual or family is seen as a loss to others, and the person who makes what the Western world lauds as 'progress' is viewed as a threat to the stability of the entire community" (1972, 169).

The key here is the perception that everything good is already distributed and cannot be increased. Foster suggests that when people view the world in this way, two things will happen: (1) people "are reluctant to advance beyond their peers because of the sanctions they know will be leveled against them"; (2) anyone "who is seen or known to acquire more becomes much more vulnerable to the envy of his neighbors" (1972, 169). Social relations become heavily dependent not just on maintaining what one has in life but also on avoiding the perception of gaining more. To gain is to steal from others. Thus peasants will not tolerate neighbors who acquire beyond what they have. Because goods are limited, envy follows acquisition as surely as night follows day. Two things, then, are at stake in our discussion of John 3:25–30: (1) the perception of limited good, such that one's gain comes at another's expense; (2) the reaction of envy to prevent this gain/loss.

Cultural Illustrations of "Limited Good" in Antiquity

Although the notion of limited good was formulated by a modern scholar studying modern peasant societies, it has direct relevance for interpreting a host of ancient texts, both Greco-Roman and biblical. The following examples, once appreciated, illustrate the presence of the concept in antiquity and thereby confirm the utility of an anthropological model for the interpretation of biblical documents. Thus our argument is that ancient expressions of limited good can serve as interpretative parallels for understanding John 3:25–30.

We begin with an ancient saying of Iamblichus that fully expresses what we saw in regard to the attitude of John's disciples: "People do not find it pleasant to give honor [τιμή] to someone else, for they suppose that they themselves are being deprived of something" (*Anonymus Iamblichi* 2.400). Evidently, those described here ("people") perceive the world in the same way as do Foster's peasants: everything is limited, especially honor, such that another's gain comes at one's own loss. Of course, this naked quotation tells us nothing of the reaction of those who are "deprived of something," but since this gain is perceived as an injury or insult of some sort, the common social reaction would likely be anger and/or envy to stop the loss and restore the former balance.

Plutarch describes a situation of limited good when he remarks that some persons hear a speaker and react in envy at the speaker's success: "As though commendation were money, he feels that he is robbing himself of every bit that he bestows on another" (*Rect. rat. aud.* 44B). Here again the issue is one of reputation or respect, and the perspective is that of limited good. Another's gain means "robbery" of oneself. Although Plutarch does not say that this situation results in agonistic behavior, it remains a distinct possibility. In another place Plutarch states, "And whereas men attack other kinds of eminence and themselves lay claim to good character, good birth, and honor, as though they were depriving themselves of so much of these as they grant to others" (*An seni* 787D). Obviously, honor is to be both sought and defended. But a pattern is also emerging here: a grant of honor to another means depriving oneself of honor in equal measure. The perspective is one of limited good, and agonistic reactions would likely follow.

In a number of places Josephus also describes situations that presume some sort of perception of limited good. First, when he describes the envy of John, son of Levi, at his own rise in fortune, he comments,

> Believing that my success involved his own ruin, he gave way to immoderate envy. Hoping to check my good fortune by inspiring hatred of me in those under my command, he tried to induce the inhabitants of Tiberias, Sepphoris, and Gabara—the three chief cities of Galilee—to abandon their allegiance to me and go over to him, asserting that they would find him a better general than I was. (*Life* 122–123)

The issue is once again honor or reputation, and the perception is again that of limited good. Josephus's "success" meant John's "ruin." The result was "envy" and an attempt by John to win back what he saw Josephus as taking from him.

In another place Josephus reports how Herod demanded that his sons be treated each according to his particular honor, because to give honor unfairly to one son was to take it unjustly from a deserving son: "Let the honors you award them be neither undeserved nor unequal [ἀνώμαλος], but proportioned to the rank of each; for in paying deference to any beyond the deserts of his age, you gratify him less than you grieve the one whom you slight" (*J.W.* 1.459). Once more, the focus is honor, and the perception is that of limited good: the deference given one son is seen as loss of deference to another. Feuding among the royal sons is sure to result in an attempt to redress the perceived wrong.

Josephus's account of Moses' peril (*Ant.* 2.254–257) clearly reflects his own appreciation of limited good. Even as certain Egyptian nobles urged Pharaoh to put Moses to death, "He [Pharaoh] on his own part was harboring thoughts of so doing, alike from Moses' generalship and from fear of seeing himself abased, and so, when instigated by the hierarchy, was prepared to lend a hand in the murder of Moses" (*Ant.* 2.255). As we have come to expect, honor is the limited good: Pharaoh perceived that Moses' reputation came at his own expense ("fear of seeing himself abased"), and the appropriate envious reaction was to kill Moses and thus restore himself to prominence.

Finally, in the account of Korah's revolt (*Ant.* 4.24–34) Josephus comments, "It is monstrous that Korah, in coveting this honor, should deprive God of the power of deciding to whom He would accord it." Not accidentally, the issue is over honor, and the perception, at least by Josephus, is that of limited good: Korah's acquisition of status and honor in this regard comes at God's expense. The deity must and will respond to this threat.

In one place Philo (*Drunkenness* 28) compares and contrasts people of insight with those with mere earthly vision. The wise and all-seeing soul, he says, stretches toward God and interprets created things as benefactions of God; moreover, such a person honors God as the only Cause of these material benefactions. In contrast, the person of undiscerning vision, whose eye is blinded, does not perceive the Cause at all but rather considers material benefits as causes of what he or she hopes to receive. Hence, such a person worships many gods, building idols of stone and wood. Philo then makes a claim that relates this material to his perception of limited good: "Polytheism creates atheism in the souls of the foolish, and God's honor is set at naught by those who deify the mortal. . . . They even allowed irrational plants and animals to share in the honor which belongs to things imperishable" (*Drunkenness* 110). As we have come to see, honor—in this case, God's honor—is proportionately diminished as more creatures are honored as gods; the honor of the imperishable God wanes insofar as honor is given to perishable beings. It is clear, therefore, that there is only so much honor in the cosmos, and when honor is unworthily given to some, it diminishes the legitimate honor of others. For this reason, Philo labels the just honoring of God as ὁσιότης, whereas the improper honoring of creatures is ἀσέβεια.

Fronto's letter to the emperor Marcus Aurelius (*Correspondence* 4.1) provides another striking illustration of the phenomenon that we are investigating. Fronto begins by comparing Orpheus's ability to charm "sheep and doves with wolves and eagles" with that of a political leader who gathers together different nations endowed with diverse characteristics. Orpheus's following, nevertheless, lived sociably together in unity and concord, "the gentle with the fierce, the quiet with the violent, the meek with the proud, the sensitive with the cruel." Fronto exhorts the emperor to the same achievement, but he concedes that at court the emperor faces "a far harder task than to charm with the lyre the fierceness of lions and wild beasts." His endeavors, then, should be focused on this:

> Set yourself to uproot and utterly stamp out one vice of mutual envy and jealousy among your friends, that they may not, when you have shown attention or done a favor to another, think that this is so much taken from or lost to themselves. Envy among men is a deadly evil and more fatal than any, a curse to enviers and envied alike.

The stage is the imperial court, where clients seek the emperor's patronage, thus climbing the fragile ladder of honor and shame. Despite the fact that Fronto talks about imperial elites and not peasants, the social perception is the same: all things are limited, and the success of one person is perceived as another's loss. However, a new element emerges here: the explicit remark that envy follows the perception of another's success. That is so because all are grasping for the same prize. All seek a high reputation in the eyes of their peers.

At this point we turn from the Greco-Roman world to examine some of the evidence in the Hebrew and Christian Scriptures. The story in Gen 27:30–40 of Esau's lost blessing provides a good example. Esau returns from hunting and asks his father's blessing. But as a result of Jacob's deceit, Isaac has already blessed his younger son. When Esau returns, and Isaac recognizes him, he is distraught. Esau pleads, "Bless me, me also, father!" But Isaac cannot. There is only one blessing, and it has already been distributed. So too are the servants, grain, and wine that go with it and sustain it. Esau's second plea to his agitated father is even more telling. It makes clear the limited nature of the good: "Have you only one blessing, father?" (27:38 NRSV). Indeed he does. Esau receives a curse instead.

Once, when Gideon and his army were prepared to go into battle, the Lord said to him, "The people with you are too many for me to give the Midianites into their hand, lest Israel vaunt themselves against me, saying, 'My own hand has delivered me'" (Judg 7:2 RSV). The point of view is that of the person who stands to lose honor by the actions of another. The deity perceives that if Gideon wins the victory with a large army, the likely result is the rise of Gideon's reputation as a great warrior and Israel's reliance on him. This, it is implied, comes at God's expense. Hence the command is given to reduce Gideon's troops by two-thirds so that the victory remains with God.

Similarly, David was returning to Saul from "slaying the Philistine" and was acclaimed in city after city by women who came out "singing and dancing . . . with timbrels, with songs of joy, and with instruments of music" (1 Sam 18:6 RSV). And they sang, "Saul has slain his thousands, and David his ten thousands" (18:7 RSV). When Saul heard this, he was "very angry, for this saying displeased him. He said, 'They have ascribed to David ten thousands, and to me they have ascribed thousands; and what more can he have but the kingdom?'" (18:8 RSV). This represents a classic situation of the birth of envy. Saul, like so many other figures we have seen, perceives that David's success comes at his own expense. Moreover, the issue continues to be one of honor, in this case a reputation for military valor and success. Obviously, Saul calculates that David will not be satisfied with this honor and will in time aim to have Saul's very throne: "What more can he have but the kingdom?" Thus from that time on, we are told, "Saul eyed David," indicating that he continued to interpret David's every plan or success as wounding his own honor.

Next we turn to Mark's account of Jesus' teaching in the synagogue of his home village (6:1–6 [cf. Matt 13:53–58; Luke 4:16–30]). His public act of speaking in so formal a setting as the synagogue at the most significant of times (on the sabbath) embodies a claim of qualification to do something that he apparently did not have prior to his departure. Now, disciples follow him! Evidently, Jesus has changed radically since he left Nazareth, and he has become a person of considerable stature and honor. But his public speech immediately provokes a negative reaction: "They were astonished." In a string of questions the villagers voice their objections to Jesus' public behavior. First, they call attention to what they find most offensive in Jesus, namely, his newly found capabilities and the corresponding honor that they bring him: "Where did this man get all this? What is the wisdom given to him? What mighty works are wrought by his hands!" (6:2 RSV). Such actions would hardly be expected of a peasant artisan. They are perceived as increases in Jesus' status vis-à-vis his former neighbors. Such a quantum leap in honor is apparently processed via the perception of limited good, which adequately explains the hostile reaction to Jesus. His gain is interpreted as their loss.

In antiquity the chief cultural grounds for an individual's status are pegged to kin, since one's origin and birth ordinarily provide a reliable index of worth for one's entire life (Malina and Neyrey 1996, 23–27, 158–60). Hence, the question "Where did he get all this?" implies that Jesus could not have gotten wisdom and powers from his family, who are ordinary peasants: "Is not this the carpenter, the son of Mary and brother of James and Joses and Simon and Judas, and are not his sisters with us?" (Mark 6:3 RSV). This means that their social location in the village environment is that of typically poor peasants and artisans. Born of humble stock, Jesus has no means in their eyes to deserve any new honor. Being an artisan, he had received no schooling (John 7:15), and so the qualifications for his public voice in the village synagogue remain uncertain. And yet, here he is enjoying a most favorable and increasing reputation. Jesus' increase in respect throughout Galilee lifts him high above his village peers, a situation that his neighbors perceive as an intolerable and unbalancing force that means their corresponding loss of honor in proportion to Jesus' gain (Rohrbaugh 2000, 200–214). Although the term *envy* does not appear here, the complete ingredients for it are present, as we will soon see.

What do people do who perceive a serious imbalance in the zero-sum game of honor and status? Luke concludes his version of Jesus' teaching in his hometown synagogue with the report of an attempt on Jesus' life (Luke 4:29). Resort to violence is an open admission of loss (Rohrbaugh 1995, 185–86). Matthew and Mark both record a hostile reaction, although not life-threatening: "They took offense [ἐσκανδαλίζοντο] at him." In short, they deny his claim to public voice; they attempt to cut him down to size. Jesus has the final word, quoting a common proverb: "A prophet is not without honor except in his own country and in his own house" (Matt 13:57 RSV). Granted that Jesus' remark is a generic sort of maxim that is sufficiently broad to apply to many situations, it nevertheless does have to do with role and status ("prophet"), honor, and peer envy—items regularly found in a perspective of limited good. We do not think it far from the mark to translate Jesus' remark as "A person of distinction [prophet] lacks no acknowledgment of his role/status [honor] except in situations of limited good, where his closest associates and relatives [in his own country and in his own house] perceive themselves as losing honor precisely as his increases."

In Mark's gospel we find several other stories that reflect the perception of limited good (7:24–30; 9:38–41; 10:35–45). In the story about the Canaanite woman (7:24–30) Jesus first refuses her request, saying, "Let the children first be fed, for it is not right to take the children's bread and throw it to the dogs" (7:27 RSV). The plain meaning of his words states that there is only so much bread, and it belongs to the "children." To give any to the dogs means that the children's share will necessarily shrink. But the woman argues in response, "even the dogs under the table eat the children's crumbs" (7:28 RSV). She effectively neutralizes the limited good perspective by stating that she is not encroaching on the children's portion (bread) but rather wishes to share in that part of the portion that has always been fed to dogs (the bread crumbs). The story depends on the audience understanding limited good in order to grasp both Jesus' words and the woman's argument.

In Mark's gospel we also hear John the son of Zebedee reporting to Jesus about a situation that resembles the dialogue between John the Baptizer and his disciples. John and others saw a man who was not a disciple use Jesus' name in successfully casting out a demon (9:38), and they forbade him. Jesus' disciples evaluate what they observe in terms of some notion of limited good, and so the focus is on the "name" of Jesus and the honor that this nondisciple gains. His success means that Jesus (and his disciples) suffers some corresponding loss; to staunch this flow, the disciples "forbade him." Jesus, however, does not perceive the incident in terms of limited good and criticizes the disciples' actions: "Do not forbid him." Far from being a proclamation of tolerance, Jesus' words admit of a different interpretation: Jesus continues to gain an honorable reputation when another uses his name. When and until this other person speaks ill (κακολογῆσαι) of Jesus, he the teacher experiences a net gain in honor. What is clear is that the disciples evaluate the episode in terms of limited good, seeing the exorcist's success coming at their and Jesus' expense. Jesus does not contradict the evaluation of limited good so much as indicate that currently he and his disciples continue to experience a net gain in honor. Hence, "Do not forbid him" indicates that Jesus does not feel envy and thus hostility.

One further example from Mark 10:35–52 concludes our survey of parallel materials. James and John, two disciples who are already prominent among the Twelve (5:37; 9:2), approach Jesus and request further special favors: "Grant us to sit, one at your right hand and your left hand, in your glory" (10:37 RSV). We today consider someone at the right hand of the boss to have extraordinary status; so also in antiquity. Psalm 110:1 states it quite clearly: "The LORD said to my Lord, 'Sit at my right hand'" (RSV). Thus James and John have asked for a truly unique honor. However, Jesus persuades them to accept his new calculus of honor, which is "the cup" of sufferings that he will drink and the "baptism" of his passion and death. Instead of receiving what they asked for, James and John are given the honor of sharing Jesus' fate.

But the damage has been done. The other ten disciples hear of the request and react in anger. Their reaction makes perfect cultural sense in terms of limited good because if James and John were to receive the honor status that they requested, there would be little or no special honor left for them. The success of two would come at the expense of ten. Thus the ten understand that they themselves will be hurt by the request of James and John. Moreover, the indignation and anger (ἀγανακτεῖν) with which they react was understood as the appropriate emotional response to a sense of injury. The episode, Mark tells us, does not escalate into a situation of envy and agonistic behavior because Jesus intervenes (10:42–45). But all of the elements of a battle born of perceptions of limited good are present.

Yet, as Jesus did with James and John (Mark 10:38–40), he now does with all of the Twelve (10:43–45). He redefines honor such that limited good will make no sense. He criticizes positions of power and status by reminding the Twelve that people in such situations despoil those below themselves. In his circle of disciples, Jesus states, the "great" one is the servant of the rest, and the "first" person is the slave of all. Ambition for these particular status positions is acceptable, for no one loses anything; all gain. Jesus then concludes by presenting himself as an honorable example of what he is saying: "The Son of man came not to be served but to serve, and to give his life a ransom for many" (10:45 NRSV).

In sum, the ancient illustrations of limited good that we have examined exhibit the following three traits. First, they all clearly indicate the perception of a zero-sum game in which one's success means another's failure. A causal connection is invariably perceived between the gains of one person and the losses of another. Second, almost all of the illustrations indicate that the commodity being contested is "honor"—that is, commendation by another, reputation, precedence, role and status, attention or favor from a high-ranking person. The result is that in most instances those who perceive themselves as losing because of another's success take hostile action to redress the imbalance. Sometimes it is active harm that is done, including gossip and vilification, or murder or dismissal and disdain. Third, many of the illustrations describe a situation of envy, a most important element in the social dynamics of ancient Greeks, Romans, and Israelites. The data thus appear as follows:

AUTHOR AND WORK	EXPRESSION OF LIMITED GOOD	COMMODITY IN DISPUTE	REACTION (ESPECIALLY ENVY)	AGONISTIC REDRESS
Iamblichus	clearly stated	honor	not mentioned	not mentioned
Plutarch, *Rect. rat. aud.* 44B	clearly stated	honor	implied	not mentioned
Plutarch, *An seni* 787D	clearly stated	honor	implied	attack
Josephus, *Life* 122–123	clearly stated	success, good fortune	immoderate envy	inspiring hatred and defection
Josephus, *Ant.* 4.32; 4.51	clearly stated	honor	not mentioned	divine judgment
Philo, *Drunkenness* 110	clearly stated	honor	not mentioned	not mentioned
Fronto, *Correspondence* 4.1	clearly stated	attention, favor	explicitly mentioned	"deadly and fatal"
Judg 7:2	clearly stated	honor	not mentioned	not mentioned
1 Sam 18:9	clearly stated	reputation, honor	implied	"eyed" David
Mark 6:1–5	implied	reputation, honor	implied	"took offense at him"
Mark 7:24–30	implied	patronage, honor	not mentioned	bestowed favor
Mark 9:38–41	implied	reputation, honor	implied	"they commanded him to stop"
Mark 10:35–45	implied	status, honor	implied	"they became angry at James and John"

Figure 19: Ancient illustrations of limited good

"Limited Good" and Envy

Although only two of the passages discussed above explicitly state that envy follows the perception of limited good, we assert that it is implied in all of the others. We base this on our analysis of envy in the ancient world as well as our investigation of limited good. Here we briefly examine envy in terms of five issues: (1) what is envy, (2) what is envied, (3) who envies whom, (4) how one envies, (5) how one avoids envy.

(1) In his analysis of the emotions that speakers typically arouse Aristotle defines envy as "a kind of pain at the sight of [another's] good fortune," a distress that comes not from any effort to match the success of the person envied but simply "because others possess it" (*Rhet.* 2.10.1). Cicero repeats this centuries later: "Envy is distress incurred by reason of a neighbor's prosperity" (*Tusc.* 4.8.17). In Plutarch's words, "Envy is pain at another's good" (*Curios.* 518C). Envy, then, is pain or distress at another's success, a sense of being injured, which seeks redress.

(2) The object of envy seems always to be "honor" in one of its manifestations. Rhetoricians declare that "success" (εὐπραγία) is envied, a judgment verified by authors who describe the arousal of it. We suggest that whatever patronage someone received, wealth one acquired, status one enjoyed, reputation one earned, prowess one displayed—in short, the Greco-Roman contents of the cultural value of honor—caused the distress and pain that constitute envy.

(3) Who envies? Basically peers, as Aristotle said: "Envy is defined as a kind of distress at the apparent success of one's peers" (*Rhet.* 2.10.1). Cicero echoes this: "People are especially envious of their equals, or of those once beneath them, when they feel themselves left behind and fret at the other's upward flight" (*Or. Brut.* 2.52.209). Envy, we are told, also arises within families: "Kinship, too, knows how to envy" (Aristotle, *Rhet.* 2.10.5). Foster, in his excellent study of envy, indicates that "every society designates those of its members who are deemed eligible to compete with each other for desired goals"—that is, "conceptual equals" (1972, 70).

(4) Although Cicero (*Tusc.* 4.8.17) states that envy does not always translate into harmful behavior toward the envied person, we find in numerous instances that it does. When we ask how enviers typically envy, the research indicates six ways: (a) ostracism, (b) gossip and slander, (c) feuding, (d) litigation, (e) the evil eye, (f) homicide (Hagedorn and Neyrey 1998). Saul's "eyeing" of David after hearing of "Saul's thousands and David's ten thousands" likely illustrates ocular malevolence (Elliott 1988; 1990), which festered until Saul attempted to kill David. Jesus' endless controversies with Pharisees and others represent feuding at its most savage level, for Jesus cannot say or do anything without incessant criticism and carping from his rivals. Likewise, the various reactions to Jesus at Nazareth are examples of either ostracism (Mark and Matthew) or attempted homicide (Luke). Jesus' enemies spread slanderous gossip about his empty tomb (Matt 28:11–15). And Jesus is the formal object of judicial proceedings before the Sanhedrin and the Roman procurator.

(5) How does one avoid envy? Foster's study indicates four ways to avoid envy: (a) concealment, (b) denial, (c) the "sop," (d) true sharing. If one does noble deeds in secret and hides one's prowess, then no one will know of any reason for feeling envy. But Jesus' mission is to proclaim the kingdom of God (Mark 1:14–15) in all the towns of Galilee (Mark 1:35–39), for which he must be as public as possible. Moreover, Jesus instructed his disciples in a parable about putting a lamp on a

lamp stand and not under a bushel basket (Mark 4:21–23), virtually prohibiting them from concealment—a strategy he himself followed. Second, Jesus appears to use the strategy of denial when he refuses the compliment of the rich man: "Good Teacher, what must I do?" (Mark 10:17 RSV). He instructs this man, "Why do you call me good? No one is good except the one God" (Mark 10:18). Third, a "sop" refers to some form of forced sharing of goods meant to placate a group likely to envy the success that earned the goods, such as the "liturgies" in ancient Greece (Llewelyn 1994). One can only speculate about the remarks in Mark 6:5–6 that Jesus "could not work any power there because of their unbelief." No possibility of sharing his benefaction of wisdom and power is available to Jesus, and it is odious to imagine that Jesus allowed himself to be a victim or to be pressured into buying off his critics. Jesus, then, offered no "sop" to avoid envy. Finally, the rich deposit of Markan references to Jesus' healing power and his lavish feeding of the multitudes argue that Jesus almost continually engaged in true sharing of God's benefaction. Thus, except for Jesus' refusal of the compliment in Mark 10:17, he does not appear to have engaged in any of the classical strategies of avoiding envy.

We remarked earlier about the widespread prevalence of the perception of limited good in the ancient world. Now we argue that in the context of limited good, envy is the logical and social next step in the sequence of events that occur when the ancients perceive that another's gain means their own loss. This is expressed and clearly implied in the catalogue of materials that both illustrate the existence of a perception of limited good in antiquity and lay bare its anatomy. This implies a continually agonistic social dynamics, which modern scholars label as an agonistic society. For example, biblical scholars readily point out how the principal literary form of the Gospels, the *chreia* (an expanded saying or deed), embodies agonistic behavior. The "responsive" type of *chreia* typically begins with criticism of a sage's behavior and teaching or with a hostile question put to him. Thus provoked, the sage must respond with sharp wit. This native rhetorical form corresponds to what cultural anthropologists describe as situations of challenge and riposte, where the claims of some to honor (prowess, precedence, power) are challenged, generally by a peer who finds the other's honor painful or distressing.

When one reads the narrative of Mark and identifies the responsive *chreiai* and their cultural shape as challenge-riposte episodes, it becomes clear that the narrative episodes in the story of Jesus contain a pervasive sense of antagonism, whether the reader analyzes them in terms of rhetoric as responsive *chreiai* or in terms of cultural anthropology as challenge-riposte exchanges. Thus, we conclude, there was a widespread perception of limited good by the ancients generally and by the characters of the Gospels specifically. This perception generally aroused envy in the perceiver, which frequently issued in hostile behavior to cut down to size the person perceived as gaining honor. This gives rise to the constant tension between claimants of honor and those who envy them that is typical of an agonistic society. These perceptions, the envy that they arouse, and the agonistic behavior that they give rise to are expressed in the ubiquitous rhetorical form of the responsive *chreia,* an exercise taught to young students. Thus both the model of social dynamics drawn from cultural anthropology and the forms of ancient rhetoric tell a similar story.

John 3:22–30 in Cultural Context

The materials that we have just surveyed and the model of agonistic social dynamics that we have described can be brought to bear on John 3:22–30 with considerable profit. First, the ζήτησις in which John's disciples are involved should be described as an envious reaction. They perceive the situation in terms of limited good, in that they interpret Jesus' rise in reputation and fame as causing decrease in that of John the Baptizer and thus of their own. Their complaint that "All are going to him" means that fewer are flocking to John or that John is losing popularity. This perception, then, causes in them what is expected in that society: pain at another's good fortune and distress at his success. Since injury must be answered, they are poised to act out their envy in some hostile way.

That, of course, is exactly what happens in 11:45–52. There, we get the culturally expected response when the perception of loss (limited good) leads to envy and eventually to hostile action. In 3:27–30, however, John stops the spiral of envy. He corrects one part of his disciples' perception when he declares that God is the source of Jesus' honor and success (3:27); human beings should in no way challenge God's sovereignty as benefactor. When God is gracious and causes an increase, no fault accrues to the recipient of his favor. Thus John reminds his envious disciples that he himself has never felt injured or distressed by Jesus; in fact, his greatest honor has been to witness to Jesus (1:19–23). In other words, he, unlike his disciples, does not perceive the present situation in terms of limited good. Jesus' success means his own success as herald of or witness to the Lamb of God (1:29–34). Indeed, John himself pointed Jesus out to two of his disciples who then heard and followed Jesus (1:35–39). Evidently, John was pleased that Jesus succeeded, even if it meant the "loss" of two of his own disciples.

By way of the metaphor of a wedding party, John totally denies any rivalry between himself and Jesus. John, the friend (φίλος) of Jesus the bridegroom, listens to the bridegroom's voice and "rejoices with joy" at it (3:29a). No pain at Jesus' good fortune here! No distress at his success! "My joy is now filled" (3:29b). If there is no perception of limited good, then there is likewise no sense of pain or distress, nor is any envy aroused that leads to agonistic behavior. John, then, completely contradicts his disciples' perception of the situation.

John concludes his response to his disciples with an utterly countercultural remark: "He must increase, I must decrease" (3:30 NRSV). Most commentators read the "must" here as a statement of divine necessity, signaling God's will that Jesus increase. This final remark repeats what John said earlier about the contentment that the φίλος should have at the bridegroom's taking of a wife. But it also addresses the heart of the cultural model that we have been studying. Jesus' success in fact means that John's reputation and significance wane. The fundamental perception of limited good is again validated, but in this case it does not lead to envy and hostility. In this way it is countercultural. For John insists that he is neither pained nor distressed at Jesus' "increase." And so, he readily surrenders his reputation and honor, which belong to Jesus by right. Rarely does one find in Greek or Israelite literature a public figure who willingly and peacefully allows his honor and prestige to diminish without envy and hostile reaction. Therefore, it is only when readers appreciate the cultural perception of limited good, which leads to a sense of pain and distress and issues in envy, that they hear what the characters are saying and understand the strikingly unusual response of John to his disciples.

BIBLIOGRAPHY

Cohen, David. 1991. *Law, Sexuality, and Society: The Enforcement of Morals in Classical Athens.* Cambridge: Cambridge University Press.

Elliott, John H. 1988. The Fear of the Leer: The Evil Eye from the Bible to Li'l Abner. *Forum* 4:42–71.

———. 1990. Galatians and the Evil Eye. *Currents in Theology and Mission* 17:262–73.

Faraone, Christopher. 1991. The Agonistic Context of Early Greek Binding Spells. Pages 10–17 in *Magika Hiera: Ancient Greek Magic.* Edited by C. A. Faraone and Dirk Obbink. Oxford: Oxford University Press.

Foster, George M. 1965a. Peasant Society and the Image of Limited Good. *American Anthropologist* 67:293–315.

———. 1965b. Cultural Responses to Expressions of Envy in Tzintzuntzan. *Southwestern Journal of Anthropology* 21:24–35.

———. 1972. The Anatomy of Envy: A Study in Symbolic Behavior. *Current Anthropology* 13:165–202.

Hagedorn, Anselm C., and Jerome H. Neyrey. 1998. "It Was Out of Envy That They Handed Jesus Over" (Mark 15:10): The Anatomy of Envy and the Gospel of Mark. *Journal for the Study of the New Testament* 69:32–54.

Llewelyn, S. R. 1994. The Development of the System of Liturgies. Pages 93–111 in vol. 7 of *New Documents Illustrating Early Christianity: A Review of the Greek Inscriptions and Papyri Published in 1982–83.* Edited by G. H. R. Horsley and S. Llewelyn. 9 vols. North Ryde, NSW: Ancient History Documentary Research Centre, Macquarie University, 1981–1998.

Malina, Bruce J. 2001. *The New Testament World: Insights from Cultural Anthropology.* 3d ed. Louisville: Westminster John Knox.

Malina, Bruce J., and Jerome H. Neyrey. 1996. *Portraits of Paul: An Archaeology of Ancient Personality.* Louisville: Westminster John Knox.

Neyrey, Jerome H. 1998. Questions, Chreiai, and Challenges to Honor: The Interface of Rhetoric and Culture in Mark's Gospel. *Catholic Biblical Quarterly* 60:657–81.

Rohrbaugh, Richard L. 1995. Legitimating Sonship: A Test of Honor; A Social Science Study of Luke 4:1–30. Pages 183–97 in *Modelling Early Christianity:*

Social-Scientific Studies of the New Testament in Its Context. Edited by Philip F. Esler. London: Routledge.

———. 2000. Locating Jesus: Strategies for Persuasion. Pages 198–230 in *The New Testament World.* Edited by Philip F. Esler. London: Routledge.

Walcot, Peter. 1978. *Envy and the Greeks: A Study in Human Behavior.* Warminster: Aris & Phillips.

Part Four

MODAL
PERSONALITY

Modal Personality

14

M odern Americans are individualists. They value the accomplishments of the individual and see someone's accomplishments as being all the more impressive if they have been attained without the help of others. This individualism, with its accompanying ethnocentrism, is a historical development that comes out of modernism: "The fundamental assumption of modernity, the thread that has run through Western civilization since the sixteenth century, is that the social unit of society is not the group, the guild, the tribe, or the city but the person" (Bell 1976, 16).

Modern and ancient peoples from the Middle East, however, are "group-oriented" or "collectivist." The ancient Mediterranean "modal personality"—the ways they lived and how they understood their humanity—was not at all individualistic. In that culture individuals were embedded in a series of relationships: family, tribe, trade, association, and so forth. As such, their basic identity was in relationship to others: "son of So-and-So" or "Zacchaeus, the chief tax collector" or "Caiaphas, the high priest" or "a disciple of Moses."

We access knowledge about these ancient group-oriented persons from miscellaneous remarks made about individuals, which themselves must be assessed in terms of the social system in which they live. People are described in terms of their geography (place of birth), generation (parents, ancestors), formation and training, manner of life, bodily constitution, natural dispositions, and fortune. The same set of identifiers is used in Greek oratory and becomes codified in instructions on forensic and epideictic rhetoric (Cicero, *Inv.* 1.24, 35–25.36; Quintilian, *Inst.* 5.10.24–29).

These are the data that orators and authors considered sufficient for presenting an ancient person to an audience, and they often used such identifiers as abbreviated ways to sum up a person's significant traits, relying on stereotypes of the time. For example, "The Egyptian disposition is by nature a most jealous and envious one" (Philo, *Flaccus* 26); "Cretans are always liars, evil beasts, lazy drunkards" (Titus 1:12). As regards geography, it was considered noble for an Israelite to have been born in Jerusalem (Ps 87:6) and superior for one to have been born in Greece. How honorable a child from Tarsus (Acts 21:39), and how ignoble one from Nazareth (John 1:46)!

BIBLIOGRAPHY

Bell, Daniel. 1976. *The Cultural Contradictions of Capitalism.* New York: Basic.

Bruce J. Malina
and Jerome H. Neyrey, SJ

Ancient Mediterranean Persons in Cultural Perspective: Portrait of Paul

INTRODUCTION

We can identify three native sources of information about how persons were perceived and portrayed in the ancient Mediterranean world. The authors of the rhetorical, progymnastic ("school exercise"), and physiognomic (describing physical features of persons) literature serve us adequately as native informants about what they consider important to know about a person. A journey through this literature will indicate that these materials attest to nonindividualistic, group-oriented persons. Collectivistic, group-oriented ancient Mediterraneans followed a scenario in which they viewed themselves "sociologically" in terms of gender, generation, and geography, with constant concern for public awards of respect and honor. This scenario suggests that Paul and his audience perceived human beings quite differently from the way modern Americans view human beings, and so they thought quite differently about who a person might be and what might be the expected range of human behavior.

STRONG GROUP PERSONS

To begin with, we recall the fact that all people the world over use the word "I," and those who use this word with meaning make reference to their "selves." But the dimensions of this "I" are not the same in all cultures. As Triandis has noted,

> The self is coterminous with the body in individualist cultures and in some of the collectivist cultures. However, it can be related to a group the way a hand is related to the person whose hand it is. The latter conception is found in collectivist cultures, where the self overlaps with a group, such as family or tribe. (1989, 77–78)

Thus when "I" is thought of in terms of individualistic or collectivistic cultures, it will mean quite different things in each.

Individualism means that individual goals precede groups goals. In contrast, collectivism suggests that group goals naturally precede individual goals. As a cultural orientation, American individualism was, and still is, a way of being a person that is totally alien to the scenarios of the ancient Mediterranean world. In the contemporary world individualism can be found among the affluent, socially, and geographically mobile segments of society. Individualistic cultures as a whole emerged only where Enlightenment values have permeated society and agriculture has become the occupation of extremely few people. Since the contemporary version of the individualistic self emerges rather late in human history, it surely was not available in the first-century-c.e. Mediterranean area. Hence, to imagine persons of that time and place in terms of contemporary American personal experience would be highly inaccurate, to say the least. If we wish to be historically and culturally accurate in understanding collectivist models of personality, we must turn to native models of that understanding that are adequately contained in rhetorical, progymnastic, and physiognomic literature (Malina and Neyrey 1996, 19–152). Failure to use these native descriptions of our ancient Mediterranean informants will inevitably result in the errors of anachronism and ethnocentrism.

How prevalent are collectivist societies? In today's world, Triandis (1989, 48) observes, 70 percent of the world's population remain collectivistic, while the remaining 30 percent are individualistic. As a matter of fact, individualism seems totally strange, esoteric, incomprehensible, and even vicious to observers from collectivistic societies. Again, Triandis (1989, 50) notes that what is of most importance in the United States—individualism—is of least importance to the rest of the cultures of the world. Clifford Geertz, moreover, when confronted with the modern anomaly of individualism, has tried to develop a definition of it as it appears in current U.S. usage. Geertz describes that individual as "a bounded, unique, more or less integrated motivational and cognitive universes, a dynamic center of awareness, emotion, judgment and action organized into a distinctive whole and set contrastively both against other such wholes and against its social and natural background" (Geertz 1976, 225). He notes that this way of being human is, "however incorrigible it may seem to us, *a rather peculiar idea* within the context of the world's cultures" (225, italics added).

The point of all these observations is to demonstrate that any self that we might encounter in the New Testament, Jesus or Paul, should be understood as a collectivistic self or as a group-oriented person, not as an individualistic self. We repeat: to understand the persons who populate the pages of the New Testament, we must not consider them as individualistic. The personal, individualistic, self-concerned focus typical of contemporary American experience was simply unavailable in to people in antiquity. Given their cultural experience, such self-concerned individualism would appear deviant and detrimental to other group members. For group survival it would be dysfunctional, hence dangerous. If those people were not individualistic, what or how were they?

For people of that time and place, the basic, most elementary unit of social analysis is not the individual person considered alone and apart from others as a unique being; rather, it is the collectivistic person, the group-embedded person, the person always in relation with and connected to at least one other social unit, usually a kinship group. Contrast, for example, how a modern American and how Paul would explain why they might regard someone as abnormal. First, the American will look to psychology, childhood experiences, personality type, or some significant event in the past that affects an adult's dealing with the world. Biography in the United States, moreover, tends to contain a description of an individual's psychological development in terms of singular events of a unique person passing through the psychological stages of life. Hence, an "abnormal" person in the United States is assessed as one who is psychologically "retarded," or who is deviant, "neurotic," or "psychotic" because of "having been an abused child," and the like. The collectivistic Mediterranean person, however, is nonpsychologically minded and anti-introspective. For elite ancients, basic personality derives largely from generation, geography, and gender, hence from ethnic characteristics that are rooted in the water, soil, and air native to the ethnic group. Being "abnormal" for them would mean not measuring up to the social and cultural expectations or stereotypes that constitute the identity of such persons. A Mediterranean person such as Paul would label someone as "abnormal" and mean by that "she was a sinner," "he submits to Satan," "he was possessed." Such designations of abnormality indicate that "the person is in an abnormal position because he is embedded in an abnormal matrix of relationships" (Selby 1974, 15). The problem is not within a person but rather outside a person, in faulty interpersonal relations. There really is nothing psychologically unique, personal, and idiosyncratic going on within a person at all. All people in a family (generation) and in a distinctive city or region (geography) are presumed to have the same experiences. If any distinctions hold, such are based on region and gender.

Note the ideal set of relationships in which a "normal" person is embedded: "The nurse rules the infant, the teacher the boy, the gymnasiarch the youth, his admirer the young man who, when he comes of age, is ruled by law and his commanding general. No one is his own master, no one is unrestricted" (Plutarch, *Amat.* 754D). "No one is his own master!" Alternately this might be illustrated by the value placed on concern for others:

> Our sacrifices are not occasions for drunken self-indulgence—such practices are abhorrent to God—but for sobriety. At these sacrifices prayers for the welfare of the community must take precedence of those for ourselves; for we are born for fellowship, and he who sets its claims above his private interests is specially acceptable to God. (Josephus, *Ag. Ap.* 2.195–196)

Plutarch and Josephus illustrate what we mean by a collectivist person "set in relation" to others and "set within" a given social background. Thus we describe such persons as strongly group-oriented or group-embedded persons. And so, here we will call them "strong group persons," persons who define themselves almost exclusively in terms of the groups in which they are embedded. Their total self-awareness emphatically depends upon such group embeddedness.

Embeddedness

Ancient Mediterranean people identified and defined themselves as situated in and embedded in various others persons or unities. Such unities were groups held together by the social glue of loyalty or solidarity and were symbolized by blood, birth, or fictive birth. Ancient Mediterraneans considered themselves embedded in a range of in-groups with varying degrees of loyalty: family, fictive family (school, faction, guild, clientele), *polis,* and the like. Let us look more closely at the range of such groups.

Family

The dominant social institution for most people in the first century c.e. was the family, whether the immediate household of father, mother, children, and servants, the imperial household, or fictive-kinship groups. Males, for example, are known in terms of their father and his extended family. How commonly we read of people introduced in New Testament documents as the "son of So-and-So": Simon, son of John (Matt 16:17); James and John, sons of Zebedee (Matt 4:21); Levi, son of Alphaeus (Mark 2:14). Although Jesus' genealogy serves a variety of purposes, it primarily functions to proclaim his embeddedness in the clans and traditions of Israel (Matt 1:1–16). Identity, however, resides not just in one's father, but also in one's grandfather, their clan, and ultimately in the aetiological ancestor of the extended family (see Josh 7:16–18; 1 Sam 1:1). John the Baptizer's father was a priest of the division of Abijah, and his mother a daughter of Aaron (Luke 1:5); Barnabas was a Levite (Acts 4:36); Paul, a Benjaminite (Phil 3:5). Membership, protection, and other benefits can be rightfully claimed on the basis of such kinship.

Similarly, females are known in terms of another person, generally a male member of their family. First, females are embedded in their father's family and so are known in terms of him: Rebekah, daughter of Bethuel (Gen 24:24); Judith, daughter of Beeri the Hittite (Gen 26:34); Aseneth, daughter of Potiphera, priest of On (Gen 41:45); Zebidah, daughter of Pedaiah of Rumah (2 Kings 23:36). But once married, females become embedded in their husbands: Milcah, wife of Nahor (Gen 24:15); Anah, daughter of Zibeon, Esau's wife (Gen 36:14); Abigail, widow of Nabal of Carmel (1 Sam 30:5). Herodias is known to us as the wife of two men, first Philip and then Herod (Mark 6:17; see also Luke 8:3).

Fictive Family

A household in antiquity certainly differed from the typical nuclear family common in the modern United States. It included married sons and their wives and families, as well as a host of servants and retainers. Moving up the social ladder, households would correspondingly contain a greater variety of people needed for its proper functioning. The "household of Caesar" (Phil 4:22) comprised a host of civil servants, bureaucrats, slaves, and the like. The followers of

Jesus, moreover, described themselves as a "household," albeit a fictive family. They are "the household of God" (1 Pet 4:17), and they address one another as "sister" and "brother" (see Mark 3:31–35).

School and Teacher

Disciples had a dyadic relationship to their teachers and mentors. Disciples were subsequently known as the students of the teacher in question, a relation not unlike that of father and son. We know from forensic rhetoric and the encomium that "education" constituted an important piece of information about a person (Malina and Neyrey 1996, 70–75), for it indicated whether that person was in fact trained in a group's understanding of virtue and honor. Just as Luke was quick to point out that Paul was a student of Gamaliel (Acts 22:3), so other ancient persons are identified in terms of their mentors or teachers (Neyrey 1994, 191). For example, Achilles was a student of Chiron; Alexander, of Aristotle; Cicero, of Posidonius. The same pattern emerged in later Pharisaic scribalism, called rabbinism. Not only did disciples study under specific teachers, but also they entered certain gatherings of disciples called "schools," thus taking on the identity, ideas, and behavior of the tradition emerging from such a school. In doing this, an individual's identity is encapsuled in group identity. To know the teacher or mentor is to know the student.

Factions and Coalitions

A person's membership in a faction or coalition constitutes a third form of embeddedness. Scholars have called our attention to groups at the time of Jesus that clustered around social-crisis leaders called "prophet" and "messiah." Various figures recruited followers to join them, such as Theudas (Acts 5:36), Judas the Galilean (Acts 5:37), and a certain Egyptian (Acts 21:38). John the Baptizer gathered a large group of followers, among whom was Jesus. There even seems to have been some competition and rivalry between John's disciples and those of Jesus (see Mark 2:18; John 4:25–30). Such groups, recruited by a central person for some specific purpose, are given the label "faction."

We hear of competition between factions in the synagogue: one group acclaims itself as "disciples of Moses" in opposition to another group who are "disciples of Jesus" (John 9:28). The New Testament, of course, refers to a number of such groups: Pharisees, Sadducees, Zealots. Only occasionally do we know the name of a Pharisee (e.g., Nicodemus [John 3:1]), because the ancient writers thought it sufficient simply to indicate that this or that person was a Pharisee (Mark 7:1; 10:2; Luke 7:36; 11:37; 18:10). The point is that people who were recruited into factions or other coalitions became embedded in them to such an extent that they took their major identity as disciples or followers of the central personage of the group. Jesus, of course, is a case in point. At times it seems that Paul also expected the members of his churches to act in the same way—that is, to consider themselves as his disciples; after all, he claimed to be their "father" (1 Cor 4:14–15; 2 Cor 11:3) and "founder" (1 Cor 3:10).

Trade, Collegia, and Synagogues

A fourth type of embeddedness might be one's trade or the association of similar tradesmen. This should be immediately evident from the way in which persons are identified in the New Testament: Simon and Andrew, fishermen (Matt 4:18); Zacchaeus, tax collector (Luke 19:2); Simon, tanner (Acts 10:6); Lydia, seller of purple goods (Acts 16:14). As Rohrbaugh (1991, 125–49) has shown, when allowed in cities, artisans and merchants tended to live together in the same quarter and on the same street. Paul, for example, sought lodging with other workers of leather (Acts 18:3). Silversmiths, who presumably lived together in a certain quarter of Ephesus, united as a group against Paul (Acts 19:24–27). These tradesmen and artisans gathered together to form their own associations, such as collegia, synagogues, and the like. The ancient world was populated with many types of groups and associations gathered around specific crafts and trade. Sons were socialized to learn their father's trade, with its shared viewpoint and social relations. Thus, when we know the trade of individuals, we know a significant piece of information about them. This presumes, however, that we learn the cultural meaning of being such an artisan or tradesman.

Patron-Clients

People might also be embedded in a web of patron-client relationships. Receiving goods, influence, and the like from a patron, people would then be known as "the friend of So-and-So" and would owe loyalty and commitment in return. The accusation against Pilate if he releases Jesus makes mention of this feature: "If you release this man, you are not Caesar's friend; every one who makes himself a king sets himself against Caesar" (John 19:12). The core of Pilate's identity, then, rests in his being known as Caesar's loyal client—that is, his "friend."

The U.S. myth of the Western frontier idealizes American independence and individualism. But nothing could be more foreign to the first-century-C.E. Mediterranean, where individuals were constantly reminded that they stand in some sort of dependent relationship to landlords, kings, and God. If they speak of "freedom," they generally understand it as both freedom from slavery to one lord or master and freedom to enter the service of another lord and benefactor (Malina 1978, 62–76). For example, individuals are reminded that in regard to their own bodies, "you are not your own" (1 Cor 6:19 NRSV). The sense of belonging to another is expressed in various ways. Paul insists, "You were bought with a price" (1 Cor 6:20; 7:23 NRSV). This means that individuals are the property of Christ: they are his servants. In other places Paul stresses how individuals were freed from being slaves of sin and death and became slaves of God and slaves of righteousness (Rom 6:16–22). Although the language of "freedom" is used, converts to Jesus become free to join the service of a faithful and noble Lord. In fact, the premier confession of Paul, the very prophet of freedom, is "Jesus is Lord" (Rom 10:9; 1 Cor 12:3; Phil 2:11), thus expressing his total embeddedness. Moreover, Paul himself is always "servant of God" or "steward of God's mysteries."

Polis

For elite males it seems that the prevalent form of defining group embeddedness consisted in terms of being a member of the πόλις ("city")—that is, a πολίτης ("citizen" of such a social unit). "Paul of Tarsus," "Jesus of Nazareth," and "Philo of Alexandria" are examples of such designations. Obviously, the significance of the person in question derives from the significance of the *polis*. Of course, nonelite village people do not have the exalted aura of "citizen," hence they derive their honor from family or occupation as previously described. But others, such as Paul, are to be valued more highly because they were born in a "metropolis" or in "Tarsus, no mean city." But as we have seen, geography is a primary contributor to the identity of a person, as well as gender and generation.

SOCIALIZATION, TRADITION, AND LOYALTY

A group-oriented or group-embedded person must in some way learn the code of behavior expected of his or her role and status and geographical location. We turn now to the cultural importance given in antiquity to learning the traditions of one's social group. Deference to the group is evident in the reverence given to what the Romans called the *mos maiorum,* the customs of those greater than us by birth—that is, the tradition of our ancestors. The tradition handed down by former members of the group is presumed valid and normative. Power arguments might be phrased thus: "We have always done it this way!" *Semper, ubique, ab omnibus* ("Always, everywhere, by everyone!"). "The old ways are the best ways." This would be true of ideas, social structures, and cultural values, as well as crafts and trades.

Paul appeals to just this point when he prefaces his account both of the Eucharist (1 Cor 11:23) and the resurrection (1 Cor 15:3) with an appeal to traditional authority: "I hand on . . . what I received." He expects the church to "maintain the traditions even as I have delivered them to you" (1 Cor 11:2), and he is critical of behavior that flaunts them (1 Cor 14:33–36). The Pharisees occasionally criticize Jesus precisely because he did not hew to the "tradition of the elders" (Mark 7:3–5). Hence we find the exhortation to "stand firm and hold fast to the traditions that you were taught by us, either by word of mouth or by our letter" (2 Thess 2:15; cf. 3:6 NRSV). Likewise, the chief duty of Timothy is to "Follow the pattern of the sound words which you have heard from me. . . . guard the truth" (2 Tim 1:13–14; cf. 3:14 RSV).

Clearly, the past is held in great esteem by the group. Anthropological studies of time indicate that people in the U.S. view time quite differently from those of other cultures, in particular peasant societies and among Mediterraneans (Malina 1989, 4–9). Whereas Americans tend to be future-oriented, these others give proportionate value to the past. Rituals and ceremonies, for example, function in such cultures to confirm the values and structures of the past and make them relevant in the present (Malina 1986, 140–43; Neyrey 1995, 200–201). The preferred model of time in the ancient world was one of social devolution, with the distant past as the golden age, followed by silver and bronze ages. The best lies in the distant past, and everything subsequent is a degeneration. In contrast, moderns might be said to espouse a developmental model in which everything is evolving toward some future perfection ("It's getting better all the time," according to a popular song by the Beatles).

The value placed on the past and tradition shows up in the constant injunction that disciples imitate their masters. Paul tells the Corinthians, "Be imitators of me as I am of Christ" (1 Cor 11:1 RSV). Paul himself imitates Christ by embodying the hymn in Phil 2:6–12; like Jesus, who gave up equality with God in obedience to the deity, Paul forgoes the former value found in the law and seeks only to be conformed to the dying and risen Jesus (Phil 3:7–10, 17). The "clouds of witnesses" in Heb 11 illustrate the meaning of "faith" for imitation. Jesus commands his disciples to be like him by "denying themselves." The ancient collectivistic self was embedded in a family. Hence, self-denial means leaving one's family, siblings, and land—the dearest features of a first-century person's life. This is what taking up the cross (or yoke) and following Jesus entails (Mark 8:34 [see Malina 1994]). The disciples must be like the master, either in acts of service (John 13:13–16) or in imitation of the master's fate (John 15:18–20). The best that one might hope for is to live up to the model presented—that is, to the social expectations to which one is socialized. Group-oriented people, then, tend to be oriented to the past, hoping to embody the traditions of their ancestors and striving to imitate them and live up to the expectations created by those past cultural figures.

SANCTIONS AND REWARDS: VIRTUES, DUTIES, PIETY

If individuals are embedded in others, and if they are socialized into roles and shared traditions, this is manifested in the corresponding system of sanctions and rewards that protect this process. We ask now particularly about the general code of social education of individuals—that is, their socialization into the values, duties, and piety of their respective kinship or fictive-kinship groups. Here we take up issues stemming from gender and generation: the social expectations of gender identity and birth into a particular family or clan.

Duties

The collectivistic, group-oriented person did not have any rights in any legal sense. Human rights are a product of the Enlightenment. But such a person surely did have duties. Where roles and status are perceived as ascribed by God and part of "nature," these entail reciprocal social expectations. For our purposes, we examine now only the duties into which embedded persons are socialized. We focus primarily on the duties encoded in their understanding of the family, the dominant institution of the ancient world. It comes as no surprise that sons and daughters, both of which are embedded in their father, are enjoined to "honor" them. The importance of this is manifested by its important place in the Ten Commandments: "Honor your father and mother" (Exod 20:12; Deut 5:6; Mal

1:6; Eph 6:1–3). Honor is manifested by obedience to one's father (Gen 27:8, 13, 43; 28:7; Col 3:21; Eph 6:1) and by the support given an aged parent (Sir 3:11–16). Alternately, the biblical authors censure all forms of disrespect to one's father and record a variety of ways in which this figure can be dishonored: cursing one's father (Exod 21:17; Prov 20:20), shaming him (Prov 28:7), dishonoring him (Deut 27:16; Mic 7:6), robbing him (Prov 28:24), mocking him (Prov 30:17), striking him (Exod 21:15), disobeying him (Prov 5:13). A father is particularly shamed by a rebellious son (Deut 21:18–21) and by an unchaste daughter (Deut 22:21; see also Lev 21:11, 19). Hence, it is the duty of children to treat a father honorably in the ways in which that culture defined respect and honor.

By the first century C.E., lists of household duties formally expressed reciprocal duties among the various members of a family (Eph 5:21–6:9; Col 3:18–4:1; 1 Pet 2:13–3:7). Husbands must treat their wives with the respect owed to blood relatives, even though she may not be his kin. She in turn must show loyalty to the male in whom she is now embedded, transferring to him the loyalty formerly owed to her father. Children are to obey their parents, in particular their father; slaves must obey their masters. Of course, we would expect great praise to attend obedience, and it does (Mark 14:36; Rom 5:19; Phil 2:7–8; Heb 5:8). Thus duties, especially those that define roles within the primary institution of the family, were clearly articulated and inculcated.

Piety

By "justice" the ancients meant the loyalty owed to the gods, one's parents, and the dead. Devotedness to these personages was labeled in Greek as εὐσέβεια and in Latin as *pietas*. These words cover what we moderns generally call "religion." A religious, a faithful, devoted person was εὐσεβής or *pius*. Scholars regularly discuss εὐσέβεια/*pietas* in terms of religious loyalty and devotion to the gods, but we focus on the second aspect, devotion to parents and family. Performing one's duty to parents and family was no less εὐσέβεια than that directed to the gods or God. This is recognized in authors such as Plato (*Resp.* 615c) and Lucian (*Somn.* 10) and is recorded in numerous ancient inscriptions. In the New Testament when children and grandchildren are instructed to see to the needs of their widowed mother and grandmother, this devoted loyalty is called "piety" (1 Tim 5:4). In a more general exhortation, the author of 2 Peter lists the ideal virtues that a pious person should have, and these include self-control, steadfastness, piety, brotherly affection, and love (1:6–7 [see Neyrey 1993, 54–55]). Where family looms as the major institution and where people are known in terms of embeddedness in the family group, their respect for and devotion to the family are celebrated as a major virtue, piety.

Faithfulness, Loyalty, Altruism

We are so accustomed to translating the word πίστις as "faith" in terms of religious creed that we tend to miss its basic meaning as "faithfulness" or "loyalty."

Faithfulness and loyalty are owed to the basic personages in whom one is embedded: God and one's kinship group. Furthermore, given a person's embeddedness in family and other social groups and the constant awareness of prescribed duties toward those in whom one in embedded, it is not surprising to learn how concern for others, especially the group, is valued here. Earlier we noted this remark by Josephus: "At these sacrifices prayers for the welfare of the community must take precedence of those for ourselves; for we are born for fellowship, and he who sets its claims above his private interests is specially acceptable to God" (*Ag. Ap.* 2.195–196). Faithfulness or loyalty, then, emerges as a distinct value among group-oriented persons.

Group orientation indicates that individuals should always seek the good of the neighbor (1 Cor 10:24 RSV) and not pursue individualistic objectives. Paul structures many of his arguments in 1 Corinthians in light of this. His persistent argument is that if a certain individualistic behavior harmed the body or acted against the common good, it was censured. For example, freedom to eat idol meat must be proscribed if it causes a weak person to stumble (8:9–13); knowledge puffs up, but love builds up (8:1). Promoting the interests of one's own group or one's own status expectations, then, offends the larger group. Self-indulgent behavior at the Eucharist profanes the ceremony so much that "it is not the Lord's supper that you eat" (11:20 RSV). Other people at Corinth luxuriated in their charismatic gifts, a behavior that Paul sought to moderate in terms of the good of the group. Prophecy is better than tongues because it "builds up" the group, whereas those who speak in tongues "edify" only their own group (14:3–4). Yet both prophecy and tongues should be normed and subjected to controls for the sake of the larger group, its "edification" (14:26–33).

Summary

We conclude this part of the essay by recalling that first-century-C.E. Mediterranean persons were fundamentally embedded in kinship and other groups. They were not individualistic personalities; they were collectivistic or group-oriented personalities. As they passed through stages of psychological awareness, they were constantly shown that they exist solely because of and for the group in which they found themselves. Without that group, they would not have any identity (Selby 1974). Such persons perceive themselves as always interrelated to other persons, while occupying a distinct social position both horizontally (with others sharing the same status, ranging from center to periphery) and vertically (with others above and below in social rank).

Group-oriented persons, moreover, internalize and make their own what others say, do, and think about them because they deem it necessary, if they are to be human beings, to live out the expectations of others. Such persons need to test this interrelatedness, which focuses attention away from their own egos and toward the demands and expectations of others who can grant or withhold reputation or honor. Group-oriented persons rely on others to the tell them who they are ("Who do people say that I am?" [Mark 8:27 NRSV]). Their "conscience" depends on others to tell them who they are, what is expected of them, and where they fit.

PAUL: FIRST-CENTURY MEDITERRANEAN PERSON

From all that we have considered, it seems rather obvious that Paul and his contemporaries did not understand themselves as individualistic persons. They knew one another, although not very well by our standards, for they did not know one another psychologically, as unique, idiosyncratic, singular persons. Rather, for them, according to our native Mediterranean informants, a person's social standing, social identification, and social worth derived from one's group orientation in terms of generation, geography, and gender.

Encomium and Paul's Self-Presentation

One of the most important ways of presenting an ancient person for public consideration was the formula for describing a person's life found in the rules for the encomium. Here our native informants tell us what topics are significant as well as what they meant by them. The encomium encodes a set of expectations and values derived from the social system shared by both Paul and his audience. In that social system, persons were publicly praised and thus accrued honor according to culturally valued praiseworthy features. These features both constrained and liberated. They constrained because they forced persons to see themselves and others only in limited, stereotyped terms, but they liberated because they set forth quite clearly and unequivocally what is required of a person to be a decent human being in that society.

By following this genre in his letters, Paul obviously set out all the information of social relevance that he could: birth, manner of life, education, and the like. "Relevance" here refers to the code of honor into which all males were socialized in Paul's society (see Malina 2001, 27–57). In this perspective, Paul presented himself as the quintessential group-oriented person, controlled by forces greater than he: God ascribes his role, status, and honor at birth; Paul is duly group affiliated, a Pharisee, a member of a specific group; he insists that he learned nothing on his own but rather received everything from God; he was totally group-oriented: loyal, faithful, and obedient, seeking God's honor and group benefits; he is ever sensitive to the opinions of others: his detractors, his Galatian audience, the Jerusalem "pillars." For this group-oriented person, the acknowledgment by the Jerusalem "pillars" was a matter of the highest significance.

Then, in the formal defense speeches of Acts 22–26, Luke presents all of the vital information about Paul that would portray him most favorably, organizing it according to the same categories that structure the encomium. In this depiction Paul comes across as an outstanding person, with all proper, group-based credentials. By setting forth Paul's education, piety, and authorization, Luke shows him to be a witness of reputable social standing, upright, stable, and pious, whose testimony deserves a fair hearing in court.

Paul's Self-Presentation

Consider the salient and consistent highlights of Paul's self-presentation as they emerged from our study. Paul himself appreciates the importance of the encomiastic categories of (1) pedigree (generation, geography), (2) education and training, (3) accomplishments and moral decisions, (4) deeds of the body, the soul, and fortune, (5) patrons and "friends." He chooses to present himself in these stereotypical terms that all would know and understand (Neyrey 1994). In doing so, he presents himself as a group-oriented person of the integrity.

Pedigree

Paul himself tells us in his own letters about his honorable origins: "of the people of Israel, of the tribe of Benjamin, a Hebrew born of Hebrews" (Phil 3:5 NRSV) and "Hebrew . . . Israelite . . . descendant of Abraham" (2 Cor 11:22). Luke records similar information: "a Judean, born at Tarsus [no mean πόλις!] in Cilicia, brought up in this πόλις [Jerusalem]" (Acts 22:3 RSV). By knowing his gender, geography, and generation, we are directed to identify Paul as an honorable and full member of an ancient, honorable ethnic group, as well as a person rooted in noble πόλεις, Tarsus and Jerusalem. In their respective contexts, both sets of remarks function precisely as honor claims—that is, claims to the honor that resides in others, either ethnic or geographical groups. Moreover, Paul boasts of these claims to excellence and thereby affirms that he too accepts them as indicators of his basic personhood.

Education and Training

In his own letters Paul speaks only obliquely of his formation when he says of himself, "as to the law, a Pharisee" (Phil 3:5 RSV; see also Gal 2:14). By his own admission, he is a Pharisee's Pharisee: "as to righteousness under the law, blameless" (Phil 3:6 RSV). He boldly admits, then, that he accepted his socialization into the Pharisaic way of life; by this he attests his embeddedness in group values and traditions, even to the point of being "blameless." But since his career depended on changing the focus of his formation from being zealous for God's law to being zealous for God's Christ, it is not surprising that Paul speaks so infrequently of his primary formation except to say that it now counts as rubbish for the sake of Christ (Phil 3:7–8). Yet in Acts, Luke makes much of Paul's formation: "brought up in this πόλις at the feet of Gamaliel, educated according to the strict manner of the law of our fathers" (22:3 RSV; see also 26:4). In the elite Jerusalem temple setting this is vital information about Paul because it indicates that he was not a boor or a rustic or a maverick individualist but rather was an educated person of considerable standing who embodies one of the great, honorable ways of being a servant of God. We know him to be knowledgeable of the traditions of his ethnic group, obedient to them, and embedded in the group's values and structures. He is, in short, a decidedly group-embedded person.

Accomplishments and Moral Decisions

Paul's earliest life choice was to be zealous for God as a strict Pharisee: "as to the law, a Pharisee; as to zeal, a persecutor of the church; as to righteousness under the law, blameless" (Phil 3:6 RSV). This zeal manifests itself in his lifelong dedication to purity and perfection (Neyrey 1990, 21–55), which represent the *conscientia* ("shared knowledge") that Paul derived from his Pharisaic father and from membership in the Pharisaic group: "I am a Pharisee, the son of a Pharisee" (Acts 23:6). Note that Paul has sufficiently identified himself by proclaiming himself a member of a group, which both he and Luke presume is understood in terms of some stereotype (see Acts 23:7–8; Neyrey 1990, 129–33). Paul's life is characterized, then, by a formation in and dedication to a disciplined way of living as a follower of God's will. He boasts only of his excellence in assimilating the education and discipline into which he was socialized, for he is at core a group-oriented person, not an individualist.

Most importantly, his Pharisaic dedication led him into conflict with the followers of the Jesus movement, whom he perceived as deviant (1 Cor 15:9; Gal 1:13, 23; Phil 3:6; Acts 9:4–5; 22:4, 7–8; 26:11, 14–15). Of course, the praiseworthy significance of his zeal will be assessed differently, depending on whether his audience consists of followers of the Way or of its Judean opponents. Yet he is fully and adequately identified as a thoroughgoing party member, whether as a Pharisee persecuting or preaching the Way: "The churches in Judea . . . only heard it said, 'He who once persecuted us is now preaching the faith he once tried to destroy'" (Gal 1:23 RSV).

From where did the obvious change in Paul's behavior from persecutor to preacher derive? It was not the result of individual investigation or study. It did not derive from his individual and personal anguish, anxiety, uncertainty, distress, or any other psychological state that we normally associate with soul-searching decision-making or "conversion." Paul simply had no individualistic "soul" to search. Rather, the change in his life was mandated to him from the outside, by God, who revealed new information to him (Gal 1:15–16), or by God's Messiah, Jesus, who commanded Paul to alter the thrust of dedication to God and so to change the way he lived his life (Acts 22:7–10; 26:14–18). In Damascus God's prophet Ananias serves as his new mentor, as Paul had been told: "there you will be told all that is appointed for you to do" (Acts 22:10 RSV). Paul's zeal, then, is always directed by others to new tasks. Paul is essentially obedient to group norms and group-sanctioned persons. He accepts the directives given to him, and thus he manifests himself once more as a group-oriented person, a loyal "party member." He was transformed from being a figure who defended God's honor by applying sanctions to those deviants whom he believed challenged God's honor to one who defended that same honor by proclaiming a gospel given him directly by God. God's patronage and favor are subsequently made known to Paul in manifestations of great favor: (1) revealing Israel's Messiah to him (Gal 1:16); (2) ascribing the role and status of prophet to him (Gal 1:15; Acts 26:16–18). Basically, then, Paul's style is to concur with the decisions of others, either Pharisees (against the Way) or God (on behalf of the Way). It would be quite difficult to call Paul's transformation a "conversion" in any modern sense of the term. It really was God who changed by raising Jesus from the dead, not Paul!

Deeds of the Body

In this regard, Paul tells us not of deeds of the body that bring him honor but rather of his shameful physical condition. Instead of strength, Paul acknowledges only weakness to the church at Corinth: "I was with you in weakness and in much fear and trembling" (1 Cor 2:3 RSV). In later communications he writes, "Who is weak, and I am not weak? Who is made to fall, and I am not indignant? If I must boast, I will boast of the things that show my weakness" (2 Cor 11:29–30 RSV). This is expanded upon later in the letter:

> On my own behalf I will not boast, except of my weaknesses. . . . [God] said to me, "My grace is sufficient for you, for my power is made perfect in weakness." I will all the more gladly boast of my weaknesses, that the power of Christ may rest upon me. . . . I am content with weaknesses, insults, hardships, persecutions, and calamities; for when I am weak, then I am strong. (2 Cor 12:5, 9–10)

Instead of beauty as defined by the canons of his culture, he is stigmatized as a person with weak bodily presence: "His letters are weighty and strong, but his bodily presence is weak and his speech of no account" (2 Cor 10:10 RSV). Instead of health, he admits to bodily ailments, but these work quite providentially: "You know it was because of a bodily ailment that I preached the gospel to you at first" (Gal 4:13 RSV). And it seems that Paul is continually afflicted with illness: "We are . . . always carrying in the body the death of Jesus" (2 Cor 4:8–10 RSV), presumably a bodily ailment of some sort. Paul has no deeds of the body to recommend him—quite the opposite.

Cultural conventions in the Greco-Roman world would interpret such phenomena negatively. Without strength, a man could hardly claim or defend honor. In comparison to others, especially the elite ecstatics at Corinth, Paul is faulted for notably lacking the valued bodily skill of public speaking. He preaches the power of God's Spirit, but he himself is weak, and this calls into question either the message (thus shaming God) or his suitability for his role (thus shaming himself). Elliott (1990) has underscored Paul's bodily ailment in Gal 4:12–16 in terms of the evil eye. He notes how Paul might have been feared and avoided because of his physical failings, thus highlighting the potential shame in his bodily ailment. In short, the radical absence of deeds of the body normally would betoken a lack of honor. Yet Paul turns dishonor into honor by using his weakness as his boast. Paul's physical body is socially perceived and described; it is classified in terms of group meanings that Paul accepts.

Deeds of the Soul

The category of deeds of soul entails the four cardinal virtues as indices of a person's behavior. The traditional quartet bears the labels "prudence, justice, temperance, fortitude." What these refer to are practical know-how, fairness, a sense of shame, and courage, which, as we have seen, are very much cultural categories that express group values and ideals. All through his letters Paul sprinkles his claim to these; here we offer a sampling. Of the four, Paul makes the strongest claim for courage: "So we are always of good courage [θαρροῦντες]; we know that while we are at home in the body, we are away from the Lord. . . . We are of good courage, and we would rather be away from the body and at home with the Lord" (2 Cor 5:6–8 rsv). He couples courage with the concern for honor that a sense of shame entails. For, as a group-oriented person bent on the main collectivistic goal of group integrity, Paul rests assured "that I shall not be at all ashamed, but that with full courage [παρρησία] now as always Christ will be honored in my body, whether by life or by death" (Phil 1:20 rsv). Fitzgerald (1988, 87–91) views Paul's repeated endurance of hardships in 2 Corinthians as examples of courage.

Surely Paul also considers himself endowed with wisdom, as is apparent from his sarcastic remarks to Corinthians who claim superior wisdom: "We are fools for Christ's sake, but you are wise in Christ. We are weak, but you are strong. You are held in honor, but we in disrepute" (1 Cor 4:10 rsv). Paul is wise, indeed, but not by Corinthian norms:

> I did not come proclaiming to you the testimony of God in lofty words or wisdom
> . . . and my speech and my message were not in plausible words of wisdom. . . . Yet
> among the mature we do impart wisdom, although it is not a wisdom of this age or
> of the rulers of this age, who are doomed to pass away. But we impart a secret and
> hidden wisdom of God, which God decreed before the ages for our glorification.
> (1 Cor 2:1–7)

Nevertheless, he claims to be a "wise" master builder (1 Cor 3:10).

Furthermore, Paul knows and insists on justice. Since justice pertains to what is owed to God, ancestors, and parents, Paul can claim in all candor to be a just person. In his incessant repetition of his divine commission, Paul presents himself as a person of exceptional justice (δικαιοσύνη): he demonstrates faithfulness (πίστις) to his celestial Patron and constant reverence (εὐσέβεια), both being elements of justice. In regard to his ancestors, Paul followed their traditions with blamelessness: "circumcised on the eighth day" (Phil 3:5; see also Acts 22:3). Although Paul never speaks of his own parents, he presents himself as "father" and defends the rights and duties of a father, thus illustrating his appreciation of this cultural aspect of justice: "For though you have countless guides in Christ, you do not have many fathers. For I became your father in Christ Jesus through the gospel" (1 Cor 4:15 rsv). As a father, he jealously guards the church at Corinth as a father protects his daughter from evil suitors (2 Cor 11:2). Beyond the classical three loci of justice, Paul also acknowledges justice toward those who have legitimate authority, even local magistrates: "Pay all of them their dues, taxes to whom taxes are due, revenue to whom revenue is due, respect to whom respect is due, honor to whom honor is due" (Rom 13:7 rsv).

Deeds of Fortune

As regards the deeds of fortune listed in the encomium and forensic rhetoric, Paul claims very few, and he acknowledges what might be called "deeds of ill fortune." For example, as regards reputation, fame, and honor, Paul calls attention to his shame. In what follows here, we will include parallel references from

Acts. Even though these pieces of information are not formally contained in the encomium or forensic rhetoric, notice of the lack of deeds of fortune is a major element in Luke's presentation of Paul.

Dishonor, Not Fame or Reputation. Paul calls himself "a spectacle" (1 Cor 4:9); "a fool" (1 Cor 4:10); "in disrepute and dishonor" (1 Cor 4:10; 2 Cor 6:8); "slandered" (1 Cor 4:13; Acts 17:4–5; 18:12–16; 21:21–29); "refuse of the world, off-scouring of all things" (1 Cor 4:13 RSV); "an imposter" (2 Cor 6:8); "unknown" (2 Cor 6:9); and he is called "mocked, reviled" (Acts 17:32; 18:6).

Wealth. Paul knows of persistent lack as he catalogues the absence of wealth and riches in his life: "hunger and thirst" (1 Cor 4:11; 2 Cor 6:5; 11:27); "ill clad, homeless" (1 Cor 4:11; 2 Cor 11:27); "toil, labors" (2 Cor 6:5; 11:27); "hardships" (2 Cor 11:27).

Power. Especially in regard to power, Paul tells us of his afflictions at the hands of others and of his shameful physical treatment: "persecution" (1 Cor 4:12; 2 Cor 4:9; Acts 13:50; 20:3); "buffeting" (1 Cor 4:11); "affliction" (2 Cor 4:8; 6:4); "beatings" (2 Cor 6:5; 11:23–25; 12:7); "imprisonment" (2 Cor 11:25; Phil 1:12–14, 17; Philemon; Acts 16:19–24; 22:22–26:31); "dangers" (2 Cor 11:26); "death threats" (1 Cor 4:9; 2 Cor 11:32; Acts 9:23–25, 29; 14:5; 19:21–41; 21:31; 23:12–22; 25:3); "shipwrecks" (2 Cor 11:25; Acts 27:9–44).

Patrons and "Friends"

Paul boasts that while in residence, he does not allow the local church to support him and thus act as "friends" to him (1 Cor 9:4–12; 2 Cor 11:7–9). Marshall (1987, 101–5, 165–77) has argued that part of Paul's crisis at Corinth is precisely his refusal to accept local patronage and thus lower status there. To accept patronage from persons at Corinth would make Paul beholden to them. Whereas Paul categorically resists "friends," at least at Corinth, Philippi entered into partnership with him (Phil 4:15–19). But Paul himself prefers to act as the broker of God's patronage and as the dispenser of God's favor. His exclusive claims to be God's broker has put him at odds with various church members.

Yet, if we consider the flip side of friendship, we find very little evidence that Paul made clients of people in his churches. Paul, like Jesus, acted like a broker. Brokers connect prospective clients with sought-after patrons. And brokers do not have clients; only patrons do. Stephanus, Paul's first adherent in Achaia, is described by Paul as a leader of the Corinthian church (1 Cor 16:15–16), perhaps for his personal loyalty to Paul (16:17–18). Philemon would be a special case, for Paul requires the assistance of his slave, and this would balance Philemon's debt to Paul (Phlm 19); but this does not entirely sound as though Paul was formally a patron to Philemon. Otherwise, we know very little of Paul's friendship relationships with members of his churches, at least in ways that might be cited as marks of honor.

Relative to another feature of fortune, marriage, Paul tells us that he was not married, at least at the time he wrote his first letter to the Corinthians (1 Cor 7:7–8). And he tells us nothing of his children, whether numerous, accomplished, or well-married themselves. Finally, Paul's letters, obviously, do not tell us of his death, yet neither does Luke in Acts. We know only of a persistent wish on his part to die as a transforming experience (2 Cor 5:1–5; Phil 1:19–26); and we are alerted to numerous death threats and plots. Thus Paul is singularly lacking in the honorable marks of divine favor as conventionally understood.

Despite his specific lists of deeds of ill fortune, Paul claims God's singular favor and thus the honor of God's patronage. How frequently he celebrates the "gift" or "grace" given him by God! (Malina 1989, 3–11). First, he never tires of proclaiming and defending the role and status that God has ascribed to him—apostle, prophet, master builder, father, and so on. In 2 Corinthians Paul, while acknowledging his ill fortune, maintains that God defended his honor in these challenges and repeatedly vindicated him. He was not crushed, not driven to despair, not forsaken, not destroyed (4:8–9). Even his most shameful list of ill fortune (11:23–33) is cited as the boast of a "madman," in that such shameful events are actually his "boast" (11:30). For in weakness he is "strong" (12:10), and through weakness he is made "perfect" (12:9). As we noted previously, these catalogues of ill fortune resemble the lists of trials that philosophers overcame and are mentioned as proof of the excellence of their teaching (Fitzgerald 1988, 114–16). Although philosophers underscored their courage and discipline in overcoming such hardships, Paul attributes his victories to divine favor as well. Hence his deeds of ill fortune actually serve as proof of his ultimate good fortune and favor from God.

Conclusion

Paul presents himself as utterly dependent on group expectations and the controlling hand of forces greater than he: ancestors, groups, God. He was a typically group-oriented person. In fact, "independence" of any group authorization would have been a major liability to him. From the viewpoint of modern biography, we must admit that we know little of his character, personality, idiosyncrasies, likes and dislikes, and other vast sections of his life. The most we can say is that he was a group-oriented person, not at all individualistic. But in terms of ancient Mediterranean concerns, we do not need to know any more than we do, for from what he tells us, we can fill in all that is necessary to know the man in his society.

All in all, the most significant determinants of who or what a person is derive from outside the individual person. Everyone was an "other-made" man or woman; "self-made" persons simply did not exist. Moreover, one is not permitted to forget that everything in life that counts has been received from other. Hence, one actually has no control over anything of importance, certainly not over generation, geography, and gender. They have little if any control over who forms them, over the stages of growth that they undergo, over the events and persons that they encounter. What situates a person socially befalls passively on him or happens to her. Achievements flow from ascribed status and are not produced by the individual achiever as we understand "self-made" persons. Instead of a "vanity wall" with plaques marking personal accomplishments such as we see in the modern American home, the first-century Mediterranean home would feature masks, busts, and memorials of ancestors who made the residents who they were, thanks, of course, to the God(s) of these ancestors. We conclude, then, with a cultural truism noted by Paul: "What have you that you did not receive? If then you received it, why do you boast as if it were not a gift?" (1 Cor 4:7 RSV).

BIBLIOGRAPHY

Bellah, Robert, et al. 1985. *Habits of the Heart: Individualism and Commitment in American Life.* Berkeley: University of California Press.

Elliott, John H. 1990. Paul, Galatians and the Evil Eye. *Currents in Theology and Mission* 17:262–73.

Fitzgerald, John T. 1988. *Cracks in an Earthen Vessel: An Examination of the Catalogue of Hardships in the Corinthian Correspondence.* SBL Dissertation Series 99. Atlanta: Scholars Press.

Foster, George. 1961. The Dyadic Contract: A Model for the Social Structure of a Mexican Peasant Village. *American Anthropologist* 63:1173–92.

Geertz, Clifford. 1976. "From the Natives' Point of View": On the Nature of Anthropological Understanding. Pages 221–37 in *Meaning and Anthropology.* Edited by Keith H. Basso and Henry Selby. Albuquerque: University of New Mexico Press.

Hui, C. Harry, and Harry C. Triandis. 1986. Individualism-Collectivism—A Study of Cross-Cultural Researchers. *Journal of Cross-Cultural Psychology* 17:225–48.

Hui, C. Harry, and M. J. Villareal. 1989. Individualism-Collectivism and Psychological Needs: Their Relationship in Two Cultures. *Journal of Cross-Cultural Psychology* 20:310–23.

Malina, Bruce J. 1978. Freedom: The Theological Dimensions of a Symbol. *Biblical Theology Bulletin* 8:62–76.

———. 1986. *Christian Origins and Cultural Anthropology: Practical Models for Biblical Interpretation.* Atlanta: John Knox.

———. 1989. Dealing with Biblical (Mediterranean) Characters: A Guide for U.S. Consumers. *Biblical Theology Bulletin* 19:127–41.

———. 1992. Is There a Circum-Mediterranean Person? Looking for Stereotypes. *Biblical Theology Bulletin* 22:66–87.

———. 1993. *Windows on the World of Jesus: Time Travel to Ancient Judea.* Louisville: Westminster John Knox.

———. 1994. "Let Him Deny Himself" (Mark 8:34//): A Social Psychological Model of Self-Denial. *Biblical Theology Bulletin* 24:106–19.

———. 2001. *The New Testament World: Insights from Cultural Anthropology.* 3d ed. Louisville: Westminster John Knox.

Malina, Bruce, and Jerome H. Neyrey. 1991. First-Century Personality: Dyadic, Not Individualistic. Pages 67–96 in *The Social World of Luke-Acts: Models for Interpretation.* Edited by Jerome H. Neyrey. Peabody, Mass.: Hendrickson.

———. 1996. *Portraits of Paul: An Archaeology of Ancient Personality.* Louisville: Westminster John Knox.

Marshall, Peter. 1987. *Enmity at Corinth: Social Conventions in Paul's Relations with the Corinthians.* WUNT 2.23. Tübingen: J.C.B. Mohr.

Neyrey, Jerome H. 1990. *Paul, in Other Words: A Cultural Reading of His Letters.* Louisville: Westminster John Knox.

———. 1993. *2 Peter, Jude.* Anchor Bible 37C. New York: Doubleday.

———. 1994. Josephus' *Vita* and the Encomium: A Native Model of Personality. *Journal for the Study of Judaism* 25:177–206.

———. 1995. The Footwashing in John 13:6–11: Transformation Ritual or Ceremony. Pages 178–213 in *The Social World of the First Christians.* Edited by L. Michael White and O. Larry Yarbrough. Minneapolis: Fortress.

———. 1996. Luke's Social Location of Paul: Cultural Anthropology and the Status of Paul in Acts. Pages 251–79 in *History, Literature, and Society in the Book of Acts.* Edited by Ben Witherington III. Cambridge: Cambridge University Press.

Rohrbaugh, Richard L. 1991. The Pre-industrial City in Luke-Acts: Urban Social Relations. Pages 125–49 in *The Social World of Luke-Acts: Models for Interpretation.* Edited by Jerome H. Neyrey. Peabody, Mass.: Hendrickson.

Selby, Henry. 1974. *Zapotec Deviance.* Austin: University of Texas Press.

Triandis, Harry C. 1989. Cross-Cultural Studies of Individualism and Collectivism. Pages 41–133 in *Nebraska Symposium on Motivation 1989: Cross-Cultural Perspectives.* Edited by in Richard A. Diensbier and John J. Berman. Lincoln: University of Nebraska Press.

Eric C. Stewart

Afterword

The occasion for putting this book together was the twentieth anniversary of the Context Group's first meeting (Esler 2004). During that time the Context Group has grown substantially with friends and colleagues across the world. Although "membership" in the group is somewhat fluid as people come and go, the core group of scholars has been remarkably consistent for twenty years, meeting annually in March, in November with their section on Social-Scientific Criticism of the New Testament under the auspices of the Society of Biblical Literature, and in the summer with their Social Task Force within the Catholic Biblical Association. What unites the members of the group is the conviction that the ancient Mediterranean context in which the texts that now compose the Jewish and Christian Scriptures is vastly different from the modern Western world in which many of the group's members live and work.

The majority of the members of the Context Group teach primarily undergraduate students. The aim of this book has been to communicate clearly the models of the social-scientific approach to this audience with the hope that these studies can introduce students to the social-scientific reading of biblical texts. Such readings ideally will help to bridge the gap between what our modern cultures tell us about the texts and what ancient cultural cues and scripts might have told the first hearers/readers of these texts.

The perceptive reader will have noticed that the essays in this volume cover a wide variety of institutions, values, and concepts in mutually interconnected ways. Not all the authors in this book agree on every point, but all of them share a basic recognition that social systems are necessary for language to have meaning. The essays on the institutions of the ancient world, kinship, patron-client, and the agrarian world of the eastern part of the Mediterranean demonstrate the basic conviction of this volume. "Family" takes on a different meaning in different cultures. Patronage is considered taboo in modern American society in which it is the (in ideal terms) merit of the individual that allows promotion and social mobility. Finally, the notion of agrarian society is now lost to most of those in the modern Western world. We are not, by and large, making our living from tilling the soil, nor are we village artisans. Modern Western societies are largely urban, in strong contrast to ancient Mediterranean society. Finally, the essay on group-oriented personhood addresses the fundamentally different way in which modern Western people understand themselves compared to those people of collectivist cultures.

The work of the Context Group continues at a furious pace, with several new books and articles every year by the core members of the group. The work of the group has also started to involve a number of younger members who are working on or have recently completed doctorates. Many of these scholars continue to probe the social sciences for new models and methods to enable us to better understand the world in which the texts of the New Testament were composed. Esler notes that scientists distinguish between "background technology" and "foreground technology." "For many of us cultural anthropology is now background technology" as we pursue new theories and models, but "we believe that it is helpful, or even necessary, to read the Bible with eyes attuned to honour and shame, patron and client, androcentric gender relations, group-orientation, envy and the evil eye, purity concerns and so on" (2004, 54). The Context Group as a whole remains committed to the principle that it is necessary to understand the meaning of any given expression within its own historical and cultural context in order to ascertain the meaning that it was intended to convey.

BIBLIOGRAPHY

Esler, Philip F. 2004. The Context Group Project: An Autobiographical Account. Pages 46–61 in *Anthropology and Biblical Studies: Avenues of Approach.* Edited by Louise J. Lawrence and Mario I. Aguilar. Leiden: Deo.

Select Bibliography

Elliott, John H. 1993. *What Is Social-Scientific Criticism?* Minneapolis: Fortress.

Hagedorn, Anselm C., Zeba A. Crook, and Eric Stewart, eds. 2007. *In Other Words: Essays on Social Science Methods and the New Testament in Honor of Jerome H. Neyrey.* Sheffield: Sheffield Phoenix Press.

Malina, Bruce J. 2001. *The New Testament World: Insights from Cultural Anthropology.* 3d ed. Louisville: Westminster John Knox.

Malina, Bruce J., and John J. Pilch. 2000. *Social-Science Commentary on the Book of Revelation.* Minneapolis: Fortress.

———. 2006. *Social-Science Commentary on the Letters of Paul.* Minneapolis: Fortress.

Malina, Bruce J., and Richard L. Rohrbaugh. 1998. *Social-Science Commentary on the Gospel of John.* Minneapolis: Fortress.

———. 2003. *Social-Science Commentary on the Synoptic Gospels.* 2d ed. Minneapolis: Fortress.

Neyrey, Jerome H., ed. 1991. *The Social World of Luke-Acts: Models for Interpretation.* Peabody, Mass.: Hendrickson.

———. 2004. *Render to God: New Testament Understandings of the Divine.* Minneapolis: Fortress.

———. 2007. *Give God the Glory: Ancient Prayer and Worship in Cultural Perspective.* Grand Rapids: Eerdmans.

Pilch, John J., and Bruce J. Malina, eds. 1998. *Handbook of Biblical Social Values.* Peabody, Mass.: Hendrickson.

Rohrbaugh, Richard L. 1996. *The Social Sciences and New Testament Interpretation.* Peabody, Mass.: Hendrickson.

———. 2007. *The New Testament in Cross-Cultural Perspective.* Matrix: The Bible in Mediterranean Context. Eugene, Ore.: Cascade Books.

Index of Modern Authors

Index of Subjects

Index of Ancient Sources